Labor Demand

Daniel S. Hamermesh

PRINCETON UNIVERSITY PRESS

PRINCETON, NEW JERSEY

Library of Congress Cataloging-in-Publication Data

Hamermesh, Daniel S.
Labor demand / Daniel S. Hamermesh.
p. cm.
Includes bibliographical references and index.
1. Labor demand. 2. Labor market. I. Title.
HD5706.H36 1993 331.12′3—dc20 92-23775

ISBN 0-691-04254-3

This book has been composed in Linotron Palatino

Princeton University Press books are printed on acid-free paper,
and meet the guidelines for permanence and durability of the
Committee on Production Guidelines for Book Longevity of the
Council on Library Resources

Printed in the United States of America

10 9 8 7 6 5 4 3 2 1

To my parents, with love and respect

Contents

Figures

Tables

Preface

THERE IS no need for the usual prefatory *apologia pro libro suo* here. That is done in great detail in the introductory chapter. Rather, I would like to explain the intellectual and policy origins of my work on and interest in the topic of labor demand. Much of this study is a compilation, extension, and exposition of a number of related ideas on which I have worked in a variety of ways and contexts over the years. My doctoral dissertation at Yale University (1969) dealt mainly with the dynamics of gross flows of employment, including gross flows of hires. It was thus a precursor to my interest in the topics of Chapters 6 and 7.

I spent fifteen months as Director of Research in the Office of the Assistant Secretary of Labor for Policy, Evaluation and Research in 1974 and 1975. During that time of rapidly deepening recession one of the ideas I pushed very hard was a marginal employment tax credit (an idea, for which I was only partially responsible, that eventually became the New Jobs Tax Credit of 1977). This proposal was discussed at a White House meeting on measures to combat the recession. I was questioned by the then deputy director of the Office of Management and Budget, Paul O'Neill, who asked what justification there was for the estimates of the elasticity of demand I had used to underlie my results simulating the effect of the tax credit. I had no comprehensive justification. That absence led to my initial recognition of the relative lack of systematic work on labor demand, and my interest in summarizing what we know. It resulted in an early publication (Hamermesh 1976) presenting the literature on this parameter and demonstrating its usefulness. A companion piece on heterogeneous labor and the analysis of multifactor production functions, written with James Grant, appeared in the same journal in 1979.

My interest in static labor demand continued during the early 1980s with work on substitution among demographic groups, including related studies of the employment effects of a subminimum wage. This culminated in my contribution to the *Handbook of Labor Economics* (Hamermesh 1986), which is the basis for part of the expanded and extended discussion in Chapters 2 and 3.

In the mid-1980s my interest in dynamic labor demand was rekindled. That renascence arose partly from my feeling that the sterility of the convex-adjustment literature was stultifying research, and partly from my involvement with the growing number of European labor economists and policy analysts concerned about the effects of policies regulating labor-market adjustment. Small parts of Chapters 6 and 7 reflect my interest in expanding beyond the standard model of quadratic adjustment costs and include modified versions of material published in the *American Economic Review* in 1989, the *Review of Economics and Statistics* in 1992, and the proceedings of a conference in Holland published in 1992.

Chapter 4, in some ways a bridge between static and dynamic labor demand, stemmed from my interest in policies relating to worker displacement and includes some material that appeared in the *Review of Economics and Statistics* in 1988. Chapter 8 deals with the impact of policies on labor-market adjustment and is partly based on work published in the volume *Employment Security and Labor Markets* in 1992. The material on unemployment insurance in that chapter is a modified version of work in *Research in Labor Economics*, 1990. It reflects my longstanding interest in the important arcane panoply of unemployment insurance policies and my belief that on this topic, as on so many others, there has been a severe imbalance between the study of its effects on labor supply and labor demand. The discussion of necessary data in Chapter 11 is based in part on my contribution to *Fifty Years of Economic Measurement* in 1990.

Beyond these germs, nuggets, and chapter sections, the material in this volume is entirely new, if not always original. The book is designed to explain what we know and do not know about labor demand, and to offer ideas for research to increase the former and decrease the latter. I do not claim that the book is comprehensive, that is, that it summarizes every published study on every topic I discuss. It does, I believe, contain the only comprehensive discussion of labor demand, and it links theory, empirical work, and policy in a way that is essential for an applied subdiscipline like labor economics.

Someone whose chief concern is with theoretical fine points will no doubt be dissatisfied that not all of them are explicated. Someone who is only interested in finding out what we know from the econometric evidence will find the theory useless. Someone interested only in policy implications will not be concerned, and indeed will be mystified by the discussions of theory and econometric problems. Within any of these groups, someone who wishes a thorough discussion of only the latest developments will be disappointed and should instead rely on a few narrow articles.

Anyone falling into any of these three categories should recognize that concern with theory alone removes labor economics from policy. Concern for empirical results only guarantees that those results cannot be taken seriously, since they are necessarily divorced from the underlying theory that is crucial for conditioning how the data are organized. An interest in policy alone removes the labor economist from his or her comparative advantage—the careful testing of models derived from the behavior of underlying microeconomic agents. While no one person can be theorist, empirical worker, and policy analyst, a comprehensive study of a major topic like labor demand requires the integration of all three components of labor economics.

During the academic year 1990–91 I drafted Chapters 7 through 11 while on sabbatical leave from Michigan State University. In addition to thanking my institution, I also thank the Alfred P. Sloan Foundation for a small grant that partially supported that time away from classroom teaching. The Research School of Social Sciences of Australian National University offered extremely competent support during my tenure as a Visiting Fellow in spring 1991.

Any effort of this magnitude and duration necessarily owes a lot to many different people. Particularly helpful with their comments on large sections of the manuscript have been: Katharine Abraham, Steven Allen, Mark Berger, Ernst Berndt, George Borjas, Mark Killingsworth, Jonathan Leonard, Andrew Oswald, and John Strauss. Belton Fleisher, Robert Hart, Gerbert Hebbink, Harry Holzer, Edward Montgomery, John Pencavel, Gerard Pfann, and Mark Roberts offered useful comments on individual points. At Michigan State Lori Austin, Kari Foreback, and Terie Snyder helped with the drawings and the typing. Shirley Kessel prepared the index. Jack Repcheck, formerly of the Princeton University Press, shepherded this project (with a very willing sheep) from its inception in 1987 as an idea for a book.

Labor Demand

CHAPTER ONE

The Study of Labor Demand

I. What Is the Demand for Labor?

The simplest answer to this question is that the demand for labor is any decision made *by an employer* regarding the company's workers—their employment, their compensation, and their training. This broadest definition of labor demand implicitly divides the study of labor economics into just two parts, labor supply and labor demand. While this decision may have made sense before 1960, before the burgeoning of empirical and theoretical work in labor economics, it is not very helpful now. There are too many variations that have themselves been so differentiated that they have now become major themes in their own right.

In Marshall's statement of neoclassical economics (1920) much of the focus in analyzing labor markets was on employers' decisions about how many workers to employ and how many hours they should work. The demand for labor was viewed as derived from consumers' demands for final goods and services, and as being concerned with the availability of employment. This view of labor demand is the one I adopt here to delimit the study. The study of the demand for labor has, for historical reasons and because of the divergence of research on employers' behavior in a variety of contexts, become the study of the number of jobs offered, the hours that employees are required to work, and the responses of these quantities to external shocks.

Much of Marshall's discussion of labor demand was concerned with what, after Hicks's developments (1932), became the formal study of the structure of production and its implications for employment and hours. Indeed, this broad strand of research has become the core of the modern subfield of labor demand and is often viewed as synonymous with it. This core has been thoroughly studied. We know a lot about the nature of production, both conceptually and, as a result of the rapid growth of statistical work, empirically. In this book I synthesize these developments and what we have learned.

There is more to the study of labor demand than the neoclassical theory of the comparative statics of employers' responses to marginal changes in product demand and factor prices. The study of the responses of employment and hours to nonmarginal changes—large shocks that are not readily analyzed using the standard mathematical tools—surely belongs in the subfield of labor demand, even though there has been little work in this area as yet. So too, examining the time paths of adjustment of employment and hours to both marginal and nonmarginal shocks—the comparative dynamics of employment and hours—deserves inclusion.

II. Is Labor Demand Merely a Branch of Production Theory?

Having shown that there is more to labor demand than neoclassical comparative statics, I have not shown what, if anything, is unique about the study of labor demand. Why should labor demand be studied separately from the demand for other productive inputs? The same neoclassical theory of factor demand applies, and has been applied to, the study of the demand for investment goods, energy, materials, and other inputs. Similarly, the same theory of the dynamics of employment has been used to study the dynamics of investment; and there is the same dearth of analysis of nonmarginal changes in investment as there is in the study of employment.

Some of the characteristics of labor demand that seem so unusual are common to other productive inputs. While workers can be distinguished by age and skill (including education, training, and other forms of human capital), so too can investment goods. These latter differ in age and complexity, and studying employers' choices among heterogeneous investment goods is not different from examining their decisions about employing workers with different characteristics. Admittedly, we are much more interested in the extent to which, for example, an influx of unskilled immigrants might affect the wages or employment opportunities of unskilled native workers than we are in whether introducing laser-guided lathes reduces the returns on conventional lathes. Qualitatively, though, these are very similar issues. The employment-hours distinction might seem unique, but it is not: Many machines can be worked at varying intensities; and among the firm's stock of machinery, only a varying fraction may be utilized.

Among productive inputs labor is the most important in its share of factor payments. Labor's share of national income grew rapidly during the Great Depression in the United States; but in 1959 compensation of employees was only 68.7 percent of national income. By 1990 labor's share had risen to 73.4 percent. This growth is typical of Western economies (Paldam 1979). Yet size alone does not make the subject interesting or, more important, any different analytically from the study of other inputs. It is true that we care more about people than we do about machinery; and much of government policy has to do with people, not with machinery. Yet the machinery does after all yield streams of income to the people with whom we are concerned. To the extent that our interest is in providing people with the income required to maintain consumption at least at some commonly agreed upon minimum level, income received from renting capital goods could be of as much concern as that received from selling labor services.

Labor is the only productive input that requires, as Marshall (1920, bk. 6, chap. 4) noted in his list of the peculiarities of labor, that the owner of the services, "present himself where they are delivered." The provision of labor services automatically engages workers' attention and affects not only their income, but also many nonpecuniary aspects of their existence. Time must be spent earning labor income, time that is thus unavailable for other purposes; the workplace can provide a focus for workers' socializing; workers may expose themselves to dangers on the job.

Even this unique aspect relates more closely to the worker's use of time, and thus to supply decisions, than to labor demand. What then is unique about labor as an input? The best answer is that though none of these aspects of labor demand—our interest in policies that affect different types of workers, labor's importance in production, and the requirement that workers be physically present on the job—is sufficient to make the study of labor demand a subtopic in its own right, taken together they are.

Interestingly, the originators of neoclassical economics recognized that labor demand was not merely a matter of examining how employers responded to exogenous changes (though they were concerned about that too). Marshall (1920, bk. 6, chaps. 2 and 13) expounds at length on the variability of workers' effort and its relation to productivity and hence to the demand for labor. This early recognition of the uniqueness of labor as a productive input has recently returned to vogue among economists concerned with the microeconomic foundations of macroeconomic fluctuations. To some extent I try in this volume to integrate it into the theory of labor demand; but most of the exposition deals with the standard factor-demand theoretic issues and with issues reflecting our interest in various disaggregations of employment.

III. Why Synthesize the Study of Labor Demand, and Why Do It Now?

The Marshallian scissors, as students of basic economics know, has two blades. Even though it makes sense to divide the field of labor economics more finely than is indicated by the supply-demand scissors, a brief analysis of patterns and trends in economists' study of labor demand and supply alone can help in understanding the relative importance of these areas in recent economic research. One bit of evidence is a three hundred-page book on empirical labor economics that is divided into "halves" dealing with supply and demand (Devine and Kiefer 1991), the second of which is fourteen pages long.

A more detailed consideration of the relative importance attached to the two areas measures the number of contributions included under the two rubrics in the *Handbook of Labor Economics* (Ashenfelter and Layard 1986), the first major compendium produced for labor economics. Seven syntheses are included under the heading labor supply: labor supply of men, and of women; demographics of marriage and fertility, and household production; retirement; the demand for education; and one study of data used to examine labor supply. Under labor demand only two syntheses were included, one on comparative statics, the other on dynamics. Even if we exclude the demand for education as having by now become part of the separate subfield of the economics of education, it is clear from this summary that there is more interest in supply, and presumably more research on labor supply, to be synthesized.

Stafford (1986) has summarized the direction of research in labor economics by subfield from 1965 through 1983. His results, and my updating of them for 1984–90, are shown in Table 1.1.[1] They underscore the conclusion that the economics profession has shown much more interest in labor supply than in labor demand. They do, though, indicate that the relative extent of professional interest in the two areas has changed at least somewhat.

Why has labor demand been relatively ignored? One major reason is that the creation of large sets of microeconomic data based on household surveys has spurred and been spurred by the development of new theoretical and econometric techniques for studying labor supply. We would know a lot less, and labor economists' infatuation with problems of labor supply would be less intense, if these data did not exist and if the resources devoted to their collection had gone into data more appropriate for studying other labor-market issues. Much less effort has been channeled into collecting comprehen-

---

[1] In classifying articles published during 1984–90, I tried to follow the same technique that Stafford used. The only potential ambiguity is with studies of factor demand generally. I followed the rule of including these in the category "basic labor demand" if they produced estimates of labor demand elasticities and/or of substitution between labor and other inputs.

TABLE 1.1
Articles in Major Economics Journals, by Subject, 1965–90

	Years				
	1965–69	*1970–74*	*1975–79*	*1980–83*	*1984–90*
Labor Demand					
Basic labor demand	10	11	11	10	19
Adjustment and dynamic demand	6	4	6	10	14
Minimum wage	1	2	4	4	4
Labor Supply					
Population size and structure	7	14	19	10	13
Household production	0	11	8	8	11
Labor supply of men	2	5	7	6	9
Labor supply of women	0	3	9	6	7
Labor supply of others and income support disincentives of UI, NIT, taxes, or other	2	7	16	15	14
Retirement	0	1	4	1	6
Educational demand	3	11	9	2	6
Migration	13	9	14	4	9

Sources: Columns (1)–(4) are from Stafford (1986). Column (5) is tabulated using the same six journals counted by Stafford, the *American Economic Review, Econometrica, International Economic Review, Journal of Political Economy, Quarterly Journal of Economics*, and *Review of Economics and Statistics*. Only articles are included; notes and comments are not.

sive data describing establishments that might be readily usable to study labor demand. To the extent that the causation in research in empirical economics runs from data to analysis, this dearth can explain the relative paucity of research on labor demand.

Another possible reason has to do with the intellectual source of much of the development of modern labor economics. A disproportionate amount of contemporary thought about labor markets has arisen out of the tradition of neoclassical economics identified with the Chicago School defined broadly. While no quick characterization of Chicago-style labor economics is possible, it is reasonable to conclude that it is denoted by beliefs that long-run supply curves to industries and occupations are horizontal, and that the long-run supply of skills is close to horizontal. To the extent that interest focuses mainly on explaining long-run differences in wages, these assumptions lead one to ignore the role of labor demand as being irrelevant.

The demand blade of the labor-market scissors has became like the Cheshire Cat: It is there, but it is often difficult to spot.

Modern research on labor supply has been surveyed frequently (e.g., Cain and Watts 1973); and a comprehensive synthesis of theoretical and empirical work in this subfield has been produced (Killingsworth 1983). Even if one believes that the supply blade of the scissors is more important than its counterpart, one must admit that there exist readily available loci for discovering what we know about it. No single locus exists for the demand blade. All we have are three surveys of parts of the subfield (Hart 1984, on employment-hours substitution; Hamermesh 1986, on static labor demand; and Nickell 1986, on some aspects of dynamic labor demand), and detailed summaries of empirical research on a few of the policies that can be viewed as affecting labor demand (Brown, Gilroy, and Kohen 1982, on the minimum wage; Ehrenberg and Schumann 1982, on the overtime premium). There is no comprehensive treatment of labor demand as there is of labor supply. One is needed to provide intellectual balance and to bring together what is, in fact, a great deal of material on a variety of important topics that are related to one another.

There are a number of reasons why this type of synthesis is now timely. The neoclassical theory of production has led modern economists to devise ever more complex representations of the engineering relationships underlying production. From the Cobb-Douglas function (1928), to the CES function (Arrow et al. 1961), to complex forms such as the generalized Leontief function (Diewert 1971) and the translog frontier (Christensen, Jorgenson, and Lau 1973), economic theorists have successively removed restrictions on substitution possibilities among inputs. Increasingly complex methods of estimating the production relationships characterized by these decreasingly restrictive assumptions about the underlying technologies have been devised. The methods have been applied at an increasing rate to a variety of sets of data from numerous countries, and to an increasing variety of disaggregations of the labor force, of capital services, and other inputs.

During the 1960s rapid developments in the theory of economic growth and the recognition (Oi 1962) that transactions costs mean that employers' demand for labor cannot be characterized by spot markets led to the growth of theoretical and empirical studies of the dynamic adjustment of employment and hours. Simple studies of employment adjustment have in turn led to increasingly complex research that embeds dynamic optimizing decisions about employment and hours in complete models of dynamic factor adjustment. More recent work has distinguished between these decisions and the effects of employers' expectations about the paths of factor and product prices. These models have generated a substantial empirical literature that has shown us the relative rates at which employers adjust their demand for different types of workers and for hours as compared to workers.

Government intervention in labor markets expanded rapidly in industrialized countries during the twentieth century. Many of the policies generated by this intervention change the incentives facing employers making decisions about employment and hours. The study of the impacts of these policies has increasingly relied on the theoretical and empirical tools that have arisen out of the growth of research in neoclassical production theory and in the dynamics of factor demand. From minimum wages to employment subsidies, and from overtime pay premiums to subsidized training, there are substantial modern analytical literatures on the effects of the policies, especially in the United States, but increasingly in other industrialized countries too. We now know a lot about how these and other policies affect employment through their impact on labor demand. That knowledge allows us to predict with greater confidence the potential impact on employment of changes in these policies.

All of these areas represent "success stories" of modern labor economics. The importance of these successes alone justifies an attempt to exposit exactly what we have learned from this broad area of research. It is not true that there are no worlds left to conquer in the study of labor demand; but much of the empirical analysis of neoclassical production theory has become routinized, and the development of the theory has been reduced to increasingly arcane generalizations. Similarly, while the study of employment and hours adjustment is still changing rapidly, it is fair to say that it too is characterized by generalizations of the basic theory of the employer's dynamic optimizing choices of inputs and by estimation of increasingly generalized paths of adjustment of these inputs.

The subfield of labor demand is thus at a crossroads. In addition to synthesizing the knowledge produced by these successes, this summary also indicates which paths should be taken from this crossroads. In general the answer should be based on considering what aspects of labor-market problems related to labor demand have been ignored. Part of the answer suggests studying those characteristics of labor demand that rely on the kind of detailed microeconomic establishment-based data that has been so fruitful in generating advances in the study of labor supply. The other part relates to the uniqueness of labor vis-à-vis other factors of production. Thus, while this book deals at length with the standard approach to labor demand, it also intermingles the few strands of research that have recently begun to analyze the theory of the demand for labor in light of workers' behavior.

IV. What Will Be Considered, and What Will Not Be?

Most of the focus in the book is on the microeconomics of labor demand; but I repeatedly link the microeconomic theory and evidence to macroeconomic issues, and devote one chapter (Chapter 9) entirely to them. This book is divided into three main parts. The first deals with aspects of labor demand in static equilibrium. The focus of this part is mostly on issues of substitution among inputs into production. Although they are at least as important in terms of their impacts on labor demand, issues of scale effects and the impacts of changes in product demand receive less attention here. This is because they are analytically less complex, they have received less attention in empirical research, and most policies affecting labor demand alter relative input prices.

Chapter 2 presents the theory of demand for homogeneous labor in a two-factor model, the demand for different types of labor in a multifactor model, the nature of demand for homogeneous workers whose hours of work can vary, and the demand for several types of workers with different hours. These are developed using both the standard assumption that the employer maximizes profits in the face of exogenous factor prices, and then taking into account alternative criteria for determining employment.

Chapter 3 synthesizes the results of the vast literature of empirical estimates of labor-demand elasticities and of estimates of substitution among types of labor, and between groups of labor and other productive inputs. It examines evidence on the determinants of firms' choices about the appropriate inputs of workers and hours to use in generating labor services. In this chapter, and in others that summarize empirical evidence, I provide tabular surveys of the research and evaluate it critically on its implications about the underlying parameters. The major focus is an effort to infer the magnitudes of the parameters describing the demand for homogeneous labor, for workers of different types, and for hours and workers separately.

Research on labor demand has begun to focus on such changes as the opening and closing of establishments, which laypeople have long recognized as being major sources of employment change and as accounting for a large share of job losses. Chapter 4 presents some modifications of standard theory that can generate these nonmarginal changes. It reviews empirical work on the magnitudes of the gross changes in employment resulting from plant openings and closings, infers how much of any net change in employment is due to changes among continuing firms, and studies the effect of changes in factor price on these nonmarginal decisions.

Chapter 5 examines the theory and evidence on such employment policies as the minimum wage, overtime penalty rates, employment subsidies, and payroll taxes. Except for the first two cases there has been no major review of the evidence, and no review that uses more general findings about labor demand to infer the effects of these policies. To render the policy analysis less parochial and less ephemeral, the specific policies studied are offered as examples of general types of policy measures that affect the long-run demand for labor.

Part II deals with the dynamics of labor demand. Chapter 6 examines how the demand for labor adjusts in both one-factor and multi-factor cases under various specific assumptions about the nature of expectations and adjustment costs. It then considers the role of factor utilization in affecting adjustment and discusses the dynamics of hours and employment in response to shocks. Finally, a discussion of models of implicit contracts is presented that stresses them as depicting employment adjustment in response to external shocks and that accounts for idiosyncratic behavior of workers.

Chapter 7 summarizes evidence on the rates at which labor demand responds to shocks that affect long-run equilibrium, in particular, estimates of the speeds of demand adjustment when wages or expected product demand change. Implications for cyclical changes in labor productivity are discussed, based in part on evidence on asymmetry in employment adjustment. The chapter presents evidence on the interrelated dynamics of employment and hours adjustment and on the speed with which employers alter their demand for different types of workers. Also considered is evidence on the size and structure of adjustment costs and on returns to scale.

Chapter 8 considers the effects of the growing number of policies that can affect the adjustment of labor demand, including advance notification of layoffs, imposed severance pay, taxes that finance unemployment benefits—in short, anything that might change the cost of adjusting employment or hours. Again I examine the policies in the context of a general typology, based on the kinds of adjustment costs that they affect. Their prospective impacts are analyzed in the context of the models of Chapter 6, and the available econometric evidence on them is presented and evaluated.

Part III consists of two unrelated chapters that broaden the discussion of labor demand still further by going beyond the microeconomic theory and the analysis of labor markets in industrialized economies. Chapter 9 examines various macroeconomic aspects of labor demand, including whether it makes sense to speak of a labor-demand relationship and what the evidence in Chapters 3 and 7 implies for different theories of macroeconomic adjustment. I also discuss whether the notion of "job creation" means anything beyond subsidies to labor costs or macroeconomic stimuli.

Chapter 10 considers whether the theories that have been presented and developed need any modifications in low-skilled economies in which apparent surpluses of labor exist. I analyze labor demand in the context of the prevalent farmer-laborer agricultural household and consider various issues of demand in the smaller modern sector of developing economies. I summarize the empirical research on labor demand that applies to these questions and relate the broader set of research results discussed in Chapters 3 and 7 to them.

The difficulty with even this broad set of topics is whether it is broad enough. Limits must be set, though, because the discussion will not encompass the determination of all labor-market outcomes in which employers participate. Thus, much of the heterogeneity of labor that is of interest here stems from employers' actions through their joint investment in training with workers. While I do examine substitution among heterogeneous workers, I do not inquire into the sources of their different characteristics. On-the-job and other forms of training are not studied. Similarly, employers spend substantial amounts of time and money searching for and screening potential new employees. While the book does examine the results of this search, the economic determinants of employers' search behavior are not considered.

Much of the interest in labor demand among economists who do not specialize in studying labor markets is in the effects of cyclical fluctuations in product demand on employment and unemployment. Their concerns relate to broader macroeconomic outcomes, ones that will not be dealt with directly here. The reader will, though, be able to infer much of what we know about those outcomes. In several places, particularly in Chapters 6 and 7, the discussion deals at length with what we know about microeconomic determinants of employers' responses to such shocks. I cannot be sure that their reactions aggregate up to an economy-wide relationship, and I will not attempt to embed labor demand in a complete macroeconomic model; but I will consider whether macroeconometric evidence is consistent with microeconomic theory and evidence.

The entire discussion proceeds in the context of a closed economy.

While issues of regional variation in employment demand are interesting and important, there is very little that is specifically regional about the formal study of labor demand. That study does inform regional analysis; but the obverse is not true. Similarly, the increasing openness of industrialized economies has increased the potential effects on employment of transnational shocks to product demand. These are considered, but only as part of the examination of how employers react to other demand shocks.

There is no specifically international focus about the discussion, though the analysis of the empirical research covers all available evidence from many economies. Drawing on this broad evidence means that any conclusions reached about specific parameters or effects are likely to be uncontaminated by the idiosyncratic aspects of one country's labor market or institutions. The analytical results and the synthesis of what we have learned about employment adjustment and labor substitution should suffice to enable researchers interested in international changes in patterns of product demand to infer their effects on domestic labor markets.

The scope of this study, then, is the presentation and critical analysis of all that we know about the impact of employers' choices about employment and hours of work on labor-market outcomes—wages, employment, and work intensity. Because workers are diverse, and because their diversity stimulates much of the interest in labor-market policy, special attention is paid to the heterogeneity of the labor force and its implications for these outcomes and the policies that affect them. The end result is a complete statement of the current status of the subfield of labor demand: what we know, and the implications of that knowledge; what we do not know, but should; and some indications of future research necessary to obtain that knowledge.

PART ONE

The Static Demand for Labor

CHAPTER TWO

The Static Theory of Labor Demand

I. Introduction

In this chapter I demonstrate how parameters describing employers' long-run demand for labor can be inferred from data characterizing their employment, wages, product demand, and in some cases the prices and quantities of other inputs. Much of the exposition in Sections II–V is the standard neoclassical theory of factor demand, in which the effects on factor demand of small changes are analyzed. The purpose is not, however, to rehash this theory, but rather to show that it can be used to infer parameters of interest. Toward that end I spend a substantial amount of time indicating how the theory can be specified explicitly to enable one to infer the structure of production. More mathematical complexity can be found in Varian (1984); still more is available in the essays in Fuss and McFadden (1978).

The entire discussion assumes that a demand curve exists at the level of the firm. There is a longstanding controversy over the existence of an aggregate production function, and by inference therefore an aggregate labor-demand curve; but there is no long history of objections to the notion of a firm-level labor-demand relationship (Harcourt 1972). There are more recent objections, not so much to the underlying theoretical notion but rather to the usefulness of the construct in describing employment-wage outcomes (e.g., Oswald 1985). I discuss some of these objections in detail in Chapter 9 in the context of applying the results to aggregate labor markets. In the end, though, like any other internally consistent theory, its validity rests on its usefulness in describing measurable real-world phenomena.

For considering the appropriate form of the theory to use in deriving estimating relationships, there are two essentially polar ways of viewing labor demand. Neither is always correct; neither may ever be entirely correct. But both are useful for bracketing the likely responses of wages and employment to exogenous shocks. The first takes the view from the level of the individual employer that the wage is, in most cases, exogenous. Consider the firm shown in Figure 2.1a. It views supply as infinitely elastic at S^0, at a wage W_0. An increase in supply to S^1 produces a rise in employment from E_0 to E_1

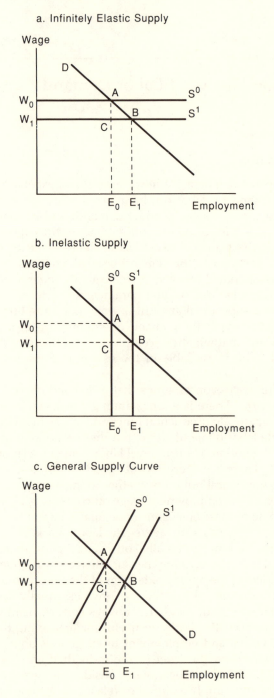

a. Infinitely Elastic Supply

b. Inelastic Supply

c. General Supply Curve

2.1 Alternative Labor Supply Assumptions

because the wage has dropped to W_1. The entire direct effect of the shock is on wages, and that in turn produces an impact on employment that can be inferred if we know the slope of the labor demand curve, AC/CB.

Even in broader instances than at the level of the small firm—for example, in a unionized firm that operates on its demand curve, or where the supply of labor to a subsector is perfectly elastic—the wage can be viewed as unaffected by labor demand. In such cases being able to infer the magnitudes of wage elasticities of labor demand allows one to infer the effects of exogenous changes in wage rates on employers' labor demand. The impact of changes in the price of one type of labor on its employment and on the employment of other types of labor (cross-price effects) can be discovered using estimates of labor-demand relations alone. The assumption that wages (and other factor prices) are exogenous clearly presents problems when one tries to move from a firm, a small industry, or a unionized sector to the entire economy. If the particular type of labor under study has its wages *effectively* fixed by government, perhaps because it is paid an effective minimum wage; or if there is sufficient unemployment among workers of this type that the supply *to the market* is perfectly elastic, then it is reasonable to ask what will happen to employment when the exogenous wage is changed. Under this polar assumption about labor supply the static theory can be used to analyze the impact on employment of imposed changes in the wage of any one type (or types) of labor, in other factor prices, or in product demand.

In the alternative polar case one can in many instances assume that the employment of workers of a particular type is fixed (and determined solely by the completely inelastic supply of such workers to the market). Perhaps the economy is at full employment, so the supply curve of this (or any other) type of labor is completely inelastic, as shown by S^0 in Figure 2.1b. In this case employment is E_0, entirely determined by the supply of labor. The demand for labor determines the wage rate W_0 that workers of this type are paid. If, for example, there is an exogenous increase in the supply of labor, perhaps because of an increase in population in the group, or a greater taste for market work, the supply shifts out to S^1. The wage falls to W_1. Here again, knowing the slope AC/CB of the demand curve D provides the information needed to infer the effect of the shock on the market, but in this case the entire effect is on the wage rate. If one believes that, unless governments interfere by setting wage floors, labor markets must be characterized by full employment in the long run, this is the approach to use to analyze the comparative statics of supply shocks. Even with a less strictly new classical view of macroeconomics, this case is still clearly suited to analyzing the effects of supply shocks on those labor markets, and at those times, where and when there is full employment.

In general, neither perfectly elastic nor completely inelastic supply characterizes labor markets. Instead, the situation is such that supply has a positive finite slope, as shown by S^0 in Figure 2.1c. In this case an increase in supply to S^1 produces both an increase in employment and a reduction in the wage rate. Without knowing the slopes of *both* the supply and demand curves, one cannot infer the size of the changes in wages and employment. For a given supply shock, one can, though, still place an upper bound on the effect of the supply shock on employment (wages) using the demand curve alone, as in Figure 2.1a (2.1b).

How serious is ignoring supply by restricting the assumptions about supply to the two polar cases? There is no theoretical difficulty; the theory derived in this chapter applies regardless of what supply responses look like. The problem is the standard one of identification in econometrics, coupled with a desire to link the theory and estimation as closely as possible (Klein 1974, 137–45).

In many important instances problems of identification can be ignored. First, there are numerous cases where the first polar approach is appropriate because the wage of the particular type of labor is set by fiat. Second, that approach can also be useful in analyzing the effects of subsidies to (or taxes on) employment in particular occupations, for both economic theory and empirical work suggest that the elasticities of supply to particular occupations are quite high. Third, there is substantial evidence that for many groups of workers labor supply to the market is very inelastic (e.g., Killingsworth 1983). That being the case, the effect of population changes on those workers' wages can be studied using the second polar approach. For these reasons the theory can be viewed not only as specifying one of the two joint determinants of employment and wages. It is also directly useful in determining long-run impacts on employment or wages because in many cases the other is fixed.

Throughout Sections II–V I assume that labor is homogeneous in terms of hours worked and effort per hour. There is no consideration of the possible effects on the demand for labor of different types of workers or differences in their supply of hours, their willingness to expend effort or how these combine with the size of the work group to affect output. In Sections VI and VII I relax these assumptions. This departure necessitates a lengthy discussion of the nature of labor costs, for what makes the distinction between workers and hours in production interesting is the effect of changes in the relative importance of the components of labor cost.

The purposes of this entire chapter are to exposit the theory of labor demand generally, and to show specifically how we can infer the effects of exogenous labor-market changes on the employment and/or wage rates of a group or groups of workers. The theoretical discussion of the static demand for labor is in Sections II–IV: demand for labor in the one-factor case, the two-factor case, and in the multifactor case. In the latter two sections I first derive the results generally, then proceed to specific functional forms. Section V examines the results in the context of nonprofit organizations. The theoretical discussion of the demand for workers and hours in Sections VI and VII is necessarily somewhat less formal. Partly the difference in treatment stems from the formal similarity between many of the issues treated there and those handled in Sections II–IV, and from the relative sparseness of the literature and narrowness of the topic. Partly, too, much of the literature has developed very specific models that provide few general insights about the issues of concern.

The focus throughout is on the relations between exogenous wage changes and the determination of employment, and between exogenous changes in inelastically supplied labor and the structure of relative wages. I generally assume that the typical firm maximizes profits, though Section V does analyze how the theory of labor demand is affected by alternative assumptions about what the enterprise maximizes. I also assume throughout that employers are perfect competitors in the labor market. Most of the discussion assumes that the employer is also a perfect competitor in the product market. While this latter assumption may not be correct, the analysis applies mutatis mutandis to employers who have some product-market power.

II. Labor Demand with One Input

Though the basic theorems of labor demand require assuming that there are at least two inputs into production, some very useful results can be derived when only one input is assumed. Included among these is a motivation for the downward-sloping labor-demand curves in Figures 2.1a–c.

Let L be the homogeneous labor input, W the nominal wage, and P the product price. In this section I assume that output is produced by a production function that transforms labor services into output, $\phi(L)$, with $\phi' > 0$, $\phi'' < 0$. In other words, there are diminishing returns to the single input, labor. This can be assumed to be a short-run production function in which all other input amounts are held constant. Assume for the moment that the firm is competitive in all markets. It attempts to maximize profits

$$\pi = P\phi(L) - WL,$$

which it does by setting

$$\phi'(L^*) - w = 0, \qquad (2.1)$$

where $w = W/P$ is the real wage and L^* is the profit-maximizing demand for labor. Condition (2.1) is the standard rule that the profit-maximizing firm sets the value of the marginal product equal to the real wage. It yields a maximum, for $\phi'' < 0$. The result shows that for a firm that is competitive in the product market we need only consider changes in real factor prices.

The condition also leads us to infer the downward-sloping demand curve of the figures. Differentiating in (2.1) and rearranging terms:

$$\frac{dL^*}{dw} = \frac{1}{\phi''(L^*)} < 0. \qquad (2.2)$$

The negative slopes of the demand curves in the figures are based on the concavity of the one-factor production function. The more rapidly diminishing are the returns to labor (the more negative is ϕ''), the steeper is the demand curve for labor.

If the product market is not perfectly competitive, profits become $P(\phi(L)) \cdot \phi(L) - WL$, with P now a decreasing function of output. The profit-maximizing demand for labor is now determined by $P'(L^*)\phi'(L^*)\phi(L^*) + P\phi'(L^*) - W = 0$, which, by multiplying the first term by P/P and remembering the definition of an elasticity, is

$$\phi'(L^*)[1 - \frac{1}{\eta}] = \frac{W}{P}, \qquad (2.3)$$

where $\eta \geq 0$ is the absolute value of the elasticity of product demand. Notice that the only difference between (2.3) and (2.1) is that the inverse of the product demand elasticity is subtracted. The condition now states that the firm chooses employment by setting the marginal revenue product equal to the real wage. For a perfectly competitive firm, $\eta \to \infty$, so (2.3) reduces to (2.1). This derivation shows that, other things equal, labor demand is also more steeply sloped the less elastic is the demand for the product.

III. Labor Demand with Two Inputs

The important results that the labor-demand curve slopes downward and that the elasticity of product demand affects labor demand are not a useful theoretical basis for serious empirical research in this area. First, the assumption of only one input is patently unrealistic and leaves unanswered the question of why there should be diminishing returns to the (single) factor. Second, the crucial notion of factor substitution, which underlies most empirical work, is impossible to discuss when only one input is assumed.

Many useful insights beyond those of the previous section come from examining the demand for homogeneous labor when there is only one cooperating factor. The convention is to assume that capital services are the other factor, which makes sense given the role of those services as the second biggest component of value added in most industries. Many of the specific mathematical forms for the production and cost functions from which labor-demand functions are derived were initially developed for the two-factor case and make more economic sense applied to only two factors than generalized to several.

Assume that production exhibits constant returns to scale, as described by the linear homogeneous function F, such that:

$$Y = F(L,K), \; F_i > 0, \; F_{ii} < 0, \; F_{ij} > 0, \tag{2.4}$$

where Y is output, and K is homogeneous capital services. In this initial part of the derivation, I assume the firm maximizes profits

$$\pi = F(L,K) - wL - rK, \tag{2.5a}$$

where r is the exogenous price of capital services, and I assume the competitive product price is one. Maximizing (2.5a) yields

$$F_L = w \tag{2.5b}$$

and

$$F_K = r. \tag{2.5c}$$

The competitive firm sets the value of the marginal product of each factor equal to its price. The ratio of (2.5b) to (2.5c),

$$\frac{F_L}{F_K} = \frac{w}{r}, \tag{2.5d}$$

is the familiar statement that the ratio of the values of marginal products, the marginal rate of technical substitution, equals the factor-price ratio.

Allen (1938, 341) defines the elasticity of substitution between the services of capital and labor as the effect of a change in relative factor prices on relative inputs of the two factors, *holding output constant.* (Alternatively, it is the effect of a change in the marginal rate of technical substitution on the ratio of factor inputs, defined as an elasticity.) Intuitively, this elasticity measures the ease of substituting one input for the other when the firm can only respond to a change in one or both of the input prices by changing the relative use of the two factors without changing output. In the two-factor linear homogeneous case the elasticity of substitution is

$$\sigma = \frac{dln(K/L)}{dln(w/r)} = \frac{dln(K/L)}{dln(F_L/F_K)} = \frac{F_L F_K}{Y F_{LK}} \tag{2.6}$$

(Allen 1938, 342–43). By this definition σ is always nonnegative.

Following Allen (1938, 372–73), the price elasticity of labor demand with output and r constant is

$$\eta_{LL} = -[1-s]\sigma < 0, \tag{2.7a}$$

where $s = wL/Y$, the share of labor in total revenue. η_{LL} measures the *constant-output labor-demand elasticity*. Intuitively, η_{LL} is smaller (less negative) for a given technology σ when labor's share is greater, because there is relatively less capital toward which to substitute when the wage rises. Equation (2.7a) reflects the first of Marshall's four laws of derived demand, that the own-price elasticity is higher the more easily the other factor is substituted for labor.

The *cross-elasticity of demand for labor* in response to a change in the price of capital services is

$$\eta_{LK} = [1-s]\sigma > 0. \tag{2.7b}$$

The intuition for including [1-s] here is that if capital's share is very small, a 1 percent change in its price cannot induce a large percentage change in labor demand, because the possible change in spending on capital services is small relative to the amount of labor being used. Both (2.7a) and (2.7b) reflect substitution between inputs, the crucial element missing in the previous section.

When the wage rate increases, the cost of producing a given output rises. In a competitive product market a 1 percent rise in a factor price raises cost, and eventually product price, by that factor's share. This reduces the quantity of output sold. The *scale effect* is thus the factor's share times the product-demand elasticity. To obtain the total demand elasticities for labor, scale effects must be added to (2.7a) and (2.7b):

$$\eta'_{LL} = -[1-s]\sigma - s\eta, \tag{2.7a'}$$

and

$$\eta'_{LK} = [1-s][\sigma - \eta]. \tag{2.7b'}$$

The term $s\eta$ in (2.7a') reflects Marshall's second law of derived demand: Input demand is less elastic when the demand for the product is less elastic, as we saw in the one-factor case. Equation (2.7a') is the fundamental law of factor demand. It divides the labor-demand elasticity into substitution and scale effects.[1] It can be derived using the

---

[1] The discussion here is based on constant returns to scale. The case of input demand with decreasing returns to scale (obversely, increasing marginal cost) is dis-

production-function analysis employed thus far; but the derivation is much simpler using cost functions, so that I delay it until those have been introduced.

The representations (2.7a′) and (2.7b′) are best thought of as describing effects on labor demand in competitive firms that have the same production function and demand elasticity, η, for the industry's product. These results and (2.7a) and (2.7b) are the most important in the theory of labor demand. (Clearly, if we are dealing with factor demand by one competitive firm that *alone* experiences a change in a factor price, η'_{LL} and η'_{LK} approach $-\infty$, since the drop [rise] in the factor price leads the firm to expand [contract] forever.)

Both (2.7a) and (2.7b), and (2.7a′) and (2.7b′), are useful, depending on the assumptions one wishes to make about the problem under study. For competitive firms in a particular industry, which can expand or contract as the wage changes, scale effects on employment demand are relevant. In that case (2.7a′) and (2.7b′) are more appropriate for inferring the potential effects of changes in input prices. If the typical firm's output supply is constrained, or, more interestingly, if we wish to apply these definitions to an entire closed economy operating at full employment, (2.7a) and (2.7b) are the correct measures of the long-run effect on labor demand of changes in the wage rate and the price of capital services.

All of these measures assume that both labor and capital services are supplied elastically to the firm. If they are not, the increases in employment when the wage decreases cannot be complete: The labor that is demanded may not be available; and the additional capital services whose presence raises the marginal product of labor ($F_{LK} > 0$) also may not be. In such cases the demand elasticities are reduced (Hicks 1932, Appendix). The example of a limit on the supply of capital services illustrates Marshall's third law of input demand.[2] These cases may be important, but I ignore them in the discussion. I do, though, deal with the polar case that assumes that employment is fixed but wages are flexible.

A dual approach is based on cost minimization. At the start total cost is assumed to be the sum of products of the profit-maximizing input demands and the factor prices. Total cost is linear homogeneous in input prices (doubling all nominal prices just doubles total

---

cussed by Mosak (1938). Though the analysis clearly differs (and is more complex), the distinction between substitution and scale effects still applies.

[2] The fourth law, which is based on the conditions describing the other three, is that the demand for an input that accounts for a small share of costs will be less elastic, other things equal, because the scale effect will be very small. A good intuitive discussion of these laws is provided by Stigler (1987).

cost, regardless of the degree of homogeneity of the production function). It can be written as

$$C = C(w,r,Y), \; C_i > 0, \; C_{ij} > 0, \; i,j = w,r, \tag{2.8}$$

since the profit-maximizing input demands were themselves functions of input prices, the level of output, and technology. By Shephard's lemma (see Varian 1984, 54) the firm's demand for labor and capital can be recovered from the cost function (2.8) as

$$L^* = C_w, \tag{2.9a}$$

and

$$K^* = C_r. \tag{2.9b}$$

Taking the ratio of these two conditions,

$$\frac{L^*}{K^*} = \frac{C_w}{C_r}. \tag{2.9c}$$

Intuitively, the cost-minimizing firm uses inputs in ratios equal to their marginal effects on costs.

The forms (2.9) are particularly useful for estimation purposes, since they specify the inputs directly as functions of the factor prices and output. One can write (2.9a) as

$$L^* = L^d(w,r,Y), \tag{2.9a$'$}$$

which can be written in logarithmic form for easy estimation as a log-linear equation. In such a form it yields the constant-output elasticity of demand for labor, η_{LL}, the cross-elasticity of demand, η_{LK} and the employment-output elasticity. Similarly, many researchers have rewritten (2.9c) as

$$\frac{L^*}{K^*} = l^d(w,r,Y). \tag{2.9c$'$}$$

Unlike (2.9a$'$), estimating (2.9c$'$) does not provide direct measures of the demand elasticities.

Using equations (2.9) and the result that $C(w,r,Y) = YC(w,r,1)$ if Y is linear homogeneous, the elasticity of substitution can be derived:

$$\sigma = \frac{CC_{wr}}{C_w C_r} \tag{2.10}$$

(see Uzawa 1962). The form one uses to measure σ, (2.6) or (2.10), should be dictated by convenience.

The constant-output *factor-demand elasticities* can be computed as

$$\eta_{LL} = -[1-m]\sigma, \tag{2.11a}$$

and

$$\eta_{LK} = [1-m]\sigma, \tag{2.11b}$$

where m is the share of labor in total costs. Since, by the assumptions characterizing perfect competition, factors are paid their marginal products, and since the production and cost functions are linear homogeneous, $m = s$, and (2.11a) and (2.11b) are equivalent to (2.7a) and (2.7b).

With this apparatus it is now easy to prove the fundamental law of factor demand, (2.7a'). Following Dixit (1976, 79), continue to assume constant returns to scale, so that we can treat the firm as an industry. Industry factor demands are just the right-hand sides of (2.9a) and (2.9b) multiplied by industry output. Under competition firms equate price, p, to marginal and average cost:

$$p = C.$$

Noting that if markets clear, so that output equals industry demand $D(p)$,

$$\frac{\partial L}{\partial w} = YC_{ww} + D'(p)C_w^2.$$

Because C is linear homogeneous, $C_{ww} = (-r/w)C_{wr}$. Substituting for C_{ww}, then from (2.10) for C_{wr}, and then for C_w and C_r from (2.9a) and (2.9b),

$$\frac{\partial L}{\partial w} = \frac{rK}{Y}\frac{\sigma L}{wC} + \frac{D'(p)L^2}{Y^2}.$$

To put this into the form of an elasticity, multiply both sides by pw/pL:

$$\eta'_{LL} = -\frac{rK}{pY}\sigma + \frac{pD'(p)}{Y}\frac{wL}{pY} = -[1 - s]\sigma - s\eta,$$

by the definition of factor shares under linear homogeneity. This is (2.7a').

The production or cost functions can also be used to define some concepts that are helpful for studying markets where real factor prices are flexible and endogenous, but factor supplies are fixed (and because of the flexibility of input prices, the second polar case in the introduction to this chapter, are fully employed). The converse of asking, as we have, what happens to the single firm's choice of inputs in response to an exogenous shift in a factor price is to ask what happens to factor prices that the representative firm must pay in response to an exogenous change in factor supply, as in Figure 2.1.b. Define the *elasticity of complementarity* as the percentage responsiveness of relative factor prices to a 1 percent change in relative inputs:

$$c = \frac{\partial ln(w/r)}{\partial ln(K/L)}. \tag{2.12}$$

This is the inverse of the definition of σ. Thus,

$$c = \frac{1}{\sigma} = \frac{C_w C_r}{CC_{wr}} = \frac{YF_{LK}}{F_L F_K}. \tag{2.13}$$

In this two-factor case with a linear homogeneous production technology, one can find the elasticities of substitution and of complementarity equally simply from the production and cost functions. Having found one, the other is immediately available.

With constant marginal costs, an assumption that is analogous to the assumption of constant output in (2.7a) and (2.7b), the *elasticities of factor price* (of the wage rate and the price of capital services) are defined as

$$\epsilon_{ww} = -[1-m]c, \tag{2.14a}$$

and

$$\epsilon_{rw} = [1-m]c. \tag{2.14b}$$

Equation (2.14a) states that the percentage decrease in the wage rate necessary to accommodate an increase in labor supply with no change in the marginal cost of the product is smaller when the share of labor in total costs is larger. This occurs because labor's contribution to costs—a decrease—must be fully offset by a rise in capital's contribution in order to meet the condition that marginal cost be held constant.

Consider now some examples of specific production and cost functions. These are the main specific forms that have been used to infer the sizes of the crucial parameters, σ, η_{LL}, and η'_{LL}, in empirical studies of various industries, labor markets, and economies.

A. Cobb-Douglas Technology

The production function is

$$Y = AL^\alpha K^{1-\alpha}, \tag{2.15}$$

where α is a parameter, and A is some scale parameter that I assume hereafter equals one. The marginal products are

$$\frac{\partial Y}{\partial L} = \alpha \frac{Y}{L}, \tag{2.16a}$$

and

$$\frac{\partial Y}{\partial K} = [1 - \alpha]\frac{Y}{K}. \tag{2.16b}$$

Since the ratio of (2.16a) to (2.16b) is w/r if the firm is maximizing profits, taking logarithms and differentiating with respect to $ln(w/r)$ yields $\sigma = 1$. Equations (2.7a) and (2.7b) imply

$$\eta_{LL} = -[1-\alpha] \text{ and } \eta_{LK} = 1 - \alpha.$$

Minimizing total costs subject to (2.15), one can derive the demand functions for L and K, and thus the cost function. The latter reduces to

$$C(w,r,Y) = Zw^{\alpha}r^{1-\alpha}Y, \tag{2.17}$$

where Z is a constant. Using Shephard's lemma for both L and K in this specific case, one can derive

$$\frac{L}{K} = \frac{\alpha}{1 - \alpha} \frac{r}{w}. \tag{2.18}$$

Taking logarithms,

$$\ln\left(\frac{L}{K}\right) = \alpha' + \ln\left(\frac{r}{w}\right), \tag{2.18'}$$

where α' is a constant. This form is very easy to use for estimation. It is trivial to show in (2.18') that $\sigma = 1$ and also that $c = 1$. Moreover, it is clear from (2.18) alone that $\eta'_{LL} = -1$.

While the Cobb-Douglas function is easily used, the severe restrictions on all the interesting parameters render it of little current interest, since the purpose usually is to discover the sizes of labor-demand elasticities, not to assume that they equal $-[1-\alpha]$ and -1. Its only real advantage, given current computing technology, is its simplicity in providing a theoretical basis for inferring the size of labor's contribution to output. Indeed, that was its original purpose (Douglas 1976).

B. Constant Elasticity of Substitution Technology

The linear homogeneous production function is

$$Y = [\alpha L^{\rho} + (1 - \alpha)K^{\rho}]^{1/\rho}, \tag{2.19}$$

where α and ρ are parameters, $1 > \alpha > 0$, $1 \geq \rho \geq -\infty$. Marginal products are[3]

$$\frac{\partial Y}{\partial L} = \alpha\left(\frac{Y}{L}\right)^{1-\rho}, \tag{2.20a}$$

and

$$\frac{\partial Y}{\partial K} = [1 - \alpha]\left(\frac{Y}{K}\right)^{1-\rho}. \tag{2.20b}$$

[3] The trick to derive (2.20a) and (2.20b) is to remember that, after having done the arithmetic, the numerator is just Y raised to the power $1 - \rho$.

Letting the ratio of (2.20a) to (2.20b) equal to the factor-price ratio, taking logarithms, and differentiating with respect to $ln(w/r)$ yields

$$-\frac{\partial ln(K/L)}{\partial ln(w/r)} = \sigma = \frac{1}{1 - \rho}. \tag{2.21}$$

The CES is sufficiently general that σ is free to fluctuate between 0 and ∞, so that one can infer its size and that of the η_{LL}.

Among special cases of the CES are: (1) the Cobb-Douglas function ($\rho = 0$, as is clear if one lets $\rho \to 0$ in (2.21)); (2) the linear function ($\rho = 1$). From (2.19) $F_{LK} = 0$ if $\rho = 1$, so that from its definition $\sigma \to \infty$. In this case L and K are perfect substitutes; and (3) the Leontief function ($\rho \to -\infty$), in which case output is the minimum function $Y = min\{L, K\}$, and $\sigma = 0$, so the inputs are not substitutable at all.[4] The constant-output factor-demand elasticities follow immediately from the definitions and the recognition that α is labor's share of revenue if the factors are paid their marginal products.

The CES cost function can be derived (Ferguson 1969, 167) as

$$C = Y\left[\alpha^{\sigma}w^{1-\sigma} + [1-\alpha]^{\sigma}r^{1-\sigma}\right]^{1/(1-\sigma)}$$

where, as before, $\sigma = \dfrac{1}{[1 - \rho]} \geq 0$. The demand for labor is

$$L = \frac{\partial C}{\partial w} = \alpha^{\sigma}w^{-\sigma}Y. \tag{2.22}$$

Taking logarithms in (2.22) yields

$$ln\ L = \alpha'' - \sigma ln\ w + ln\ Y, \tag{2.22'}$$

where α'' is a constant. The form (2.22') is very useful for estimation.

In these examples it is straightforward to derive c first, then to derive σ as its inverse. It is worth noting for later examples and for the multifactor case that c is more easily derived from equations (2.20) and the factor-price ratio (since w/r, the outcome, appears alone) than from (2.22) and the demand for capital. σ is more readily derived from the cost function, since the ratio L/K appears alone. Obviously, in the two-factor case the simple relation (2.13) allows one to obtain c or σ from the other; but the ease of initially obtaining c or σ differs depending on which function one starts with, a difference that is magnified in the multifactor case.

A variant on the CES function is the *variable elasticity of substitution function*, in which $\sigma = h(L/K)$, where h is some continuous function (e.g., Lovell 1973). This assumption maintains the linear homogene-

---

[4] The arithmetic that demonstrates this is in Varian (1984, 18).

ity of the function in (2.19) while allowing the elasticity of substitution to change as the ratio of inputs changes. Probably because it is difficult to develop any intuition about h', and because it is not easy to use in estimating equations like (2.22'), this formulation has only rarely been used in studies of labor demand.

Several other specific functional forms, the generalized Leontief form of Diewert (1971), the translog form (Christensen, Jorgenson, and Lau 1973), and the CES-translog of Pollak, Sickles, and Wales (1984), are second-order approximations to arbitrary cost or production functions. Like the variable elasticity function, each has the advantage over the CES function in the two-factor case that σ (or c) is not restricted to be constant, but instead depends on the values of the factor inputs or prices.

C. Generalized Leontief

This approximation specifies

$$C = Y\{a_{11}w + 2a_{12}w^{.5}r^{.5} + a_{22}r\}, \tag{2.23}$$

where the a_{ij} are parameters. Applying Shephard's lemma to (2.23) for each input,

$$L/Y = a_{11} + a_{12}[w/r]^{-.5}, \tag{2.24a}$$

and

$$K/Y = a_{22} + a_{12}[w/r]^{.5}. \tag{2.24b}$$

As can be seen by taking the ratio of (2.24a) to (2.24b), in general σ depends on all three parameters and the ratio w/r. Equation (2.24a) is easily estimated in logarithmic form by itself or jointly with (2.24b), providing estimates of the constant-output labor-demand elasticity that vary with the ratio of input prices. If $a_{12} = 0$, (2.23) becomes a Leontief function (since the ratio of L to K is always a_{11}/a_{22}).

D. Translog and CES-Translog

The translog cost function is

$$\ln C = \ln Y + a_0 + a_1\ln w + [1-a_1]\ln r + .5b_1[\ln w]^2 \tag{2.25}$$
$$+ b_2[\ln w][\ln r] + .5b_3[\ln r]^2,$$

where a_1 and the b_i are parameters. Applying Shephard's lemma to the labor input, and taking the ratio of both sides to total costs,

$$s = a_1 + b_1\ln w + b_2\ln r. \tag{2.26}$$

Here too σ depends on all parameters and both factor prices. If $b_i = 0$ for all i, the cost function reduces to a Cobb-Douglas technology.

Equation (2.26) alone is ideally suited for estimating purposes and provides all the available information about the structure of production (since $b_1 + b_2 = b_2 + b_3 = 0$, due to the linear homogeneity of the cost function in w and r).

The CES-translog is a variant of the translog function that replaces the terms a_1 and $[1 - a_1]$ with

$$ln\left\{ a_1 w^{1-\sigma} + [1-a_1]r^{1-\sigma} \right\}^{1/[1-\sigma]}.$$

The equation for labor's share becomes

$$s = \frac{a_1 w^{1-\sigma}}{a_1 w^{1-\sigma} + [1-a_1]r^{1-\sigma}} + b_1 ln\ w + b_2 ln\ r. \qquad (2.26')$$

The only difference between this equation and (2.26) is in the first term, which specifies a nonlinearity that permits estimation of an additional parameter that allows somewhat more generality in the elasticities. This formulation takes off from the CES function, for if all the b_i are zero, the cost function reduces to that of a CES.

All three of these formulations may be useful for empirical work, even when written out as in (2.23) and (2.25). Each has the virtue of allowing flexibility and containing some simpler forms as special cases. That suggests that they should supplant the Cobb-Douglas and CES functions even for empirical work involving just two inputs.

Throughout this section we have assumed the production function is linear homogeneous. Linear homogeneous functions are a subset of *homothetic* functions. In this broader class factor demand is such that the ratio of inputs is independent of scale at each factor-price ratio. This assumption may not always make sense. For example, large firms may increase efficiency by using a more capital-intensive process than small firms at given w and r. Alternatively, a particular firm facing the same factor prices may combine resources more efficiently in different proportions as its scale of operations changes.[5]

In the general case heterotheticity means that the production function cannot be written as $Y = G(F[L,K])$, where G is monotonic and F is linear homogeneous. Still more restrictively, the cost function cannot be expressed as

$$C(w,r,Y) = C^1(Y) \cdot C^2(w,r).$$

---

[5] My favorite example of heterotheticity is leaf raking on my own campus. Three technologies are used: (1) one worker with a rake cleaning up leaves behind bushes and next to buildings; (2) one worker with a lawnmowerlike machine in small open areas; (3) one worker with a giant fan on a flatbed truck blowing leaves into huge piles whence they are vacuumed into a compactor mounted on another truck, used in large open areas.

If production is heterothetic, output is not separable from factor prices; instead, the effect of factor prices depends on the scale of output. Some special cases are useful for estimation; and heterothetic CES-type functions (Sato 1977) and translog forms (Berndt and Khaled 1979) have been used. The latter involves the addition of the terms

$$\delta ln\ Y \cdot ln\ w$$

and

$$[1 - \delta]ln\ Y \cdot ln\ r$$

to (2.25), which results in the addition of $\delta ln\ Y$ to (2.26). Alternatively, if one does not wish to impose a particular functional form, examining whether the term in output belongs in a loglinear version of (2.9c') provides a test for homotheticity. These additional generalizations of production are useful if one believes that demand parameters depend on scale *and if* the underlying data show sufficient variation to allow one to test for heterotheticity by, for example, including the terms in $ln(Y)$ in the estimating equations.

Throughout this and the next section the maintained assumption is that the product price is constant at 1. This also implies that w and r are measured in real units. One could just as easily replace F_L and F_K in (2.5b) and (2.5c) by PF_L and PF_K and derive the implications for labor demand of shifts in industry demand. These modifications produce only scale effects as long as F is homothetic. Indeed, generalizing still more by assuming that the firm is noncompetitive, so that the price the firm charges depends on its output, still produces only scale effects if F is homothetic. Thus unless one abandons homotheticity, the derivations of constant-output factor-demand and other elasticities in this chapter are generally applicable.

IV. Labor Demand with Several Inputs

The derivation of factor-demand relationships with more than two inputs is of general interest to economists and should be of particular interest to labor economists when labor is one of those inputs. In that case we can tell, for example, how employment or wages are affected when the price or quantity of any one of several other inputs changes. It is useful to labor economists when we disaggregate labor along some interesting dimension, for example, age, race, sex, education, immigrant status, skill, occupation. In that case the theory of production with several inputs allows us to infer how changes in the wage rate of one group of workers affect the demand for labor in other groups (following the first polar approach to studying demand, that factor prices are exogenous); or how changes in the supply of one group affect the returns to other types of workers (following the second approach, with factor quantities exogenous).

Mathematically the theory of demand for several inputs is just a generalization of the theory of demand for two factors. Empirically, though, the generalization requires the researcher to examine a related aspect of factor demand that is missing when the set of inputs is classified into only two aggregates. The issue is illustrated by considering a three-factor world, for example, three types of labor, L_1, L_2, and L_3. One could assume that production is characterized by

$$Y = F(G(L_1, L_2), L_3), \tag{2.27}$$

where F and G are two-factor production functions of the kind we discussed above. The difficulty with (2.27) is that the aggregation of L_1 and L_2 by the function G is an arbitrary description of technology. Far better to devise some method to test the validity of this particular aggregation.

This problem, one of *separability of inputs*, provides the major reason why labor economists must be interested in multifactor labor demand. For example, does the effect of a subsidy to employing low-skilled workers on the relative employment of workers by skill level differ depending on the preexisting capital intensity of production? Nonseparability means that one should not combine pairs or groups of labor subaggregates on the basis of prior beliefs about how closely related the groups are. Intuitively, this is because changes in the amount of one type of labor in a particular subaggregate can affect the ease of substitution between two groups of labor that are arbitrarily included in another subaggregate. Doing so will lead to incorrect inferences about the ease of substitution between the latter two factors (and about cross-price demand elasticities).

Consider a firm using N factors of production, $X_1, \ldots, X_N$. Let the production function be

$$Y = f(X_1, \ldots, X_N), f_i > 0, f_{ii} < 0. \tag{2.28}$$

Then the associated cost function, based on the demands for X_1, $\ldots, X_N$, is

$$C = g(w_1, \ldots, w_N, Y), g_i > 0, \tag{2.29}$$

where the w_i are the input prices. Similar to the two-factor case,

$$f_i - \lambda w_i = 0, \qquad i = 1, \ldots, N; \tag{2.30}$$

and using the cost function,

$$X_i - \mu g_i = 0, \qquad i = 1, \ldots, N, \tag{2.31}$$

where λ and μ are Lagrangian multipliers.

The technological parameters can be defined using either the equilibrium conditions based on the production function ((2.28) and

(2.30)) or those based on the cost function ((2.29) and (2.31)). Allen (1938) used f to define the *partial elasticity of substitution*, designed to measure the ease of substituting one input for another holding output and other input prices constant, as

$$\sigma_{ij} = \frac{Y}{X_i X_j} \frac{F_{ij}}{|F|},$$ (2.32)

a generalization of (2.6), with $|F|$ the bordered-Hessian determinant of the equilibrium conditions (2.28) and (2.30), and F_{ij} the cofactor of f_{ij} in F.

The definition in (2.32) is quite messy. An alternative based on the cost function is

$$\sigma_{ij} = \frac{Cg_{ij}}{g_i g_j}.$$ (2.33)

This is a straightforward generalization of the definition of σ in the two-factor case (shown in (2.10)). It has the virtue that it relies on only a few derivatives of the cost function, unlike (2.32), which requires a complete description of the production function. The measure σ_{ij} has been used extensively in empirical research on multifactor substitution. It has a severe difficulty, though, in that its magnitude (but not its sign) depends on the particular values of the input prices (Blackorby and Russell 1989). It is useful mainly for classifying pairs of inputs according to the sign of σ_{ij}, as discussed below.

The own- and cross-*partial elasticities of factor demand* are

$$\frac{\partial \ln X_i}{\partial \ln w_j} = \eta_{ij} = \frac{f_j X_j}{Y} \cdot \sigma_{ij} = s_j \sigma_{ij},$$ (2.34)

where the last equality results from the assumptions that factors are paid their marginal products and f is linear homogeneous.[6] The η_{ij} can be calculated using either definition of σ_{ij}, (2.32) or (2.33).[7]

Since $\eta_{ii} < 0$ (and thus $\sigma_{ii} < 0$), and since $\sum_j \eta_{ij} = 0$ (by the zero-

---

[6] These can be derived by differentiating (2.28) and (2.30) totally, yielding the comparative-static equations

$$[F] \begin{bmatrix} d\lambda/\lambda \\ dX_1 \\ \vdots \\ dX_N \end{bmatrix} = \frac{1}{\lambda} \begin{bmatrix} \lambda dY \\ dw_1 \\ \vdots \\ dw_N \end{bmatrix}.$$

Then holding constant Y and all the w_k except w_j yields

$$\frac{\partial \ln X_i}{\partial \ln w_j} = \frac{F_{ij}}{\lambda |F|}.$$

Multiplying the numerator and denominator by $w_j X_i X_j Y$ gives (2.34).

[7] One might wonder how, if $\eta_{LL} = -[1 - s_L]\sigma$ in the two-factor case, $\eta_{LL} = s_L \sigma_{LL}$ in the

degree homogeneity of factor demands in all factor prices), at least one $\eta_{ij} > 0$, $j \neq i$. What makes the multifactor case interesting is that some of the η_{ij} may be negative for $j \neq i$. This means, for example, that an increase in the wage rate of one group of workers with output constant might reduce employment of one or more other groups of workers as well as that of the workers whose wage rate has increased.

The *partial elasticity of complementarity* between two factors is defined using the production function as

$$c_{ij} = \frac{Yf_{ij}}{f_i f_j} . \tag{2.35}$$

This definition is a straightforward generalization of (2.13). The c_{ij} show the percentage effect on w_i/w_j of a change in the input ratio X_i/X_j, holding marginal cost and other input quantities constant. They provide a general way of analyzing the effects implicit in the polar case illustrated by Figure 2.1b. Just as the σ_{ij} are not invariant to changes in relative factor prices, the c_{ij} are not invariant to the relative amounts of the inputs, though their signs are. As the obverses of the partial elasticities of substitution, the c_{ij} can also be defined from the cost function (from the system of equations (2.29) and (2.31)) with much more complexity as

$$c_{ij} = \frac{CG_{ij}}{w_i w_j |G|} , \tag{2.36}$$

where $|G|$ is the determinant of the bordered-Hessian matrix that results from totally differentiating (2.29) and (2.31), and G_{ij} is the cofactor of g_{ij} in that matrix.[8]

Unlike the two-factor case, in which $c = 1/\sigma$, $c_{ij} \neq 1/\sigma_{ij}$. One cannot even infer the sign of the partial elasticity of complementarity from that of the partial elasticity of substitution between the same two factors. While σ_{ij} is calculated on the assumption that output is constant, calculating c_{ij} assumes marginal cost is constant. It is possible that changes in relative wages change marginal costs in such a way as to cause the equality to disappear. As an example, employers would react to an increase in the relative wage of young workers (perhaps the abolition of a subminimum wage for youths) by substituting adult female workers for youths, so that $\sigma_{ij} > 0$. An influx of

---

multifactor case when we assume $N = 2$. Remembering that $s_L \sigma_{LL} + s_K \sigma_{KL} = 0$, $\eta_{LL} = -s_K \sigma_{KL}$. Since $s_K = 1 - s_L$, and σ_{KL} is just alternative notation for σ, the two representations are identical.

[8] Sato and Koizumi (1973, 48) derive the c_{ij} from a cost function.

adult women into the labor force could lower the relative wages of young workers, so that $c_{ij} < 0$.

Analogous to a factor-demand elasticity is

$$\frac{\partial \ln w_i}{\partial \ln X_j} = \epsilon_{ij} = s_j c_{ij} , \qquad (2.37)$$

the *partial elasticity of factor price i* with respect to a change in the quantity X_j.[9] Since $\epsilon_{ii} = s_i c_{ii} < 0$, and $\Sigma_j s_j c_{ij} = 0$, $\epsilon_{ij} > 0$ for at least one input. It is possible, though, that there are factors for which $\epsilon_{ij} < 0$ for some $j \neq i$, that is, for which an exogenous increase in the quantity of input j reduces the price of input i at a constant marginal cost. For example, an influx of new immigrants into a labor market must raise the wage rate of at least one other group of workers, or increase the rate of return to capital; but it could lower the wage received by some other group of workers (presumably a group that competes for jobs with the new immigrants).

The partial elasticities of demand and of factor prices can be used to classify the relationships within pairs of factor inputs, with a terminology based on whether quantities (q) or factor prices (p) are assumed to shift exogenously. Using the ϵ_{ij}, inputs i and j are said to be *q-complements* if $\epsilon_{ij} > 0$. They are *q-substitutes* if $\epsilon_{ij} < 0$. It is possible for all input pairs (i,j) to be q-complements, but the interesting case arises when inputs in at least one pair are q-substitutes. Using the η_{ij}, inputs i and j are said to be *p-complements* if $\eta_{ij} < 0$. They are *p-substitutes* if $\eta_{ij} > 0$. It is possible for all input pairs (i,j) to be p-substitutes, but the problem is more interesting if inputs in one pair are p-complements. If there are only two inputs, they must be q-complements and p-substitutes. An increase in the price of capital must induce firms to use more labor at a constant output; an increase in the amount of capital in a market raises the productivity of labor and hence its wage.

[9] This can be derived by totally differentiating (2.29) and (2.31) under the assumption that G is linear homogeneous to obtain

$$[G] \begin{bmatrix} dY/Y \\ dw_1 \\ \vdots \\ dw_N \end{bmatrix} = \begin{bmatrix} Y d\mu \\ dX_1 \\ \vdots \\ dX_N \end{bmatrix} .$$

Solving in (2.29) for $\partial w_i/\partial X_j$ yields

$$\frac{\partial w_i}{\partial X_j} = \frac{G_{ij}}{|G|} .$$

Multiplying both numerator and denominator in this expression by $C w_i w_j X_j$ gives (2.37).

Some examples may help demonstrate the use of these definitions. If educated and uneducated workers are p-substitutes, one may infer that a rise in the cost to employers of employing the low-wage, uneducated labor, perhaps resulting from an increase in the minimum wage, will increase the fraction of educated workers used at each level of production. These two factors may also be q-complements. If so, an increase in the relative supply of educated workers (perhaps resulting from increased awareness of the nonpecuniary benefits of acquiring a college education) will raise the relative wage of uneducated workers by making them relatively more productive.

These derivations and the specific examples illustrated below provide explicit ways of inferring the underlying production parameters that determine the relevant own- and cross-partial factor-demand elasticities, and the own- and cross-partial factor-price elasticities. If one is less interested in the formalism and simply wishes to examine demand elasticities absent the theoretical structure, one can use Shephard's lemma in (2.29) to derive

$$X_i^* = X_i^d(w_1, \ldots, w_N, Y), \quad i = 1, \ldots, N, \tag{2.38}$$

a generalization of (2.9a'). The logarithm of (2.38) for a particular input k yields a reasonable loglinear form for estimation, though by ignoring the other N-1 equations in (2.38) the researcher discards substantial amounts of information that could be relevant for the factor-demand elasticities η_{ki} of interest.

A. Multifactor Cobb-Douglas and CES Functions

These are just logical extensions of the two-factor cases. The N-factor Cobb-Douglas cost function can be written

$$C = Y \prod_i w_i^{\alpha_i}, \quad \Sigma \alpha_i = 1. \tag{2.39}$$

Each $\sigma_{ij} = 1$ (as can be seen by applying (2.33) to (2.39)), making this function quite uninteresting in applications where one wishes to discover the extent of p-substitutability (measure cross-price elasticities) or examine how substitution between X_i and X_j is affected by the amount of X_K used. That $c_{ij} = 1$ can be readily derived from a generalization of the argument in (2.16)–(2.18). The only reason for estimating an N-factor Cobb-Douglas function is to discover the shares of output accounted for by each of the inputs. The production parameters can then be estimated using data on costs, output, and factor prices in an equation that takes logarithms of both sides of (2.39).

The N-factor CES production function is

$$Y = \left[\Sigma \beta_i X_i^\rho \right]^{1/\rho}, \quad \Sigma \beta_i = 1. \tag{2.40}$$

As with the N-factor Cobb-Douglas function, the technological parameters are identical for all pairs of inputs and thus not very interesting:

$$c_{ij} = 1 - \rho \text{ for all } i \neq j.$$

A slightly more interesting case is Sato's (1967) two-level CES function containing M groups of inputs, each of which contains N_i individual inputs:

$$Y = \left\{ \left[\sum_1^{N_1} \alpha_i X_i^{\rho_1} \right]^{v/\rho_1} + \cdots + \left[\sum_{N_{M-1}}^{N_M} \alpha_k X_k^{\rho_M} \right]^{v/\rho_M} \right\}^{1/v}, \sum_1^{N_M} \alpha_i = 1, \quad (2.41)$$

where v and the ρ_m are parameters to be estimated. Equation (2.41) is the same as (2.40), except that groups of factors aggregated by CES subfunctions are themselves aggregated by a CES function with the parameter v. Let $\sigma_v = 1/[1 - v]$, and $\sigma_m = 1/[1 - \rho_m]$. Then for pairs of inputs i,j in different subgroups, $\sigma_{ij} = \sigma_v$. For factors i and j within the same subaggregate m,

$$\sigma_{ij} = \sigma_v + \frac{1}{s_m}[\sigma_m - \sigma_v], \ m = 1, \ldots, M,$$

where s_m is the share of inputs in group m in total cost. Each level of this production function can be estimated, for example, using a version of (2.21), to show substitution within each pair of inputs and then between each pair of aggregated inputs. The multilevel CES form is still quite restrictive, though. It retains the assumption that the ease of substitution is the same between all pairs of factors not in the same subgroup. It also imposes separability—substitution within a subgroup is unaffected by the amount of inputs from other subgroups; and most seriously, it requires the researcher to choose how to group inputs into particular subgroups.

B. Generalized Leontief

The cost function, an expanded version of (2.23), is

$$C = Y \sum_i \sum_j a_{ij} w_i^{.5} w_j^{.5}, \ a_{ij} = a_{ji}. \tag{2.42}$$

The technological parameters are estimated from the system of linear equations:

$$\frac{X_i}{Y} = a_{ii} + \sum_{j \neq i} a_{ij} \left[\frac{w_j}{w_i} \right]^{.5}, \ i = 1, \ldots, N. \tag{2.43}$$

This approach has the virtue for studies of the demand for different types of labor that one can easily add nonwage variables that might affect the number of workers in a labor market or industry. The partial elasticities of substitution are

$$\sigma_{ij} = \frac{a_{ij}[w_i w_j]^{.5}}{2 s_i s_j},$$

and

$$\sigma_{ii} = \frac{w_i}{2 s_i^2}\left[a_{ii} - \frac{s_i}{w_i}\right].$$

To calculate the σ_{ij}, only those parameters that involve factors i and j are used.[10] A production function similar to (2.42) yields an analogue to (2.43) that has the ratio of a factor price to cost on the left side of each equation and ratios of quantities on the right side. With this version one can derive the c_{ij} using only the parameters involving the terms in X_i and X_j. It is particularly useful (and is used in most of the empirical work based on this function) if the only inputs are various types of labor, so the production system has wage rates as functions of relative labor inputs.

C. Translog and CES-Translog

In general the translog cost function is

$$ln\ C = ln\ Y + a_0 + \sum_i a_i ln\ w_i + .5\sum_i \sum_j b_{ij} ln\ w_i ln\ w_j, \qquad (2.44)$$

with

$$\sum_i a_i = 1;\ b_{ij} = b_{ji};\ \sum_i b_{ij} = 0,\ \text{for all } j.$$

The first and third equalities in (2.44) result from the assumption that C is linear homogeneous in the w_i (proportionate increases in the w_i raise costs proportionately); the second assumption stems from the requirement on the cost function (2.29) that $g_{ij} = g_{ji}$. With some manipulation one can derive a set of share equations that are linear in the production parameters:

$$s_i = a_i + \sum_{j=1}^{N} b_{ij} ln\ w_j,\ i = 1,\ \dots,\ N.^{[11]} \qquad (2.45)$$

---

[10] To derive σ_{ij}, perform the required differentiation, remember that $g_i = X_i$, and that the s_i equal the share of X_i in cost and revenue.

[11] By Shephard's lemma in (2.44)

$$\frac{\partial ln\ C}{\partial ln\ w_i} = \frac{X_i w_i}{C} = s_i,\ i = 1,\ \dots,\ N,$$

where both sides of the factor demand equation have been multiplied by w_i/C, and we have assumed factors receive their marginal products. Differentiating yields (2.45).

In this system the partial elasticities of substitution are

$$\sigma_{ij} = \frac{b_{ij} + s_i s_j}{s_i s_j}, \quad i \neq j; \tag{2.46a}$$

and

$$\sigma_{ii} = \frac{b_{ii} + s_i^2 - s_i}{s_i^2}. \tag{2.46b}$$

The σ_{ij} can also be calculated from a translog production specification, using (2.32) and thus the determinant of what could be a large matrix. To derive the c_{ij} easily a production function analogous to (2.44) can be specified and manipulated to yield share equations like (2.45), but with terms in the logarithms of the input quantities on the right-hand sides. The definitions of the c_{ij} are identical to (2.46), except the parameters are based on these alternative share equations.

The multifactor CES-translog representation departs from the translog in the same manner as in the two-factor case by replacing $\sum_i a_i \ln w_i$ in the cost function (2.44) with

$$\ln \left[\sum_i a_i w_i^{1-\sigma} \right]^{1/1-\sigma}.$$

In the ith share equation the a_i is replaced with

$$\frac{a_i w_i^{1-\sigma}}{\sum_j a_j w_j^{1-\sigma}}. \tag{2.47}$$

Though the system of share equations becomes nonlinear once these terms are included, it can be estimated by nonlinear techniques. The gain is greater generality in the estimates of the partial elasticities of substitution.[12]

As in the two-factor case, the assumption of homotheticity can be readily relaxed by specifying that unit costs, C/Y, depend on Y. In the translog case this means adding terms $\delta_j \ln Y \cdot \ln w_j$, $j = 1, \ldots,$ N, with $\Sigma \delta_j = 0$, to (2.44). Each share equation (2.45) then includes a term in $\delta_i \ln Y$. This extension of the translog function is readily suited for empirical work, though it has not been very widely used by labor economists.

Throughout I have strictly divided the discussion of the two polar cases implicit in Figures 2.1a and 2.1b. Either factor prices have been

---

[12] The partial elasticity of substitution between factors i and k is

$$\sigma_{ij} = \left\{ (\sigma - 1) \left[\frac{a_i w_i^{1-\sigma}}{\sum_j a_j w_j^{1-\sigma}} \right] \left[\frac{a_k w_k^{1-\sigma}}{\sum_j a_j w_j^{1-\sigma}} \right] + b_{ik} + s_i s_k \right\} \Big/ s_i s_k.$$

assumed to be exogenous (the production-function approach), or factor quantities have been assumed to be given (the cost-function approach). In a variety of cases one might, for example, wish to calculate the effect of an exogenous increase in the size of one group of workers on the wages of other groups of workers and on the numbers of workers employed in still other groups whose wages are rigid.

As an example, consider a world in which employment of factors $i = 2, \ldots, N$ is exogenous at X_i^*, but the wage of workers of type 1 is fixed at w_1^*. What is the effect of an exogenous increase in the number of workers of type k, ΔX_k^*, on employment of type 1 workers and on the wages of the other N-2 types of workers? Marginal productivity conditions analogous to (2.30) are

$$w_1^* = f_1(X_1, X_2^*, \ldots, X_N^*), \tag{2.48a}$$

and

$$w_i = f_i(X_1, X_2^*, \ldots, X_N^*), i = 2, \ldots, N. \tag{2.48b}$$

Substantial differentiation and manipulation of (2.48) yield

$$\frac{\partial \ln X_1}{\partial \ln X_k^*} = -\frac{s_k c_{1k}}{s_1 c_{11}}, \tag{2.49a}$$

and

$$\frac{\partial \ln w_i}{\partial \ln X_k^*} = \frac{s_k[c_{ik}c_{11} - c_{1i}c_{1k}]}{c_{11}}, i = 2, \ldots, N. \tag{2.49b}$$

If one knows the factor shares and partial elasticities of complementarity, one can multiply the elasticities in (2.49) by $\Delta X_k^*/X_k^*$ to obtain the percentage changes in employment of the one factor and the factor prices of the others.[13]

V. Labor Demand in Nonprofit Organizations

The increasing importance of government and other nonprofit organizations justifies at least a brief look at how the static theory of employment demand needs to be modified when one moves away from profit maximization. Consider first a firm that is just like the archetype of the previous three sections, but that does not seek to maximize profits. It does minimize costs, and it does hire the same types of productive factors as the profit-maximizing firm. Its goals could be

---

[13] This example is modeled on Grant and Hamermesh (1981). The general case in which some input prices are rigid while others can vary freely is described by Johnson (1980).

avoiding losses (maintaining nonnegative profits) or maximizing revenue. A wide range of other goals is possible (Reder 1975), but these very straightforward ones probably characterize a lot of nonprofit industry. Whether they describe government employers, who may get intrinsic rewards from hiring workers of different groups, is unclear. In the case of government the applicability of the results of this chapter has to rest on their being a good approximation to what government employers do.

If the nonprofit firm is a cost minimizer, its cost function is qualitatively the same as (2.8). Under the same assumption (that production is linear homogeneous in the inputs) labor demand can be described by (2.9a), with demand depending only on factor prices. More generally, as long as the production function is homothetic, we can write labor demand as

$$L^* = C_2(C^1(Y) \cdot C_w^2(w,r)), \tag{2.50}$$

so that any effects of changes in factor prices are separable from those of changes in output. Thus, in this case η_{LL} and η_{LK} are the same as before (given the description of technology in the particular production function).

The η'_{LL} and η'_{LK} will differ from the profit-maximizing case, because scale effects will not be the same. In the competitive case it is difficult to examine what will occur. But between profit-maximizing and revenue-maximizing noncompetitive firms that have the same production functions, the former will take account of changes in revenue and increases in cost as it expands, while the latter will only consider revenue. The latter will thus raise output more in response to a given drop in an input price, so that scale effects will be greater so long as average costs eventually increase.

The situation is more complicated still among cooperative firms, where the goal may be to maximize net revenue per cooperative member. The stylized ideal here is the labor-managed firm (Vanek 1970), which is assumed to maximize revenue minus other input costs per worker:

$$\text{Net revenue} = \frac{PF(X_1, \ldots, X_N, L) - \Sigma X_i}{L}. \tag{2.51}$$

In the multifactor case the results of Section IV are unchanged if production is separable in cooperative members L, for then L can be treated exactly as entrepreneurs are in the case of the profit-maximizing firm: They maximize an analogue to profits in full awareness that the size of their own input does not affect substitution possibilities among other inputs.

The assumption of separability of labor (co-op members) from other inputs is not very credible; but dropping it makes it hard to draw many inferences about factor demand. Assume the co-op is small, and let the price of its product be one. Then, following Meade (1972), consider the simple case in which it hires capital services to work with its members and maximizes:

$$\text{Net revenue} = \frac{F(L,K) - rK}{L}. \tag{2.51'}$$

In this case the net-revenue-maximizing conditions are

$$F_K = r, \tag{2.52a}$$

and

$$F_L = \frac{F(L,K) - rK}{L}. \tag{2.52b}$$

Condition (2.52a) is identical to (2.5c): The co-op hires capital services until their marginal product equals their rental price. It expands its membership until the marginal product of another member equals the net revenue that each member can draw from the co-op. The only exogenous factor price is r.

None of the long-run factor-demand elasticities (with respect to r) is the same as in the profit-maximizing case. With output constant the response to an increase in r is affected by the change in the numerator in (2.52b). If output can vary, the responses are still more complex, with even the directions of the effects on K and L being indeterminate.[14] Other than being sure that at a constant output an increase in r will lower K and raise L, we cannot say very much about labor demand in this case.

VI. The Distinction between Workers and Hours, and the Cost of Labor

Throughout the previous sections we assumed that all workers exerted the same amount of effort in the workplace and, even more

[14] In this situation

$$\frac{dK}{dr} = \frac{[-LF_{LL} - KF_{LK}]}{\Delta},$$

and

$$\frac{dL}{dr} = \frac{[LF_{LK} + KF_{KK}]}{\Delta},$$

where $\Delta = F_{LK}^2 - F_{LL}F_{KK} < 0$. The directions of the responses to a change in r depend on the shape of F and on the capital-labor ratio.

important, that this amount was not subject to choice by either the worker or the employer. Indeed, the term "labor" was never strictly defined. Once we wish to talk of hours, more precision is necessary. Therefore throughout the rest of the volume the term "labor" denotes a particular subaggregate of workers, or the total input of time from that subaggregate. "Worker-hours" denotes the product of "employment," the number of employees in the group, and their "hours," the amount of time they work per period. A similar lack of precision has attached to the "wage," which has implicitly thus far been just the "price of labor" in the long run. That too no longer suffices, so that in discussing choices between workers and hours here, and in analyzing adjustment in Chapter 6, I distinguish among various components of labor costs.

Essentially we have implicitly assumed for each type of labor i that

$$L_i = E_i H_i, \tag{2.53}$$

where E is employment, and H is the hours they work per time period. The assumption that effective labor input is multiplicative in employment and hours masked any need to consider differences in the prices of these two possible ways of altering the input of labor. The assumption is clearly unrealistic, particularly along the hours dimension: Doubling weekly hours from 60 to 120 will probably not double the amount of effective labor. Indeed, whether effective labor would even increase is questionable. Given the absurdity of the behavioral assumption implicit in (2.53), it makes sense to see what additional insights can be gained from generalizing about how workers and hours are combined.

Moving beyond (2.53) means that we view employers as facing interesting choices about how much labor to employ at the *extensive margin* of additional employment and the *intensive margin* of planning for a work force that can expend more or fewer hours per time period. We measure the intensity of production solely by H, therefore ignoring the realistic possibility that effort per hour worked can vary. Perhaps most important, we do not deal with variations in hours worked in response to short-run changes in derived demand or with the time path of hours between long-run equilibria. These questions have provoked much of the study of the demand for hours, and they are dealt with in Part II. This means, though, that we cannot assume that the firm's capital stock is fixed (though it may be reasonable to assume that the demand for workers and hours is separable from the demand for capital services).

Hours H are measured per time period; but per *what* time period— day, week, month, year, lifetime? The convention is to measure H as

TABLE 2.1
Weekly Hours of Work by Industry, United States, 1990

Industry	Hours
Mining	44.0
Construction	38.2
Manufacturing	40.8
Transportation and Public Utilities	38.9
Wholesale Trade	38.1
Retail Trade	28.8
Finance, Insurance, and Real Estate	35.8
Services	32.6

Source: *Employment and Earnings*, March 1991, table C.2.

hours per week, and I stick with that convention. Nonetheless, it is important to recognize that scheduled weekly hours need not equal 1/52 of scheduled annual hours and, more important, that there are differences in employers' costs of varying hours per week and weeks per year that will affect decisions about these dimensions of the intensity with which employees are used.

That employers do have sufficient scope for substituting hours for workers is demonstrated by the very sharp differences in weekly hours even among the broadly defined industries shown in Table 2.1. (See also Lilien and Hall 1986.) The data suggest that technology differs among industries in ways that dictate differences in work intensity, that there are interindustry differences in the relative costs of workers and hours, or some combination of both explanations.

The designation of all labor costs in Sections II–IV as a wage, w, must be abandoned when we move to examining choices about workers and hours. Regrettably, there is no clear-cut typology for labor costs, though some have been suggested (Rosen 1968; Hart 1984). Here, I concentrate on developing a new description of costs that seems parsimonious, yet is sufficiently exhaustive to provide all the distinctions necessary for the analysis here and in subsequent chapters.

The main distinction is between costs that vary with E, *fixed costs*, measured throughout this section on a per-worker basis as F, and those that vary with hours, *variable costs* V. This distinction is the basis for the two major branches of the typology shown in Figure 2.2; yet attempts to pigeonhole specific aspects of labor costs even at this low level of distinction require care. In the United States the payroll tax that finances state unemployment insurance benefits has a ceiling on the taxable annual wages that averaged (in 1991) roughly $9,000.

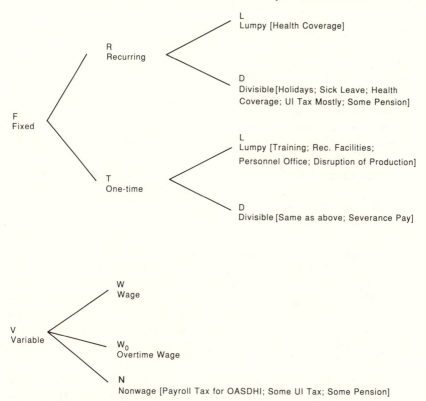

2.2 Typology of Labor Costs

This means that for most workers this tax represented a fixed cost, since additional hours worked did not raise the employer's tax liability. For very low-wage workers, though, it was a variable cost, for extra hours raised the tax bill.[15] Near the other extreme in the United States is the payroll tax for Old Age Survivors' and Disability Insurance (OASDI), which has a very high maximum taxable earnings ($53,400 in 1991). On all but the highest-wage workers this tax is a variable cost to employers; but in considering whether to employ high-wage workers and how intensively to use them, it is a fixed cost.

Within the category of fixed costs a useful distinction exists between *recurring* costs, *R*, and those that are incurred at *one time*, *T*,

[15] The UI tax is also a good example of a labor cost that differs along the dimensions of weekly hours and weeks per year.

usually when the worker is hired. Employer-provided health insurance is a good example of recurring fixed costs. Covered workers generate the same premium cost regardless of their work hours, and the premium is paid every month. Pension costs do vary in part with hours worked, but under many plans the variation is not linear or even constant, so that part of these costs is also fixed and recurring. One-time fixed costs include the reduction in output that occurs as inexperienced workers are trained up to full capacity, the costs of operating a personnel office, and at the other end of some workers' tenure, any severance pay.

A still finer distinction exists within both recurring and one-time costs between those fixed costs that are *lumpy*—that are invariant to the number of workers—and those that are *divisible* and thus that vary with employment. Among recurring costs much of health coverage can be viewed as lumpy: There clearly are some economies of scale in providing such coverage. Holidays and sick leave are good examples of divisible recurring costs, since the extra costs vary linearly with the size of the work force. Making the distinction between lumpy and divisible onetime costs is more difficult, because most of these, and particularly the direct and indirect costs of training, are hard to observe. Nonetheless, there are some economies of scale in hiring and in the activities of the personnel office that result from spreading out lumpy costs. Some government-imposed reporting requirements, including some produced by affirmative-action rules, generate costs only if a hire occurs, and the same forms can be used for each hire. The distinction between lumpy and divisible costs is not used here; but it is important for examining employment dynamics in Part II.

The distinctions among variable costs are less well articulated, since such costs are less diverse. It is useful, though, to distinguish among standard and overtime wages, and between wages and such nonwage costs as parts of pension, OASDI, and unemployment insurance payments. These distinctions necessitate examining how the price of an additional hour per week varies with hours.

All of the one-time costs are identical analytically to the costs of capital: They are incurred only once during the tenure of the worker in the plant, and they generate per-period costs equal to $r+q$, where q is the quit rate.[16] The typical firm thus faces fixed costs per period of

$$EF = E\{R + [r+q]T\}.$$

[16] If workers quit at a rate q per period, the initial costs they generate can be recovered with a sinking fund requiring periodic payments of q cents per dollar.

The borrowing rate r is exogenous to the firm's choice between workers and hours; but the quit rate may well not be, as higher onetime fixed costs may lead firms to alter their wage policy in order to reduce turnover costs (Hamermesh and Goldfarb 1970; Pencavel 1972). Though no doubt correct, this extension is not central to the results on the worker-hours distinction. Also, while empirical work requires distinguishing between R and T, there is no gain to doing so in the theoretical exposition. In sum, throughout the rest of this chapter I parameterize fixed costs per worker as F, recognizing that any results on the effects of higher F can reflect higher values of R, r, q, or T.

Conventional analysis of the choice between workers and hours treats the various components of labor income, in particular the wage rate and any premium for overtime work, as exogenous to the firm. I analyze briefly that type of model at the end of this section. But that view is quite inconsistent with the huge corpus of literature on labor supply. If typical workers are asked to work additional hours, they will require a higher wage rate to do so. Indeed, if workers have identical tastes, the firm will face a wage

$$w = w(H), \ w' > 0, \tag{2.54}$$

with w' equaling the marginal rate of substitution of income for leisure in the typical worker's utility function at the equilibrium wage rate and weekly hours. The theory of labor supply suggests we should not treat the wage as invariant to employers' hours decisions. That in turn implies that imposed changes in one aspect of the wage-hours package will affect the other through demand *and* supply (Trejo 1991). That view conditions the discussion of the effects of overtime laws in Chapter 5. In the meantime, the general model recognizes this interdependence by using (2.54) to specify the wage-hours relationship.

The typical firm is constrained by supply to pay workers a wage $w^* = w(H^*)$ determined by (2.54). I assume the firm is small enough that it faces an infinitely elastic supply of potential employees; but each potential employee has an upward-sloping reservation wage that must be paid to retain the worker's services at H^* per week. Coupled with the other assumptions, this means that the firm's labor costs are

$$\text{Labor cost} = EHw(H) + EF. \tag{2.55}$$

The cost of capital services is, as before, rK per time period.

In much of the discussion I assume that choices about workers and hours are separable from capital. This assumption is clearly not always correct: On an assembly line capital and employment may be highly p-complementary, while they may be jointly p-substitutable against hours (and the rate of utilization of the capital). Nonetheless, the initial assumption of separability may be valid and makes the analysis easier.

The second issue is the shape of the labor aggregator:

$$L = L(E,H).$$

In the firm's output maximization subject to the constraint that labor cost is C^0, it makes sense that $\dfrac{\partial H}{\partial C^0} = 0$, that is, that the firm's optimal hours be independent of scale. There is no evidence that weekly hours of full-time workers at General Motors differ substantially from hours of workers at the local steel fabricator. This assumption requires that

$$L = \phi_1(E)\phi_2(H), \quad \phi_i' > 0.$$

Ehrenberg (1971a) has suggested a specific example of this function that is particularly easy to use:

$$L = aE^b g(H),$$

$a, b > 0$, and $g' > 0$. These functions are clearly quite restrictive, but the restriction seems consistent with the observation that weekly hours are basically invariant with scale.

To make the exposition easier, I present the firm's problem as one of maximizing L subject to the constraint that labor cost equals C_0. This yields, after some manipulation,

$$\frac{L_E}{L_H} = \frac{wH + F}{wE[1 + \epsilon]}, \tag{2.56}$$

where ϵ is the elasticity of wages with respect to hours. As is standard, the ratio of the marginal products of employees and hours is set equal to the ratio of their relative prices when the firm maximizes its labor input with a cost constraint.

Notice that the exogenous variables facing the firm are the fixed costs, F, and the (constant) elasticity of the wage rate, ϵ. I assume that the former is determined by technology and the latter by workers' preferences. From (2.56) it is clear that an increase in F raises the price of employees, while an increase in ϵ raises the price of hours. Since the marginal products of each are positive and decreasing, the demand functions are

$$E^* = E(\overset{-}{F}, \overset{+}{\epsilon}, \overset{+}{C^0}), \tag{2.57a}$$

and

$$H^* = H(\overset{+}{F}, \overset{-}{\epsilon}, \overset{0}{C^0}), \tag{2.57b}$$

where the superior signs denote the effects on employment or hours of increasing the parameter in question. These are the fundamental

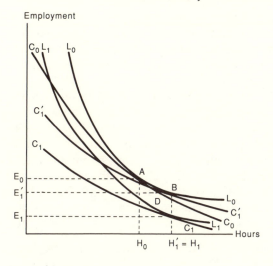

2.3 Substitution and Scale Effects in the
Worker-Hours Choice

results of the discussion in this section. If choices of workers and hours are separable from capital, an exogenous increase in fixed employment costs reduces the ratio of employment to hours at a given scale. An exogenous increase in the elasticity of wages with respect to hours raises this ratio. An increase in scale will, by assumption, affect only employment in the long run.

These substitution effects, and the scale effects that also result, can be illustrated by Figure 2.3. The initial labor input is L_0, consisting of employment E_0 and hours H_0. The labor isocost is C_0, which is convex as long as w' is not too positive.[17] Consider the effect of an increase in fixed employment costs. This shifts the isocost to C_1, both lower and flatter than C_0. The firm moves from A to D in the diagram, reducing employment to E_1 and increasing hours to H_1. The substitution effect along the isolabor curve L_0 to its tangency with the isocost C_1' that is parallel to C_1 is AB, an unambiguous increase in hours and cut in employment. In addition, the increase in fixed costs increases the cost of each worker-hours combination, so that the scale of operations is reduced. This leads to the scale effect BD. By assumption there will be no scale effect on hours, consistent with observation, though it is possible theoretically that the scale effect could change hours. It is certain that employment will be reduced and that EH, worker-hours, are reduced by this increase in fixed costs.

[17] The degree of convexity of C_0 must be less than that of the isolabor curve L_0 to obtain an internal maximum.

It is worth noting how changes in the parameters F and ϵ affect the equilibrium wage rate (remembering that in this general model the wage is determined by the interaction of the typical worker's labor-leisure choice and the firm's decision about employment and hours). The rise in equilibrium hours that is produced by an increase in fixed costs must in this model be accompanied by an increase in the average wage. (Otherwise, the supply of hours to the firm would not be forthcoming.) This conclusion is unaffected by any scale effects, since we assumed that scale effects have no impact on equilibrium hours.

Thus far I have assumed that workers and hours can be aggregated into the input "labor," so that choices about employment and hours are separable from choices about labor and capital inputs. If this is not so, most of the conclusions about the directions of the effects of higher fixed costs, or a higher wage-hours elasticity, no longer hold. Only the result that $\frac{\partial E^*}{\partial F} < 0$ is still valid (Hart 1984, 77–78); the effect of F on H^* is ambiguous. The reasons for these results can be seen by referring back to the discussion in Section IV. With more than two factors of production the increase in fixed costs, which is an increase in the price of E only, produces the usual negative own-price effect on E. Without knowing the relative p-substitutability or complementarity among the inputs, we cannot generally infer the impact on H.

The impacts of an increase in ϵ in (2.57a) and (2.57b) both become ambiguous once the separability of capital from labor is no longer assumed. The reason is that a higher ϵ represents an increase in two prices, those of employment and hours, relative to the price of capital services. Thus there is no unambiguous own-price effect. It is likely that the demand for hours falls, but if hours and capital are sufficiently relatively p-complementary compared to hours and workers, the demand for hours will rise. The effect on employment is ambiguous, since while its price falls relative to that of hours, it rises relative to the price of capital services.

Most of the theoretical work on the employment-hours decision has not used the general cost specification in (2.55). Instead, researchers (Rosen 1968, 1978; Ehrenberg 1971a; Hart 1984) have specified costs as

$$C^0 = EwH_s + Ew[H - H_s][1 + p] + EF, \qquad (2.58)$$

where w is the exogenous straight-time wage, p is the overtime premium, and H_s is standard hours, above which additional hours must be paid at the overtime rate. This respecification of labor costs changes the isocosts in Figure 2.3 by introducing a kink at H_s, with the isocost having a steeper slope to the right of H_s.

Assuming that all firms use some overtime, and redefining ϵ to be the elasticity of variable labor costs (the elasticity of all the terms in (2.58) except EF) with respect to H, yields

$$\epsilon = \frac{H[1 + p]}{H[1 + p] - pH_s} \geq 1,$$

with a strict inequality as long as the overtime premium is positive. This respecification of variable labor costs makes little sense as a model of labor-market equilibrium, since it completely ignores how workers' supply behavior might be affected by changes in H occasioned by altering p or F. Since it has been widely used, though, it is worth examining the implications for H^* and E^* of changes in the parameters of C^0.

The general results carry through this specific model in the case in which capital services are separable from labor. In particular, notice that a higher overtime premium raises the hours elasticity of labor costs. This means that an increase in p induces substitution away from hours and toward employees. A reduction in standard hours reduces the labor-cost elasticity and thus produces the opposite effects on employment and hours. Finally, as before, higher fixed costs reduce the ratio of employees to hours.

All of these inferences are made under the assumption that there are no scale effects on employment. (That there is none on hours is the maintained assumption throughout this and the next section.) All three changes—a higher overtime premium, lower standard hours, and higher fixed costs—produce negative scale effects on the demand for employment. Thus, the negative substitution effects on employment of lower standard hours and higher fixed costs are exacerbated by the scale effect; and the positive substitution effect of higher overtime premia is mitigated, and perhaps even reversed, by the negative scale effect it induces. The negative scale effect generated by lower standard hours is likely to be especially large, since it produces a large increase in the cost of inframarginal labor services.

These conclusions can only be drawn readily under the assumption that the typical firm works its homogeneous labor force some amount of overtime hours. In a more general model, in which some firms are in an overtime regime while others are not, a rise in fixed employment costs causes some firms to shift out of the straight-time regime and to use overtime hours. The possibility that firms shift regimes in response to changes in the cost parameters complicates the analysis. However, the regime shifts are in the same directions as the marginal changes made by firms that continue to use overtime. Thus, the conclusions about the directions of the substitution effects and the total impacts still hold.

The same cannot be concluded about the responses to a drop in standard hours. That change will cause some firms to shift to the straight-time regime, implying that total hours in those firms are reduced. This shift may be sufficient to outweigh the positive impact on hours among firms that remain in the overtime regime, so that the substitution effect on hours becomes ambiguous. Coupled with the scale effect on employment, though, it means that dropping the assumption of identical firms reduces and may even reverse the overall negative impact on employment.

As in the general model, when the separability of capital services from labor is not assumed, nearly all predictions about factor substitution become ambiguous. Unless one specifies the possibilities for substitution among employees, hours, and capital services, only the result that higher fixed costs reduce employment still holds. The reasons are the same as before: Most of the changes can operate on two margins, between workers and hours, and between workers (or hours) and capital services.

As noted above, workers' supply responses, which require that a higher wage rate must be paid to elicit additional weekly hours, make it unlikely that the wage rate remains fixed when the firm's cost parameters change. Assume the firm must offer a wage-hours package that maintains the typical worker's utility at

$$U(wH_s + w[1 + p][H - H_s], \bar{T} - H) = \bar{U}, \qquad (2.59)$$

where $\bar{T}$ are the total weekly hours available to the typical worker, $\bar{U}$ is the utility level available in other firms, and $U_i > 0$, $U_{ii} < 0$. Then if capital services and labor are separable, the negative substitution effect of a higher overtime premium on hours raises the second argument in U. As long as employment-hours substitution is not very large, the first argument will also increase. The firm can then reduce the wage and still attract workers, for it can maintain $U = \bar{U}$. At the very least this means that some part of the negative scale effect on employment generated by the increased overtime premium is eliminated by the action of the market. In this broader, labor-market view of the worker-hours decision a higher overtime premium results in lower straight-time wages, and because of that the reduction in hours produced through the substitution effect will be smaller.

Some ambiguity exists with fixed costs. On the demand side higher fixed costs result in higher weekly hours, thus reducing utility through the second argument of U; but the increase in hours raises income, thus raising utility in (2.59). Presumably, following our assumption of an upward-sloping labor supply schedule earlier in this section, the wage must increase with hours worked to hold utility at $\bar{U}$. Since an increased wage raises the cost of an hour of labor relative to that of another employee, this additional impact means that a higher overtime premium will reduce the extent of substitution toward workers and produce still larger negative scale effects on employment than in the standard model. It is possible that the wage adjustment will be sufficient so that the only impact of higher fixed costs is the negative scale effect on employment.

As we saw, a reduction in H_s generates substitution toward increased hours and away from workers and produces a negative scale effect on employment. Whether this conclusion is modified when a labor-market view is taken is ambiguous. The higher hours reduce the second argument of U in (2.59), thus reducing utility; but the reduction in H_s raises the first argument, thus increasing utility. If these labor-leisure choices are important, it is possible that the market will generate a change in the wage rate that could alter the conclusions about scale effects.

VII. The Demand for Hours in a Heterogeneous Work Force

If we abandon the assumption that workers are identical in production, the theory of labor demand offers very few concrete results. Those that can be drawn are illustrated by a model with only two types of workers, an assumption I maintain in this section. The workers are assumed to be distinguished by their skills, and this distinction means that each group of workers has its own wage-hours relation, with $w_1(H_1) < w_2(H_2)$, so that by assumption Type 2 workers are more skilled than Type 1 workers. Labor costs are

$$C^0 = \sum_{i=1}^{2} [E_i H_i w_i(H_i) + E_i F_i]. \tag{2.60}$$

The production technology can be written like (2.28):

$$Y = f(E_1, H_1, E_2, H_2, K), \tag{2.61}$$

a form that is so general that, without further specification, we cannot infer anything beyond the conclusions of Section IV. Therefore, consider the first and probably most interesting issue: Is there substitution between E_i and H_i independent of E_j? If not, can each type of labor be aggregated so that (2.61) can be rewritten as

$$Y = f(L_1(E_1, H_1), L_2(E_2, H_2), K), \tag{2.61'}$$

so the issue becomes one of first examining employment-hours substitution within each type of labor, as in Section VI, and then examining substitution among the three inputs L_1, L_2, and K, as in Section IV? If so, all the conclusions of Section VI apply to each type of labor. For example, higher fixed costs of Type 1 labor induce substitution toward hours of Type 1 workers and away from employing Type 1 workers, as does a lower wage-hours elasticity among these workers.

It is difficult to believe that the technology in (2.61') describes reality. Increased hours of unskilled workers may increase the productivity of each hour worked by skilled workers. To some extent the weekly work schedule functions as a public good within the plant (Stafford 1980), so that H_1 and H_2 cannot be separable. For example, if semiskilled workers spend more hours on the assembly line, the firm may benefit by increasing the daily or weekly hours of the skilled machine repairers who keep the equipment in satisfactory operating condition.

This counterargument suggests the interesting specific possibility that workers and hours are separable:

$$Y = f(E(E_1, E_2), H(H_1, H_2), K). \tag{2.61''}$$

If this alternative describes production well, the analysis of Section VI applies mutatis mutandis to the firm's choice between its total employment aggregate and the aggregate of hours. Combined with a discussion of how E_1 and E_2 are aggregated to generate employment (and similarly for the aggregation of hours), that analysis would provide helpful insights into the effects of changes in fixed costs or wage-hours elasticities of each type of labor.

Let the two types of labor be production workers and managers, and assume that the cost of hiring or training production workers falls, producing an increase in their employment. The increased ratio of production workers to managers raises the productivity of *both* the hours and the number of managers. This shows that employment and hours are not generally separable, and that (2.61'') will also not always be a good description of production.

These examples suggest that there will be substitution between E_i and H_j independent of E_j. It means that in general nothing can be concluded about the effects of, say, higher F_1 on the demand for hours of Type 1 workers, or on hours or employment of Type 2 labor. The own-price effects of wage-hour elasticities still hold if labor is separable from capital services; and the own-price effects of fixed costs hold if even it is not. But the direction of the substitution effects on the other components of labor input cannot be determined generally.

Based on the evidence that weekly hours do not vary systematically with firm size, I assumed in Section VI that there are no scale effects on hours. This assumption is presumably equally valid (or invalid) when labor is disaggregated into several types. Whether the demand for hours is homothetic in the intensity with which each type of labor is used is less clear. If the firm can vary continuously the amount and utilitization rate of each type of worker, there is no reason a priori to reject homotheticity. Nonetheless, there are no obvious facts that allow one to assume that the demand for hours is homothetic.

Throughout this section I have assumed heterogeneity exists only along the dimension of workers' skills. Workers' tastes for weekly hours were assumed to be identical, both here and in Section VI. What if they are not, and instead there is a continuum of workers arrayed by their marginal rates of substitution of income for leisure at each wage rate? In that case the market will generate an upward-sloping locus of wage-weekly hours equilibria (see Rosen 1974, 1978). The typical firm will still see itself as confronting the same wage-hours function as in Section VI, and the results derived there will still be valid. The only difference is that, rather than only generating changes in hours worked by the typical employee, parametric changes in labor costs alter the sorting of workers among firms.

VIII. Summary, and Prospects for the Theory of Static Labor Demand

The neoclassical theory of static labor demand has provided a framework and a number of specific predictions for studying how changes in exogenous factor prices and their components affect the relative and absolute amounts of labor inputs and their components. It has also generated predictions about how changes in exogenous factor quantities affect the relative and absolute wage levels of different groups of workers. The major conclusions are:

1. The effect of an increase in the wage of one group of workers on the amount of their labor demanded is negative. This negative response consists of a negative effect at a constant level of output, and a negative scale effect. An exogenous increase in the quantity of one type of labor available in the labor market produces a negative effect on those workers' wage rates. This response consists of a negative effect at a constant rate of marginal cost and a negative cost effect.

2. If there are only two inputs—say, labor and capital services—an increase in the wage raises the amount of capital services demanded at each output level; but the negative scale effect may still result in an overall decline in the firm's demand for capital services. Obversely, an increase in the supply of labor to the market raises the

return on capital services at a fixed cost of output, though the cost effect may produce an overall decline in the return to capital. If there are several inputs, perhaps several groups of workers and capital services, at least one input must see its employment increase at a fixed level of output if the wage of another group of workers rises. Similarly, the wage of at least one group of workers, or the return to capital, must rise at a given marginal cost if the available number of workers of another group increases.

3. The theory provides us with a useful framework and terminology for classifying demand relationships. Discovering whether particular pairs of inputs are p-substitutes or complements and q-complements or substitutes is helpful for evaluating the impact of a wide variety of policies, for analyzing the potential effects of changes in those policies, and for predicting how new policies will affect employment and/or wages. An increasingly elaborate superstructure of forms for estimating the underlying production relations has been built that can enable econometric research to provide estimates of these substitution relationships.

4. An increase in fixed costs of employment causes employers to alter the mix of worker-hours toward using more hours and fewer workers. An increase in the wage elasticity of additional hours (less generally, an increase in required premium wages for overtime work) produces the opposite effect. In all these cases, though, the increase in costs generates a negative scale effect that reduces total worker-hours. When combined with the substitution effect, this scale effect may be sufficiently large to cause total employment to fall when an overtime premium is increased.

The main message here is the central point of microeconomics: Price changes affect behavior. In the case of labor demand, this means that imposed increases in labor costs reduce labor demand, changes in relative wages shift relative worker-hours in the opposite direction, and relative changes in the components of labor cost alter the mix of employment and hours in the opposite direction. The changes may not be immediate. Indeed, there may not be any response if decisions about employment are lumpy, as I discuss in Chapter 4. How large the responses are is an empirical question, on which a huge amount of research has been produced (see Chapter 3). But that there is a *tendency for firms to reduce employment when wages increase and to shift relative employment toward workers who become relatively less expensive* is undeniable. Readers who are not convinced of this should close this book, as the vast body of empirical work and policy analysis is unlikely to sway them further.

Much of the development of the theory of labor demand from 1960 through 1990 was in the area of constructing functional forms for describing production technology. As Sections III and IV showed, these have been aimed at providing increasingly general methods for empirical research to infer the substitution parameters. No doubt still more complex functional forms can be invented, as the continued eruption of such forms during the 1980s (Pollak, Sickles, and Wales 1984; Considine and Mount 1984) shows. These will be useful, because they will allow further refinements of estimates of substitution relations. Despite that, extensions of this approach do not seem likely to be very fruitful in the sense of substantially broadening understanding of labor markets.

Further extensions in the long-run demand for employees and hours will undoubtedly also take place. Still more complex models of employment-hours choices along the lines of Hart (1984) can and will be built; and they may be able to provide an expanded framework that will allow careful empirical work to yield useful insights into firms' decision making and the impacts of changes in labor-market policy. Here too, though, these are extensions, amendments, and modifications rather than the basic novel research that is likely to revise and expand knowledge of the central issues in labor demand.

The most necessary theoretical work would link the demand and supply of labor. In Sections VI and VII I indicated how this approach might proceed in the context of the employment-hours choice and how it might modify conclusions about those decisions. Substantial work has proceeded since the development of contracting models in the mid-1970s (Baily 1974; Azariadis 1975). However, contracting models, which recognize how important it is to consider labor-market equilibrium rather than focus on supply and demand separately, have not been integrated into the theory of labor demand, and vice versa.

Aside from its implications for the progress of economic knowledge, this lack of communication among economists working in areas that are related can and, in this case, has resulted in serious problems when changes in policy are undertaken without paying attention to both relevant areas.[18] With that integration, and with only the data

---

[18] Federal legislation effective beginning in 1985 required state unemployment insurance systems in the United States to increase sharply the range of the experience-rated taxes that finance unemployment benefits. The intellectual origin of this change was the demonstration using contracting models of the disincentive effects produced by limits on tax rates under experience rating (e.g., Feldstein 1976). There was no change, though, in the very low ceiling on an employee's annual earnings that were taxable. In some states and for some employers superimposing the broader range of tax rates on the continued low base produced effective tax rates as high as 10 percent on the

now available for estimating substitution relations, much more can be learned about factor substitution. In particular, it should be possible to derive a set of estimating forms that enable one to infer the extent of factor substitution in the general context of Figure 2.1c rather than under the restrictive assumptions of perfectly elastic or inelastic supply depicted in Figures 2.1a and 2.1b. Similarly, it would enable us to understand the extent to which worker-hours outcomes are affected by both demand and supply forces.

The other area where important work on the theory of labor demand can and should proceed is what one might call the "new wage theory." This approach includes such work as the examination of efficiency wage models (e.g., Akerlof and Yellen 1986a) and the study of wage and employment outcomes that result from formal or informal bargaining over the rents generated by investments that are shared by workers and their employers (e.g., Kuhn 1988). In all this work the demand side of the models is rudimentary: A simple production function is assumed, with one type of labor at work in the typical firm. How would the conclusions of these models be altered by assuming several types of labor, especially if the extent of substitution among them and with capital is specified in ways consistent with existing empirical evidence? Obversely, bringing these models into the corpus of labor demand theory should enable us to draw better inferences about the nature of substitution among inputs.

Though the basic neoclassical theory of long-run labor demand has been well developed since the 1930s, and the major framework for applying it stems from the early 1970s, the theory need not be viewed as moribund. By integrating it into recent literatures that examine the relationships between workers and their employers, we can enhance our ability to draw useful inferences. More important from the point of view of this book, our ability to infer how employers substitute among workers and between workers and hours will also improve.

---

labor of their low-wage workers, as compared to rates of perhaps 2 percent on that of high-paid employees (Hamermesh 1990c). While probably reducing incentives for employment fluctuations, the modification of experience rating increased incentives to substitute high- for low-skilled employees. A dynamic imperfection was mitigated, while a static imperfection was worsened.

CHAPTER THREE

Wage, Employment, and Substitution Elasticities

I. WHAT WE NEED TO INFER

In Chapter 2 I developed the theory of labor demand, showing how production theory provides a framework within which empirical research can generate estimates of interesting parameters. Most important among these, and most widely studied by economists, is η_{LL}—the constant-output demand elasticity for homogeneous labor. Also included have been the total demand elasticity for homogeneous labor, η'_{LL}; the demand and factor-price elasticities for various groups of workers; partial elasticities of substitution and of complementarity between these groups, and for capital; and elasticities of substitution between workers and hours worked. In this chapter I assess critically the available estimates of these parameters and infer what we know about their magnitudes.

Empirical research on labor demand has progressed beyond being able to determine that the elasticity of substitution between labor and capital is definitively between zero and infinity (a level of knowledge that Johnson [1976, 107] claimed for it). How much further we have gone needs investigating. Achieving a consensus in this area is crucial if the theory presented in Chapter 2 is to provide an understanding of how labor markets actually work and of the likely impacts of existing and potential policies that affect them.

No single empirical study can provide definitive measures of a particular parameter. This guarantees that substantial numbers of empirical studies of the more important parameters describing labor demand will have been produced. The multiplicity of estimates imposes the burden of evaluating the design of each empirical study and, most important, of assessing whether the data allow researchers to draw the inferences they wish to make. In what follows I therefore first consider the appropriateness of various types of data, disaggregations of the labor force, and approaches to estimation for inferring labor-demand parameters. After determining the general outline of the empirical approaches that are likely to yield useful estimates, I present a detailed classification and critique of the available estimates of the parameters describing employers' demand for labor.

II. Problems of Data, Method, and Classification

A. Choices about Data and Aggregation

In evaluating empirical research on labor demand we must first determine precisely what should be estimated. For example, in the case of homogeneous labor, is it the demand elasticity for labor in the aggregate, or is it the typical firm's demand elasticity that we seek to estimate? The former is one step removed from the theory of production, for it is the result of aggregating individual firms' demand elasticities. The latter is explicitly tied to the theory, but is broadly useful only if the firm is truly "typical"—representative of the entire economy. I assume throughout that the desideratum is to obtain estimates of underlying production parameters. Thus, estimates based on aggregated data must be used with the caveat that the aggregation procedure does not bias the parameters describing production within the units of the aggregate.

Underlying all the considerations about data and aggregation should be the goal of identifying the demand parameters. In each study there should be enough exogenous variation in factor prices to allow the author to infer the demand elasticities of interest. Readily identifiable structural shocks, including natural experiments, form one regrettably infrequent source of this variation. More commonly, authors are forced either to claim (explicitly or implicitly) that for some reason there is exogenous variation in factor prices or quantities, or to attempt to account for the simultaneity of demand and supply.

The first general issue in evaluating the data used to generate estimates of demand parameters is the choice of time-series or cross-section data. For the moment let us ignore problems of spatial aggregation, of whether we observe firms, industries, or the aggregate economy, and of temporal aggregation, and assume that data at the appropriate level of disaggregation are equally easily available in cross-section or time-series form. Assume we seek to estimate an equation like (2.9a') describing the elasticity of demand for homogeneous labor. Then if the extent of randomness in the right-hand-side variables in the empirical version of this equation is the same in both cross-section and time-series data, both sources will yield equally good estimates of η_{LL}.[1]

---

[1] This does not mean that time-series and cross-section estimates are completely interchangeable. Kuh (1959), among others, showed that cross-section estimates will generally not provide good information on the dynamics of factor demand. All I claim

One might argue that randomness—in particular, measurement error—will be greater in the usual cross-section data sets than in time-series data. That is correct if we compare aggregate time-series data to cross-section data describing individual plants or particular households. But if we compare estimates generated from a time series describing one plant to those produced on a cross section of industry aggregates, the opposite inference would be correct. In fact, as the tables in this chapter show, most time-series studies are based on industry or aggregate data, and most cross-section studies are based on data covering industries or geographical subdivisions. Any measurement errors at the micro level will average out within these units (though nonrandom errors may be a problem here too).

For our purposes the only important distinction between time-series and cross-section data is dictated by the characteristics of each type of data that are generally available to the researcher. Time-series data on individual plants or establishments are rarely available, but time series of industry or even economywide aggregates form the basis for many of the studies analyzed here. While cross-section data are often available as industry or geographical aggregates, there are few sets of cross-section data describing plants or firms. For purposes of inferring demand parameters, a greater degree of disaggregation is generally possible with cross-section than with time-series data. In sum, in estimating long-run relationships there is nothing inherently more attractive in cross-section or time-series data. Rather, the choice depends on the degree of spatial aggregation in each type of available data and on the effects of aggregation on the parameter estimates.

The second general issue is whether to use data based on establishments or households. The immediate answer is to use establishment data—after all, we are seeking to estimate the parameters of *firms'* production technologies. Ignoring problems of measurement error and of the availability of data (or the cost of collecting data), though, it probably does not matter which choice is made. For example, if we seek to infer factor-demand elasticities using some form of (2.43), we can either observe wages reported by employers in a variety of geographic areas characterized by differing relative supplies of labor or by workers in those areas.

Differences in the kinds of data available from establishment and household surveys cannot be ignored. For purposes of estimating demand parameters, using household data implies cross-section estimation, either based on individuals in different geographic areas or

---

here is that a properly specified static labor-demand equation (or cost or production function) can produce unbiased parameter estimates.

on aggregates across these areas. In both cases the data represent workers in establishments that may have substantially different production technologies. With carefully chosen establishment data this problem can be mitigated. For example, a cross section of establishments in a particular industry can be examined, or a time series describing the aggregate of an industry's establishments can be analyzed. As with the choice between time-series and cross-section data, choosing between household- and establishment-based data in the end depends on the importance of problems of aggregation.

Ignoring for the moment the choice of an appropriate labor aggregate, there are several issues of aggregation over units of observation that require consideration. In discussing them it is important to keep in mind that the purpose is to infer the parameters characterizing labor demand at the level of establishments. Researchers have used: (1) actual observations on individual firms or establishments; (2) establishment (or, less often, household data) aggregated to the level of an industry; and (3) the same data aggregated for an entire economy.

The first issue here is the well-known problem of linear aggregation of nonlinear relationships (Theil 1954). Even if all the constituent establishments have identical technologies that generate versions of (2.22') like

$$ln\ L_i = \alpha - \sigma ln\ w_i + ln\ Y_i, \tag{3.1}$$

where i is an establishment, the estimate of σ will contain errors if (3.1) is estimated over data representing aggregates of those establishments. The equation is estimated on aggregated data as

$$ln(\Sigma L_i) = \alpha' - \sigma' ln(\Sigma w_i) + b ln(\Sigma Y_i). \tag{3.1'}$$

There is no reason to expect that $\sigma' = \sigma$, or $b = 1$. Without, for example, knowing the distribution of the w_i by size of establishment, we cannot infer the existence or direction of any biases.[2]

This difficulty does not dictate using microeconomic data to the exclusion of industry or economywide observations. If the former are less readily obtainable (are more expensive to acquire), we may be thrown back on the latter. A tradeoff must be made between the ease of acquiring data and errors induced when the more readily available data are used to estimate demand parameters. The discussion suggests that equally competent research based on carefully measured microeconomic data is likely to yield better estimates of the parameters of interest than that based on aggregated data. Whether one in-

---

[2] This problem is discussed at length as part of the general issue of aggregating capital stocks in Sato (1975).

tervenes to measure employment and wages at the establishment or with the worker, or considers observations arrayed in cross section or time series, more reliable estimates of production parameters are produced if microeconomic data form the units for estimation.

Aggregation over microeconomic units is only one aspect of the aggregation problem in studying labor demand. The other is the choice of how to aggregate the labor of the workers in a particular plant, industry, or economy. No two workers are perfectly substitutable; but estimating separate demand equations for Joseph Jones, Albert Smith, and so on is neither feasible nor of any great economic interest. Compromises must be made so that the estimation problem can be limited and the estimates allow generalization to other workers.

The general approach is to aggregate workers who one believes to be very close p-substitutes or q-complements (ideally, with $\sigma_{ij}, c_{ij} \rightarrow \infty$). This aggregation almost always involves simply summing the number of workers, so that the even stronger assumption that the workers are equally productive is also implicit. It also implies that the individuals who are aggregated are separable from the other inputs. Without estimating the demand for each particular individual, it is impossible to know how closely one's choices approximate the ideals of close substitution, equal productivity, and separability. This means that researchers must rely on their intuition about these issues when aggregating groups of workers.

It is extremely difficult to discover whether a particular aggregation of labor is appropriate. We should, though, at least estimate demand relationships describing aggregates of labor that are of intrinsic interest, either in terms of some labor-market policy, because of the sizes of groups chosen, or because understanding substitution relations among them could provide evidence on a theoretical controversy. As a somewhat negative example, easy availability of the data has led many researchers to estimate substitution relationships between production and nonproduction workers. Knowing the degree of substitution between them is of little inherent policy interest. Also, because there is a remarkably large overlap in the earnings of these two groups, this knowledge tells us relatively little about substitution between high- and low-skilled workers.[3] This particular aggregation may, though, be of theoretical interest insofar as one wishes to ex-

[3] For example, in 1980 49 percent of white-collar workers earned less than $10,000 per year, while 59 percent of blue-collar workers did. At the other extreme, 35 percent of white-collar workers earned more than $20,000 per year, but so did 25 percent of blue-collar workers. (Computed from *Census of Population*, 1980, PC80-1-D1-A, Table 281.)

amine issues of labor hoarding and employment dynamics that may differ between blue- and white-collar workers (see Chapter 7).

An example of a useful aggregation for purposes of analyzing static labor demand is that of workers classified by experience or age. The huge literature on human capital makes it clear that this is also an aggregation by skill. It is thus interesting for any policy issue that relates to the differential taxation/subsidy of wage rates by skill, and to the impacts on relative wage rates of training programs that change relative supplies of labor by skill. It is also useful for analyzing the impact on relative wages of changes in cohort size and thus in the age structure of the labor force. Indeed, the impact on relative wages of any policy that would change relative labor supply by age can be analyzed using the parameter estimates based on this aggregation.

A way to circumvent the problems of aggregating individual workers was proposed by Welch (1969) and elaborated by Rosen (1983), Stapleton and Young (1984), and especially Heckman and Sedlacek (1985). The approach yields an amalgam of workers' characteristics based on variations in the returns to those characteristics in different sectors. The labor input is then a weighted average of workers' characteristics, with different weights in each sector. Probably because it does not yield easily identifiable aggregates the demand for which, and substitution among which, can be linked to policy, this approach has not been widely applied.

In practice that cumbersome approach is unlikely to be used frequently to solve the aggregation problem; but its use at least tries to account for the aggregation of skills. In nearly all other studies workers are just added up (aggregated linearly); their earnings are simply summed and divided by worker-hours to yield the group's wage rate; and the two measures are used to estimate the demand parameters for the group of workers (perhaps for all labor together). This approach is partly dictated by the availability of the data; partly, too, it reflects an unwillingness of most researchers to consider how the data they use are generated. The implication of linear aggregation of workers i and j is that $\sigma_{ij} \to \infty$, which hardly seems correct for all workers even within a narrow group, for example, high school graduates ages twenty-five to forty-four. If it were correct for all labor lumped together, there would be no interest in the theory of Section 2.IV or in the empirical work discussed in Section 3.IV.

Among those studies that worry about aggregation, the nearly universal approach is to take the particular disaggregation provided in the data as given. Various aggregations of the data are then examined and tested for whether groups of workers i and j are separable in production (whether $\sigma_{ik} = \sigma_{jk}$ for all other factors k). This approach has the virtue of making the choice of aggregator endogenous to the production process rather than a priori in the collection of data. It suffers, though, from the fault that it begins with data that are already highly and perhaps inappropriately aggregated, so that much of the potential difficulty with aggregation is never examined.

Studies that create their own aggregates by examining substitution among very narrowly defined groups of workers, or even among individuals, are more believable than those that take published aggregates and analyze the demand for them. However, the work entailed in choosing appropriate and interesting aggregates is immense. If each new study does not make its own choices about aggregating data on individuals, we can at least hope that each pays some attention to aggregation and the problems it can cause.

The availability of data also dictates that many studies exclude measures of the stock of capital. For the same reason other studies concentrate on the demand for one or several types of worker and exclude much of the total input of labor from the estimation. In these cases a problem of interpretation arises. Let, for example, the true production function for two types of labor (assumed to be aggregated appropriately) and capital be

$$Y = F(K, G[L_1, L_2]), \tag{3.2}$$

where I assume that G aggregates the two types of labor and that this aggregate is separable from capital. Then estimates of a system of labor-demand equations that ignores capital, or of the labor aggregator

$$L = G(L_1, L_2), \tag{3.3}$$

implicitly measure substitution along an isolabor curve, not an isooutput curve.

The factor-demand elasticities computed from (3.3) are thus not constant-output elasticities. Instead (Berndt 1981), they are *gross elasticities*; constant-output labor-demand elasticities differ from these, for any rise in a wage—for example, w_1—will induce a reduction in L (because the price of aggregate labor has risen). If, for example, the L-constant demand elasticity for L_1 is η_{11}^*, the constant-output labor-demand elasticity η_{11} is

$$\eta_{11} = \eta_{11}^* + s_1 \eta_{LL}. \tag{3.4}$$

In general (see Berndt and Wood 1979),

$$\eta_{ij} = \eta_{ij}^* + s_j \eta_{LL}.$$

The constant-output demand elasticity is more negative (greater in absolute value) than the gross elasticities, η_{ii}^* that such studies produce. The true cross-price demand elasticities are more negative than those based on estimates of substitution using (3.3) as the underlying production relation, because they also allow for capital-labor substitution.

There is nothing inherently wrong with ignoring capital or some part of the work force, assuming problems of separability are resolved. Estimates of factor-demand or factor-price elasticities are readily interpretable, but they must be interpreted carefully. Otherwise, one will, for example, underestimate own-price demand elasticities and infer that two groups of labor are greater p-substitutes than they in fact are. In the simplest case, if we include only two factors out of many, empirical work must show them to be p-substitutes no matter what their substitutability is in a complete model.

B. Specific Measurement and Estimation Problems

Having weighed the pros and cons of using cross-section or time-series and establishment or household data, and after determining the degree of spatial aggregation and the appropriate labor subaggregates to use, empirical researchers must still determine how to measure labor inputs and their prices, or at least be aware of problems with their choice of data. The simpler issue is the choice of a measure of the quantities L or L_i. In the literature the alternatives have mostly been total employment and worker-hours. Clearly, if workers are homogeneous, working the same hours per time period, the choice is irrelevant. If they are heterogeneous along the single dimension of hours worked per time period, using employment to represent the quantity of labor will lead to biases if hours per worker are correlated with factor prices or output. In studies using cross-section data, in which there may be substantial heterogeneity among plants, firms, or industries in hours, this suggests that worker-hours be used. In time series (on which most estimates of η_{LL} are based) the choice is less important if the sole concern is estimating long-run elasticities, since variations in worker-hours over time are highly correlated with variations in employment.[4]

In most cases one has data on hours at work, as opposed to hours on the payroll, which include paid vacations, sick time, and the like. Since we wish to measure productive inputs, hours at work are clearly the better measure to use if both are available, since they reflect actual inputs of labor into production. Unlike in most countries,

[4] Of course, if long-run elasticities are sought, time-series estimation is fraught with problems (noted above) unless the lag structures that are imposed are extensive.

though, until the 1980s the generally available time series for manufacturing in the United States were on hours on the payroll. If the ratio of hours paid for to hours worked varies over time, as it has with increased paid time off, any study using worker-hours that ignores these changes will generate biased estimates of η_{LL} in an equation relating worker-hours to real wages and output.

Choosing a measure of the price of labor is more difficult. Most of the published data from developed countries reflect average hourly earnings or average wage rates. A few countries publish data on compensation (employers' payments for employee benefits and wages per hour a worker is on the payroll). While most of the studies of the demand for homogeneous labor use one of the first two measures, none of these three is completely satisfactory. There are two problems: (1) variations in the measured price of labor may be the spurious result of shifts in the distribution of employment or hours among subaggregates with different labor costs, or of changes in the amount of hours worked at premium pay; and (2) data on the cost of adding one worker (or one hour of labor services) to the payroll for one hour of actual work are not available.

The first problem can be solved in studies of labor demand in the United States using the adjusted earnings series covering most of the postwar period for the private nonfarm economy. The second problem is soluble (except for labor costs resulting from inputs into training) for studies of the U.S. labor market beginning in 1977 by the Employment Cost Index produced by the Bureau of Labor Statistics. Clearly, future work using aggregate time series should increasingly rely on that index. The potential importance of the distinction is shown by Hamermesh (1983), whose broader measure of labor cost per hour worked generates higher estimates of own-price demand elasticities than do average hourly earnings or compensation measures.

In examining substitution between workers and hours still more difficulties arise in measuring labor costs. Ideally one would measure the marginal cost of an additional employee as the compensation per time period plus the user cost of hiring and training *plus* the marginal change that adding this worker induces in the cost of employing all other workers. (Without assuming monopsony, one might well still imagine that an extra worker changes the per-worker cost of providing training or certain employee benefits.) The marginal cost of an extra hour of work should be measured as the wage rate defined as a function of hours of work (equation 2.54) at the existing input of hours. Much research on employment-hours substitution takes the *relative average* costs of employment and hours as the ratio of per-worker benefit costs to the average price of an hour of overtime work. Few studies go beyond this to examine the *marginal costs* of the two components of labor input in detail.[5] This failure, which is dictated by the limited availability of data and by the difficulty of using available data to approximate marginal input costs, means that the measured relative cost of workers and hours usually contains substantial measurement error. Prior choices about measuring the relative price of employment and hours make it difficult for most studies to discover the degree of complementarity (or substitutability) between them.

Beyond explicit issues of measurement the researcher must decide what variables to treat as exogenous. Ideally the production or cost function, or labor-demand equation, will be embedded in an identified model including a labor-supply relation or some specification of workers' choices. In that case methods for estimating a system of equations are appropriate, and the problem is obviated: Both the price and quantity of labor may be treated as endogenous. In reality this is not always done in studies of the demand for homogeneous labor.[6] If a complete system of equations, or a mechanism describing workers' supply behavior, cannot be specified, one may have sufficient variables that are not in the equation based on the cost or production function and that can be used to produce an instrument for the endogenous right-hand side variable. However, given the difficulty of specifying a labor-supply relation in the aggregate data on which most studies of labor demand are based, it seems unlikely that a good set of variables can be found.

If the problem is severe for studies of homogeneous labor, it is essentially insolvable when one examines heterogeneous labor. Accordingly, one must be able to argue that supplies of each type of labor are either completely inelastic or completely elastic in response to exogenous changes in demand.[7] For both homogeneous and heterogeneous labor the choice usually boils down to whether price or quantity can be viewed as exogenous in the problem under study. (This is the identification problem noted in the introduction to Chapter 2.) If the data describe small units—plants, firms, or perhaps even geographic areas—one can reasonably argue that supply curves are nearly horizontal in the long run. The wage rate may then be treated

---

[5] The best example of greater care on this issue is Hart and Kawasaki (1988).

[6] The few exceptions are Black and Kelejian (1970), Heckman and Sedlacek (1985), and Kennan (1988).

[7] This is an economic issue, not a problem of inferring the partial elasticities of substitution or complementarity. In the translog case, for example, those can always be inferred, either easily or by inverting a matrix involving all the coefficients estimated.

as exogenous; and estimates of cost functions, labor-demand equations, or share equations based on factor prices are appropriate (for they include the wage instead of the quantity of labor as an independent variable). In studies using aggregate data this assumption has not been considered valid since Malthusian notions of labor supply were abandoned. If the supply of labor to the economy is quite inelastic even in the long run, demand parameters are best estimated using specifications that treat the quantity of labor as exogenous. Production functions and variants of second-order approximations that include factor quantities as regressors should then be used.

Since the supply of labor to the units being studied is generally neither perfectly elastic or inelastic, any choice other than estimating production parameters within a complete system including supply is unsatisfactory. The difficulties of doing this force the researcher to rely on beliefs about the likely elasticity of supply to the units, the availability and quality of data, and whether factor-demand elasticities or elasticities of factor prices are of interest. In practice the best guide to choosing between treating wages or quantities as exogenous is the link between this choice and the researcher's beliefs about the supply elasticities of the inputs (and thus how the misspecification that is induced can be minimized).

Consider the example of determining the extent of substitutability among adult women, adult men, youths, and capital. Studies of labor supply suggest it is reasonable to treat the quantity of adult men in the work force as exogenous, and increasingly also of adult women; but that assumption hardly makes sense for youths, whose labor supply appears to be more elastic. (The supply elasticity of capital may also be a problem.) The overwhelming shares of output are accounted for by the first two groups, whose supply of effort is relatively inelastic. That being so, treating factor quantities as exogenous is probably the better choice. This also means that one should focus the analysis on the elasticities of complementarity and of factor prices, which are estimated more readily using production rather than cost functions (see Section 2.IV).

Like the aggregation problems discussed above, this difficulty also dictates that the resulting estimates be interpreted carefully. We are unlikely to solve problems of exogeneity in estimating demand relations, and there are more fruitful avenues of inquiry in estimating labor demand. We should at least, though, be aware of the issue and consider it in assessing any estimates.

A major issue is the choice of a theoretical framework to use for estimating the parameters of interest. The first approach to estimation generates measures of σ. One way of doing so relies on the production or cost function "directly." In the case of the Cobb-Douglas function this method produces the distribution parameters. (If, for example, data on factor prices are unavailable, these parameter estimates are necessary to compute the factor-demand elasticities. If data on shares can be computed, there is no reason to estimate this function.) Estimating a CES function directly is, as inspection of (2.19) shows, not easy; and directly estimating more complex forms, such as the generalized Leontief and translog approximations, is still more difficult. For that reason little work has relied on this approach, though it is quite feasible in the two-factor case. In the multifactor case multicollinearity ($N+1$ terms involving each factor are included in the translog approximation, N in the generalized Leontief approximation) becomes severe (but see Klotz, Madoo, and Hanson 1980). With more than two inputs included, direct estimation should not be done unless one arbitrarily imposes a multifactor Cobb-Douglas technology. As Chapter 2 showed, though, if that is done we cannot answer any questions about factor substitution.

A second way of generating estimates of σ, if one is interested only in a two-factor production function, is to estimate a version of the marginal productivity condition (3.1). This produces estimates of the degree of homogeneity of the production function along with the estimate of σ. Together with information on s_L the estimate of σ generates η_{LL}.

Yet a third way of estimating σ directly is to use the ratio of factor inputs. In the two-factor CES case this just involves estimating (2.21), with $\ln \dfrac{L}{K}$ as a dependent variable. The elasticity with respect to relative factor prices provides the estimate of σ, and η_{LL} can be calculated by multiplying by $[1 - s_L]$. The relative factor-demand method should not be used in the multifactor case, though this has been done. That involves the estimation of all pairs of equations like (2.21) in the CES case, or all ratios like those of (2.24a) and (2.24b) in the generalized Leontief case. While there is nothing inherently wrong with this approach, it requires imposing the restrictions that factor demand be homogeneous of degree zero in all factor prices. That is easily done, but the studies that have used this method to examine multifactor substitution have not done so.

The fourth way of estimating σ directly is the method offered by Arrow et al. (1961) in the original exposition of the CES function. The authors proposed estimating value-added per worker as a function of the real wage. This method is probably the most widely used way of generating estimates of σ. However, because it has been used mostly in research not designed to estimate parameters describing labor demand (though it obviously does this), and because there are many surveys of that empirical literature, I do not discuss it here.

A second approach uses labor-demand conditions from the Shephard conditions (2.9). With even two factors this means estimating

$$ln \; L_j = \Sigma b_i ln \; w_i + a_1 ln \; Y, \; \Sigma b_i = 0, \tag{3.5}$$

an empirical form of (2.38). Clearly, (3.5) should be viewed as part of a complete system of factor-demand equations. If data on all factor quantities are available, a complete system should be estimated. If not, though, (3.5) will provide all the necessary estimates, for

$$\frac{\partial ln \; L_j}{\partial ln \; w_i} = \frac{s_i}{s_j} \frac{\partial ln \; L_i}{\partial ln \; w_j}.$$

The multifactor labor-demand approach provides an easy way of using information on all available inputs to estimate the desired parameters. Constraints that are dictated by theory (symmetry and homogeneity) can easily be imposed on the b_i. A similar approach can be used to examine a wage equation specified as a linear function of the logarithms of all factor quantities to calculate partial elasticities of factor prices.

The third approach is to estimate the demand for labor or a particular type of worker as a part of a system of equations based on one of the approximations, like the generalized Leontief, translog, or CES-translog forms. While this is not generally done in the two-factor case, a single equation like (2.26) could be estimated. In the case of heterogeneous labor, though, using one of these approximations is an easy way to impose the restrictions implied by production theory.

In estimating substitution between workers and hours, researchers have rarely used the third (system) method. They have frequently used all other methods, with much of the research concentrating on the relative factor-demand approach. The problems inherent in these methods when they are applied to substitution among groups of workers, or between a group of workers and capital, also exist when they are used to estimate employment-hours substitution. The added difficulties imposed by problems of measuring relative prices in this case, though, strengthen the argument for estimating production functions involving employment and hours directly (since measures of input prices are not necessary).

Most of the discussion thus far has dealt with constant-output demand elasticities η_{LL}. This is appropriate, given that the theory is based on long-run equilibrium, which for an entire economy implies that output is fixed. In Chapter 2, though, I noted that in the short run, or for individual firms, sectors, or industries, a change in the price of labor will induce a change in output (especially if a small industry is the unit of observation). In that case one may wish to estimate the size of the scale effect on labor demand (alternatively, estimate the total labor-demand elasticity η'_{LL}).

An indirect approach simply takes some extraneous estimate of the demand elasticity for the product of the industry and uses (2.7a') to derive a labor-demand elasticity that includes the scale effect. For an entire economy no such demand elasticity is likely to be available. In that case, or if no good estimates of industry product-demand elasticities are at hand, a direct approach is required and is taken in a few of the studies discussed in this chapter. That approach estimates equations like (3.5), with wages and (perhaps) other factor prices, but with output (Y) deleted.

C. A Schema for Classifying Studies of Labor Demand

The ideal classification of a large group of studies organizes the results so that one can determine which ones provide the better estimates of the underlying parameters of interest. The discussion in Subsection A above suggested that the greatest difficulties in studies of labor demand should arise from differences in the extent of aggregation of the data. Accordingly, as Figure 3.1 shows, at the top of the hierarchy of classification is the threefold distinction among studies by the level of the data: (I) an entire economy, or a major industry, is the unit of observation; (II) small industries, or a geographic area or areas, are observed; and (III) firms, establishments, or individuals are the units of observation.

We saw that the choices between time-series or cross-section and establishment- or household-based data need not yield different estimates of the same underlying production process if the estimating equations are specified carefully. The specification is not always so careful, though, so that distinguishing among studies along these two criteria is necessary to evaluate the results. Accordingly, in each table I classify studies according to whether they use (A) time-series data, or (B) cross-section data, and whether they are based on (1) establishment data, or (2) household data. Where studies use panel data they are denoted by A–B.

The fourth level of classification is the method used to estimate the parameters, one of the three discussed above in Subsection B. These are: (a) direct estimation of a cost or production function, or of σ; (b) labor-demand conditions; and (c) system estimation, usually one of the approximations to a generalized cost or production function.

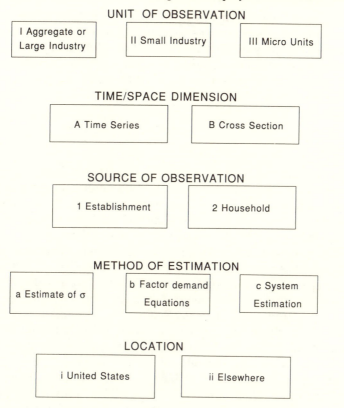

3.1 Schema for Classifying Studies of Labor Demand

The final level of classification distinguishes the source of the data by country. While much of the literature covers the United States, there is a large and rapidly growing corpus of studies based on data from other countries. Even if technology is easily transferable, the parameter estimates that researchers produce using data from various countries will differ due to international differences in the patterns of exogenous shocks and in the kinds of data that are collected and the way that national statistical agencies collect them. We can expand our knowledge of labor demand by considering cross-national differences in parameter estimates. The studies are therefore classified by whether they use (i) U.S. data, or (ii) non-U.S. data.

Tables 3.1 through 3.6 organize the available estimates of the demand for homogeneous labor according to the three levels of data aggregation I–III. Tables 3.7 through 3.10 organize studies of heterogeneous labor in the same way, except that each table presents all the estimates for a particular disaggregation of the labor force or on a particular issue of labor-labor substitution. Table 3.11 presents all the estimates of employment/hours substitution. Within each of these tables the analysis is organized by the parameter (or concept) being measured; and within that, by the type of study in question and by chronological order.

III. Estimates of the Elasticity of Demand for Homogeneous Labor

In this and the next two sections I examine the evidence on the demand for homogeneous labor, substitution among different types of workers, and substitution between workers and hours. The literature surveyed does not exhaust all studies that have been made of these topics, since I cannot claim to have searched through all available journals and especially through all possible nonjournal sources. Instead, searches were made through a broad range of scholarly journals before 1975 (see Hamermesh 1976), through a wider range of journals from 1975 to 1982 (see Hamermesh 1986) and through a still wider range from 1983 to 1990.[8] References were followed up from the studies in these sources. Unless otherwise noted, where I summarize estimates for several industries from a particular study I take employment-weighted averages of those estimates if employment weights are available in the published study or could be obtained from the author. Where that was not possible, I present the median of the estimates for the industries. Where I summarize estimates for different countries from one study, I present simple averages. In a few cases where one study produced alternative estimates by equally plausible methods I present the range of results. In Tables 3.1 through 3.5 I present the negative of the estimates of the various labor-demand elasticities. Thus, most of the estimated constant-output labor-demand elasticities are listed as positive, because they are measuring $-\eta_{LL}$.

The studies of union wage effects surveyed by Lewis (1986) and of labor supply summarized by Killingsworth (1983) were mostly de-

---

[8] The journals searched for this period are: *American Economic Review, Canadian Journal of Economics, Econometrica, Economic Inquiry, Economic Journal, Economica, Industrial and Labor Relations Review, International Economic Review, Journal of Human Resources, Journal of Labor Economics, Journal of Political Economy, Quarterly Journal of Economics, Review of Economic Studies, Review of Economics and Statistics,* and *Southern Economic Journal*. No doubt a few studies have been missed. Also, in many cases the published versions mentioned but did not provide estimates of the appropriate elasticities. In several cases attempts to obtain from the authors the necessary information to compute the elasticities were not successful, so the studies are not presented in the tables.

signed to produce estimates of the wage effects or of labor supply parameters. The studies of labor-labor substitution analyzed in Section IV and those of employee-hours substitution discussed in Section V are mostly aimed at providing estimates of those substitution parameters. In most studies of the demand for homogeneous labor, however, the estimate of η_{LL} or of η_{LX_j}, where X_j is another input, is a by-product of the investigator's interest in some other topic. Some of the studies surveyed in this section are designed solely to predict the path of employment; others seek to model and examine the dynamics of employers' demand for workers and hours. (These form the basis for much of the survey in Chapter 7.) Still other research has aimed at testing the properties of alternative specifications of production functions or at examining the effects of embedding various functions in dynamic models. Yet other strands of research seek to study the demand for other inputs, particularly energy, and include labor as one of several inputs in cost or production functions. Very few studies focus on η_{LL}, so that in many cases estimates of it produced by a particular study must be calculated from other information.

A. Studies Using Highly Aggregated Data

The first group of studies (Group I in the schema) is based on data aggregated over an entire economy (or economies) or a major sector (usually manufacturing). With this high degree of aggregation the authors are by inference producing estimates of η_{LL} that are net of all shifts of employment that occur among firms in the economy (or sector), including those that are induced by changes in relative costs across firms or industries that differ by factor intensity. As such, the estimate is not the same as the firm-level demand elasticity that asks how a particular firm's employment would change if its wage alone were shocked. That suggests that, ignoring any other difficulties, the estimates produced by these studies will understate the true firm-level value of η_{LL}.

The first set of Group I studies produces direct estimates of σ. These estimates, which must be multiplied by $1 - s_L$ to obtain estimates of η_{LL}, are presented in Table 3.1. While it is clear from the specification of these studies and from the discussion in Chapter 2 that it is in fact σ that they are estimating, several of them refer to the estimates as "demand elasticities for labor." They are not, and I have summarized them accordingly.

Most common among these direct estimates are those based on the marginal productivity condition (3.1). This specification has often

TABLE 3.1
Estimates of σ Using Data on Aggregates or Large Industries (Group I.a Studies)

Study	Category	Description	σ_{LK}
Dhrymes (1969)	I.A.1.a.i	Total private hours, quarterly, 1948–60; MP condition	0.75
Hamermesh (1983)	I.A.1.a.i	Private nonfarm, quarterly, 1955–78; MP condition, attention to measuring labor cost	0.47
Drazen, Hamermesh, and Obst (1984)	I.A.1.a.ii	Manufacturing worker-hours, quarterly, 10 OECD countries, mostly 1961–80; MP condition	0.21
Lucas and Rapping (1970)	I.A.1.a.i	Aggregate production-worker-hours, annual, 1930–65; MP condition, supply-demand system	1.09
Black and Kelejian (1970)	I.A.1.a.i	Private nonfarm worker-hours, quarterly, 1948–65; MP condition, supply-demand system	0.36
Liu and Hwa (1974)	I.A.1.a.i	Private worker-hours, monthly, 1961–71; MP condition, supply-demand system	0.67
Beach and Balfour (1983)	I.A.1.a.ii	Manufacturing operatives worker-hours, quarterly, 1956–78; U.K.; MP condition, supply-demand systems	(0.49, 0.79)
Lewis and Kirby (1988)	I.A.1.a.ii	Nonfarm employment, quarterly, 1967–87; Australia; MP condition	0.78
Rudebusch (1986)	I.A.1.a.i	Nonfarm business worker-hours, quarterly, 1952–81; MP condition, disequilibrium supply-demand model	1.16
Quandt and Rosen (1988)	I.A.1.a.i	Private worker-hours, annual, 1932–83; MP condition, disequilibrium supply-demand model	0.69
Hall, Henry, and Pemberton (1990)	I.A.1.a.ii	Total employment, quarterly, 1966–88; U.K.; disequilibrium supply-demand model	6.86
Brown and de Cani (1963)	I.A.1.a.i	Private nonfarm worker-hours, annual, 1933–58; capital-labor ratio	0.47

TABLE 3.1 (*cont.*)

Study	Category	Description	σ_{LK}
David and van de Klundert (1965)	I.A.1.a.i	Private worker-hours, annual, 1899–1960; capital-labor ratio	0.32
Schaafsma (1978)	I.A.1.a.ii	Manufacturing employment, annual, 1949–72; Canada; capital-labor ratio	0.42
Symons (1985)	I.A.1.a.ii	Manufacturing employment, quarterly, 1961–76; U.K.; KL and import prices	2.40

been used where the researcher cannot obtain satisfactory measures of the prices or quantities of other inputs. When zero-degree homogeneity in factor prices is imposed on the demand for labor (a term in w/r is entered into an equation describing the demand for labor), measurement error in r will bias the estimate of η_{LL} toward zero. Thus, problems of measuring the price of capital services in particular have led researchers to estimate condition (3.1) rather than a labor-demand equation.

The first three studies summarized in Table 3.1 simply estimate condition (3.1) without worrying about other factors or about factor supply. (Remember, the supply of labor may be elastic to the firm, but it is unlikely to be elastic to the economy or to a large sector.) All three studies find that $\sigma < 1$. Their use of aggregate data and their failure to account for the simultaneity of supply and demand mean they are not by themselves very informative. They do, though, provide a benchmark for comparing studies that consider these problems.

One set of extensions to the simple marginal productivity condition specifies some kind of equilibrium model in which a supply condition is estimated jointly with the MP condition. The supply equations in Black and Kelejian (1970), Liu and Hwa (1974), and Beach and Balfour (1983) really just provide ways of obtaining instrumental variables for estimating the MP condition. Lucas and Rapping (1970), however, do provide a full-blown equilibrium model of the labor market that lays special stress on the formation of expectations. In terms of estimating the MP condition, though, it too is used mainly to provide instrumental variables. None of these estimates of σ is outside the range produced by the first group of studies using the MP condition. The reason may be that the assumption of equilibrium is incorrect. It may also be that the time-series supply equations are not well specified due to their inability to model the major causes of shocks to aggregate labor supply. (Measures of per-capita assets that are included in time-series labor-supply equations do not capture much of the income effect they are designed to reflect.)

To account for one of the problems in the supply-demand studies several authors have estimated disequilibrium models of the labor market. In these studies the condition that actual employment be the minimum of the amounts supplied and demanded is used to estimate the probability that the economy is operating on its labor-demand or labor-supply curve. The estimates of σ produced by Quandt and Rosen (1988) (and in their several earlier studies) and by Rudebusch (1986) are consistent with Cobb-Douglas production and are not that different from those generated by the studies of MP conditions using equilibrium supply-demand systems. Here too the reason may be that the aggregate labor-supply equation is not estimated very precisely. While the same inability to specify supply and demand adjustment jointly is present in Hall, Henry, and Pemberton (1990), the authors pay more attention to the time-series properties of the data. Why the estimate of σ is much higher in their data for the United Kingdom is not clear.

The final four studies presented in Table 3.1 used (2.21) to obtain estimates of σ. With the exception of Symons (1985), who includes import prices as well as w and r, they are quite low, implying constant-output labor-demand elasticities between 0.10 and 0.15. Part of the difficulty here may again be that the independent variable, w/r, has substantial measurement error due to the inclusion of an imperfectly measured cost of capital services in its denominator. That Symons's estimate is so much larger is consistent with this interpretation, since his equation does not constrain the coefficients on w and r.[9]

Considering all of the results in Table 3.1, an appropriate inference is that direct estimation of σ is not a very promising route. It may give estimates that differ little from broader approaches; but that should be tested. The difficulties for inferring η_{LL} of including an imperfectly measured price of capital can be overcome in a labor-demand equation by specifying w and r separately. The real problem is that the rudimentary state of knowledge about the effects of changes in the returns to work on variations in labor supply over the relatively short time periods used means that little additional knowledge

---

[9] Some other potential difficulties with the studies in this early literature are discussed in Berndt (1976).

has been gained from embedding demand equations in standard supply-demand models.

The second group of studies using highly aggregated data provides estimates based on factor-demand equations. These are presented in Table 3.2. In this table, and throughout the rest of this section, M refers to materials and E refers to energy (the latter for this section only). Except for one study in the final group in the table, each includes a measure of w and at least one other input price.

The archetypal studies, the first nine listed in the table, include wages and the price of capital services. Clark and Freeman (1980) are especially careful in testing different specifications of the input prices and show very clearly the pitfalls of measurement error in r. Michl (1987) shows that the estimate of η_{LL} is sensitive to how output is measured. Six of the nine studies in this group generate estimates of η_{LL} that are within the range of those implied in Table 3.1. That is not true for Tinsley's (1971) estimates. The difference may result from the very short time period Tinsley used; or it may stem from the unusual specification of his equations, which involve complex and varying lag structures. It is also not true for Bucher's (1984) (wrong-signed) estimates for France, for reasons that are not clear from the author's explanation of his methods.

Chetty and Heckman's (1986, but substantially completed in the early 1970s) estimates are far above the range of estimates in most of the other studies. This study imposes a very tight structure on the usual series of aggregate output, employment, wage, and capital-rental price data to infer a variety of parameters reflecting aggregation, labor supply, and firms' entry and exit. While the standard errors that are presented are small, the model imposes a complex structure on a set of data that, as in most aggregate time series, exhibits only small variations around trends, so that the estimated demand elasticity is questionable.

The second group of factor-demand studies using aggregate data is diverse in terms of specification and the economy under study, but each study includes output as shifting labor demand. Heckman and Sedlacek's (1985) study has been described, but it is worth noting that their measure of labor input based on workers' characteristics produces estimated demand elasticities that, while higher than those in most other studies, are below unity. Bruno and Sachs (1982) embed the factor-demand equation in a system that determines output and factor prices; Pencavel and Holmlund (1988) specify a standard equation that includes a combined price of energy and materials as well as w and r; Nickell (1984) pays special attention to how employers form their expectations about future demand for their product;

TABLE 3.2
Estimates of η_{LL} or η'_{LL} Based on Factor-Demand Equations Using Data on Aggregates or Large Industries (Group I.b Studies)

Study	Category	Description	$-\eta_{LL}$
Tinsley (1971)	I.A.1.b.i	Private nonfarm, quarterly, 1954–65; KL prices. Employment: worker-hours:	0.04[a] 0.06[a]
Chow and Moore (1972)	I.A.1.b.i	Private worker-hours, quarterly 1948:IV–1967; KL prices, large forecasting model	0.37[a]
Kollreuter (1980)	I.A.1.b.ii	Manufacturing worker-hours, quarterly, 1971–77; West Germany; KL prices	0.20
Clark and Freeman (1980)	I.A.1.b.i	Manufacturing production workers, quarterly, 1950–76; KL prices. Employment: worker-hours:	0.33 0.51
Bucher (1984)	I.A.1.b.ii	Employment, quarterly, 1963–80; KL prices. France: West Germany:	−3.61 0.63
Chetty and Heckman (1986)	I.A.1.b.i	Manufacturing production-worker hours, quarterly, 1947–69; KL prices; accounts for aggregation, entry/exit, supply-demand model	3.88
Michl (1987)	I.A.1.b.i	Manufacturing production-worker-hours, quarterly, 1950–78; KL prices; special attention to measuring real output	(−0.02, 0.34)

Flaig and Steiner (1989)	I.A.1.b.ii	Manufacturing employment, quarterly, 1963–86; West Germany, KLM prices	0.14
Hsing (1989)	I.A.1.b.i	Manufacturing, annual, 1953–78; KL prices, tests of functional form	0.70
Coen and Hickman (1970)	I.A.1.b.i	Private worker-hours, annual, 1924–40, 1949–65; KL prices	0.18
Bruno and Sachs (1982)	I.A.1.b.ii	Manufacturing, annual, 1956–78, U.K.; system of output, factor-price frontier and labor-demand equations	0.08[a]
Epstein and Denny (1983)	I.A.1.b.i	Manufacturing worker-hours, annual, 1947–76; KLM prices, complex dynamics	0.07[b]
Nickell (1984)	I.A.1.b.ii	Manufacturing, quarterly, 1958–74; U.K.; LEM prices, careful specification of expectations	0.19
Heckman and Sedlacek (1985)	I.A.2.b.i	"Tasks," annual, 1968–81; KLEM prices; transformed labor-demand relation.	
		Manufacturing:	0.49
		Nonmanufacturing:	0.93
Franz and König (1986)	I.A.1.b.ii	Manufacturing, quarterly, 1964–83; West Germany, KLM prices	0.96
Kokkelenberg and Bischoff (1986)	I.A.1.b.i	Manufacturing production-worker-hours, quarterly, 1959–77; KLE prices, nonstatic expectations about K adjustment; interrelated adjustment of KL	0.13

TABLE 3.2 (cont.)

Study	Category	Description	$-\eta_{LL}$
Pencavel and Holmlund (1988)	I.A.1.b.ii	Blue-collar, manufacturing and mining, annual, 1950–83; Sweden; KLEM prices	0.75
Pencavel (1989)	I.A.1.b.ii	Aggregate, annual, 1953–79; U.K.	
		KLM prices:	0.40
		With K stock:	0.51
		With alternative wages:	0.03
Nadiri and Rosen (1973)	I.A.1.b.i	Manufacturing employment, quarterly, 1948–65; interrelated adjustment of E,H,K,K utilization, inventories.	
		Production workers:	−0.11
		Nonproduction workers:	0.14
Schott (1978)	I.A.1.b.ii	All industry, annual, 1948–70; U.K.; KL prices, interrelated adjustment of K,E,H.	
		Employment:	0.82
		Hours:	0.25
Harris (1985)	I.A.1-2.b.ii	Engineering worker-hours, quarterly, 1968–81; U.K.; KL prices, interrelated adjustment; special attention to capital	0.21

			Short-run $-\eta'_{LL}$
Nadiri (1968)	I.A.1.b.i	Manufacturing, quarterly, 1947–64; K held constant. Employment: worker-hours:	0.12 0.14
Meese (1980)	I.A.1.b.i	Private production-worker employment, quarterly, 1947–74; KL prices, K held constant	1.73
Layard and Nickell (1986)	I.A.1.b.ii	Aggregate, U.K.; import prices, K held constant: annual, 1954–83 quarterly, 1957–83	0.93 1.19
Andrews (1987)	I.A.1.b.ii	Aggregate, annual, 1950–79; U.K.; supply-demand system, KLEM prices; K held constant	0.51
Burgess (1988)	I.A.1.b.ii	Manufacturing, quarterly, 1964–82; U.K.; EM prices, international competitiveness; K held constant	1.85
Harris (1990)	I.A.1.b.ii	Private worker-hours, quarterly, 1965–87; New Zealand; K held constant	0.24
Nickell and Symons (1990)	I.A.1.b.i	Manufacturing employment, quarterly, 1962–84; MP condition, K held constant; attention to measuring w	1.92

TABLE 3.2 (cont.)

Study	Category	Description	$-\eta'_{LL}$
Symons and Layard (1984)	I.A.1.b.ii	Manufacturing employment, quarterly, 1956–80; 5 OECD countries; LM prices; no Y or K	1.54
Wadhwani (1987)	I.A.1.b.ii	Manufacturing employment, quarterly, 1962–81; U.K.; KLM prices; no Y or K	0.38[b]
Kennan (1988)	I.A.1.b.i	Manufacturing production-worker-hours, monthly, 1948–71; MP condition, supply-demand system; no Y or K	11.58
Begg et al. (1989)	I.A.1.b.ii	Employment, annual, import prices, attention to dynamics; no Y or K.	
		U.K., 1953–85:	0.40
		Japan, 1953–86:	0.45
		West Germany, 1953–86:	c

[a] Estimates are calculated at the sample end points.
[b] 1971 elasticity.
[c] Explosive dynamics.

and Coen and Hickman (1970) estimate the adjustment of the demand for both labor and investment jointly.

In all nine studies the estimated $-\eta_{LL}$ is below unity, though in Franz and König (1986), one of the few available studies for West Germany, it is nearly that large. The extremely low value in Bruno and Sachs's study, which uses the same data employed in other studies of the U.K. manufacturing sector, must result from the inclusion of the other, nonstandard equations that are estimated jointly within the same model. The similarly low estimate in Epstein and Denny (1983) is surprising given the consistently higher estimates of $-\eta_{LL}$ produced on this data set using other methods (see Table 3.3). Again, the imposition of a very complex dynamic structure on these time series, which represent mostly trends, may be generating this result.

The next three studies listed in Table 3.2 all specify employment (or worker-hours) as an input whose adjustment is simultaneous with one or more other inputs. All specify the demand for at least three factors. The most complete specification, Nadiri and Rosen (1973), estimates a system with the inputs and their rates of utilization (in the case of labor, employees, and hours) adjusting along with inventories. Except for Schott's (1978) employment elasticity, all of these studies produce fairly low estimates of η_{LL}. As some of the authors note, and as Section 2.VI made clear, it is extremely difficult to specify and measure the price of the utilization rates of each input correctly. Since the estimates of η_{LL} from these studies are produced in a system that includes these hard-to-measure prices, they may be biased.

The next group of Type b studies estimates labor-demand equations including several factor prices (of which one is w), but with K instead of Y held constant. Because K is held constant but Y is not, the estimated elasticities are short-run measures of η'_{LL}. Nadiri's (1968) very early study predated most of the work summarized in this chapter. Its motivation was to remove the restrictions on the relative factor-demand condition by specifying L as a function of w, r, and K. One motivation for the three studies using U.K. data, and for Nickell and Symons (1990), was concern that output could not be treated as exogenous.

The interesting result is that, despite the very wide variation in the estimated η'_{LL}, even in the four British studies that use almost identical data, most of the estimates are higher than the estimates of $-\eta_{LL}$ discussed already. Except for Harris's (1990) study of the highly regulated New Zealand economy, and Nadiri's early work, the implied short-run scale effect is around one. This suggests a very large elasticity of aggregate demand with respect to prices. Even if the estimates were more believable, the approach is not recommended: If one wishes to infer short-run behavior, explicitly specifying dynamics in a system of adjustment toward a long-run equilibrium is preferable (see Chapter 6), since it is based in theory rather than imposed on an ad hoc basis.

The final group of studies holds neither Y nor any input quantity constant. All the authors in this group implicitly measure η'_{LL}. Particularly thoughtful is Kennan's examination of a supply-demand system in which shocks are modeled as part of the error terms rather than as deterministic. Kennan's approach generates the highest estimate in Tables 3.1 through 3.5. The estimate may be correct; but it suffers from an insufficient link between the aggregate data that are used and the behavior of the micro agents whose maximization is modeled so carefully.

The estimates by Symons and Layard (1984), Wadhwani (1987), and Begg et al. (1989) of η'_{LL} are not wildly inconsistent with the sum of the range of other estimates of η_{LL} and a scale effect. Their wide range, especially the wide range within Symons and Layard's estimates, gives pause about the robustness of this approach. In the end, though, the empirical value of this approach to estimating η'_{LL} really depends on whether in fact output should be treated as endogenous at the level of aggregation chosen. Endogeneity (if expectations about sales are modeled carefully) is surely not a problem at the micro level; and the only evidence using aggregate data (Quandt and Rosen 1989) suggests it is not a difficulty at the macro level either. If output is endogenous, the appropriate method of dealing with it to make structural inferences (as opposed to predictions) is to specify and estimate a disequilibrium model (as in the third group of studies in Table 3.1) rather than simply exclude it. Nonetheless, this approach is useful for predicting the long-run effect on employment of a change in the real wage. Also, the difficulties I have noted in specifying supply restrictions properly are a good justification for using it.

The third group of studies based on aggregate data estimates the labor-demand elasticity as part of a production system, in most cases a translog cost-share system, as in equation (2.45). A single coefficient in a cost-share system can be used with an estimate of s_L to measure σ_{LL} and η_{LL}. The economic motivation for most of the studies in this group was the examination of the demand for energy (spurred by the "energy crisis" of the 1970s) and its substitutability/complementarity with other inputs.

Much of the research on this issue proceeded on the same set of aggregate time-series data that measured inputs of capital, worker-hours, energy, and materials (denoted by KLEM in the tables) that was produced by Berndt and Wood (1975). These data performed for researchers developing and examining complex descriptions of production technologies and dynamics a role similar to that of certain pure-bred strains of laboratory mice used in biomedical research. The first thirteen studies listed in Table 3.3 use these data or their extensions to later time periods or additional inputs. With very few exceptions the estimates of $-\eta_{LL}$ hover around 0.5, toward the higher end of the range implied by most of the studies summarized in Tables 3.1 and 3.2.

The estimates do not appear particularly sensitive to alternative assumptions about functional forms (Diewert and Wales); to different estimation procedures (Chung); to these two variations jointly (Segerson and Mount); to the inclusion of additional inputs in the translog KLEM system (Harper and Gullicksen; Segerson and Mount); to inclusion of the translog cost system in a dynamic model (Berndt and Khaled; Pindyck and Rotemberg; Norsworthy and Harper); to attempts to account for simultaneity (Anderson); or to very careful attention to the derivation of the translog cost system in the presence of stochastic shocks within the firm's optimization problem (McElroy).

The one study that produces unusual (low) estimates (Morrison 1986) concentrates on the formation of employers' expectations about the path of capital inputs. As we saw in several of the studies summarized in Table 3.2, attention to this issue leads to very low estimates of $-\eta_{LL}$. That is apparently true whether one estimates a factor-demand condition or share equations in a dynamic translog cost system. Why this should be generally so is unclear. We do know, though, that the specification of expectations is by no means a settled issue in macroeconomics, nor, as I discuss in Chapter 6, in the study of dynamic factor demand. Part of the problem may be that these studies generate expectations endogenously rather than specify them based on extraneous information from surveys of employers.

The remaining seven studies all estimate translog cost systems, but do so on a variety of sets of data, some of which include inputs of materials along with inputs of capital, labor, and energy. Particularly interesting in this group are the studies by Griffin and Gregory (1976) and Pindyck (1979), which estimate the same system for a variety of countries. While there is substantial variation in the estimated η_{LL} among economies, the average estimates are in line with those based on the KLEM data. There is nothing special about that set of data or about examining technology in the U.S. economy using translog methods.

The Berndt and Wood KLEM data are time series. Yet pooling

TABLE 3.3
Estimates of η_{LL} Based on Equation Systems Using Data on Aggregates or Large Industries (Group I.c Studies)[a]

Study	Category	Description	$-\eta_{LL}$
Berndt and Wood (1975)	I.A.1.c.i	Manufacturing, annual, 1947–71; KLEM, translog cost	0.45
Berndt and Khaled (1979)	I.A.1.c.i	1947–71; KLEM, translog cost	
		Homogeneous, neutral technical Δ:	0.46
		Heterothetic, nonneutral change:	0.17
Norsworthy and Harper (1981)	I.A.1.c.i	1958–77; KLEM, translog cost, complex dynamics	0.74
Anderson (1981)	I.A.1.c.i	1948–71; KLEM, translog cost, concentrates on endogeneity	0.42
Morrison and Berndt (1981)	I.A.1.c.i	1952–71; KLEM, translog cost	0.35[b]
Pindyck and Rotemberg (1983)	I.A.1.c.i	1948–71; KLEM, translog cost, concentration on adjustment paths	0.57
Segerson and Mount (1985)	I.A.1.c.i	1958–81; selected years; KLEM and management, AIDS and other systems	(0.50, 0.62)
Morrison (1986)	I.A.1.c.i	1949–80; KLEM, translog cost, various specifications of expectations on quasi-fixed capital	(0.03, 0.12)
Chung (1987)	I.A.1.c.i	1947–71; KLEM, translog cost, alternative estimation methods	(0.66, 0.95)
Diewert and Wales (1987)	I.A.1.c.i	1947–71; KLEM, various functional forms, translog cost	(0.19, 0.72)
McElroy (1987)	I.A.1.c.i	1947–71; KLEM, translog cost, concentration on stochastic optimization	0.34
Kim (1988)	I.A.1.c.i	1948–71; KLEM, indirect translog production (allows for endogenous output)	0.26
Harper and Gullickson (1989)	I.A.1.c.i	1949–86; KLEM and business services, translog cost	0.61

Griffin and Gregory (1976)	I.A–B.1.c.ii	Manufacturing employment, quality (education) adjusted, 1955, 1960, 1965, 1969; 9 OECD countries; KLEM, translog cost	0.23
Fuss (1977)	I.A–B.1.c.ii	Manufacturing worker-hours, annual, 1961–71; Canadian regions; KLEM, translog cost	0.49[c]
Magnus (1979)	I.A.1.c.ii	Enterprise sector, annual, 1950–76; Netherlands, KLE, translog cost	0.30
Pindyck (1979)	I.A.1.c.ii	Aggregate, annual, 1963–73; 1963–73; 10 OECD countries; KLE, translog cost	0.43
Tarhouni (1983)	I.A.1–2.c.ii	Aggregate, annual, 1962–78; KL, translog production. Egypt: Libya:	0.64 0.35
Garofalo and Malhotra (1984)	I.A–B.1.c.i	Manufacturing, production-worker-hours, states, 1974–77; KLE, translog cost	0.74
Morrison (1988)	I.A.1.c.i–ii	Manufacturing, annual; KLEM, generalized Leontief. U.S., 1952–81: Japan, 1955–81:	0.41 0.66

[a] Unless otherwise noted, parameter estimates refer to the last year or quarter in the sample, here and in translog estimates in Tables 3.4 through 3.10.

[b] Estimate at the sample midpoint.

[c] Estimate for Ontario.

cross-section and time-series data, as in Fuss (1977) and Garofalo and Malhotra (1984), does not alter the conclusions about the magnitude of η_{LL}. Estimates of η_{LL} based on highly aggregated data in translog and other systems are remarkably robust to the choice of data, the economy being studied, the method of estimation, and the particular specification of the technology.

Tables 3.1 through 3.3 summarize nearly seventy studies, most of which generate estimates of the constant-output demand elasticity for homogeneous labor. Taking all of these together, do we learn anything about its magnitude? A simple mean of the estimates of σ is 0.75, while the mean estimate of $-\eta_{LL}$ is 0.39. Ignoring for the moment issues of aggregation, nearly all of the studies produce estimates below 1, and in most the estimates are below 0.75. At the other extreme, few studies produce estimates below 0.15. Most of the very low estimates arise when the authors concentrate on allowing the data to reflect the process by which employers form expectations about future sales or inputs (but see Nickell 1984 for an exception). Since our theories of expectations are somewhat speculative, the estimates generated by these studies should be discounted.

These considerations and an estimate that $s_L \cong 0.70$ in developed economies suggest that a reasonable confidence interval for $-\eta_{LL}$ in the aggregate is [0.15, 0.75]. We can be fairly sure that the true value *at the aggregate level* is in this range. If one were to choose a point estimate for this parameter, 0.30 would not be far wrong (though picking a single estimate is not a good idea). This value is quite close to the combined means of the direct estimates of $-\eta_{LL}$ and the indirect estimates based on $\eta_{LL} = -[1-s_L]\sigma$. Interestingly, with this value of s_L, the "best guess" value of $-\eta_{LL} = 0.30$ is consistent with Cobb-Douglas production (since the implied σ is 1.0). The immense literature that estimates the constant-output demand elasticity for labor in the aggregate has truly led us "to arrive where we started and know the place for the first time."[10]

B. Disaggregated and Microeconomic Studies of Homogeneous Labor

By their nature the studies summarized in this subsection are more diverse than those discussed above. Not all are based on manufacturing establishments or on data describing the aggregate economy that form the basis for the Type I studies. The type of labor thus may differ by skill from the typical manufacturing worker (or the typical worker economywide). Also, there is no reason to expect that factor

[10] T. S. Eliot, *Little Gidding* (London: Faber and Faber, 1942).

substitution is equally easy in all industries, so that underlying differences in technology will generate different estimates because the true values of the parameters differ.

The studies are summarized in Table 3.4 in the same logical order as the aggregate studies presented in Tables 3.1 through 3.3. Four of the seven studies using the MP condition are based on data covering workers in nonprofit industries. They thus provide the best link to the theory of labor demand in such industries, though all four regrettably use this simple representation of technology. Freeman's (1975) estimates for university faculty, Ashenfelter and Ehrenberg's (1975) estimates for government workers, and Thornton's (1979) results for teachers are within the same range as the bulk of the estimates using this approach on aggregate data. Stapleton (1989) produces very low estimates (for economists). Whether this is due to the nature of the occupation or, as in the studies using aggregate data, to the complexity of the expectations that are specified in the study is not clear. These four studies support the notion of a downward-sloping labor-demand curve in nonprofit industry. They do not suggest, as the theory in Section 2.V showed, that the demand elasticity is higher than in for-profit firms. Without more research we cannot tell if that is caused by the simple specification that is used, by the nature of the particular industries/occupations chosen, by problems of measurement, or by some deficiency in the theory.

Three studies use Type a methods to examine factor substitution in disaggregated manufacturing industries. The MP conditions used by McKinnon (1962) and Bernanke (1986) produce estimates of σ that are comparable to those presented in Table 3.1. It is especially worth noting that Bernanke's estimates for manufacturing industries pre–World War II differ little from those for the postwar period generated by other studies. Lovell's (1973) cross-section estimates of σ based on the VES function are also similar to aggregate estimates, suggesting that this particular extension of the CES function has little effect on what we infer about factor substitution.

Three studies examine disaggregated industries using Type b methods with the prices of labor and other factors included. Waud's estimates of η_{LL} exceed the top of the range we inferred from Tables 3.1 through 3.3, while Faini and Schiantarelli's (1985a) estimate is below the bottom of that range. Both of these studies use very short time series. That brevity could be causing the results for Italy, since the absence of major shocks to relative prices increases the relative importance of measurement and other random errors that bias the estimated elasticities toward zero. That Waud's estimates are so high is difficult to understand given the low estimates found in the aggre-

TABLE 3.4
Estimates of Demand Parameters Using Data on Small Industries (Group II Studies)

Study	Category	Description	Various Parameters
			σ
McKinnon (1962)	II.A.1.a.i	2-digit SIC manufacturing, annual, 1947–58; MP condition	0.29
Lovell (1973)	II.B.1.a.i	2-digit manufacturing, production-worker employment, states, 1958; VES production function	0.75
Ashenfelter and Ehrenberg (1975)	II.A–B.1.a.i	State and local government activities, states, 1958–69; MP condition	0.67
Freeman (1975)	II.A.1.a.i	University faculty, annual, 1920–70; MP condition	0.26
Thornton (1979)	II.B.1.a.i	Public-school teachers, states, 1968–74; MP condition	0.63
Bernanke (1986)	II.A.1.a.i	Small manufacturing industries, production-worker employment, monthly, 1923–39; MP condition, supply-demand system.	0.58
Stapleton (1989)	II.A.1.a.i	Ph.D. economists, annual, 1960–85; MP condition; supply-demand system with specification of suppliers' expectations	0.06

			$-\eta_{LL}$
Waud (1968)	II.A.1.b.i	2-digit manufacturing, production-worker-hours, quarterly, 1954–64; KL prices	1.03
Faini and Schiantarelli (1985a)	II.A–B.1.b.ii	Five two-digit industries, employment, annual, 1970–79; southern Italy; KL prices	0.09
Lewis (1987)	II.A–B.1.b.ii	Hired labor, annual, 1964–82; prices of variable inputs. Sheep farms: Beef farms:	0.23 0.37
Field and Grebenstein (1980)	II.B.1.c.i	10 2-digit SIC manufacturing industries, employment, states, 1971; KLE, and working capital, translog cost	0.51
Denny, Fuss, and Waverman (1981)	II.A.1.c.i–ii	2-digit manufacturing, annual; KLEM, quadratic cost function. U.S., 1948–71: Canada, 1962–75:	0.56 0.46
Denny et al. (1981)	II.A.1.c.ii	Bell Canada, annual, 1952–76; KLM, translog cost, several outputs	0.40[a]
Harper and Field (1983)	II.B.1.c.i	2-digit SIC manufacturing industries, states 1974–76; KLEM, heterothetic translog cost	0.27
Evenson and Binswanger (1984)	II.A–B.1.c.ii	Farm labor, 1954–72; India, four regions; M prices, K, output price, generalized Leontief	0.61
Halvorsen and Smith (1986)	II.A.1.c.ii	Metal mining, annual, 1954–74; Canada; KLE and natural resources, translog cost	0.51[b]

Study	Category	Description	Various Parameters
			$-\eta_{LL}$
Santoso (1988)	II.A–B.1.c.ii	Rice farming, hired labor, annual, 1976–85; Indonesia provinces; prices of variable inputs, translog cost	(0.23, 0.33)
Nakamura (1990)	II.A–B.1.c.ii	Iron and steel, employment, annual, 1964–82; Japan; KLM, heterothetic generalized Leontief	(0.87, 1.61)
Wylie (1990)	II.A.1.c.ii	Four 2-digit manufacturing industries, employment, annual, 1900–29; Canada, KLE, translog cost	0.52
			$-\eta'_{LL}$
Carruth and Oswald (1985)	II.A.1.b.ii	Coal mining employment, annual, 1950–80; U.K.; KLE prices, no Y or K	(1.0, 1.4)

[a] Estimated at sample mean.
[b] Median estimate.

gate studies that used short time periods. Lewis's (1987) estimates on an unusual set of data covering relatively small sectors of the Australian economy are consistent with the aggregate estimates.

The next set of studies based on industry data estimates translog cost or other systems for capital, labor, and one or more other inputs. These studies run the gamut from time-series to cross-section to panel data and cover a large variety of industries and countries. What is remarkable about the estimates is their clustering in the middle or toward the high end of the range found in Tables 3.1 through 3.3. Remarkably, too, despite the theoretical requirement that $\sigma > -\eta_{LL}$, these estimates are roughly equal to the estimates of σ presented earlier in the table.

Carruth and Oswald (1985) examine a contracting model on industry time-series data. While their purpose is not to generate estimates of labor-demand parameters, their study does produce an estimate of the long-run η'_{LL} (because they hold neither Y nor K constant). Estimating this parameter makes more sense in the context of the disaggregated data they use than in the studies in Table 3.2, since assuming that output can vary in the long run is more reasonable. Given this view, and assuming that η_{LL} in this industry is around -0.3, the scale effect is consistent with a fairly elastic demand for the product.

The disaggregated estimates presented in this table avoid some of the problems of the data underlying Tables 3.1 through 3.3. Even with them, though, the authors cannot completely avoid the endogeneity of input prices that may bias the estimates. Because of that difficulty, unless the purpose is to estimate demand parameters for a particular industry *and* microeconomic data are not obtainable, the Type II approach offers nothing that cannot be obtained using other types of data.

Studies that produce estimates of labor-demand elasticities using microeconomic data offer the greatest hope for inferring the nature of production and its implications for the demand for labor. They are, though, necessarily quite diverse in the establishments chosen for analysis. In some cases a series of establishments within a narrowly defined industry is studied. The estimates presumably reflect choices about technology facing producers at a point in time. In other cases a wide variety of firms is chosen, with the parameters reflecting an average of substitution possibilities among a large set of technologies in different industries.

In discussing these studies I use the same general schema as before. An additional way of analyzing them is necessary, though. In some of the studies the major purpose was estimating production parameters; but another group of studies sought to examine how employment and wages are determined within a bargaining model. As in the Carruth and Oswald (1985) study, labor-demand parameters are generated by these models as a by-product of testing whether wage-employment outcomes are on a demand curve or whether the parties to collective bargaining reach a joint-maximizing rent-sharing agreement to the right of the demand curve.

Among the studies using microeconomic data, the first shown in Table 3.5 use Type a methods on remarkably diverse sets of data. Jones and Pliskin (1989) estimate an MP condition for a very long pooled time series of cross sections in a few British industries, while Sosin and Fairchild (1984) cover modern manufacturing firms in Latin America. Despite their different methods the two studies generate very similar estimates of σ and clearly show that the constant-output demand for labor slopes downward. It is worth noting that Sosin and Fairchild's results, which are based on data from developing countries, are similar to the estimates produced for developed economies.

A number of studies have used Type b and c methods to examine substitution at the micro level. Among the three studies using Type b methods, Mairesse and Dormont (1985) use random samples of manufacturing firms, Rich (1990) uses specific occupations of airline employees, and de Pelsmacker (1984) examines auto manufacturers. The estimates in all three demonstrate a downward-sloping constant-output labor-demand curve, though with a fairly high elasticity.

Five studies estimate translog systems on data describing utility plants. Among the four studies that estimate a translog cost system, the range of estimates is very much what was shown in Table 3.3. Casual inspection suggests that substitution will not be particularly easy in this industry. The estimates are thus somewhat larger than one might expect. That is especially so for the estimates of ϵ_{LL} in Karlson (1986). If we make the heroic assumption that $\eta_{LL} \cong [\epsilon_{LL}]^{-1}$, the implied labor-demand elasticity is very large.

The two studies of the trucking industry, one using two cross sections of data, the other using an eight-year panel, produce estimates of η_{LL} that are in the middle of the range of aggregate estimates. Allen's (1986) carefully constructed set of data describing particular construction projects also produces estimates well within that range. Allen's estimates are especially valuable since, by virtue of the definition of the observations, there is very little problem of endogeneity of output.

Among the twelve Type b and c studies, only Kokkelenberg and Nguyen's (1989) estimate for flat-glass plants suggests almost no substitution of labor for other factors. It is unclear why this estimate is so low, since the estimation methods are standard, the time period

TABLE 3.5
Estimates of Demand Parameters Using Data on Firms or Plants (Group III Studies)

Study	Category	Description	Various Parameters
			σ
Sosin and Fairchild (1984)	III.B.1.a.ii	Latin American firms, 1970–74; capital-labor ratio	0.50
Jones and Pliskin (1989)	III.A–B.1.a.ii	Profit-sharing and other firms in printing, footwear, and clothing, employment, annual, some starting in 19th century; U.K.	0.48
			$-\eta_{LL}$
Atkinson and Halvorsen (1984)	III.B.1.c.i	Electric utilities, employment, 1984; KLE; efficient production, heterothetic translog cost	0.15
Nelson (1984)	III.A–B.1.c.i	Steam-generating plants, annual, 1951–78; KLE, translog cost	0.52
de Pelsmacker (1984)	III.A–B.1.b.ii	Five auto manufacturing firms, production workers, annual, 1976–82; Belgium; KL prices	0.44
Mairesse and Dormont (1985)	III.B.1.b.ii	Manufacturing firms' employment, changes over 1970–79; KL prices. France: West Germany:	0.82 0.83
Allen (1986)	III.B.1.c.i	Construction projects, early 1970s; KLM, translog cost	(0.36, 0.53)
Karlson (1986)	III.B.1.c.i	Utility companies, 1978; KL fuel, bought power; multiple outputs, translog production	(0.5, 0.9)[a]
Kokkelenberg and Choi (1986)	III.B.1.c.i	Utility companies, 1978; KLE, translog cost	0.30

TABLE 3.5 (cont.)

Study	Category	Description	Various Parameters $-\eta_{LL}$
Baltagi and Griffin (1988)	III.A–B.1.c.i	Steam-generating plants, annual, 1951–78; KLE; concentration on technical change, translog cost	0.45
Daughety and Nelson (1988)	III.A–B.1.c.i	Trucking firms, employment, selected years, 1953–82; KLE, purchased transport, two outputs, translog cost	0.33
McMullen and Stanley (1988)	III.A–B.1.c.i	Trucking firms, employment, 1977, 1983; KLE, purchased transport, translog cost	0.38
Kokkelenberg and Nguyen (1989)	III.A–B.1.c.i	Flat-glass plants, production-worker employment, 1972–81; KLM, electricity, other fuels, translog cost	0.03
Rich (1990)	III.A–B.1.b.i	Airline pilot employment, annual, 1971–84; KLEM prices	0.51
Dertouzos and Pencavel (1981)	III.A–B.1.b.i	Typographers, small newspapers, 1946–65; KLM prices	(0.25, 5.59)
Brown and Ashenfelter (1986)	III.A–B.1.a.i	Typographers, estimated employment, 1948–65; MP condition, alternative wages	(0.22, 1.21)
Card (1986)	III.A–B.1.a.i	Seven airlines, maintenance-worker employment, quarterly, 1969–76; MP condition, alternative wages	0.39
MaCurdy and Pencavel (1986)	III.A–B.1.c.i	Typographers, small newspapers, 1945–73; two types of capital, translog production	(0.75, 1.24)[a]

Bean and Turnbull (1988)	III.A–B.1.a.ii	Coal mines, annual, 1967–83; U.K.; MP condition, alternative wages	0.21
Card (1990c)	III.A–B.1.b.ii	Union contracts, employment, 1968–83; Canada; LM prices; attention to employment-contract-wage simultaneity	0.62
Christofides and Oswald (1991)	III.A–B.1.a.ii	Union contracts, 1978–84; Canada; MP condition, alternative wages	(< 0; 0.22)
Currie (1991)	III.A–B.1.a.ii	Ontario teachers' contracts, 1975–83; Canada; MP condition; alternative wages in a supply-demand model	(0.53, 0.68)
			Short-run $-\eta'_{LL}$
Wadhwani and Wall (1990)	III.A–B.1.b.ii	Manufacturing firms, employment, 1974–82; U.K.; K held constant, ML prices	0.53
Benjamin (1992)	III.B.1.b.ii	Preharvest farm labor, 1980; Java; fixed land	0.30
			$-\eta'_{LL}$
Blanchflower, Milward, and Oswald (1991)	III.B.1.b.ii	Employment, large sample of plants, 1984; U.K.; no Y or K	0.93

[a] Estimate of ϵ_{LL}.

covered is as long as that in some of the other studies using micro data, and the data are constructed as carefully as those used in other studies. (They are the establishment data underlying the Annual Survey of Manufactures.) Perhaps, unlike in the other small industries used in these studies, there just is not much possibility for substituting against labor when the wage rises in this industry.

The studies of airlines, electric utilities, construction, and trucking are important, for they show that the substitution observed using industry or aggregate data does not just reflect output substitution across industries. Here we have solid microeconomic evidence of factor substitution within a narrowly defined industry. The aggregate results may reflect some output substitution; but they also reflect substitution among inputs within particular industries.

Eight studies have used panels of collective-bargaining contracts and additional published data to examine union-management rent sharing. In each case part of the model involves an equation that resembles a demand curve but includes, among other variables, a measure of the alternative wage facing employees. The five studies that are based on MP conditions generate estimates of η_{LL} that are consistent with those produced in other micro studies and with the estimates based on aggregate data. The three studies using other methods produce similarly standard estimates, though the estimates for some of the union locals examined by Dertouzos and Pencavel (1981) are very large.

In many of these studies the parameters that generate the estimates of σ or η_{LL} are not strongly significantly different from zero. There are two reasons why these studies will underestimate σ or η_{LL}. First, to the extent that wage rates in a specific contract are affected by the alternative wage, unless substantial care is taken some of the effect of the contract wage on employment will be attributed to the alternative wage. Thus Currie's (1991) study, which embeds the contracting model in a carefully specified supply-demand system, suggests that the results from the other contracting studies can be interpreted as implying a fairly standard estimate of σ. The second source of downward bias in these estimates is their restriction to unionized employment. Unions achieve their goals partly by restricting managerial discretion, including presumably discretion to substitute against labor when wages are raised. (See the discussion of Freeman and Medoff's (1982) results below.) That being so, the true values of the substitution elasticities are likely to be below those characterizing nonunion workplaces in the same industries.

Benjamin (1992) estimates the short-run η'_{LL} to be quite low compared to what the aggregate data showed for this parameter. Those estimates were, though, very large; and with Benjamin's estimate based on traditional peasant agriculture, it is perhaps surprising that any price responsiveness was found. Indeed, Wadhwani and Wall's (1990) estimate of the same parameter on a small sample of British firms is somewhat closer to the estimates based on aggregate data. Blanchflower, Milward, and Oswald (1991) estimate the long-run value of η'_{LL} using one of the best available sets of data for this purpose, a random sample of establishments covering the entire British economy. Here there are no problems of endogeneity entering the estimates as in the studies using aggregate data that excluded Y and K. With these data, and without these potential problems, the estimate of η'_{LL} turns out to be remarkably close to what one would expect with Cobb-Douglas production and a unitary price elasticity of product demand.

The rough corroboration of the aggregate estimates by those based on microeconomic data might suggest that the effort of obtaining establishment data is not worthwhile. That would be wrong. First, as the sensitivity of aggregate estimates to assumptions about employers' expectations shows, they are not robust with respect to at least some interesting extensions. Second, and more important, aggregate time series are inherently incapable of providing many different realizations of the processes that generate choices about technology. It is quite possible that similarities among estimates based on aggregate time series reflect only the lack of variation in the few time series that are used. Third, microeconomic data from a particular industry allow the researcher to avoid averaging a huge array of unrelated technologies. These studies may show that there is substitution among firms with differing labor intensities; or, as I assume but cannot demonstrate, they may show that firms with nearly identical technologies alter their factor demands when factor prices change. If so, the estimates are more closely linked to the underlying theory of production. Even if not, the estimates at least also reflect varying labor demand resulting from interindustry shifts in product demand induced by changes in relative factor prices.

Examining estimates of labor-demand elasticities based on microeconomic data does not alter the conclusion reached from aggregate data. While the mean of the estimates of $-\eta_{LL}$ in Tables 3.4 and 3.5 is 0.45, a bit higher than the average in Tables 3.1 through 3.3, the mean estimate of σ is somewhat lower, 0.49. Concluding that $-\eta_{LL}$ is probably between 0.15 and 0.75 for the typical firm remains warranted. There is clearly a wide range of actual values of this parameter, depending on the nature of the industry; thus there is no typical firm or industry. But for a randomly chosen industry this range should bracket reasonable estimates of the elasticity quite well. The constant-output demand curve for homogeneous labor slopes down. There is a neoclassical labor-demand relation.

C. Substitution between Homogeneous Labor and Energy/Materials

A by-product of the many Type b and c studies that focus on the demand for energy is a set of estimates of the degree of p-substitutability of energy for labor. If we assume wages are rigid, then the estimates of σ_{LE} and η_{LE} presented below can be used directly to infer the effects of an increase in the relative price of energy on employment or worker-hours. Alternatively, as the discussion in Chapter 2 makes clear, one must use factor-price elasticities to infer how an energy price shock will affect the returns to labor. None of the studies took the latter approach, though in the long run for nonrenewable energy resources it must be correct. Thus, the estimates I summarize, which allow us to infer whether energy and labor are p-substitutes or p-complements, are most useful only in the short and intermediate run.

All but a few of the studies were presented in Tables 3.2 through 3.5, so that Table 3.6 does not reproduce descriptions of them, a practice I follow throughout this volume. Those few that were not included before were excluded because there was no way to infer a labor-demand elasticity from their results. Finally, in addition to presenting results on labor-energy p-substitution, Table 3.6 summarizes estimates of p-substitution between labor and materials inputs in those studies that permit it.

Regardless of the size of σ_{LE}, we should expect that η_{LE} will be small, for s_E is a small fraction. In fact, most of the estimates of η_{LE} presented in Table 3.6 are fairly small. Looking first only at the studies using the aggregate U.S. KLEM data, the estimates of this elasticity are all less than 0.2 and, with the exception of Morrison (1986), are positive. Unless one delves into employers' expectations, this data set produces small positive values of η_{LE} no matter what reasonable additions are made to it or how one proceeds with estimation.

The next eleven studies listed in Table 3.6, which use other KLEM or KLE data based on economywide or industry aggregates, lead to the same inference. With the exception of Fuss (1977) and Morrison (1988), all indicate that labor and energy are p-substitutes, and that the cross-elasticity of demand is quite small. The next six (Type III) studies presented in the table also corroborate this result: In five of them the implied values of η_{LE} are positive but small. Only Kokkelenberg and Nguyen (1989), who generally found that firms in the flat-glass industry use an essentially fixed-coefficients technology, find no p-substitution between labor and energy.

Among the five Type b studies that present estimates of η_{LE}, Kokkelenberg and Bischoff's (1986), Andrews's (1987), and Wadhwani's (1987) estimates are in line with or a bit more negative than those in most of the Type c studies. The estimates from Sweden (Pencavel and Holmlund 1988) and from five developed economies (Symons and Layard 1984) are wildly different from any others presented in the table. Not only do they not imply that labor and energy are p-substitutes; they suggest an extremely high degree of labor-energy complementarity in light of the very small share of output accounted for by energy. Partly they may stem from the authors' use of an energy-materials composite price index, so that they are not strictly comparable to all of the other studies (except Andrews). Even with that observation, though, they are extremely large and negative. Why they arise is unclear from an examination of the descriptions contained in the studies.

The plethora of evidence based on aggregate and industry data, and the more recent evidence from sets of microeconomic data, make it clear that the question of *LE* p-substitution is as closed as any in empirical economics. Labor and energy are p-substitutes; and the labor-demand elasticity with respect to energy prices is small. Additional work from the same studies summarized in Table 3.6 also demonstrates, though less conclusively, that capital and energy are p-complements and are jointly p-substitutable for labor.

The evidence from the studies in Table 3.6 suggests that labor and materials are p-substitutes, with a small cross-price elasticity. This parameter is of much less interest for predictive or policy purposes than is η_{LE}, since the materials input is a loosely defined aggregate of many inputs. It is worth knowing, though, that labor is a p-substitute for this input too. This underscores the following general conclusion: *Homogeneous labor is in general a p-substitute for each other large aggregate input that has been defined in studies of production.*

IV. Studies of the Demand for Heterogeneous Labor

The variety of disaggregations of the labor force used in studies of labor-labor substitution and of the demand for particular groups of workers prevents detailed comparisons among the individual studies. There just are not enough different estimates of substitution within a particular disaggregation to learn how alternative specifications affect the results. Rather, all that can be done is to consider

TABLE 3.6
Estimates of Substitution of Labor for Energy and Materials

Study		η_{LE}	σ_{LE}	η_{LM}
Type c Studies: U.S. KLEM Time Series				
Berndt and Wood (1975)		0.03		0.37
Berndt and Khaled (1979)		(0.02, 0.11)		(−0.06, 0.39)
Anderson (1981)		0.05		0.34
Morrison and Berndt (1981)		0.07		0.34
Norsworthy and Harper (1981)		0.03		0.66
Pindyck and Rotemberg (1983)		0.11		0.50
Pollak, Sickles, and Wales (1984)		0.03		0.38
Manufacturing, annual, 1947–71; KLEM, CES-translog cost				
Morrison (1986)		(−0.02, −0.01)		(0.05, 0.14)
Diewert and Wales (1987)		(0.05, 0.18)		(−0.01, 0.61)
Chung (1987)		(0.02, 0.04)		(0.63, 0.88)
McElroy (1987)		0.07		0.32
Kim (1988)		0.06		0.08
Harper and Gullickson (1989)		0.07		0.03
Type c Studies: Other KLEM and KLE Data				
Griffin and Gregory (1976)		0.11		
Fuss (1977)		0.55		
Magnus (1979)		0.05		−0.02
Pindyck (1979)			0.96	
Field and Grebenstein (1980)		0.24		
Denny, Fuss, and Waverman (1981)	U.S.:	0.015		
	Canada:	0.005		
Harper and Field (1983)			0.24	

Study			
Garofalo and Malhotra (1984)		0.21	
Turnovsky and Donnelly (1984)	Iron and steel, annual, 1959–79; Australia; translog cost.		
KLEM:		0.03	0.48
KLE:		0.21	
Halvorsen and Smith (1986)		0.01	0.40
U.S.:		−0.06	0.59
Morrison (1988) Japan:		−0.05	1.04
Nelson and Wohar (1983)	Steam-generating plants, 1950–78; KLE; translog cost	0.41	
Atkinson and Halvorsen (1984)		0.07	
Pollak, Sickles, and Wales (1984)	Steam-generating plants; KLE; CES-translog	0.87	
McMullen and Stanley (1988)		1.17	
Daughety and Nelson (1988)		0.02	
Kokkelenberg and Nguyen (1989)		0.00	0.01

Type b Studies

Study		
Symons and Layard (1984)	−2.00	
Kokkelenberg and Bischoff (1986)	0.13	
Andrews (1987)	−0.09[a]	
Wadhwani (1987)	0.29	
Pencavel and Holmlund (1988)	−2.19[a]	
Martinello (1989) Wood products worker-hours, 1963–83; British Columbia; KLE prices, alternative wages		0.19

[a] Elasticity of employment with respect to the composite price of energy and materials.

general patterns of similarities among the groups of studies, and perhaps to draw some conclusions about particular disaggregations.

The motivations for the disaggregations chosen are varied. In some cases the interest has been in choosing one that allows examination of how the level of skill affects factor-demand or factor-price elasticities. Other studies have focused on the degree of competition among particular groups of workers, for example, on how an increase in the relative supply of one group affects the wages of another, or on how a subsidy or tax on the wages of one type of worker affects the demand for the labor of another type. A general interest that cuts across most disaggregations of the work force is in the relative degree of p-substitutability of capital for various types of labor.

Because most countries' statistical agencies do not collect establishment data that describe the demography of the work force in detail, most studies of heterogeneous labor have been based on household data. The only exceptions are Type I studies that focus on broad occupational categories. Within household data disaggregations by age-race-sex group, education, and occupation are easily obtained. The difficulty is that, except for cross-section studies that use entire economies as observations, data on capital stocks must then be calculated from establishment data and somehow linked to the household data. This difficulty guarantees problems in drawing inferences about capital-labor substitution (and about labor-labor substitution too, to the extent that the nonseparability of capital from labor affects it).

Study of the demand for heterogeneous labor was initially stimulated by interest in *capital-skill (p-)complementarity*—the notion that σ_{SK} (η_{SK}) < 0 and σ_{UK} (η_{UK}) > 0, where S and U are skilled and unskilled workers respectively (Griliches 1969). A weaker form of the hypothesis is that there is relative p-complementarity, that is, $\eta_{SK} < \eta_{UK}$. Concern about this issue stems from interest in the effects of subsidies to investment in physical capital on the returns to different groups of workers. Presumably, too, the hypothesis implies capital-skill q-complementarity, that $c_{SK} > 0$ and $c_{UK} < 0$. Studies of this dual view stem partly from the desire to learn the effects of capital deepening on the labor force: As the capital-labor ratio rises with economic development, what is the effect on skill differentials in wages?

A. Demand by Occupational Category

The first set of studies of heterogeneous labor examines substitution among broad occupational categories. These are summarized in Table 3.7. Where the information can be obtained, I present elasticities of substitution between capital and blue- (B) and white-collar (W) labor, as well as demand elasticities for each type of worker. In this and the succeeding tables in this section, the actual values of the η_{ii} and ϵ_{ii} are shown rather than the negatives of them that were presented in Tables 3.1 through 3.5.

The first seven studies use techniques other than the translog approximation to examine this particular disaggregation. The occupations chosen are mostly one-digit Census categories. Griliches (1969) and Dougherty (1972), both of whom used Type a methods, show evidence of capital-skill (KS) p-complementarity and of easy substitution among occupational categories. The Chiswick (1979) and McQuaid (1986) studies support these conclusions using similar sets of data and similar methods, as does Rosen (1968), who used Type b methods on various groups of railroad workers and capital.

Roberts and Skoufias (1991) do not estimate substitution among workers of different skills; and because they include both output and the stock of capital, their elasticities reflect substitution against other, unspecified inputs and between the two types of labor. With that in mind, though, the substitution possibilities that are left do suggest a greater elasticity of demand for unskilled than for skilled workers. Among studies in this group only Weiss (1977), who estimates a production system that restricted substitution elasticities to stand in constant ratios, fails to support the notion of KS p-complementarity. Because the technique (see Hanoch 1971) has been applied in only one other study of labor demand, we cannot tell whether the unusual results are produced by its restrictions or by the data chosen, or whether they in fact characterize production correctly.

The next four studies estimate translog cost approximations on aggregate time-series data for manufacturing that are similar to the KLEM data discussed in Section III.A. Clearly, they are not four independent tests of the same hypothesis. They do show, though, that production workers (B) are more highly p-substitutable for capital than is nonproduction labor (W), and that $\eta_{BB} > \eta_{WW}$ in absolute value. These conclusions are fairly robust to the choice of the time period over which the system is estimated and to whether the capital stock is disaggregated or not. The only exception to these inferences is the evidence in Berndt and White (1978) on the σ_{ij}.

Seven studies have estimated translog cost systems on Type II data. The evidence on the relative magnitudes of η_{BB} and η_{WW} is mixed. Grant (1979) and Freeman and Medoff (1982) suggest, albeit weakly, that there is relative capital-skill p-complementarity; Dennis and Smith (1978) suggest the opposite. Freeman and Medoff's work is especially interesting, as the difference between production in union and nonunion firms implies greater rigidity in the union sec-

TABLE 3.7
Estimates of Substitution of Production and Nonproduction Workers

Study	Type	Description	σ_{BK}	σ_{WK}	σ_{BW}	η_{BB}	η_{WW}
Rosen (1968)	III.B.1.b.i	Railroads, 1959–60; maintenance workers, KSU	$\sigma_{KU} > \sigma_{KS}$				
Griliches (1969)	II.B.1–2.a.i	2-digit manufacturing, states, 1954; CES	$\sigma_{BK} > \sigma_{WK}$				
Dougherty (1972)	I.B.2.a.i	All industry, states, 1960; multilevel CES, 8 occupation groups			4.1		
Weiss (1977)	II.B.1–2.c.i	2-digit manufacturing, states, 1960; 1-digit occupations, CRESH	Mixed results on σ_{KL_i}				
Chiswick (1979)	I.B.2.a.i	States, manufacturing, 1910, 1920; professionals, others; CES			2.5		
McQuaid (1986)	II.B.1.b.i	2-digit industries, states, 1977; KBW prices	$\sigma_{BK} > \sigma_{WK}$				
Roberts and Skoufias (1991)	III.B.1.b.ii	Manufacturing firms, 1983–84; Colombia; SUM prices; K, managers, Y held constant; random plant effects				−0.52	−0.28
Kesselman, Williamson, and Berndt (1977)	I.A.1.c.i	Manufacturing annual 1962–71; KBW, translog cost	1.28	−0.48	0.49	−0.34	−0.19
Clark and Freeman (1977)	I.A.1.c.i	Manufacturing, annual, 1950–76; KBW, translog cost	2.10	−1.98	0.91	−0.58	−0.22
Berndt and White (1978)	I.A.1.c.i	Manufacturing, annual, 1947–71; KBW, translog cost	0.91	1.09	3.70	−1.23	−0.72
Woodbury (1978)	I.A.1.c.i	Manufacturing, annual, 1929–71; BW, equipment, structures; translog cost				−0.70	−0.52
Dennis and Smith (1978)	II.A.1.c.i	2-digit manufacturing, annual, 1952–73; KBW, money balances; translog cost	0.14	0.38	−0.05		
Grant (1979)	II.B.2.c.i	SMSAs, 1970; KB, 2 white-collar; translog cost. Professionals, managers: Sales, clericals:	0.47	0.08 0.46	0.62 0.14	−0.32	−0.18 −0.25

Study	Section	Description		C1	C2	C3	C4	C5
Freeman and Medoff (1982)	II.B.1.c.i	2-digit manufacturing, states, 1972; KBW, translog cost:	Union:	0.94	0.53	−0.02	−0.24	−0.12
			Nonunion:	0.90	1.02	0.76	−0.43	−0.61
Berger (1984)	II.A–B.1.c.i	2-digit manufacturing, states, annual, 1971–77; KBWE prices, translog cost		$\sigma_{BK} \simeq \sigma_{WK}$		$\sigma_{BW} < 0$	−0.21	−0.14
Nissim (1984)	II.A.1.c.ii	Mechanical engineering, annual, 1963–78; U.K.; K, 3 labor; translog cost.	Skilled:					−1.06
			Semiskilled:				−1.76	
			Unskilled:				−2.31	
Turnovsky and Donnelly (1984)	II.A.1.c.ii	Iron and steel, annual, 1959–79; Australia, translog cost:	KBWEM:	0.79	3.52	−0.48		
			KBWE:	0.62	1.24	−0.04		
Bergström and Panas (1992)	II.A.1.c.ii	2-digit manufacturing, annual, 1963–80; Sweden; K, salaried, wage earners, translog cost		0.15	−0.01	1.20	−0.43	−0.47
Berndt and Christensen (1974)	I.A.1.c.i	Manufacturing, annual, 1929–68; KBW, translog production		2.92	−1.94	5.51	−2.10	−2.59
Denny and Fuss (1977)	I.A.1.c.i	Manufacturing, annual, 1929–68; BW, equipment, structures.	translog production:	2.86	−1.88	4.76		
			translog cost:	1.50	−0.91	2.06		
Klotz, Madoo, and Hanson (1980)	II.B.1.c.i	3- and 4-digit manufacturing, 1967; KBW, translog production.	highest quartile plants[a]:			6.00	−1.30	
			lowest quartile plants:			2.00	−1.50	

[a] Estimate is for the median plant within the quartile, plants ranked by value-added per worker-hour.

tor. Whether the difference results from union-imposed work rules or from differences in the kinds of plants that are most easily organized is not discernible from the cross-section analysis. A similar result was found by Maki and Meredith (1987) in their study of time-series data covering two-digit manufacturing industries in Canada.

Bergström and Panas (1992) use Swedish data that support the implications for KS p-complementarity of the disaggregated estimates of the translog cost system based on U.S. data on production and non-production workers. Nissim (1984) uses a different occupational disaggregation and shows a very clear increase in η_{ii} as the skill level decreases. Turnovsky and Donnelly's (1984) study of Australian iron and steel, however, finds evidence against KS p-complementarity whether or not materials are included as an input. Indeed, that study is alone among all those tabulated in finding a substantial amount of p-complementarity between production and nonproduction workers. Whether this is because of some inherent differences in production technology between Australia and the rest of the developed world or because of the unusual nature of wage setting in Australia is not clear. Berger, too, fails to find KS p-complementarity and, indeed, estimates that the two types of labor are p-complements. He does, though, find that the demand for skilled workers is less elastic than for unskilled workers.

The final three studies in Table 3.7 use translog production systems to generate estimates of σ_{ij} and the η_{ii}. The estimates support the inference that there is KS p-complementarity and that own-price demand elasticities decrease with skill. The difficulty is that the parameter estimates are all very large. The source of the problem is the studies' need to use all the coefficients of the production system to compute the production parameters. While there is no reason to expect biases, the accumulation of errors and randomness in the estimates means that these estimates are likely to be less reliable than others. The magnitude of the problem is shown by a comparison of the two sets of results produced by Denny and Fuss (1977).

These studies seem to confirm the KS p-complementarity hypothesis. Whether the hypothesis is correct is not completely clear, though. Part of the problem is that studies using aggregate data on the nonproduction-production worker distinction are comparing groups whose skills overlap greatly. While there is on average less human capital embodied in production workers, the distinction between the two groups is not sharp, as I showed before. In several of these studies the extent of capital-skill p-complementarity is not robust to whether assumptions of symmetry and homogeneity are imposed on the translog system. The best conclusion is that there may be p-complementarity, with the Rosen (1968) study providing the only microeconomic evidence on this. It and Roberts and Skoufias (1991) offer favorable Type III evidence on the greater elasticity of demand for less-skilled workers.

Although not shown in Table 3.7, one additional result is clear in all of the studies that examined it: Occupations cannot be aggregated consistently, for the σ_{iK} differ significantly among occupations i (in this table, blue-collar and white-collar workers). This result is not too disturbing for the studies presented here, since they do not assume separability of capital from labor. Many of the studies that disaggregate the work force by demographic group, though, exclude capital as a productive input due to the difficulty of generating satisfactory data on capital stocks in the cross sections examined. If nonseparability applies to other disaggregations of labor, other studies of labor-labor substitution may generate biases in the parameters of interest because they cannot include capital inputs. The difficulty stems from lack of data, not from inappropriate or unnecessarily restrictive methods.

B. Demand by Educational Category and for Miscellaneous Occupations

Because researchers do not disaggregate the work force in the same way, it is even more difficult to judge studies of substitution of education for raw labor than it was to compare studies of substitution among occupations. Nonetheless, there is enough research on this topic and enough similarity in the results to allow some generalizations. As in the previous section, one motivation of these studies has been to examine capital-skill p-complementarity. Subsumed under this has been an interest in examining how economic development affects the demand for (and the need to produce) educated labor.

The first five early studies summarized in Table 3.8 all are based on Type a or b methods. Using substantially different methods, Griliches (1969) and Fallon and Layard (1975) find evidence of relative capital-skill p-complementarity. Welch (1970) finds what might be viewed as the obverse—q-substitutability. The strength of substitution between highly educated and raw labor is unclear from these studies. Johnson's (1970) work implies easy p-substitution, and Bowles's (1970) estimates imply slight q-complementarity; but Fallon and Layard indicate weaker p-substitution.

The other studies of substitution by educational attainment use Type c methods to corroborate the results. Grant (1979) indicates that the extent of p-substitution for capital is greater for high school graduates than for those with at least some college education, and greater

TABLE 3.8
Estimates of Substitution by Education or Occupation

Study	Type	Description	Estimates	
Griliches (1969)	II.B.1–2.b.i	3-digit manufacturing, 1960; K,L, education	$\sigma_{ED,K} > \sigma_{LK}$	
Welch (1970)	I.B.2.b.i	Farm workers, states, 1960; nonlabor inputs (K), ED16+, 15–	$\epsilon_{ED16+,ED15-} > 0$, $\epsilon_{K,ED16+} < 0$	
Johnson (1970)	I.B.2.a.i	States, 1960; ED16+ as function of w16+/w12	$\sigma_{ED16+,ED12} = 1.34$	
Bowles (1970)	I.B.1.a.ii	Aggregate, 12 economies, late 1950s; relative L, W, ED8+, ED7–	$c_{ED8+,ED7-} = 0.17$	
Fallon and Layard (1975)	I.B.1–2.a.ii	Aggregate, 22 economies, 1963; K, ED8+, ED7–, 2-level CES	$\sigma_{ED8+,ED7-} = 0.61$ $\sigma_{ED8+,K} \leq 0$	
Grant (1979)	II.B.2.c.i	SMSAs, manufacturing, 1970; K, 3 labor, translog cost. ED13+: ED9–12: ED8–:	$\eta_{L_iL_i}$ −0.35 −0.44 −0.70	σ_{KL_i} 0.04 0.38 0.94
Brown and Christensen (1981)	I.A.1.c.i	Farm labor, annual, 1947–74; KM Owner labor: Land, translog cost[a] Hired Labor:	−0.52 −0.21	0.13 0.46
Berger (1983)	II.A–B.2.c.i	States, annual, 1967–74; K, 4 labor, translog production M, ED15–, EXP14– M, ED16+, EXP14– M, ED15–, EXP15+ M, ED16+, EXP15+ Female	$c_{L_iL_i}$ All are < 0 except young vs. old ED16+	$\epsilon_{L_iL_i}$ −0.51 −3.45 −0.80 −1.48 −0.29

			Results
Bartel and Lichtenberg (1987)	II.A–B.1–2.c.i	3-digit manufacturing, 1960, 1970, 1980; K, ED13+, ED12−, technology	$c_{K,ED13+} > c_{K,ED12-}$ for K quantity and quality
Deolalikar and Vijverberg (1987)	III.B.1.a.ii	Hired and owner farm labor, 1974–75, India; 1976–77, Malaysia; K, land, fertilizer, animals	$\sigma_{Hired,Owner} = (0.68, 1.16)$
Rivera-Batiz and Sechzer (1988)	III.B.2.c.i	Individuals, 1980; 3 labor qualities, generalized Leontief. Raw: ED: Experience:	$c_{R,ED} > 0$ $c_{R,EXP} < 0$ $c_{ED,EXP} > 0$
King (1980)	III.B.1.b.i	University departments, 1977–78; tenured, nontenured, TAs. Tenured: Nontenured: TAs:	$\eta_{L_iL_i}$ −1.15 −1.28 −4.01
Jensen and Morrisey (1986)	III.B.1.c.i	Nonteaching hospitals, 1986; translog production, beds. L medical staff: L nurses:	σ_{KL_i} 0.25 0.19 $\sigma_{L_mL_n} = 0.37$
Field (1988)	III.B.1.c.i	Cotton plantations, 1860; K, L free and slave, land, translog production. Small farms—Free: Slave: Large farms—Free: Slave:	c_{ij} $\quad$ $\epsilon_{L_iL_i}$ −1.22 0.15 Greater in small farms $\quad$ −16.82 −1.16

TABLE 3.8 (cont.)

Study	Type	Description	σ_{KL_i}	$\eta_{L_iL_i}$
Gyapong and Gyimah-Brempong (1988)	III.B.1.c.i	Police departments, 1984–85; translog cost, K.		
		L police:	0.24	−0.09
		L civilian:	−1.96	−0.45
			$\sigma_{L_pL_c} = 0.90$	
Okunade (1991)	II.A–B.1.c.i	Hospital pharmacies, 1981–89; translog cost, labor only		$\eta_{L_iL_i}$
		Pharmacist:		−0.01
		Technician:		−0.07
		Support personnel:		−0.39
Bresson, Kramarz, and Sevestre (1992)	III.A–B.1.b.ii	Manufacturing firms, 3 labor qualities, 1980–83, France.		
		Low:		−0.26
		Middle:		−0.14
		High:[a]		−0.17

[a] Average overtime period.

still for workers with at most eight years of schooling. Moreover, labor-demand elasticities decrease in absolute value with educational attainment. Similar inferences can be drawn from Rivera-Batiz and Sechzer's (1988) and Berger's (1983) dual approach. The former do not include inputs of capital services; but using a simplified version of Heckman and Sedlacek's (1985) method, they find that unskilled labor and experience (training?) are q-substitutes. The latter finds that, within each of two experience cohorts, the factor-price elasticity for more highly educated workers is greater.

I have included in this group two studies of substitution between own and hired labor in agriculture. Deolalikar and Vijverberg (1987) is a very rare example of using microeconomic establishment data on heterogeneous labor inputs in a developing country. They estimate a quadratic production function directly and find a substantial degree of substitution between the two types of labor. Brown and Christensen (1981) find greater substitution beween K and hired labor than between K and owner's labor. Both studies reinforce the conclusion of fairly easy substitution between levels of skill.

Considering these studies, it seems fairly safe to conclude that additional education reduces the degree of p-substitutability of labor with capital services and reduces the labor-demand elasticity. There is strong evidence for capital-skill p-complementarity (and relative q-substitutability). A smaller body of evidence based on the dual, q-approach corroborates the results by suggesting that c_{ii} is greater in absolute value among more educated workers.

Bartel and Lichtenberg (1987) do not estimate a production or cost system; but the equations describing the shares of output accruing to labor disaggregated by educational attainment allow one to infer the relative sizes of factor-price elasticities. The results indicate that both capital deepening and more rapid installation of newer capital equipment raise the share of more educated labor. These suggest that educated labor is relatively more q-complementary with capital *and* with newer technology than unskilled labor.

Though they do not directly generate estimates of substitution parameters, five additional studies confirm this conclusion. Osterman (1986) examined the paths of occupational employment in large manufacturing industries in response to increases in the stock of computing capability in each industry. The negative response was greater for the employment of clerks than for that of managers. Bartel and Lichtenberg (1991) examine pooled cross-section time-series data by demographic group using information on the technical progressivity (the age of capital equipment and the extent of computerization) of the worker's industry. The returns to college education are higher in industries that are more technically progressive, again implying that education and new technology are relatively q-complementary. Chapman and Tan (1992) link microeconomic data on young Australian workers to the rate of growth of total factor productivity in the industry where they work. They find that returns to investment in human capital (on-the-job training) are greater where productivity has grown more rapidly. Allen (1991) estimates a similar model on CPS data, and finds that such indicators as research and development spending, growth in total factor productivity, and others increase the returns to schooling. Krueger (1991b) also uses CPS data and shows that the growing use of computers during the 1980s increased the rate of return to education. Taken together, these studies provide fairly strong evidence that improved technology augments the relative productivity of skill.

Among the six miscellaneous studies of substitution by occupation, Field's (1988) work on cotton farms in 1860 corroborates the general results of this section. The own-quantity elasticities of factor price are larger in absolute value (implying, if we ignore other inputs, a steeper demand curve for free than for slave labor). She also explicitly tests for and corroborates the inappropriateness of aggregating different classes of labor. The Bresson, Kramarz, and Sevestre (1992) study of a broad sample of French manufacturing firms also supports the notion that the demand for the least-skilled group of workers is most elastic (though the estimates of $\eta_{L_iL_i}$ are all quite low).

King (1980) demonstrates that the demand for faculty is less elastic as the faculty's experience (skill) increases. Similar inferences may be drawn from Okunade's (1991) study of hospital pharmacies: Though the demand elasticity for each skilled category is essentially zero, it is not small for the unskilled category. Gyapong and Gyimah-Brempong's (1988) study of police departments supports this conclusion too: The demand for police is less elastic than for civilian department employees. While the estimates of own-price demand elasticities are consistent with the evidence summarized above, the estimates of σ_{KL_i} are not: Gyapong and Gyimah-Brempong imply that they are relatively less p-complementary with capital than are civilian workers; and Jensen and Morrisey (1986) find little difference in capital- (hospital beds) labor substitution for doctors and for nurses. The results of these four studies of nonprofit institutions are too varied (and too few) to allow general comparisons with results for profit-seeking firms; but they give no inkling that substitution parameters for capital, and between types of heterogeneous labor, differ between the for-profit and nonprofit sectors.

C. Demand by Age, Race, and Sex, and the Effect of Immigration

There are several reasons for analyzing the demand for labor disaggregated by demographic group. First among them has been a desire to study how changes in population and the demographic mix of the labor force affect relative wages. The major focus here has been on the impacts of increased female labor-force participation and of changes in the relative supply of young workers on their own and other groups' wages and employment. Also of interest has been the effect of changes in policy, such as the minimum wage (see Chapter 5), on the employment of younger workers. Finally, the effect of changing immigration patterns on native workers' wages and employment was of special concern as the U.S. economy became increasingly dependent on immigrant labor. It should be of interest in Europe as impediments to intra-EC migration of labor are eased, and as East-West migration increases.

The first group of studies listed in Table 3.9 used Type a methods. Imposing a multifactor CES technology, Welch and Cunningham (1978) suggest that the demand for teenage workers is elastic. Johnson and Blakemore (1979) imply that, on average, substitution between workers in any two age-sex groups is fairly easy. Kaufman (1989) and Bazen and Martin (1991) use MP conditions for young and adult workers separately. Though this restrictive technique cannot produce useful estimates of substitution between the two age groups, the estimates corroborate the general findings of Tables 3.7 and 3.8 that the demand elasticity falls with the level of skill.

The next two studies use Type b methods to focus on the demand for younger workers. The results on substitution between groups of workers are quite diverse, and Merrilees's (1982) positive own-wage demand elasticities and the implied p-complementarity of adult male workers with all other groups suggest severe problems with his work. Rice (1986), using a disequilibrium model of the market for young workers, gives the counterintuitive result that young males and adult women are p-complements. In both studies the restriction to Type b methods may be causing problems; and Rice excludes capital services from her model.

The next group of studies in Table 3.9 provides Type c estimates of substitution and own-wage demand elasticities for various demographic groups. The first two studies are complements: Anderson (1977) uses aggregate time series and Grant (1979) uses cross-section data on the same disaggregation of the labor force by age. Both estimate translog production systems and find the same very large own-wage elasticities that are produced from a system of translog produc-

TABLE 3.9
Estimates of Substitution by Age, Race, and Sex

Study	Type	Description	Group	$\sigma_{L_iL_j}$	$\eta_{L_iL_j}$
Welch and Cunningham (1978)	I.B.2.a.i	States, 1970; 4 types of labor, CES	14–15, 16–17, 18–19	All are > 0	
Johnson and Blakemore (1979)	I.B.2.a.i	Aggregate, changes 1970–77; 14 age-sex groups	Teens	1.43	−1.34
Kaufman (1989)	II.A–B.1.a.ii	Misc. industries, selected years, 1963–79; U.K; MP conditions	M F		(−0.29, −0.55) (−0.34, −0.64)
Bazen and Martin (1991)	I.A.1.a.ii	Aggregate, annual, 1968–86; France; MP conditions	Young Adult		−0.51 −0.22
Merrilees (1982)	I.A.1–2.b.ii	Aggregate, annual, 1957–78; Canada; K, 4 labor types	M young F young M adult F adult	All with M young are < 0	0.56 −0.44 −0.07 0.11
Rice (1986)	I.A.1.b.ii	Aggregate, annual, 1953–79; U.K.; M, F young, M, F adult; disequilibrium model		All young, adult > 0 except M young, F adult	
Anderson (1977)	I.A.2.c.i	Manufacturing, annual, 1947–72; K, 3 labor types; translog production	16–24 25–44 45+	All > 0	−7.14 −3.45 −3.99

Author	Code	Description	Group	$c_{L_iL_j}$	$\epsilon_{L_iL_i}$
Grant (1979)	II.B.2.c.i	SMSAs, 1970; K, 3 labor types; translog production	14–24 25–44 45+	All > 0	−9.68 −2.72 −2.48
Hamermesh (1982)	I.A.1–2.c.i	Aggregate, annual, 1955–75; K, 2 labor types; translog cost	14–24 25+	> 0	−0.59[a] −0.01[a]
Layard (1982)	I.A.1.c.ii	Manufacturing, annual, 1949–69; U.K.; K, 4 labor types, translog cost with K fixed	M < 21 F < 18 M 21+ F 18+	All > 0 except F < 18 vs. F 18+	−1.25 −0.31 −0.35 −1.59
Lewis (1985)	II.A–B.1.c.ii	2-digit manuf.; 1976–81; Australia; 4 labor types, constant-ratio σ	M < 21 F < 21 M 21+ F 21+	All > 0	−1.80 −4.58 −0.59 −2.25
Freeman (1979)	I.A.1–2.c.i	Aggregate, annual, 1950–74; K, 3 labor types; translog production	M 20–34 M 35–64 F	Only M20–34 vs. F > 0	−0.38[a] −0.49[a] −0.71[a]
Costrell, Duguay, and Treyz (1986)	I.A.1.a.i	Large industries, 1958–75; 4 labor types; 2-level CES	M < 35 F < 35 M35+ F35+	All small, most > 0	−0.18 −0.26 −0.19 −0.38
Ferguson (1986)	I.A–B.2.c.ii	Atlantic provinces, 1966–79; Canada; K, 7 labor types; translog production	M,F, 15–24, 25–34, 35–64, All 65 +	All small	All between −0.33 and −1.00

TABLE 3.9 (cont.)

Study	Type	Description	Group	$c_{L_iL_j}$	$\epsilon_{L_iL_i}$
Grant and Hamermesh (1981)	II.B.2.c.i	SMSAs, 1970; K, 3 labor types; translog production	14–24	All > 0 except	−0.03
			Blacks 25+	14–24	−0.43
			White M25+	vs. F25+	−0.13
			White F25+		−0.19
Borjas (1983)	III.B.2.c.i	Aggregate, 1975; 3 labor types; generalized Leontief	Blacks	All > 0	−0.07
			Hispanics		−0.64
			Whites		−0.001
Borjas (1986b)	III.B.1–2.c.i	Aggregate, 1979; K, 4 labor types; generalized Leontief	M white	All	−1.12
			M black	small;	2.59
			Immigrant	$c_{KL_i} > 0$	−1.36
			F		0.26

[a] Elasticities calculated at means of factor shares.

tion coefficients. In each the elasticity is largest for young workers, which mirrors the findings in Subsections A and B that the demand for less-skilled workers is more elastic. The other three studies, though they generate lower estimates of the demand parameters, generally imply the same result. Own-wage elasticities are larger for young workers (cf. Hamermesh's 1982 estimates for adult and young men, and Lewis's 1985 estimates for adult and young women). Finally, all five studies suggest that most of the various types of labor are p-substitutes for one another.

Most of the impact of changing relative supplies has stemmed from exogenous changes in population and from shifts due to shocks to tastes and household technology. That suggests that the analysis of the dual problem by the final six studies in the table is appropriate for studying substitution. Their use of diverse disaggregations of the work force prohibits any secure generalizations. They do, though, suggest most elasticities of complementarity are quite small, implying that changes in the relative supply of one group will not greatly affect wages received by workers in other groups. Also, the evidence of q-substitution between adult women and young workers in Grant and Hamermesh (1981) corroborates the results of Berger's (1983) study (presented in Table 3.8). Freeman (1979) shows no evidence of q-substitution between youths and adult women; but unlike the other two studies it is based on time-series data covering the entire economy.

Two studies explicitly examined the impact of the relative increase in the supply of young workers resulting from the "baby boom" on the relative wages of those workers. Both Welch (1979) and Berger (1985) use time-series of household data to examine analogues to own-quantity elasticities of factor prices. While they differ about the time path of the effect of changes in the relative supply of young workers, both demonstrate that the own-quantity elasticities are significant, but not large (between -0.1 and -0.2). Large changes in the size of labor-force cohorts affect the cohorts' earnings, but not very strongly.

Table 3.10 presents the results of six studies that examined substitution between migrants and other workers. There is tremendous variation in the own-factor-price elasticities; and in Borjas (1986a) some of these are even positive. Many of the estimates are imprecise, probably because of the small sample sizes underlying some of the demographic groups included in the production systems. The results in Altonji and Card (1991) may stem from their use of instrumental variables estimation, again illustrating the difficulties of accounting for endogeneity. Even without this technique, though, their esti-

TABLE 3.10
Studies of Substitution of Migrants for Other Workers

Study	Type	Description	Group	$c_{L_iL_j}$	$\epsilon_{L_iL_i}$
Grossman (1982)	II.B.2.c.i	SMSAs, 1970; K, 3 labor types; translog production	Natives	All < 0	−0.20
			Second generation		−0.03
			Foreign-born		−0.23
Borjas (1986a)	III.B.2.c.i	SMSAs, 1970; K, 6 labor types; generalized Leontief	M black	All > 0 except c_{FL_j}, some C_{HispL_j}	1.02
			F		2.90
			Hispanic native		−2.66
			Hispanic immigrant		−11.98
			M white native		−0.03
			M white immigrant		1.02
Borjas (1987a)	III.B.2.c.i	SMSAs, 1980; K, 4 immigrant types, 4 native types, generalized Leontief. Immigrant—White: Black: Hispanic: Asian:		All $|c_{L_nL_i}| < 0.05$	−1.09 −0.58 −1.40 −0.79

Bean, Lowell, and Taylor (1988)	III.B.2.c.i	Southwest, SMSAs, 1980, 6 labor types, including legal, illegal migrants; generalized Leontief	All $\lvert c_{l_i l_j} \rvert < .15$
Altonji and Card (1991)	II.A–B.1.b.i	SMSAs, 1970, 1980; less-educated natives (4 groups), immigrants; inverse factor demand, fixed effects Immigrant:	All < 0, large − 0.96
LaLonde and Topel (1991)	III.B.2.b.i	SMSAs, 1970, 1980; natives, immigrants entry date; inverse factor demand, fixed effects	All $\lvert c_{l_i l_j} \rvert < 0.03$; smaller in earlier cohorts All $\lvert \epsilon_{l_i l_j} \rvert < 0.05$

mated $c_{L_i L_j}$ are much larger than those produced in the other studies, for reasons not discernible from the published study.

Except for Altonji and Card (1991), one result pervades this line of research: The elasticities of complementarity between immigrants and natives, or between new immigrants and older cohorts of immigrants, are very small. Especially noteworthy on this issue are La-Londe and Topel's (1991) results. Their examination of factor-demand systems uses first differences in wages and employment across geographic areas to account for unmeasured cross-section differences in labor quality and other characteristics. This generalization suggests that the impact of changing flows of immigrants on the relative wages of domestic workers has been fairly small.

Additional and in some ways more powerful evidence on the issue is provided by two studies of what were almost surely exogenous shocks that generated substantial, rapid flows of immigrants. Card (1990a) used Current Population Survey data for Miami compared to the rest of the United States to examine the impact on earnings of the Mariel boatlift of Cubans to southern Florida. There was little if any discernible effect on natives' wages, even on the wages of the less-skilled, of this truly exogenous shift in relative supply. Hunt (1992) studied the impact on wage differentials across departments in France in 1968 of the influx of *pieds noirs* from Algeria in the early 1960s. There were only small negative effects compared to the wage differentials that existed in 1962, before the repatriation.

This diverse set of studies offers some general conclusions that inform us about how labor markets work and that should guide any future research. Though most studies ignore the problem, every one that formally examined the issue implies that labor-labor substitution cannot be analyzed correctly without measures of capital services. One reason for this is the very clear evidence that capital and skill—measured, for example, as education, experience, or white-collar occupation—are relative *p*-complements. This implies that the usual Type a methods are inappropriate, for they cannot reflect the complexities of substitution between workers of different types.

The overwhelming implication is that own-wage demand elasticities decrease with skill. This was generally true comparing white- and blue-collar, educated and less-educated, and older and younger workers. Cautious extrapolation of this generalization is needed; but the results should provide a framework for prediction to researchers and students of public policy wishing to examine issues in the demand for workers for whom no estimated elasticities are available. Finally, cross-elasticities of complementarity are small between nearly all pairs of groups. This means that exogenous changes in the mix of demographic groups in a labor force will not have large effects on the relative wages of other groups.

Despite the many studies summarized in Tables 3.7 through 3.10, we really know very little about the impact of different methods of estimating parameters describing labor-labor substitution or about the effects of thinking seriously about the interaction of relative supply and demand. Unlike in the research on capital-labor substitution, in which these issues have been studied using a common set of data, no such "laboratory mouse" has attracted researchers' attention in the study of heterogeneous labor. The conclusions of this section may be robust, but without more detailed attention to these technical issues we cannot know that.

The diversity of research produced so far means that not many firm conclusions have been drawn. There is also clearly a large variety of issues in labor-labor substitution that have not even been explored. As in the past, the major focus in research on labor-labor substitution should be to examine the effect of demographic and other changes as they arise and attract public attention. Prior research has, though, provided guidelines about the types of methods that are appropriate and about what results one should expect.

V. Studies of Substitution between Workers and Hours

The general purpose of this section is to examine what we know about the labor aggregator, $L = L(E,H)$, and whether it exists, that is, whether employment and hours are separable from capital services. As we saw in Section 2.VI, it is extremely difficult to distinguish empirically the costs of workers and hours, so that careful measurement and classification is even more important for this issue than for the issues of labor-capital, labor-energy, and labor-labor substitution. Even with proper measurement, not all price effects are theoretically unambiguous, so the issue is often one of estimation rather than of testing predictions of theory. Workers' supply of hours per week must be analyzed along with employers' demands for workers and hours, so that a demand-based model is not likely to produce unbiased estimates of the substitution parameters of interest.

The literature in this area has not been overly concerned with these caveats, and, indeed, its motivation has stemmed more from an interest in specific policies than from a desire to discover the nature of the substitution involved or to test theoretical propositions. One motivation in the United States is interest in the effects of mandated wage premia for overtime work on the demand for workers and hours. Studies of this issue have generally examined how differences in per-person benefit costs among firms generate differences in hours. The second motivation, which stems more from European policy concerns, is in the impact on employment and hours of reducing standard hours, H_s. Studies based in this approach have looked either directly at production functions with labor disaggregated into workers and hours, or at Type b models to which a measure of H_s has been appended. Yet a third motivation stemming from an interest in labor-market policy, and one which appears common to most industrialized economies, is in the growth of part-time employment and the effects on it of demand-side policies. The few studies arising from this source have used Type a or b methods to examine substitution between part- and full-time workers.

While an interest in policy underlies most of the studies summarized here, I leave discussion of the implications for the policies themselves to Chapter 5. I concentrate on the implications of the research for the underlying structure of production. Table 3.11 summarizes the results. The first group of studies directly estimates production functions in which E and H are considered as distinct inputs. Three studies use a generalized Cobb-Douglas technology. (They and others of this sort are discussed in detail in Hart 1987, chap. 6.) They do not inform us about substitution, but instead inquire about the relative productivity of workers and hours. Feldstein's (1967) study inspired this literature with the surprising result that $MP_H > MP_E$, and that MP_H is very large. Subsequent work, particularly Leslie and Wise (1980), who offered an economic rationale for the correlation of unobserved interindustry effects and hours and accounted for fixed effects, demonstrates the problems with Feldstein's results. Hart and McGregor (1988) also show clearly that there are not increasing returns to hours of work.

König and Pohlmeier (1988, 1989) attempt to measure the prices of hours and workers by calculating indexes of overtime premia and various employee benefits. They are the only available studies that provide direct estimates of worker-hours substitution. Their implication that workers and hours are p-complements and that they are p-substitutes for capital is crucial for inferring the likely impacts of policies. The results indicate that examining worker-hours substitution in a two-factor model will lead to incorrect inferences (since such a model assumes p-substitution). They also show that it may be possible to aggregate workers and hours, but that the aggregator is clearly not multiplicative.

The second group of studies estimates equations describing firms' use of overtime hours as a function of the ratio of the cost of what the authors believe are per-worker benefits to the wage rate. These studies can be viewed as Type b research in which the effects of fac-

TABLE 3.11
Studies of Substitution of Workers and Hours

Study	Type	Description	
Feldstein (1967)	I.B.1.a.ii	Manufacturing, 1960; U.K.; Cobb-Douglas production, KEH	$\eta_{YH} = 2.01$ $\eta_{YE} = 0.87$
Leslie and Wise (1980)	II.A–B.1.a.ii	Manufacturing industries, 1948–68; U.K.; Cobb-Douglas production, KEH, fixed effects	$\eta_{YH} = 0.64$ $\eta_{YE} = 0.64$
Hart and McGregor (1988)	II.A–B.1.a.ii	Manufacturing industries, 1968–78; West Germany; Cobb-Douglas production, KEH, K utilization, overtime	$\eta_{YH_s} = 0.87$ $\eta_{YE} = 0.30$ $\eta_{YOvertime} \simeq 0$
König and Pohlmeier (1988)	I.A.1.c.ii	Manufacturing, quarterly, 1969–85; West Germany; KEH, generalized Leontief cost	$\sigma_{EH} = -0.16$ $\sigma_{EK} = 0.62$ $\sigma_{HK} = 0.12$
König and Pohlmeier (1989)	I.A.1.c.ii	Manufacturing, quarterly, 1969–85; West Germany; KEH, various system methods	$\sigma_{EH} = (-0.40, -0.78)$ $\sigma_{EK} = (1.02, 1.41)$ $\sigma_{HK} = (0.72, 1.51)$
			Percent change in E given a one-third increase in the price of overtime
Ehrenberg (1971b)	III.B.1.b.i	Manufacturing, 1966; overtime depends on relative nonwage labor cost	1.6
Laudadio and Percy (1973)	II.B.1.b.ii	Manufacturing industries, 1968; Canada; overtime depends on relative nonwage labor cost	1.5

TABLE 3.11 (cont.)

Study	Type	Description	
Nussbaum and Wise (1978)	III.A–B.1.b.i	Manufacturing, 1966–74; overtime depends on relative nonwage labor cost	2.0
Ehrenberg and Schumann (1982)	III.B.1.b.i	1976; overtime depends on relative nonwage labor cost. Manufacturing: Nonmanufacturing:	(0.5, 1.1) (1.0, 2.1)
Owen (1979)	II.B.2.a.i	Industries and occupations, 1973; CES, supply-demand system, full-, part-time workers	$\sigma_{FP} = 4.35$
Ehrenberg, Rosenberg, and Li (1988)	II.B.2.a.i	Industries, 1984; CES, supply-demand system, full-, part-time workers	$\sigma_{FP} = 0.21$
Montgomery (1988)	III.B.1.b.i	Plants, 28 cities, 1980; full-, part-time workers	$\sigma_{FP} = 0.67$
Bernanke (1986)			$\eta_{E,p_E} = -.58$ $\eta_{H,p_H} = -.54$ $\sigma_{EK}, \sigma_{HK} > 0$; scale effects exceed subst. effects
Hart and Kawasaki (1988)	I.A.1.b.ii	Manufacturing, annual, 1951–81; West Germany; fixed, variable labor costs; K held constant	

			Elasticity of	
			H	E
Hart and Sharot (1978)	I.A.1.a.ii	Manufacturing, monthly, 1961–72; U.K.; MP condition. Benefits/wages: H_s:	−0.01 0.92	−0.05 −0.40

Reference	Code	Description			
Faini and Schiantarelli (1985b)	I.A.1.b.ii	Aggregate, quarterly, 1970–80; Italy; KL prices.	H_s:		−0.51
Franz and König (1986)	I.A.1.b.ii	Manufacturing, quarterly, 1964–84; West Germany; KLM and overtime prices.	Overtime premium:	−0.04	−0.10
			H_s:	0.99	−1.09
Wadhwani (1987)			H_s:		−0.53
de Regt (1988)	I.A.1.a.ii	Manufacturing employment, annual, 1954–82; Netherlands; MP condition.			
			H_s:	0.89	−0.41
Hart and Wilson (1988)	III.A–B.1.b.ii	Metalworking, 1978–82; U.K.; H, OH, includes K.	Benefits/wages:	−0.04	−0.28
			H_s:	0.77	−0.17
Brunello (1989)	I.A.1.a.ii	Manufacturing, annual, 1973–86; Japan; MP condition.	H_s:	0.05	−0.34

tor prices are constrained to be homogeneous of degree zero. All three American studies use waves of the same detailed set of establishment data. The elasticities shown in Table 3.11 indicate the percentage change in employment in response to an increase of one-third in the price of an hour of overtime (changing the premium from 50 to 100 percent), holding worker-hours constant.

All four studies imply that, at a constant input of worker-hours, and ignoring capital, there is some p-substitution between employees and hours. Moreover, because they provide estimates only of the gross elasticities, they suggest still more employment-hours substitution. The main difficulty with these estimates is that the only independent variation that produces the results is in the costs of employees' benefits. In these cross sections the denominator of the benefit-wage ratio cannot vary because of differences in the price of overtime hours (since that is fixed by law). Difficulties induced by simultaneity and the implied contractual relationships between workers and firms also seem particularly important here. That the same results are obtained for the United States and Canada is some encouragement that the estimates can be useful. But without additional evidence based on *imposed* variations in the price of hours, the inferences drawn from these sets of data are not very secure.

Two of the studies in the next group recognize the importance of accounting for the supply of hours, but they do so in the context of workers' and firms' choices about part- and full-time employment in models in which these are the only inputs into production. Using similar methods, Owen (1979) finds easy substitution between the two groups of workers, while Ehrenberg, Rosenberg, and Li (1988) imply substitution is much more difficult. Montgomery (1988) presents the most useful results here, since his microeconomic data obviate the need to account for possible endogeneity of supply. His data suggest some substitution between full- and part-time workers.

Taken together, if we ignore capital (which the studies summarized earlier in the table suggest is wrong, and which means we are examining gross elasticities), we may infer that hours and workers are p-substitutes. This inference is supported by Disney and Szyszczak (1984), who show that part-time employment in the United Kingdom was sharply reduced when legislation expanded employment protection for part-time workers. Because they exclude capital and fail to model the supply of hours, the research is at best suggestive that firms do choose part-time workers depending on their relative costs.

The next two studies are best thought of as miscellaneous corroborations of the results presented thus far. Bernanke's price elasticities suggest that employers view hours and workers as being equally productive relative to their prices, as they should be in equilibrium. Hart and Kawasaki (1988) measure fixed and variable labor costs more carefully than anyone else. Their finding that the effects of labor-cost increases on the demand for both workers and hours are more important than any substitution, and that both E and H are p-substitutes for capital, underscores the problems with models that ignore capital.

The final group of studies examines factor-demand systems in which the effect of changing standard weekly hours can be examined. In all but de Regt (1988) and Brunello (1989) hours are inputs into production along with capital. Taken together they imply strikingly different conclusions from those based on the studies that simply examined the use of overtime without a measure of capital services or their price. Hart and Sharot (1978) and Hart and Wilson (1988) show that increasing the ratio of benefits to wages reduces *both* hours and employment, as does an increase in the overtime premium in Franz and König (1986).

All seven studies present estimates of the effect of changes in H_s on E, and five estimate its effect on both H and E. All suggest that cutting standard hours increases the demand for workers. Except for Brunello's (1989) evidence for the institutionally different Japanese economy, the evidence implies that reducing H_s generates a nearly equal percentage effect on hours worked. Though imposing the additional cost of reduced standard hours should reduce the demand for worker-hours (in terms of the table, should have larger effects on H than E), only three of the five studies that allow this calculation (Hart and Sharot, de Regt, and Hart and Wilson) produce this result. None of the five makes a serious effort to solve the difficult problem of measuring the relative prices of H and E, though, so that the results of this calculation are suspect in all of them. Indeed, only Faini and Schiantarelli (1985b) attempt that measurement. Until we have solved that problem and also understand how changes in those prices are affected by changes in standard hours, the partial equilibrium estimates in these studies should be viewed as very first approximations.

The paucity of research and the special necessity to examine hours of work to account for workers' behavior guarantee that we cannot draw many general conclusions about issues in worker-hour substitution. Both higher overtime premia and lower standard weekly hours will increase the ratio of workers to hours per worker; but the magnitude of these relative changes is unclear (and, in any case, will necessarily differ depending not just on technology, but also on what the firm's or economy's labor cost structure (2.55) looks like at a particular time).

König and Pohlmeier examine employment-hours substitution using German data, but theirs are the only Type c studies that I have found. Their finding that workers and hours are p-complements in a three-factor model is potentially important.[11] Given the success of Type c methods in examining both homogeneous and heterogeneous labor demand, a substantial amount of useful research could be done on issues of worker-hour substitution using these methods. Such work will only be successful, though, if it is combined with careful measurement of the costs of the two dimensions of the labor input along the lines of Figure 2.2. Similarly, there are no studies of the substitution of workers for hours among several types of labor. Ignoring issues of contracting and the problems they cause for drawing inferences about this aspect of labor demand, it should not be difficult to learn something about the nature of the technology in (2.61).

There has been no attempt to examine worker-hours substitution in the context of a model of contracting. Such research may not be very important in the study of substitution of labor for other factors, or of one type of labor for another; but for examining the intensity of employers' use of their workers it is crucial, for in the long run hours worked are strongly affected by individual choice. That means that the implications for employee-hours substitution of workers sorting themselves among firms with different technologies need to be accounted for in order to extricate the effects of technology from those of the sorting.

No research has been conducted on differences between for-profit and nonprofit firms in the demand for workers and hours. Yet the common knowledge that nonprofit firms rely heavily on volunteer and part-time employees suggests that one cannot infer that this aspect of technology is the same for both types of firms. Going still farther afield from existing research, there has been no study, nor even any serious consideration, of the appropriate time period over which to measure labor intensity that I discussed in Section 2.VI. Distinguishing among hours per week, weeks per year, and number of workers as three dimensions of the labor input would be of intellectual interest and important for understanding the potential impact of a variety of policies.

VI. Conclusions—What We Know, and What We Don't Know

Although each section has summarized what we know about the empirical magnitudes of the parameters characterizing labor demand, that information merits a concise summary:

[11] Stafford (1980) presents a very thoughtful discussion of the issues involved in scheduling the utilitization of capital and employees' services.

We know that the absolute value of the constant-output elasticity of demand for homogeneous labor for a typical firm, and for the aggregate economy in the long run, is above 0 and below 1. Its value is probably bracketed by the interval [0.15, 0.75], with 0.30 being a good "best guess."

We know that labor and energy are p-substitutes.

We are fairly sure that capital and skill are p-complements.

We are fairly sure that technological change is q-complementary with skill.

We are fairly sure that the own-wage demand elasticity decreases as the skill embodied in a group of workers increases.

We are fairly sure that elasticities of complementarity of other groups of workers with migrants are fairly low.

We are fairly sure that workers and hours are both p-substitutes for capital.

Whatever issue in the demand for labor is investigated, and no matter what type of data the researcher uses, it is necessary to be aware of precisely what parameters are being estimated. A large number of the studies analyzed here purport to estimate "the elasticity of demand for labor." Some estimate σ; some estimate η_{LL}, and some estimate η'_{LL}. The estimates are of parameters that differ conceptually; but the discussions of the results are oblivious to these differences and, more generally, to the appropriate link between the estimates and the theory. In other studies authors have computed elasticities of factor prices and inferred they are elasticities of labor demand. It is essential that anyone studying the demand for labor or for groups of workers be completely clear about precisely what is being estimated.

The robustness of estimates of the demand for homogeneous labor to a large variety of possible specifications is remarkable. Especially convincing are the rapidly increasing number of studies that use individual firms as the units of observation. At this point, though, two major sets of extensions are worthwhile. First, we saw in Section III that the one sensible respecification that generated substantially different estimates of η_{LL} included endogenous formation of expectations. Are the unusual estimates a result of a real difficulty in distinguishing factor-demand parameters from parameters describing expectations, or is the problem merely that the mechanism for specifying expectations is faulty? Research that uses survey-based measures of expectations in factor-demand models could resolve this anomaly. Second, we know very little about the demand for homogeneous labor in particular industries or in firms that differ in the source of control of production. Studies that provide such knowledge will be more useful than aggregate or average estimates of η_{LL} and will allow for predictions of employment and wage behavior under changing types of control.

Knowledge of the extent of substitution among various groups of workers is not well developed. There are many possible disaggregations that can be examined, and not all of them are worth examining. But such simple and important questions as the relative q-substitutability of workers of different ages for each other and for capital, and the q-substitutability of workers by race and sex, have not been answered satisfactorily. These issues deserve more study.

The paucity of knowledge about how workers and hours enter the production function is remarkable. Rather than examining that function or forms derived directly from it, much research has skirted around the issue by examining overtime behavior or has considered very simple specifications. Without allowing for more general specifications of the labor aggregator defined over workers and hours, and without careful measurement of the prices of the two components, our rudimentary knowledge of how they affect output will not advance far.

More generally, what is required to advance the study of the static demand for labor is research that recognizes the simultaneity of wages and employment. While we saw that embedding labor demand in models that included supply did not alter our conclusions about the magnitudes of the parameters, much more than standard supply-demand models is needed. Contracting models of collective bargaining relationships go partway in this direction; but because collective bargaining covers a decreasing and in some cases small part of most industrialized economies, other approaches are required. In the case of worker-hours substitution the issue is clearly one of estimating demand in the context of a model of contracting between workers who are more or less tied to their employer. In the case of substitution among heterogeneous labor, supply-demand models are rare, and those few studies that have included them do so in a fairly cursory fashion.

This exhortation to examine contracting and supply-demand models is unlikely to be fruitful with currently available data. Our knowledge of labor demand will advance faster if we can acquire the kinds of data that allow us to examine appropriately designed models. Since the data needed to advance research in this area are part of a larger set of needs that overarches the entire subject of labor demand, I postpone discussing them until the concluding chapter.

CHAPTER FOUR

Employment Demand and the Birth and Death of Firms

I. Introduction

Chapter 2 presented the neoclassical theory of demand for labor and its components—people and the hours they work. Chapter 3 examined the massive amount of empirical evidence based on applications of this theory to data from a variety of industries and economies. Implicitly the theoretical discussion describes the behavior of a firm whose continued existence is assumed, and the empirical work assumes an infinitely lived firm. Alternatively, both chapters might be construed as describing the behavior of Marshall's representative firm, some amalgam of behavior by all the existing and potential firms in the industry or economy. Presumably, among the firms in any aggregate some are expanding while others are contracting. The immense outpouring of theoretical and empirical research on labor demand is agnostic about this pattern of changes.[1]

At the very least this view ignores the tremendous amount of job creation and destruction that occurs as firms and establishments are born or die. Consider the information for U.S. manufacturing in Table 4.1, based on changes during quinquennia and thus subject to a variety of potential biases due to this high degree of temporal aggregation (see Section IV). These data from the Censuses of Manufactures demonstrate the huge changes that occur in the number of jobs as establishments are born or die. As the last three quinquennia show, even where net changes in employment are small, the amount of churning among plants—the implied diversity of individual plants' experiences—may be very large. The table says nothing about the effects of factor prices and output shocks on the level of employment demand. It does, though, demonstrate that it is incorrect to equate the "representative firm" to the typical firm.

Does this matter? That is, would considering these changes affect the issues discussed in Chapters 2 and 3? For example, the estimated

---

[1] Specialists in industrial organization have been somewhat more interested in this issue than have labor economists, though their concern is also recent. See the summary in Carlton and Perloff (1990).

Table 4.1
Employment Changes in Manufacturing, in Percent, United States, 1963–82

Years	Net Employment Change	Arising From			
		Plant Births	Plant Expansions	Plant Contractions	Plant Closings
1963–67	14.5	14.1	19.4	-7.8	-11.1
1967–72	-2.7	19.6	10.6	-14.0	-18.9
1972–77	2.7	15.8	13.6	-11.3	-15.3
1977–82	3.8	17.6	11.7	-15.4	-17.7

Source: Dunne, Roberts, Samuelson 1989, 55.

labor-demand elasticities discussed in Chapter 3 may be incorrect because they are based on the assumption of an infinitely lived firm. By ignoring the discontinuous event of a plant's birth or death, these estimates, and the theory underlying them, might miss anomalously large or small changes in employment that might occur as factor prices or product demand are shocked. Similarly, discontinuous changes in employment could lead to surprising effects of policies designed to alter firms' employment decisions.

In what follows I examine the economic causes of the birth and death of plants and firms and the jobs that are born or die with them. The focus, as in Chapters 2 and 3, is on inferring the impact of changes in wages on levels of employment. Though births and deaths are inherently dynamic, the issues of interest are static—the long-run effects of shocks—rather than the time paths between equilibria. For that reason the subject properly belongs in this part of the book.

Mainly because workers in existing plants have established relationships with their employers, separate discussions are required to deal with plant openings and closings. Having analyzed models describing this behavior, I then examine the evidence on the contribution of these discrete changes to changes in employment demand. The theory has not been used as the basis for this (quite sparse) empirical literature. Instead, I present it as a guide for evaluating that research, particularly its very few behavioral implications, and for indicating useful areas of future empirical research.

II. The Birth of Plants

There is no standard textbook model of plant openings. Therefore, in the absence of any guide from received theory, I assume that there is

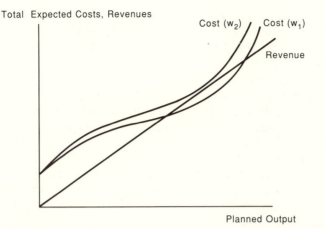

Total Expected Costs, Revenues

Cost (w_2) Cost (w_1)

Revenue

Planned Output

4.1 The Discrete Nature of Plant Openings

a set of prospective entrepreneurs who might be drawn into an industry if product prices rise high enough or input costs fall low enough. There is thus presumably a standard upward-sloping supply curve of output of the particular product. In what follows I concentrate on how the addition of new firms adds to output and employment. I thus pay little attention here to the role of existing firms' expanding output in the upward slope of this curve.

What makes the issue interesting is the possibility that there are substantial fixed costs of entering the industry. If so, very large percentage changes in output or input prices might have no impact on the decisions of potentially small-scale businesses. Obversely, very small changes in these prices can produce very large changes in the supply of output to the market and in the demand for workers in the industry.

To see the second of these possibilities, consider the potential firm depicted in Figure 4.1. Its prospective revenue per time period is assumed to be a linear function of planned output per period (because it is a perfect competitor in the product market). I draw its total cost curve as a function of the wage rate and assume technology and other factor prices remain unchanged. The curve reflects decreasing costs over the initial range of output and increasing costs subsequently. As it is drawn, the entrepreneur, or prospective entrepreneur, described by the figure will not open a plant if the wage is w_2 and expected to remain there forever. There is no positive planned output at which positive profits can be expected given existing and expected technology, factor prices and product prices.

Consider what happens if the wage falls to w_1 and is expected to remain there forever. With this *slightly lower* wage rate it pays the typical firm to enter this industry. It will plan to produce an output between the points at which $\text{Cost}(w_1)$ intersects the total revenue curve. Comparing the result in this case to the outcome at a slightly higher wage, one sees that a small drop in the wage rate has led to a discontinuous jump in employment in the firm (from zero to some possibly substantial positive amount). If all prospective entrepreneurs were identical, we would observe this industry springing full blown from an initial long-run equilibrium with no output or employment.

Obviously no industry is characterized by identical firms, despite the mystique that our textbook models hold for us. If it were, we would observe this kind of incredible movement from the initial zero-output long-run equilibrium to an equilibrium with ongoing operations and substantial labor demand. Heterogeneity among current and prospective firms renders this description incorrect. This heterogeneity makes it difficult to infer whether long-run employment decisions respond differently to small wage changes depending on whether the entrepreneur is already operating or not. Assume for simplicity that each prospective entrepreneur has static expectations about the future paths of product and input prices. (Rational-expectations forecasts would yield the same predictions, but with an accretion of notation.) Assume that the only inputs are labor and capital services, with prices w and r. Technology is assumed to be the same for each entrepreneur. This yields a profit function

$$\pi = \pi(p, w, r),$$

where p is the product price, and the average price level in the economy is assumed constant.

I assume that heterogeneity arises in this market because entrepreneurs, indexed by i, differ in the target rate of profit π_i^* below which they will choose not to enter the market. This assumption makes the exposition especially straightforward, but it could easily be modified to allow other sources of heterogeneity. Differences in their target profit rates might arise, for example, because they have different rates of time preference or different rates at which they can borrow to finance new capital purchases.[2] The ith prospective firm's decision rule is to enter the market if

$$\pi \geq \pi_i^*. \tag{4.1}$$

[2] There is strong evidence (Evans and Jovanovic 1989) that access to capital affects workers' ability to create new businesses, suggesting that borrowing rates are an important source of heterogeneity among prospective entrepreneurs. Hause and Du Rietz (1984) use heterogeneity in firms' profit functions to examine the determinants of variations in the aggregate rate of entry into an industry. I could follow this and model heterogeneity through different profit functions π_i rather than different target profit rates without affecting any conclusions.

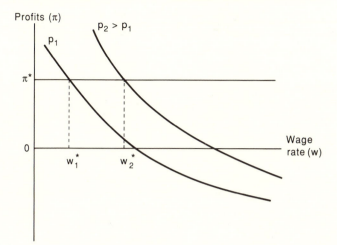

4.2 Wages and Plant Openings

This decision can be affected by changes in any of the arguments of π, but our interest is in the effect of changes in w. Accordingly, Figure 4.2 relates profits to the wage rate at fixed values of r and p. Higher wage rates reduce profits, so that the profit-wage curve slopes down. Given a target profit rate of π^* and the product price p_1, the firm will open the plant only if the wage rate is less than w_1^*, for only then will its profits exceed the target rate. If there were a permanent demand shock, so that the product price rises above p_1, say to p_2, the firm would open up even if the wage rate were above w_1^*, for its profit rate would exceed the target π_i^*. Indeed, so long as the wage is below w_2^*, the firm will begin operations.

Assume that prospective firms are arrayed by their π_i^* from lowest to highest. Then for any combination of p, w, and r only those firms that have the lowest target rate of return—whose π_i^* is below $\pi(p,w,r)$—will be in business using some amount of worker-hours L. The other, prospective firms, whose π_i^* is above $\pi(p,w,r)$, will not operate. Each increase in p or decrease in w (or r) will induce some prospective firms to expand employment from zero. Firms will be born as prices change, and in the process their labor demand may exhibit large discrete changes.

Let $f(\pi_i^*)$ be the density function of prospective firms' target profit rates, with

$$\int_{-\infty}^{\infty} f(\pi_i^*)d\pi_i^* = 1.$$

At any given time some fraction ϕ of all prospective firms will be operating. This fraction depends on the density f and the prices p, w, and r, with

$$\phi = F(\pi(p, w, r)) \leq 1.$$

ϕ is just the cumulative of the density of the π_i^* up to $\pi(p, w, r)$.

Assume now that the wage changes. Then the fraction of firms in existence from among all prospective firms will change:

$$\frac{\partial \phi}{\partial w} = f(\pi(p, w, r))\frac{\partial \pi}{\partial w} < 0. \tag{4.2}$$

The sizes of these effects will depend on the density function f and the shape of the profit function. Putting (4.2) into elasticity terms,

$$\eta_{LL}^o = \frac{f(\pi(p, w, r))}{F(\pi(p, w, r))} \cdot \frac{\partial \pi}{\partial w} \cdot w < 0. \tag{4.3}$$

The expression η_{LL}^o in (4.3) can be called the *quasi elasticity of labor demand through plant openings*. Assuming that the size of prospective firms when they do operate is independent of their target profit rates, it relates changes in worker-hours that occur as the flow of jobs created in new plants varies to changes in wages. The elasticity is between worker-hours and wages, as in Chapters 2 and 3, but not through the usual mechanism of variations within an existing plant or firm. The effects of increases in r and p can be derived similarly.

η_{LL}^o is clearly not the same as η_{LL}, for output is not being held constant. Nor is it conceptually identical to η_{LL}', since it is not definable for a particular firm. Rather, it is best viewed as the analogue for prospective firms to an industrywide measure of η_{LL}' for existing firms.

The main point to notice in all of this is that the elasticity in (4.3) could be typical of those in Section III of Chapter 3, *even though no existing firm changed worker-hours in response to a change in the wage rate*. The observed elasticities could arise solely from the birth of firms operated by heterogeneous entrepreneurs who enter the market and begin employing workers as the wage rate drops. We could observe the results predicted by standard theory even if they are not generated by movements along smooth production functions, but instead are combinations of those movements and their relation to the distribution of entrepreneurs' talents.

From this viewpoint there is no need for some of the simplifying assumptions in Chapter 2 to hold. Any regularity that characterizes most individual prospective firms—for example, a particular degree of substitutability between capital and labor—need not be apparent at the industry level. The correlation between the heterogeneity that underlies the density function $f(\cdot)$ and that in an underlying production parameter may generate an aggregate relationship of opposite sign to the average value of the parameter at the micro level. This also means that the margins along which policy can affect the demand for labor differ from the conventional ones. Employment growth can be affected both by changing the arguments of the profit function, as in the standard case, and by altering the distribution of the target profit rates (or altering entrepreneurial efficiency).

There are many unrealistic features in this derivation. No prospective employer bases a decision about whether to open a plant on the observation of a wage rate or price prevailing on a particular date. Rather, the arguments of π should be replaced by forecasts, presumably rational ones, of all three prices. As long as these forecasts are elastic with respect to permanent shocks in the prices themselves, though, discrete microeconomic responses among heterogeneous firms will still generate apparently smooth aggregate responses. Prices or wage rates may be heterogeneous, and prospective employers may have the same target profit rates. These too affect the derivation but not the general results. With initially increasing returns to scale, the basic results of this section can be reproduced as long as there is heterogeneity among prospective employers.

III. THE DEATH OF PLANTS

A simple approach to analyzing plant closings and their relationship to wage and output shocks would reverse the analysis of Section II. We could assume that there is a heterogeneous group of plants, postulate shocks to expected product or factor prices, and derive the fraction of plants that go out of business. In a simple way that is what I do in this section. A more complex approach, as in Jovanovic (1982), would take account of employers' learning about their entrepreneurial ability and use this to explain patterns of growth of firms by size and age. However, merely changing signs in the previous analysis would ignore some important differences that arise when the effect of shocks on *existing jobs* is to be considered. Jovanovic's approach, though fruitful of predictions about the patterns of growth of businesses, is less useful in discussing the demand for employees in existing firms, because it ignores contractual relationships between workers and employers.

These relationships affect how employers will respond to shocks. Employers contemplating opening a plant envision establishing such relationships, so that including contracting would be a useful way of expanding the model of Section II; but those potential contracts between prospective employers and unattached workers are less important for the labor market than are actual contracts between existing employers and the workers who are attached to their plants, because no firm-specific investments yet exist to affect firms' and workers' decisions. Accordingly, the study of the demise of plants is a good place to introduce contractual relationships between employers and workers.

In Section II I ignored the uncertainties about product and labor markets that potential employers face. Avoiding this complication is reasonable if we are studying potential employers who are considering a variety of product and labor markets in which to begin operating a plant. It is unreasonable when studying employers whose investment in industry- and firm-specific physical and human capital makes them especially concerned about the paths of wages and product prices. Accordingly, the analysis here introduces uncertainty about future prices and wages in order to focus on firm-specific human capital.

This section models the equilibrium relationship between the wage rate received by homogeneous workers and the probability that their jobs will disappear because their employer closes. I assume that once the business closes it will not reopen, an assumption that could be relaxed with the addition of substantial complexity. The assumption of heterogeneity in Section II generated a quasi elasticity of labor demand for the changes in worker-hours that are produced when firms open up a business in response to changes in wages. The analysis here generates such a quasi elasticity for changes in employment produced by shocks that affect the rate of job loss through plant closings. I assume throughout that hours of employed workers are constant, so that the quasi elasticity refers equally to employment and worker-hours.

When workers sort themselves among firms, one of the risks they consider is that their job will disappear due to exogenous negative shocks. As with any other such risk, the combination of workers' risk aversion and employers' production technologies results in a positive relation between the wage rate and the observed probability that the plant will close.[3] Workers have thus entered firms at a reservation wage w^r that makes them indifferent between choosing to work in that firm and at least one other. The market produces a compensating differential in the reservation wage at different firms that is positively related to the *ex ante* expected probability that the firm will close. (Dunne and Roberts 1989 provide evidence on the existence of this

[3] The argument is the same as Rosen (1974) and has been applied to estimating relationships between wage rates and job-related risks.

differential.) This reservation wage, including the compensating differential for the firm-specific expected risk of closing, is the basis against which workers compare the wages they receive once they have joined the firm.

Workers who have entered employment in the firm acquire firm-specific human capital that raises their wage rates above what they can obtain elsewhere, other things, including the expected risk of plant closing, being equal. Assume that such training is instantaneous, so that all workers who have joined the firm are identical. I assume that the firm employing these workers faces a known distribution of random prices p, $h(p,S)$, where $p \geq 0$ and S is an index of product demand. The index S may be viewed as an exogenous demand shock to markets in which the firm sells, with a higher S shifting the distribution of prices to the right. I ignore the firm's choice about the size of its capital stock (and thus ignore capital-labor substitution here) in order to simplify the analysis and concentrate on the effect on employment of shocks to the product market. Obviously, shocks can induce substitution between capital and labor, but there would be no qualitative differences between the analysis of that behavior in the context of plant closings and the discussion in Chapter 2. The firm's profits are thus

$$\pi = pY - wL - rK^*,$$

where production is characterized by $Y = F(L,K^*)$.

I assume that wages are set by the firm and its workers at the start of each time period in full knowledge of the state of product-market shocks, as indexed by a particular value of S, say S^*. The firm then draws from the distribution $h(p,S^*)$ and decides whether or not to shut down. Let π^* be the target level of profit that determines its continued existence. Above this level the firm will stay in business. Below it the firm will close down. Then at this level of profits the product price must be

$$p^* = \frac{\pi^* + wL + rK^*}{Y}. \tag{4.4}$$

The implied probability that the firm will close, θ, is:

$$\theta = \int_0^{p^*} h(p,S)dp. \tag{4.5}$$

Equation (4.5) implicitly defines a relationship between θ and w for a given set of exogenous conditions indexed by S. This relationship can be viewed as the set of probabilities that the firm remains in business consistent with each particular wage rate at a given S^*. The

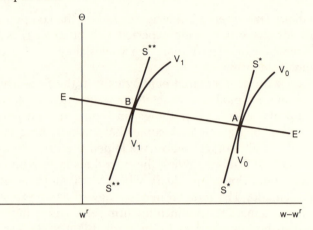

4.3 Equilibrium Combinations of Wages and the Probability of Plant Closing

probability depends on the distribution of stochastic prices, which is shifted by changes in S. The slope of the relationship is

$$\left(\frac{d\theta}{dw}\right)_{S=S^*} = h(p^*, S^*)\frac{dp^*}{dw} > 0.^4 \tag{4.6}$$

At a higher wage rate the firm is more likely to close the plant for any given draw from the distribution of stochastic product prices. We can graph the *probabilistic shutdown frontier* for $S = S^*$ in Figure 4.3. It depicts the set of all points along which probabilistic profits are at the competitive minimum given values of w and the state of the product market, S. Viewed differently, at each wage rate it shows the proba-

---

4 $\dfrac{dp^*}{dw}$ can be written as

$$\frac{dp^*}{dw} = \frac{[w - p^*F_L]\frac{\partial L}{\partial w} + L}{Y},$$

and rewritten as

$$\frac{dp^*}{dw} = \frac{L}{Y}[1 + \eta'_{LL} - \frac{\eta'_{LL}F_L p^*}{w}],$$

where η'_{LL} is the total demand elasticity for labor as derived in Chapter 2. As long as workers are not paid in excess of their marginal revenue products, we can be sure from (4.6) that $\dfrac{dp^*}{dw} > 0$, and thus that

$$\left(\frac{d\theta}{dw}\right)_{S=S^*} > 0.$$

bility that the plant will close. At points to the right of $S = S^*$ the firm will shut down; at points to the left, excess profits will be earned. Favorable shocks shift the frontier to the right.[5]

Now consider the workers in whom firm-specific investments have been made and who are thus attached to the firm. The typical worker chooses between a higher wage and a reduced risk that the firm will close. I define workers' expected utility after they have taken a job with a particular firm in terms of $w - w^r$, the excess of wages with the employer over what they could obtain outside the firm. The typical worker's expected utility increment from remaining in the firm is

$$V = [1 - \theta]U(w - w^r) + \theta U(0), \quad U' > 0, \ U'' < 0. \tag{4.7}$$

Obviously, if w falls below what can be obtained elsewhere, the worker will leave the firm voluntarily.[6] I thus implicitly examine changes in w and θ within some limited range, which is an appropriate way to make inferences about discrete responses to small shocks. Beyond that range the worker will break the contract.

Scaling U so that $U(0) = 0$ and setting the total differential of (4.7) equal to zero yield

$$\left(\frac{d\theta}{dw}\right)_{V=V^*} = [1 - \theta]\frac{U'}{U} > 0. \tag{4.8}$$

A pair of typical indifference curves V_0 and V_1 is shown in Figure 4.3. Combinations of wage rates and risks of plant closing along V_0 are preferred to those along V_1, for at each risk of losing the job the wage rate is higher along V_0. Standard assumptions about U give the indifference curves between θ and w the shapes shown in Figure 4.3.[7]

Equilibrium in the internal labor market is defined by the tangency of the indifference curve to the probabilistic shutdown frontier for fixed S^*, that is, at the point where

$$\left(\frac{d\theta}{dw}\right)_{S=S^*} = \left(\frac{d\theta}{dw}\right)_{V=V^*}. \tag{4.9}$$

Firm-specific investment to some extent insulates the average worker from shocks to product demand by giving the firm a margin over which it does not pay to close the plant. For that reason the equilib-

[5] To present both sides of the internal labor market, the frontier is drawn with w^r as the origin.

[6] To avoid specifying a quits function, I assume that workers have a knife-edge decision about voluntary turnover. Relaxing this assumption would complicate the model without changing its implications.

[7] Differentiating in (4.8):

$$\frac{d^2\theta}{dw^2} = \frac{[1-\theta][UU'' - U'^2]}{U^2} < 0.$$

rium is drawn for the average set of exogenous conditions, S^*, at point A in the first quadrant of Figure 4.3. A shock to this equilibrium, for example, a negative shock that lowers S to S^{**} such that the probability mass of h is shifted to the left, produces a new equilibrium on the new shutdown frontier $S^{**}S^{**}$ in Figure 4.3. Without specific assumptions about the shape of the zero-profit frontier, one cannot determine the slope of EE', the locus of equilibrium combinations (θ, w). However, under very reasonable assumptions it has the negative slope shown in Figure 4.3.[8]

The analysis applies better to the discussion of plant closings than to permanent layoffs from continuing enterprises. The case of layoffs is obscured by two problems. First, the possibility exists that the shared investment in firm-specific capital could be resurrected through a recall of the laid-off workers. More important, we could apply the employer's side of this analysis mutatis mutandis to analyze layoffs; but changing the worker's side appropriately would require specifying a utility map that includes both workers' beliefs about their own probabilities of being subject to layoff should S decrease and a mechanism for ordering layoffs.[9] Without these changes the model cannot go far in explaining layoff behavior.

The discussion has dealt with the contractual relationship between a worker and an employer in a firm whose continued existence is uncertain. The event under consideration, the demise of a plant or firm, is distinctly nonmarginal. Using a minimum required rate of profit and workers' attitudes toward risk, the analysis explains why some plants or firms shut down rather than make marginal changes that would allow them to continue in existence if technology were neoclassical and there were individualized wage setting.

Taking the view implicit in this model, firms shut down because they get a bad draw from the distribution of product-market conditions, a distribution whose *ex ante* risk and return sufficed to induce them to enter the market. That bad luck so affects their expectations of product-market conditions that the present value of expected profits becomes negative. Even though the investment they have made jointly with their workers in firm-specific skills partly insulates them from output shocks, sufficiently large shocks will pierce that insulation and induce the firm to close the plant.

A shock to the labor market can have a similar effect. A positive labor-market shock makes other jobs more attractive to the firm's

---

[8] If one assumes that U is isoelastic and that $\left(\dfrac{d\theta}{dw}\right)_{S=S^*}$ is a positive constant, EE' has the negative slope depicted in the graph.

[9] Wright (1986) presents an analysis embodying such a mechanism.

workers, presumably by raising their wages.[10] Such a shock can be modeled as raising the reservation wage, thus shifting the vertical axis rightward. In terms of Figure 4.3, the V_i tilt counterclockwise, producing an upward shift in the equilibrium locus EE'. The jointly optimal contract becomes one with a higher wage rate and a higher probability of plant closing. Thus even though the wage change does not originate with the firm, changes in labor-market conditions will produce a positive relationship between the probability the plant closes and the wage rate, and thus a negative *quasi elasticity of labor demand through plant closings*, η^c_{LL}.

If we make specific assumptions about the nature of the indifference maps and probabilistic shutdown frontiers, we can infer the magnitude of this quasi elasticity. The inferences clearly rest on approximations that hold only locally around the locus of equilibria, EE'; but in that region we can develop the relationship between shocks to wage rates and the fraction of jobs lost to plant closings. Throughout I assume that workers' indifference maps are homothetic around the point of equilibrium. Assume, too, that the map of probabilistic shutdown frontiers is homothetic, though that assumption can be relaxed. With both maps homothetic the slope of the shutdown frontier at any point on the equilibrium locus is the negative of the inverse of $\left(\dfrac{\partial \theta}{\partial w}\right)_{EE'}$, the slope of that locus.

The slope can be converted into the desired quasi elasticity if we assume that all existing plants in the industry are the same size and pay an average wage $\bar{w}$, and that some average fraction $\bar{\theta}$ of the plants in the industry closes down during each period. Under these assumptions, the quasi elasticity is

$$\eta^c_{LL} = \bar{\theta}\left\{\bar{w}\left\{\frac{\partial \theta}{\partial w}\right\}_{EE'}\right\}^{-1} < 0. \tag{4.10}$$

This measure is the negative of the percentage change in the probability that a plant closes in response to a 1 percent increase in the wage rate paid in the industry, holding product-market shocks constant.

If the probabilistic shutdown frontiers are not homothetic, the linear approximation to the elasticity in (4.10) is incorrect. In that case a

---

[10] The same inferences could be made if we assume that a shock reduces the probability of job loss in employment outside the firm. Anything that makes other jobs, or being out of the labor force, relatively more attractive than the current job has the same effect on the results as an increase in w^r.

second-order approximation to the changing slope of EE' can be used to correct the estimate of η_{LL}^ε. If EE' becomes flatter as $w - w^r$ increases, this correction lowers the absolute value of the quasi elasticity.

Here I have demonstrated that one can derive a quasi elasticity that relates the change in employment to a change in wage rates, in this case for employment changes occurring through plant closings. While the closings are discrete events in the plants where they occur and for the jobs that are lost, changes in the rate of plant closings and in the rate of jobs lost represent a continuum. As in Section II, what is discrete for one plant becomes smooth for the aggregate of all existing plants in an industry. There is no reason to assume that the convenient inferences about labor demand stemming from the analysis of neoclassical production functions apply to changes in labor demand resulting from these discrete events. As (4.10) implies, the quasi elasticity of labor demand through plant closings depends on the interaction of profit and utility functions (and, in a more general model, on the distribution of shocks among heterogeneous plants).

IV. Employment Shocks and the Flow of Jobs

Wedervang (1965) pioneered the analysis of gross flows of jobs that could provide the empirical counterpart of the theory of the previous sections. This was renewed beginning in the early 1980s with the development of several new sets of data that allowed researchers to decompose an industry's response to such shocks into four component parts: (B) births of new plants (or firms); (G) growth in existing plants (or firms); (D) deaths of existing plants (or firms); and (C) contraction in existing plants (or firms). Each part indicates the percentage change in employment resulting from that source. The components are linked to net employment change by the identity

$$\Delta E \equiv B + G - D - C, \tag{4.11}$$

where ΔE is the net percentage change in employment in some aggregate. Though by itself (4.11) is merely a taxonomy, with appropriate modeling it could be used to estimate the parameters from the theory in Sections II and III.

Outside the United States a variety of alternative sets of data have been assembled that can be used to produce estimates of the rates B, G, D, and C. These vary among countries in terms of coverage by industry, frequency over which the flows of jobs are calculated, basis in establishments or firms, and the amount of information available on the characteristics of the firms that are created or disappear.

In the United States these studies have been based on three different sets of data. The first was assembled by the U.S. Small Business Administration from data provided by Dun and Bradstreet (D&B) based on information that employers report to establish credit for borrowing. The data cover the majority of private firms in all industries. The second is the Longitudinal Research Database (LRD), which is based on information from manufacturing establishments in the five Censuses of Manufactures between 1963 and 1982 and the Annual Surveys of Manufactures in non-Census years. Finally, several researchers have assembled their own sets of data from unemployment insurance (UI) records in individual states. These data cover all but the smallest private establishments.

Each of these sets of data enables us to infer the relative sizes of the responses of the various components of net employment change as the economy, or a particular sector, is shocked. Estimates of these responses are not, however, strictly comparable across the various data bases. Most important, the estimates of B, G, D, and C will vary even within the same data set depending on the length of time over which the change is computed. Compare, for example, changes calculated over the five-year interval between the Censuses of Manufactures in 1977 and 1982 to those calculated annually during this period. Any plant that was born *and died* between the Censuses will not appear in the former calculation but will surely be counted in the latter if it survived one year. Similarly, any expansion of employment that took place in one year in some plant and was followed in the subsequent year by an equal cut in employment will be excluded from the former calculation but will be included in the latter. In general, estimates of annual rates of births, deaths, and the like will be larger the shorter are the time intervals over which these gross changes are calculated, assuming death rates are higher among newer plants.

Problems are also caused by comparing data covering births, deaths, expansions, and contractions of *firms* to those covering *establishments*. Plants can be born or die, and existing plants can expand or contract. At the same time there may be no measured change in the numbers of jobs stemming from each source if all these underlying changes occur within the same firm. Obversely, firms may merge or dissolve, while the plants they own continue to operate.

Whether plants or firms should be the underlying units of observation depends on where the specificity of investment lies and on the possibility of intrafirm mobility of workers. To the extent that investment is plant- but not firm-specific, or that workers do not move among plants within a firm, the plant is the more appropriate unit of observation. Thus far choices about whether to use firms or plants in analyzing flows of jobs have been constrained by the availability of data and have not had the luxury of concern about this issue. How using the more aggregated firm data instead of establishment data affects the magnitude of flows of jobs depends on the magnitude of births and deaths of plants within firms relative to mergers of firms whose plants continue to operate.

The industrial coverage of the LRD is also a problem. While a large number of the studies analyzed in Chapter 3 focus on manufacturing, and a major proportion of the available employment and other data cover that sector, manufacturing provides less than 20 percent of all jobs in the United States and similarly small percentages in other developed economies. There is nothing inherently wrong with studies using the LRD or other data on manufacturing, but any inferences from those studies must necessarily be quite limited.

Table 4.2 summarizes available studies of the sources of net changes in employment. The research is categorized by whether the data cover manufacturing or all industries and, within these categories, whether they refer to the United States or another economy. For each study the extent of employment change is shown at an annual rate. Where the changes are based on year-to-year calculations rather than comparisons over a multiyear period, the term "annual" is entered in the second column. In several of the studies the calculations did not distinguish between births and expansions and also aggregated employment reductions over deaths and contractions. For those studies only two entries are provided for gross changes. In one (Leonard and van Audenrode 1991) only changes in continuing firms are presented.

The most striking feature of the table is the sheer magnitude of the changes in employment resulting from each of the four sources. This was suggested by the data from the one study summarized in Table 4.1; but those results are by no means atypical and, indeed, because they were based on four- or five-year changes, they clearly understate the extent of the fluidity of jobs that is implied by most of the other studies presented in Table 4.2. These changes are huge in the data for manufacturing (the Dunne, Roberts, and Samuelson 1989 and Davis and Haltiwanger 1989 studies), as well as in those studies that use broader data sets. They are sufficiently large in the Organization for Economic Cooperation and Development (OECD) summary of data for four other developed countries and in the studies of Belgium, Lower Saxony, and Italy to make it clear that the phenomenon is general among labor markets in industrialized economies. That Rowter's (1990) estimates for Indonesia show even larger gross

TABLE 4.2
Studies of Sources of Job Flows

Study	Data	Annual Rate of Job Change (in percent)				
		Gross Change Due to:				Net Change
		B	G	D	C	
	Manufacturing					
Schmenner (1982)	D&B, large firms, 1972–78[a]	1.3			0.8	0.5
MacDonald (1986)	D&B, food, large firms, 1976–82[b]	1.5			1.2	0.3
Davis and Haltiwanger (1989)	LRD, annual, 1979–83[a]	8.0			13.0	−5.0
Dunne, Roberts and Samuelson (1989)	Changes between Census years, 1963–82[a]	3.5	2.9	3.3	2.5	0.6
Baldwin and Gorecki (1988)	Canada, 1970–81[a]	1.8	1.9	2.1	1.2	0.4
	annual[a]	1.5	7.7	1.8	6.5	0.9
	annual[b]	2.3		3.4		
Rowter (1990)	Indonesia, ≥ 20 workers, annual, 1975–84[b]	7.2	4.7	3.0	3.4	5.5
Leonard and van Audenrode (1991)	Belgium, Social Security records annual, 1978–83[b]	3.0			3.5	−0.5
Gerlach and Wagner (1993)	Lower Saxony Germany, ≥ 20 workers, annual, 1978–89[a]	1.2	3.1	1.4	3.5	−0.6

TABLE 4.2 (cont.)

Study	Data	Annual Rate of Job Change (in percent)				
		Gross Change Due to:				Net Change
		B	G	D	C	
	All Industries					
Armington and Odle (1982)	D&B, 1978–80[a]	3.9	7.0	3.0	3.5	4.4
Leonard (1987)	Wisconsin UI records, annual, 1977–82[a]	13.8		11.0		2.8
Jacobson (1988)	Pennsylvania UI records, annual, 1979–85[b]	6.2	2.2	6.0	2.3	0.1
OECD (1987)	Canada, tax records annual, 1979–84[b]	2.4	8.8	2.2	7.5	1.5
	France, UI records annual, 1978–84[a]	5.6	5.7	5.7	6.2	–0.6
	Germany, Social Security records, annual, 1978–84[a]	2.7	5.6	2.1	6.1	0.1
	Sweden, business register, annual, 1982–84[a]	2.6	8.8	3.4	8.7	–0.8
Contini and Revelli (1987)	Italy, Social Security records annual, 1978–80, 1981–83[b]	1.6	10.3	1.5	10.7	–0.3

[a] Based on employment changes in establishments.
[b] Based on employment changes in firms.

flows suggests that there is still more fluidity in developing economies, perhaps because of the typically lower rates of capitalization per employee.

These large gross flows of job creation and destruction do not merely reflect expansion within some industries and contraction in others. Instead, they result from simultaneous births and deaths, and expansions and contractions, within the same industry, even within industries classified at the four-digit SIC level.[11] This might mean that employers within the same industry face different price or wage shocks. It may also support the view implicit in Sections II and III that there is substantial heterogeneity among current and potential employers in the same industry in target rates of return or in the ability to earn profits when facing the same price and wage conditions.

In seven of the eleven studies in Table 4.2 that use the fourfold classification of (4.11), the absolute value of the difference $B - D$ is smaller than the absolute value of the difference $G - C$. In two of the others the differences are about equal, while in the OECD (1987) data for Sweden and in the Indonesian data the net contribution from plant entry and exit exceeds that from changes in continuing establishments. Another way of looking at this issue is to examine (4.11) using the results summarized in Table 4.2. Although the data and methods used are hardly comparable, a very rough idea of the relative importance of the various flows of jobs can be obtained simply by averaging over the eleven studies. This yields

$$1.0 \equiv 3.5 + 6.0 - 3.0 - 5.5. \tag{4.11'}$$

The contributions to net employment change within continuing firms account for roughly two-thirds of the gross flows of jobs.

These results suggest that there are always shocks that generate all four types of changes in employment; but the major source of net changes in employment within an aggregate is the difference between the expansion and contraction of employment within existing plants. This buttresses the belief that it is not completely improper to infer that the conventional estimates of *employment changes within an aggregate* that are discussed at length in Chapter 3 are based on behavior by the continuing neoclassical firm that is the archetype for the theory in Chapter 2.

The studies summarized in Table 4.2 also allow one to infer the relative contributions of B and D, and G and C, to short- and long-run changes in employment. We noted above that the inferences one

[11] Dunne, Roberts, and Samuelson (1989) demonstrate this clearly. Leonard (1987) shows a similar result for two-digit industries and for counties in Wisconsin.

draws about the relative importance of the different flows of jobs will vary depending on the time period over which one compares changes in employment. Some suggestive indirect evidence is provided by the huge annual rates of change in Leonard (1987) and Davis and Haltiwanger (1989), based on year-to-year changes in employment, compared to the other studies for the United States that calculate these changes over longer periods of time using broad-based samples from manufacturing.

Baldwin and Gorecki (1988) provide direct evidence on this issue and on the effect of defining job dynamics using data on plants or firms. Their estimates on Canadian manufacturing data suggest that most of the annual fluctuations in employment in existing plants are short-term, with increases in one year nearly offset by decreases in the same plant shortly thereafter. Indeed, like those discussed above, this study implies that the net employment changes that occur over a decade are due more to differences in $G-C$ than to those in $B-D$. It suggests, though, that long-term gross additions to employment result as much from B as from G, and long-term job losses result even more from D than from C. The study also shows that basing the calculations on firms understates the magnitude of job flows compared to what is inferred if plants are observed. Births and deaths of plants within firms exceed those that appear to arise when the ownership of continuously operating plants is transferred between firms.

In terms of generating jobs it is useful to know whether the flows in (4.11) that add to net employment change, B and G, are more responsive to shocks than are those that reduce employment, D and C. Policies designed to increase employment should differ depending on whether it is easier to produce gross increases in jobs than it is to prevent gross losses. Several of the studies in Table 4.2 also examine this issue, and the evidence is quite clear: Gross increases, $B+G$, vary much more over time and across industries than do gross declines, $D+C$.

An interesting question, given the ubiquity of data on manufacturing, is whether the results for manufacturing are typical of the entire economy. In manufacturing firms higher capital-labor ratios might lower B and D relative to G and C. On the other hand, we know that *average* fluctuations in product demand are higher in manufacturing than elsewhere. The net effect is unclear a priori. The only studies that are comparable in terms of coverage are those using the D&B data (Armington and Odle 1982, Schmenner 1982, and MacDonald 1986); and unfortunately Armington and Odle calculate job changes over a two-year period. Unless very short-lived (less than two years, but more than one year) plants in these data constitute an unusually large fraction of plants that close, though, these studies suggest that job turnover through the opening and closing of plants is less volatile in manufacturing than elsewhere.

The revival of interest in gross flows of jobs was partly stimulated by studies using the D&B data conducted by David Birch and others (Birch 1981). The main, widely heralded conclusion was that most of the net expansion of jobs was due to the creation of new jobs through the birth of *small* establishments. This finding, with its implication that policies for job creation should be targeted toward the apparently responsive small-business sector, does not imply, though, that small firms contribute more than their share to employment growth. First, it may instead be that the small establishments are owned by average-sized firms. In the one study that examined this issue (Armington and Odle 1982), this appears to be so: While small *establishments* account for a disproportionate share of job creation (in the D&B data), the share of small *firms* is the same as their share of total employment. Implicitly the large contribution of small establishments to net job growth stems from the propensity of existing firms to expand by creating additional establishments of below-average size. The locus of expansion is the small plant; but the locus of decision making is the average-sized firm. Second, Birch and others eliminate firms that die from their calculations, but oversample small firms. This means that they concentrate on employers who have low employment in the initial year of the sample, but who do not disappear. That guarantees that the remaining small firms will appear to grow rapidly, since those that do not are truncated from the sample.

More useful evidence stems from Schmenner's (1982) study of large manufacturing firms, which shows how much lower are their birth and death rates compared to those economywide. (See also Contini and Revelli 1987 and Davis 1990.) New establishments and those that disappear are both smaller than average. Small firms do not add disproportionately to net increases in employment; they do, though, disproportionately raise both B and D.

While they are extremely interesting in their own right, data on gross flows of jobs tell us nothing directly about the magnitude of the wage or output elasticities of employment changes through the births or deaths of establishments, or growth or contraction in existing establishments. All we can infer is that changes occur and that, by assumption, they must be produced by shocks that change labor demand by existing and potential employers. Whether there is sufficient variation across establishments or firms in shocks to wages, or to other factor prices or output demand, to produce the observed changes in labor demand is unclear from the available data.

In the absence of any knowledge of the sources of these apparent shocks, for the purpose of linking the inferences about these flows to factor costs let us make the heroic assumption that the responses represent what would occur if the shocks stemmed from imposed changes in wage rates. That is, assume that shocks to wages are typical of the shocks that produce the responses in these data sets. If that is true, the greater variation in $B + G$ than in $D + C$ suggests that current and prospective employers respond more to shocks that affect expansion, based on filling new jobs, than current employers respond to shocks that induce them to cut back on jobs and possibly close plants. This may perhaps reflect the insulating effect of firm-specific human capital that I noted in Section III. This evidence may imply that there is an asymmetry in the employment-wage elasticity, with larger effects of decreases than of increases in labor costs. The myriad estimates of wage elasticities discussed in Chapter 3 could be averages of larger elasticities of job creation and smaller elasticities of job destruction.

V. The Role of Wages in Plant Openings and Closings

Patterns of gross flows of jobs tell us little about η_{LL}^o or η_{LL}^c. Instead, the ideal study of the determinants of plant openings (as opposed to the magnitude of employment flows resulting from births of plants) should take the theory seriously. It should consider the potential population of entrepreneurs and examine how changes in input costs, particularly wages, and other shocks affect the fraction of that population that is actually operating in an industry and generating jobs. Reviews of the literature (Due 1961; Oakland 1978; Newman and Sullivan 1988) are replete with studies purporting to estimate the impacts of state and local taxes and of factor prices on the location of employment, in a sense presenting versions of the kinds of studies summarized in Chapter 3. However, almost none of the literature on the location of plants examines how the creation and destruction of jobs is affected by these shocks. Instead, the research relates inter-area differences in wages (or labor costs) to differences in levels of employment.

Only two studies, Carlton (1979) and Papke (1991), approach the ideal of estimating the determinants of the fraction of potential firms that come into existence at different rates of labor cost, other factor prices, and additional shocks to profit rates. Using a set of Dun and Bradstreet data covering 1967–71 and 1972–75, Carlton specifies equations relating the number of new single-plant firms in a four-digit industry in each SMSA relative to the SMSA's size to the average wage in the two-digit industry in the SMSA and to a number of other variables. The results show significant elasticities of the birth rate of new single-plant firms with respect to the wage rate, ranging from -1.0 to -1.5. These estimates are higher than the conventional estimates of η'_{LL} discussed in Chapter 3. Papke (1991) uses similar methods on a set of the D&B data describing annual rates of plant openings between 1975 and 1982 in six three-digit manufacturing industries. In four of the six industries the rates of opening new plants were significantly lower relative to an area's population in those areas that had relatively higher wage rates in the particular industry. Higher marginal tax rates on business had similar inhibiting effects on the birth of plants.

Regrettably the few other studies of the effects of wages and other input costs on the birth of plants model the process as one with a firm choosing where to locate a new branch plant among competing locations. The birth-wage elasticities generated by that approach tell us only the size of the response to *relative* wage differences conditional on the plant being opened. They do not measure η^o_{LL}. Thus Carlton (1979, 1983), using the same D&B data, examined the effects of relative wage differences across areas on firms' choices about where to locate branch plants. He found lower wage elasticities for this choice than for new births of single-plant firms. Schmenner (1982) suggests that the decision to open a new plant is often very idiosyncratic, with wage differences having little to do with where the plant is to be opened. Bartik (1985) used D&B data for all manufacturing firms on the Fortune 500 list for 1972 and 1978 to study the effect of cost differentials on the choice of where to locate new plants. He estimated that, other things being equal, each 10 percent increase in wages in an area reduces the probability that a firm will locate its new plant there by 9 percent.

One would expect that the decision about *where* to locate a plant, given that one is to be opened, is more elastic with respect to wage differences than the decision about *whether* to open a plant or firm. Admittedly only Carlton (1979) examined η^o_{LL} directly. Nonetheless, that his estimate exceeds the range of the several estimates of the relative location-wage elasticity does not add to one's confidence about our knowledge of any of these measures, particularly of η^o_{LL}. At this point we can only conclude that this elasticity may be larger than η'_{LL}, as Carlton suggests. The evidence on it is too sparse to allow any firmer conclusions about the sensitivity of changes in labor demand through the opening of new plants to changes in labor costs.

There are also few studies that allow inferences about η^c_{LL}. We are really just left with case studies of the determinants of plant closings and with attempts to infer the appropriate elasticities from miscellaneous, usually nonrepresentative data. In the former category Gerhart (1987) examines cases of union-management negotiations in response to threats of plant closings. He fails to find that wages have a major effect on whether the firm closes the plant. Whether his result is due to the unique nature of the plant-closing decision in unionized firms, or merely reflects the common result in noneconometric case studies of employment decisions that economic variables appear unimportant, is unclear.[12]

In the latter category, I used household data for 1977–81 to estimate η^c_{LL} based on the proposed calculation in (4.10).[13] The estimated value was -0.86 without the correction for heterotheticity, and -0.37 with that correction. Berger and Garen (1990) used panel data on coal mines from 1980 through 1984, including establishments that shut down when operating them was not profitable. The estimated labor-demand elasticity resulting from shocks that caused mines to open or close (essentially the weighted sum of η^o_{LL} and η^c_{LL}) was -0.94. The estimated elasticity based only on mines that were continually open (essentially η'_{LL}) was -0.42. One infers from this comparison that employment demand in the marginal coal operations was more sensitive to changes in labor cost than was demand at continuing establishments. Of course, the difference may stem from heterogeneity among the plants—those that are more sensitive to cost differences may be the ones that we observe opening up or shutting down.

Both sets of explicit estimates are well in line with or perhaps slightly higher than those characterizing the bulk of studies summarized in Chapter 3. Unlike the one available estimate of η^o_{LL}, these estimates suggest one does not go far wrong in inferring the effect of wage changes on plant closings from the literature that estimates η_{LL} or η'_{LL}. Whether this inference, based on these two estimates only, is correct is unclear without substantial additional research. At least one potential problem in comparing estimates of η^o_{LL} and η^c_{LL} stems from the inherent inability to obtain data on the entire set of potential entrants to an industry. The derivations in Sections II and III dem-

---

[12] For example, the hoary antimarginalist arguments of the 1940s and 1950s rested in part on impressionistic evidence collected in interviews with managers. (See Lester 1948.)

[13] The underlying estimates are presented in Hamermesh (1988a), which used household data. The negative effect of larger wage increases on the probability that a worker loses a job through a plant closing is consistent with the shape of the equilibrium locus EE' in Figure 4.3. The result is supported, albeit not very strongly, by Howland's (1988) study of plant closings using D&B data between 1975 and 1982.

onstrate clearly, though, that even if we could obtain better data, there would be no a priori reason to expect that $\eta_{LL}^o = \eta_{LL}^c = \eta_{LL}'$.

VI. Conclusions and Extensions

The data show that over a period of five to ten years changes in employment due to the births or deaths of plants are as important as changes due to growth or contraction within existing plants. That is less true for markets that are observed more frequently, but even there job dynamics through entry and exit of firms are a major fraction of total changes in the number of jobs. These simple facts pose stark challenges to most existing research on labor demand: Is the standard neoclassical theory of factor demand, based on a representative and presumably preexisting firm, relevant to explaining how labor demand is affected by imposed changes in factor prices? Does the massive amount of empirical research on labor-demand and substitution elasticities linked to that neoclassical model offer any predictions about the effects of wage changes on employment changes resulting from the opening and closing of plants?

On the theoretical side the answer is clear: Standard models of labor demand provide some of the basis for analyzing this issue. A firm's profit function for a potential new plant, or an entrepreneur's notional profit function for entry into a market, underlies any firm's decision about starting a plant. What is new is that there is no representative firm, so that the distribution of existing and potential firms' responses to imposed wage changes must be modeled. Thus, while the response of employment change resulting from the births and deaths of plants is based on firms' production functions, the average labor-demand elasticity resulting from this source of changes in employment depends also on the shape of the *distribution* of firms' profit functions.

This complication to the theory means that there is no reason to expect the labor-demand elasticity resulting from changes in the birth and death rates of plants and firms to equal that resulting from changes within existing plants and firms. None of the unfortunately sparse empirical research on this issue suggests that this elasticity is less than the consensus estimates presented in Chapter 3; but it is unclear whether this elasticity really exceeds the estimates inferred from comparing employment levels within aggregates or within continuously operating plants or firms over time. Very little can be concluded at this point, other than: (1) there is a great need for more study of this topic; (2) because there is no theoretical basis for expecting that these elasticities will be the same, any inferences about the potential impacts of policies designed to stimulate job creation through new plants must use standard estimates with great care; (3) inferences about any detrimental impacts of imposed increases in labor costs through their effect on plant closings must be made with similar care. The main point of all of this is that labor demand is a more complex issue than is reflected by consideration of the neoclassical theory of production, as useful as that theory has been.

All of these conclusions underscore the need for additional research in this nearly virgin area of the study of labor demand. Estimates of η^c_{LL} could ideally be produced by linking one of the sets of establishment data used in the studies summarized in Section IV to initial wage rates in the plant and the particular area and industry where each plant is located. The universe of plants would form the base against which the responsiveness of plant closings to exogenous wage shocks could be compared. This would be a significant improvement over simple cross-section studies that relate wage differentials to rates of employment growth.

Research on the effects of wages on labor demand through the entry of firms is even harder. Such studies will be much more difficult than the analogue in research on labor supply, the joint estimation of decisions about participation and hours of work. While the issue here too is one of accounting for behavior around a corner solution of non-participation (in the labor force or in a market), the appropriate data for this research are much less easily identified. The paucity of existing work and the demonstrated importance of the issues suggest, though, that further research will prove very fruitful. Given the immense number of estimates of η_{LL}, some redirection of effort toward measuring η^c_{LL} (and η^c_{LL} too) is required.

CHAPTER FIVE

Static Demand Policies

I. Introduction

In this chapter I examine government policies that can affect the wage and employment outcomes analyzed in Chapters 2 through 4. All that discussion could really have had just two purposes: allowing inferences about how natural economic events affect employment and wages, and providing guidelines for predicting how government policies can alter those outcomes. It is not worth providing an explicit description of how the results can be used to infer the impact of natural events. Inferences about their effects are easily drawn, though; and the rise in energy prices in the 1970s, and the relative growth of the female labor force in the 1970s and 1980s, were discussed in Chapter 3. The potential for public policies to affect wages and employment deserves more explicit discussion, both because they are more subject to human control and because large sections of the literature deal with them.

A standard approach to this topic would list the policies, outline the details of the legislation and administration of each, present any economic theory that is specific to evaluating the policy, and discuss what the empirical literature has shown. That approach may work with the particular policies and with the literature dealing specifically with them, but it necessarily fails to bring the more general literature on labor demand to bear. More important, its specificity means that it is limited to a few existing policies and is inapplicable to the infinite variety of policies that might be devised.

Given these difficulties, this chapter is organized by dividing policies into classes based on the discussion in the previous chapters. There are several reasons for creating yet another classification scheme in this volume. The first is that this particular typology allows the reader to use the general theoretical and empirical results of the preceding chapters to infer the actual and potential effects of a range of policies. Also, it provides a convenient way of summarizing specific research on existing policies. Finally, this makes it easier to see how research on these policies illustrates the analytical issues within the general category of policies. The typology is general enough to allow predictions about the effects of any new policy in each class or about any existing policy not discussed explicitly.

While I allude to a number of policies in the general area of labor demand, for only three—payroll taxes, minimum wage policies, and skills-training programs—do I provide detailed reviews of the sort that one would find in a standard approach. Evaluating the impact of two other specific policies—targeted and other employment subsidies, and changes in the overtime premium—is implicit in some of the discussions of Chapter 3. Because of the complexities of extending the empirical evaluation of these policies, and to illustrate how to use the syntheses of Chapter 3 to generate *ex ante* policy evaluations, I present theoretical and simulation models that analyze particular aspects of their effects. Drawing inferences from the more general literature figures as importantly in the discussion as the presentation of specific evidence. "Policy research" is very often not the most relevant or most useful way to evaluate the effects of a specific policy.

II. Classifying Policies That Affect the Equilibrium Demand for Labor

I use a three-tier classification to analyze policies affecting labor demand. The schema describing this classification is shown in Figure 5.1. The highest level of the typology divides policies into those that immediately affect factor prices (usually wage rates), called *P-policies* in line with the discussions of duality in Chapter 2. The other category consists of *Q-policies*, those that operate on the demand for labor through their effects on the quantity of labor. This distinction allows easy use of the different sets of general empirical evidence discussed in Chapters 3 and 4.

The second level of the demand-policy hierarchy distinguishes between those policies that are *general* (that apply directly to all workers) and those that are *specific* (that either de jure or de facto apply only to *particular workers*, those with certain demographic characteristics or at certain places in the distribution of earnings). This part of the typology of policies follows directly from the distinction in Chapters 2 and 3 between the demand for homogeneous and heterogeneous labor. Since those chapters were organized in part based on this distinction, this framework allows easier use of their results.

The final level of the classification distinguishes among the kinds of policy tools used. Thus, *labor policies* alter the wage rate or the amount of worker-hours that face the typical employer. *Nonlabor policies* alter the prices or quantities of other inputs that confront the employer, while *employment-hours policies* vary the relative prices of

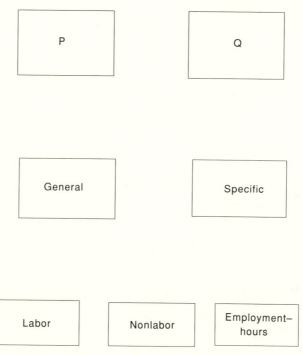

5.1 Schema for Classifying Static Labor Demand Policies

workers and hours or place limits on the amounts of each that must be used. This too follows directly from the discussions in Chapters 2 and 3. We can analyze the potential effects of labor policies using the theory and evidence on labor-demand and factor-price elasticities. The effects of nonlabor policies will in part be determined by cross-price elasticities and cross-factor-demand elasticities. Employment-hours policies must be studied using evidence on substitution between employment and hours.

Policies come and go; and it is impossible for any discussion to remain timely for very long. The main purpose of all the specific discussions in this chapter is to illustrate how to analyze any policy aimed directly or indirectly at the demand for labor. Any policy that changes the cost of employing all workers or some identifiable group of workers can be analyzed as a P-policy. A policy that alters the supply of labor generally or of a particular type of worker can be analyzed as a Q-policy. This general approach circumvents the ephemeral nature of the analysis of particular policies by letting them serve as archetypes for broader classes of intervention in the labor market.

P-general policies include general payroll taxes and subsidies as labor policies; accelerated depreciation and investment tax credits, and subsidies to develop new sources of energy, as nonlabor policies; and requirements for premium pay for overtime as employment-hours policies. *P*-specific policies include payroll taxes/subsidies that are limited by effective ceilings; policies such as requirements for a marketwide wage minimum; and requirements for pay by "comparable worth" that change the relative costs of employing male and female workers. Programs mandating the extension of coverage of employee benefits to part-time workers are *P*-specific employment-hours policies.

Q-general policies include changes in migration laws as labor policies, and changes in standard hours legislation as an employment-hours policy. Some changes in migration laws and administrative rules can be viewed as specific labor policies, as can most programs that increase the stock of trained workers. These latter include programs for developing skills through on-the-job training in the private sector, public-sector employment programs targeted to low-skilled workers, and subsidies to higher education that increase the supply of highly trained workers. Mandated minimum labor-output ratios, such as requirements for minimum staffing of day care centers, are *Q*-specific labor policies. Restrictions on hours of work by children are examples of *Q*-specific employment-hours policies.

III. *P*-GENERAL POLICIES

A. Payroll Taxes and Subsidies

Policies that affect employment by operating on the wage rate that the typical firm pays its employees form the first type of *P*-general policy. Whether they are designed to finance specific programs or raise general revenue, payroll taxes that are applicable to all employees are clearly policies that affect the demand for labor and thus equilibrium employment and wages. Their obverse, wage subsidies, are expressly designed to increase employment. All of these are *P*-general labor policies.

In the United States the payroll tax that is earmarked to finance Old Age, Survivors, Disability and Health Insurance (OASDHI, or Social Security) is by far the most important labor-market policy in terms of the size of the revenues raised and its potential impact on employment. The tax was assessed on the employer at a rate of 7.65 percent on all wages paid up to an indexed ceiling on earnings ($53,400 per year in 1991) and at an equal rate on the employee. It raised $319 billion of revenue during 1989. Because of the tax ceiling the OASDHI tax is not truly *P*-general; but in 1989 only 8.8 percent of earnings escaped the tax, and only 6 percent of employees failed to pay taxes on their marginal dollar of earnings.[1] It is thus reasonable to treat the payroll tax in the United States as *P*-general and to ignore any substitution among types of labor that the limit on taxable earnings may produce.

In many other countries payroll taxes are assessed at higher rates than in the United States. For example, in Sweden in 1986 the combined payroll tax rate for old age and disability insurance on employers and employees together could range as high as 24 percent. In Austria the combined rate was 18.5 percent.[2] The issues discussed in this section are thus even more important for many European economies than for the United States.

Targeted reductions in payroll tax rates have been the major vehicle that governments have used to provide labor-marketwide subsidies to stimulate employment demand. In the United States President Carter proposed a 4 percent credit to employers on their OASDHI taxes, with the explicit purpose of attempting to increase labor demand.[3] In Norway the payroll tax rate on employers varies from 16.8 percent in the least preferred region down to 5 percent in the most heavily subsidized.[4] Other countries have reduced or abolished payroll taxes on employers in certain regions in order to stimulate the growth of employment there.

The effects of payroll taxes and subsidies cannot be examined from the demand side alone. Instead, their impacts are a matter of tax incidence that must at least be examined in a model of labor-market equilibrium. Throughout I assume that any change in payroll taxes/ subsidies is accompanied by an offsetting change in a neutral tax that leaves total government revenue unchanged. I assume that total government spending does not change; and any effect of shifting spending from general purposes to specific programs that might be financed by the increased payroll tax has no effect on labor supply or labor demand.[5] I ignore any dynamic effects on households' alloca-

[1] *Social Security Bulletin*, Annual Statistical Supplement, 1990, Table 4.B1. Moreover, beginning in 1991 a higher earnings ceiling, $125,000, applied to 1.45 percentage points of the tax.

[2] Council of Europe, *Comparative Tables of the Social Security Schemes*, Strasbourg, 1987.

[3] This was part of the economic stimulus package submitted to Congress on January 31, 1977. The credit was not enacted. Instead, by May 1977 Congress had passed the New Jobs Tax Credit, discussed below in the section on *P*-specific policies.

[4] Council of Europe, *Comparative Tables*.

[5] Whether this last assumption is reasonable is not clear. In a world of perfect foresight and ultrarationality, the extra benefits would offset any effects of the higher taxes

tion of resources over their members' life cycles that the imposed changes in these taxes/subsidies might generate. Also excluded are any short-run dynamic impacts of the tax/subsidy policy. These depend on adjustment mechanisms and the nature of disequilibria and are left to Chapter 8.

The demand for and supply of labor are

$$L^d = f(w[1+\tau]), f' < 0; \tag{5.1}$$

$$L^s = g(w), g' > 0, \tag{5.2}$$

where τ is the percentage payroll tax or subsidy that I assume is directly assessed only on the employer, and I assume hours per worker are constant. In equilibrium $L^d = L^s$, or

$$f(w^*[1+\tau]) = g(w^*), \tag{5.3}$$

where the (*) denotes an equilibrium value. Differentiating in (5.3) with respect to the payroll tax rate, and manipulating the result to write it in logarithmic form, yields

$$\frac{\partial lnw^*}{\partial \tau} = \frac{\eta_{LL}}{\epsilon - [1+\tau]\eta_{LL}}, \tag{5.4}$$

where, as in previous chapters, η_{LL} is the labor-demand elasticity, and ϵ is the elasticity of supply of labor to the market. (See, e.g., Kotlikoff and Summers 1987.) Whether η_{LL} is the correct demand elasticity to use, or whether scale effects should be added, is not clear. Models of tax incidence usually assume full employment, though, so for expositional purposes η_{LL} is appropriate here. The impact on equilibrium employment of a change in the tax rate can be written as

$$\frac{\partial lnL^*}{\partial \tau} = \eta_{LL} \left[1 + \frac{\eta_{LL}}{\epsilon[1+\tau]^{-1} - \eta_{LL}} \right]. \tag{5.5}$$

With $\tau \cong 0$ the effects of changing the rate are easily interpreted in two polar cases. In the first the supply of labor to the economy is completely inelastic, $\epsilon = 0$. Equations (5.4) and (5.5) show that an increase in the payroll tax will have no effect on equilibrium employment and will merely produce an offsetting decrease in the wage rate. In the second polar case I assume $\epsilon \to \infty$. Then the percentage effect on employment equals the labor-demand elasticity times the change in the tax rate, while there is no impact on the equilibrium wage rate. In general the impact of a change in the payroll tax rate or

---

(ignoring issues in discounting). To the extent that workers and employers behave this way, the effects of the change in taxes over the lifetime of a typical worker are reduced, perhaps to zero.

a payroll subsidy depends on the sizes of the marketwide labor-demand and labor-supply elasticities.

This partial equilibrium analysis demonstrates that these elasticities are the crucial parameters for predicting the impacts of payroll taxes or subsidies on employment. The simplest approach to prediction would be to assume that a change in the payroll tax/subsidy generates a proportional shift in labor demand and to combine the consensus estimates of η_{LL} from Chapter 3 and some good estimates of ϵ to infer the impact on equilibrium employment and wages. For adult male workers in industrialized economies Killingsworth's (1983) extensive survey of the literature provides convincing evidence that ϵ is approximately zero. For other workers the elasticity may be positive, but it is probably not very large. That being the case, most of the long-run burden of a payroll tax increase is borne by workers in the form of lower wage rates. This is true regardless of the value of the demand elasticity. It implies that the increase generates little disemployment, and obversely that subsidizing employers' payroll tax payments generates only small rises in equilibrium employment.

This conclusion reflects the conventional wisdom about payroll taxes and the fairly widely accepted assumption that in long-run equilibrium jobs are not rationed. Using this approach of combining extraneous parameter estimates takes advantage of the results of two immense literatures in labor economics, one of which was summarized in Chapter 3. Despite the simplicity of this approach, a number of studies have attempted to measure the impact of payroll taxes on wage rates directly (and by inference their effect on equilibrium employment).

There are two general reasons why an alternative approach might be useful. First, the demand and supply elasticities for the marginal firm and worker whose behavior determines the equilibrium outcomes may differ from those describing the typical agent in the labor market. Particularly on the supply side, the marginal worker may have a very loose attachment to the labor market and a high elasticity of labor supply. The second problem is the implicit assumption that an increase in the payroll tax (subsidy) rate shifts the demand curve down (up) proportionately. Even if some employers perceive the change in the tax or subsidy incorrectly, competition in the product market would ensure that only those firms that correctly perceive any change survive.

Table 5.1 summarizes empirical studies of the incidence of the payroll tax. For each study I calculate the implied fraction of the payroll tax that is borne by labor in the form of lower earnings. One of the two main types of studies examines how changes (or differences) in

TABLE 5.1
Studies of the Incidence of the Payroll Tax

Study	Description	Fraction of Tax Shifted to Labor (s)
Studies Based on Demand or Production Relations		
Brittain (1972)	CES model, manufacturing, 1957–59; 64 countries	[1.15, 1.71]
Vroman (1974a)	CES model, economywide, 1958–67; 19 OECD countries	[0.93, 1.40]
OECD (1990)	CES model, 1974, 1986; 16 OECD countries	[0.95, 1.13]
Leuthold (1975)	MP condition, private nonfarm business quarterly, 1948–65	[−0.08, −0.02]
Beach and Balfour (1983)	MP condition, manufacturing, quarterly, 1956–78; U.K.	[0.53, 0.60]
Studies Based on Reduced-form Wage Equations		
Weitenberg (1969)	Wage rate changes, annual, 1950–66; Netherlands	0.80
Gordon (1972)	Hourly earnings changes, quarterly, 1954–70	0
Vroman (1974b)	Hourly earnings changes, manufacturing, quarterly, 1956–69	[0.46, 0.76]
Neubig (1981)	Wage changes, individual male workers, 1967–78	[0.23, 0.32]
Holmlund (1983)	Hourly earnings, males, mining and manufacturing, annual, 1951–79; Sweden	0.35
Dye (1985)	Compensation changes, private nonfarm, quarterly, 1954–77	[0.60, 1.28]
Ando, Modigliani, and Rasche (1972)	Compensation changes, private nonfarm business, quarterly, 1954–69	−0.44
Hamermesh (1979a)	Hourly earnings levels, individual white males, 1967–73	[0, 0.36]
OECD (1990)	Changes in real product wage, annual, 1955–86; average of 16 OECD countries	0.38
Cerasani (1990)	Computational general equilibrium model, mid-1980s; Australia	0.67

payroll tax rates change the demand for labor. The other uses data on wage levels or changes to examine the reduced-form effects of changes in payroll taxes. Consider first the demand studies. Those of Brittain (1972), Vroman (1974a), and OECD (1990) estimate various forms of a CES production function of the sort

$$ln\ w = \alpha_0 ln(V/L) - ln(1 + s\tau), \tag{5.6}$$

where V is value added, s is the backward-shifting parameter, α_0 is a parameter, and τ is close enough to zero that $ln(1 + s\tau)$ can be written as $s\tau$. Ignoring the term in the tax rate (assuming $\tau = 0$), equation (5.6) is the classic form proposed by Arrow et al. (1961) for estimating the substitution parameter in a CES function. In this modification, if s equals 1 there is complete shifting of the payroll tax onto labor; if s equals 0 there is no shifting. These cross-section studies imply complete backward shifting.

Standard labor-demand equations are estimated using time-series data by Leuthold (1975) and Beach and Balfour (1983). Each simply replaces w by $w[1 + \tau]$ in a marginal productivity condition and tries to infer the extent to which increases in the term τw reduce the demand for labor. Though the two sets of estimates differ greatly, neither study finds complete backward shifting. As Feldstein (1972) points out, though, no study like these can estimate the extent of shifting, since the underlying formulations focus only on labor demand. All five studies merely show the extent to which the demand for labor is altered by changes in payroll taxes, not their effects on equilibrium wages and employment.

The other strand in the literature answers Feldstein's objections by postulating a reduced-form wage equation that makes the level of money wages a function of a vector of variables, X, and the payroll tax rate. The equation is often differenced logarithmically to yield the estimating form

$$\dot{W} = F(\Delta X) - s[1 \dot{+} \tau], \tag{5.7}$$

where the superior (·) denotes a time derivative and ΔX is a vector of variables that affect the rate of change of money wages. Equation (5.7) is essentially a Phillips curve to which a term in the rate of change of payroll tax rates has been appended.

The estimates of s from the six studies based on (5.7) that are shown in Table 5.1 are calculated from the different specifications to make them comparable to one another. They vary across the entire admissible range, and even outside it! As in the demand studies, no consensus parameter estimate emerges. The estimates are highly sensitive to what appear to be small changes in the definition of the payroll tax, for example, to whether (in estimates for the United

States) only OASDHI taxes are included or other, smaller payroll taxes are added (Dye 1985). Perhaps most interesting in this group is Neubig (1981), who uses microeconomic data and thus avoids any aggregation problems and finds evidence of only very partial shifting of the tax onto workers.

A final set of studies attempts to circumvent the difficulties of estimating s using equation (5.7), particularly the noisy nature of W once the standard vector of variables X has been accounted for, by using (5.7) in levels rather than percentage changes. Ando, Modigliani, and Rasche (1972) use the same macroeconomic time series as in the Phillips curve analogues, but measure all the variables, including the total OASDHI tax rate, in levels. OECD (1990) takes essentially the same approach, but calculates an average extent of shifting over sixteen economies. Hamermesh (1979a) uses microeconomic data on individual workers and takes advantage of the limit on taxable earnings, and the lower tax rate on higher-wage workers that it implies, to infer the extent of shifting. All three studies find incomplete shifting, thus replicating the results of most of the Phillips curve studies. More complete but still partial shifting is also estimated by Cerasani (1990) using a computable general equilibrium model of the Australian economy.

It is impossible to draw any firm conclusions about the incidence of the payroll tax from these studies, and thus about its long-run effects and those of general labor subsidies on equilibrium employment and wages in industrialized economies. Existing demand studies are not even unanimous in showing that higher payroll taxes uniformly reduce the demand for labor proportionately. The absence of a satisfactory simultaneous demand-supply model of the labor market, and the problems of finding enough independent time-series variation in payroll tax rates to draw precise inferences about the effects on wages in reduced forms, make existing empirical work a very weak reed on which to rely. We are thus thrown back on the choice between using the quite robust consensus estimates of supply and demand parameters or inferring the incidence of the tax from this diverse group of not very satisfactory empirical studies.

The choice seems quite clear. While disequilibria surely exist in the labor market in the short run, over a period of a decade most shocks are dissipated. That being the case, the lack of convincing direct estimates of payroll tax shifting and the well-established values of the labor supply and demand elasticities suggest that there is only small scope *in the long run* for a payroll subsidy to increase employment, or for a payroll tax to reduce it. Barring substantial improvement in empirical studies of tax incidence, we must tentatively infer that most of the burden of payroll taxes is on wages.

B. Taxes and Subsidies to Other Inputs

The interest in these P-general nonlabor subsidies is in their potential effects on total employment and average wages, and on their specific impacts on the employment and wages of various types of workers. Throughout I deal only with subsidies to investment (to increase the stock of capital). I assume that the supply of capital is not completely inelastic, but I ignore the possibility that these subsidies might move the economy toward full employment, assuming instead that equilibrium holds in all factor markets. That such subsidies are important is shown especially clearly by the continuing debate in the United States over investment tax credits and accelerated depreciation. These incentives, which have existed in various forms since 1954, lower the cost of capital services facing the firm. There is a huge literature examining their effects on investment demand (for example, Fullerton and Henderson 1985).

We can use the theory and econometric work discussed in the previous chapters to infer their likely impacts. Chapter 2 made it very clear that these subsidies will increase the capital-labor ratio, causing the real wage to rise. Since capital and skill are relative p-complements, the empirical results in Tables 3.7 through 3.9 allow us to infer that the biggest impacts will be on the employment demand and wage offers to more skilled workers. To the extent that their supply is relatively inelastic compared to that of less-skilled workers, both demand and supply forces will combine to cause their wages to rise relative to those of less-skilled workers. Subsidies to investment are thus especially beneficial to more-skilled workers and are likely to increase inequality in the distributions of wages and earnings.

There are no direct econometric estimates of the effects of these subsidies on employment and wages, either in the aggregate or by type of worker. Inferring the effects of the policies from theory and empirical studies of factor substitution is the only available approach. Does this mean that direct studies of these subsidies' effects on the labor market are needed? The answer is probably no, and for the same reasons that direct studies of payroll tax incidence have proved to be so inconclusive. Relative to other shocks that affect the labor market, variations in these policy parameters are so small that it is exceedingly difficult to "tease out" their impacts. It is far better to rely on a model of factor demand that is based in theory, and on consensus estimates of the relevant demand and supply elasticities, to infer them. The evidence that was synthesized in Chapters 3 and 4 provides a better (and much less expensive) foundation for evaluating these policies than would specific evaluations.

C. Changes in Premium Pay for Overtime Work

The premium pay for overtime work imposed in many countries is a good example of a P-general employment-hours policy. In the United States the partial coverage of a mandatory premium pay rate of 1.5 times the hourly wage beyond forty hours of work went into effect with the Fair Labor Standards Act of 1938. A good way to evaluate the impact of this policy is to consider the suggestion, which has been strongly debated during recessions since 1945, to increase the overtime premium in order to encourage employers to increase employment.[6]

I do not outline all the issues surrounding the overtime premium here. The theory in Chapter 2 unambiguously predicts substitution away from hours and toward employees, and additional substitution away from worker-hours and toward capital. The various studies in Chapter 3 indicate that the demand for overtime hours is sensitive to the ratio of fixed employment costs to the price of an hour of overtime.

Both the theory and empirical literature deal only with substitution between employment and hours. Implicit throughout is the assumption that any increase in employment generated by a higher overtime premium is an upper bound to the effects that will be produced. While accounting for capital-labor substitution would show the complete effect on labor demand, even that is insufficient to infer the effects of changing the premium on equilibrium employment. One must, as stressed in Chapter 1 and as demonstrated in Subsection A above, also consider changes in the supply of labor that are induced by changes in the policy. This has not been attempted in the empirical literature; and the problems of accounting for the simultaneity of labor demand and supply suggest it would be very difficult.

To circumvent these problems, yet use the knowledge summarized and synthesized in Chapter 3, I simulate a partial-equilibrium model involving homogeneous labor whose hours of work can be varied. This allows use of the best extraneous estimates of the underlying parameters while avoiding problems of estimating them anew. The crucial assumption throughout is that the supply elasticity of hours

---

[6] Ehrenberg and Schumann (1982) discuss a version of this proposal.

per week equals that of workers—the employment-hours distinction is unimportant on the supply side of the labor market.[7]

In the simulation I assume that the net change in employment can be partitioned as

$$dlnE = \left.\frac{\Delta lnE}{\Delta p_H}\right|_{EH} - \left\{\frac{\Delta ln(w)}{\Delta p_H} \cdot \eta_{LL}\right\}\frac{\eta_{LL}}{[\epsilon - \eta_{LL}]}, \qquad (5.8)$$

where Δp_H is the change in the relative price of an hour of overtime, and w here includes all labor costs. The first term in (5.8) captures employment-hours substitution, holding total worker-hours constant. In the second term the bracketed quantity accounts for movement along the constant-output labor demand curve. The ratio $\eta_{LL}/[\epsilon - \eta_{LL}]$ reduces the negative impact on employment to account for any increase in labor supply produced by the greater return to a marginal hour of work offered by the higher overtime premium.

In calibrating the simulation I assume that we are evaluating the impact of increasing the overtime premium by one-third, from time and a half to double time, as in the summary in Table 3.11. Using reasonable estimates of the amount of overtime worked, this implies a 2.3 percent increase in labor costs.[8] I thus implicitly assume that there is no offsetting decrease in wages that maintains the compensation package at the same level. Such a decrease would occur if the supply of labor were infinitely elastic, and it would vitiate any effect on the demand for worker-hours. Trejo (1991) presents evidence that this negative compensating differential is produced by higher overtime premia, but the size of the effect does not fully offset the impact of higher premia.

Following the discussion in Chapter 3, I assume that the η_{LL} takes the possible values $[-0.15, -0.30, -0.75]$. The supply elasticity of worker-hours can equal $[0, 0.10, 0.50]$. In both cases the middle value is the "best guess" estimate of the underlying parameter. This means, in the case of the demand elasticity, that I am assuming there are no negative scale effects on labor demand through decreases in

[7] This assumption is clearly incorrect. On theoretical grounds, we know that income effects that affect interior solutions to the worker's choice of utility-maximizing hours do not operate on the decision about whether to enter the labor force. The distinction is confounded by the role of the fixed costs of entering the labor force, as demonstrated by Cogan (1980) and Blank (1988).

[8] Ehrenberg and Schumann (1982, 46) infer from CPS data that 69.8 million hours of overtime were worked in the reference week in May 1978. During that same week total hours worked were 3.66 billion (*Employment and Earnings*, June 1978). Combining these figures, remembering that overtime hours cost 1.5 times regular hours, and assuming that wages equaled 80 percent of labor cost yields a share of overtime in total labor cost of 2.27 percent.

TABLE 5.2
Percentage Change in Employment Due to an Increase in the Overtime Premium to Double Time

		$\dfrac{\Delta lnE}{\Delta p_H}\Big|_{EH}$					
		.005				.02	
			η_{LL}				
	$-.15$	$-.30$	$-.75$		$-.15$	$-.30$	$-.75$
0	.16	$-.18$	-1.20		1.66	1.32	.30
ϵ .10	.30	$-.01$	-1.00		1.80	1.49	.50
.50	.42	.24	$-.52$		1.92	1.74	.98

output that are induced by the imposed increase in labor costs. Thus, even these simulation results, though two steps beyond other estimates, may still overestimate the possibilities for employment creation through higher overtime premia. Finally, I assume that $\dfrac{\Delta lnE}{\Delta p_H}\Big|_{EH}$ can take values of 0.005 and 0.02, roughly bracketing the range of estimates in Table 3.11.

The results of the simulations are presented in Table 5.2 for the three sets of parameters. They show the importance of considering capital-labor substitution in evaluating the impact of changing the rate of premium pay. If labor supply is inelastic and employee-hours substitution is near the low end of the range of estimates, raising overtime premia will reduce total employment. At the middle of the range of these estimates, and with the "best guess" estimates of the elasticities of labor supply and demand, there is a negligible effect on total employment. Using the best available estimates of the extent of substitution along the various margins of labor demand, it seems clear that higher overtime pay will not expand employment, unless labor supply is far more elastic than the huge array of estimates suggests.

One might argue that these negative conclusions are unfair, in that the purpose of mandatory overtime premium pay is to spread work during a recession. That was indeed the purpose of the original legislation in the United States.[9] There is no question that such premia

[9] While various motivations no doubt lay behind the passage of the Fair Labor Standards Act of 1938, preventing excessive hours of work was important. During the floor debate on the Conference report, one legislator, Senator Thomas of Utah, remarked, "Both Houses obtained their common objective, which was to abolish traffic in interstate commerce in the products of child labor and in the products of underpaid and overworked labor" (*Congressional Record*, June 14, 1938, p. 9162; emphasis added).

will affect the dynamics of employment and hours, and I deal with these effects in Chapter 8. The policy is, though, permanent; and because of that it has permanent impacts on equilibrium outcomes—employment, hours, and wages. It may generate short-run gains during cyclical declines, and the simulation shows that it may increase equilibrium employment. These effects must, though, be offset against the negative impact on total worker-hours, and thus the reduction in living standards, that it generates because it raises employment costs.

IV. *P*-Specific Policies

The first step in analyzing a *P*-specific labor-market policy is to identify the group of workers to which it applies. Some policies are targeted specifically to a group of workers identifiable by some demographic or locational characteristic that does not depend on market outcomes. These policies are analyzed fairly straightforwardly by viewing the tax/subsidy to them as affecting the demand for a particular group of workers. This is exactly the same way that the empirical studies in Chapter 3 examined substitution between such groups and all other workers. Other policies apply to groups whose membership is defined so that it can vary, for example, to all workers with wages or earnings above (or below) some fixed threshold. In those cases the empirical literature is less informative about their potential impact, for none of the empirical studies examines substitution among workers differentiated solely by the wage they receive. (The standard econometric frameworks discussed in the previous chapters cannot allow that, though it would be possible with the approach of Heckman and Sedlacek 1985.) In this section I examine both types of policy, recognizing that the broad general literature discussed in the previous chapters is more appropriately applied to policies that designate a fixed group of workers for extra taxation or subsidization.

In discussing *P*-general policies we saw that the elasticity of labor supply to the market conditioned their eventual impact on wages and employment. That is equally true for *P*-specific policies. Also, though, their effects will be determined by the ease with which workers are able to alter their supply between the subsidized (taxed) and unsubsidized (untaxed) category of labor. The behavior of relative supply must enter into the analysis of *P*-specific policies, just as total labor supply was central to analyzing *P*-general policies. Similarly, just as the demand elasticity for homogeneous labor affected the outcomes of *P*-general policies, the signs of the elasticities of substitution between labor groups help to determine how *P*-specific policies affect labor-market outcomes here.

The synthesis of these considerations is that a tax or subsidy to a certain demographic group of workers, or to workers at a particular wage level, will affect not only their employment but the employment of other workers as well. Their equilibrium wages and those of others will also be affected by the policy. The empirical literature summarized in the preceding chapters should provide part of the information necessary for an *ex ante* evaluation of the policies' impact. The rest of the required information must come from studies of labor supply or from guesses about the responsiveness of workers' choice of occupations to changes in the relative rewards in different activities.

Here, as in the previous sections, I make no attempt to evaluate the welfare-theoretic implications of the policies. The policies may be imposed because people believe they are correcting preexisting distortions. More likely, welfare considerations do not enter the discussion, so that concerns about the impact of the policies on employment are not related to any departures from or movements toward a welfare optimum that they may produce. The sole concern in analyzing the policies is the directions of their effects on wages and employment.

Consider a partial-equilibrium model that is useful in illustrating how labor demand and supply affect the outcomes of P-specific policies. Let there be two groups of workers, Type 1 and Type 2, with Type 1 workers being by assumption inherently less productive and being taxed (subsidized) through an *ad valorem* payroll tax (subsidy).[10] Capital services are excluded from the model. Production is CES:

$$Y = \left\{ [1-\alpha]L_1^\rho + \alpha L_2^\rho \right\}^{1/\rho}, \tag{5.9}$$

with $\alpha > 0.5$. The marginal productivity conditions for the two types of workers (assuming a constant output price of one) are

$$[1-\alpha]\left[\frac{Y}{L_1}\right]^{1/\sigma} = w_1[1+\tau], \tag{5.10}$$

$$\alpha\left[\frac{Y}{L_2}\right]^{1/\sigma} = w_2, \tag{5.11}$$

where τ is the tax rate on Type 1 labor (the negative of the subsidy rate).

---

[10] The analysis could be conducted with a fixed-amount tax (subsidy), but the arithmetic would not be so simple.

The total supply of labor to the market depends on the average wage

$$L = \left[\frac{w_1 L_1 + w_2 L_2}{L} \right]^\epsilon, \tag{5.12}$$

where $\epsilon \geq 0$ is the elasticity of labor supply to the market, and

$$L \equiv L_1 + L_2$$

is the total supply of labor. Occupational choice (relative supply) is determined by

$$\frac{L_1}{L_2} = \left[\frac{w_1}{w_2} \right]^\theta, \tag{5.13}$$

where $\theta \geq 0$ is the relative supply elasticity. The model most closely approximates a tax/subsidy to workers in one occupation. To the extent that workers in one part of the wage distribution can be viewed as a distinct type of labor and the remaining workers as the other type, the model applies to the second sort of P-specific policy as well.

Let $Z = \dfrac{1-\alpha}{\alpha[1+\tau]}$. Then the model can be solved for relative wages and employment in the two groups as

$$\ln\left[\frac{L_1}{L_2} \right] = \frac{\sigma[1-\sigma]}{\sigma+\theta} \ln Z, \tag{5.14}$$

and

$$\ln\left[\frac{w_1}{w_2} \right] = \frac{\sigma}{\sigma+\theta} \ln Z. \tag{5.15}$$

Together with the solutions for $\ln L_2$ and $\ln w_2$, which are shown in the Appendix at the end of this chapter, (5.14) and (5.15) completely determine the endogenous variables.

Conditions (5.14) and (5.15) alone inform us about the determinants of the net impact of a tax (subsidy) on Type 1 labor. Note that $d(\ln Z)/d\tau \cong -1$, if τ is small. This means that the percentage change in relative wages in response to a 1 percent increase in the tax rate is

$$d\ln\left[\frac{w_1}{w_2} \right] = -\frac{\sigma}{\sigma+\theta}. \tag{5.16}$$

The percentage change in relative employment is

$$d\ln\left[\frac{L_1}{L_2} \right] = -\frac{\sigma[1-\sigma]}{\sigma+\theta}. \tag{5.17}$$

Only if $\theta = 0$—that is, if the relative supply of the two types of labor is completely insensitive to relative wages—does the net impact of the subsidy depend only on the degree of labor-labor substitution in production. In that case every tax increase on Type 1 employment is fully offset by an equal percentage decline in the relative wage of Type 1 workers. The effect on relative employment depends on whether $\sigma \gtreqless 1$.

The more interesting case is that $\theta > 0$. Unless the group targeted for taxation (subsidization) is inherently fixed in size (for example, targeting a subsidy to veterans of a past war), in the long run the size of that group will respond to the economic incentives that a tax (subsidy) generates to make membership in it less (more) attractive. Racial or ethnic boundaries are not impermeable, because subsidies alter the advantages of identifying oneself with different groups. Indeed, if the types of workers are distinguished only by skill, or by wage level, it is probable that θ is quite large: Relative supply curves between occupations are elastic in the long run. In that case (5.14) and (5.15) show that raising a tax (subsidy) will have little if any impact on relative wages or employment. The burden of any tax (subsidy) will be shared by workers of both types. Indeed, only to the extent that ϵ exceeds zero will there be any effect on the level of employment or wages if θ is large.[11]

We can apply this model to various types of payroll subsidies or taxes, considering first P-specific taxes or subsidies that are based on a worker's wage or earnings. A good example is mandating employer-provided health insurance through a payroll tax on those firms that do not voluntarily provide such benefits. Since low-wage workers are less likely to receive this benefit than other workers, the mandate amounts to a P-specific tax on the employment of low-wage workers.[12]

The two types of workers are defined as low- and high-wage. As I noted earlier, this definition does not seem to fit the model explicitly, since a particular worker can switch from being low-wage to being high-wage. In a deeper sense, though, it fits the case of a high rela-

[11] This conclusion is clearly dependent on excluding capital services from the model. A three-factor model that included them and two types of workers would generate different results; but as long as total labor supply is fairly inelastic, and the relative supply elasticity between the two types of labor is large, the conclusion does not change qualitatively.

[12] As with any other earmarked tax, the problem with this tax is the same that I noted in Footnote 5, namely the potential impact on the supply price of labor of the extra benefits that it finances. The tax that finances unemployment insurance in the United States is another good example of a P-specific tax, since the ceiling on the taxable base is very low. Analyzing its effect has the same difficulties as any other earmarked tax. In addition, its experience rating—its dependence on the particular employer's prior record of layoffs (see Chapter 8)—makes analyzing it especially complex.

tive supply elasticity quite well. As long as the change in the tax rate is small, we can imagine sufficient responses of the relative supply of workers around the tax ceiling to offset most of the impact that the change in policy might have on relative wages or employment.

The same argument applies to subsidies to increase employment that operate through payroll tax credits applicable to the first few thousand dollars of a worker's earnings, or to similar subsidies payable only on the earnings of low-wage workers. It also applies to legislated minimum wage rates: As I argue in more detail below, the minimum wage can be viewed as a tax on the employment of workers below some wage ceiling (the minimum). Stricter enforcement of the minimum wage is equivalent to a tax increase, and it produces the same effects on the wages and employment of workers earning less than the minimum relative to those of workers earning more.

Interpreted strictly, the model applies even more directly to subsidies or taxes that are targeted to particular demographic groups. Subsidizing the employment of Vietnam-era veterans is a good example of defining a target group for which the relative supply is fixed. Only the degree of substitutability in production between these veterans and other workers affects their relative wages and employment. Relative supply elasticities come into play if subsidies are targeted to workers with, for example, low educational attainment, or with prior work experience below some fixed level. In these cases the model applies perfectly, and the relative supply elasticity is positive. Such subsidies will have substantial spillovers onto the wages and employment of other workers, and their effects on the targeted workers will be mitigated.

The model can also be applied to a tax (subsidy) with a wage ceiling that itself is an instrument of employment policy. An increase in the ceiling with no change in the tax (subsidy) rate is equivalent to an increase in the tax (subsidy) on employing workers who suddenly earn less than the new, higher ceiling. Its impact on their employment and wages depends on how substitutable they are for other workers, and on whether the relative supply behavior of workers earning near the ceiling is responsive to the changed incentives.

These cases all demonstrate the crucial point of this section. We cannot evaluate the impact of a tax (subsidy) on employing a particular group of workers without knowing whether employers can substitute those workers for others, and without knowing the relative supply behavior of the taxed (subsidized) workers (and other workers too). Moreover, such knowledge and the *ex ante* evaluation that stems from it will be both more nearly complete and more likely correct than a simple, nonexperimental *ex post* evaluation of the policy.

The latter approach is always fraught with difficulties of identifying the impact of what is usually a policy change that affects a small group of workers in an always-changing labor market. It also ignores the relationship between the effects on the taxed (subsidized) group of workers and on other workers, effects produced by both demand and supply behavior.

I have discussed all the impacts of tax (subsidy) policy and the *ex ante* policy evaluations that stem from them in the context of considering relative wage and employment effects. This model and the discussion in Section III show that the net employment effects of these policies depend on workers' choices among market work, household production, and leisure—that is, on the supply elasticities of subsidized and other workers to the labor market. To the extent that these are small, none of the tax (subsidy) policies discussed in this section will have much long-run impact on total employment.

A. Minimum Wage Policies

The first application of the analysis of this section is to legislated minimum wage rates, a *P*-specific policy that involves restrictions on the right of employers to offer wages below some minimum. For the United States, and increasingly for other countries too, the literature of empirical research on minimum wages is extensive. Below I summarize what was known about the impacts of the minimum wage on employment in the United States as of 1982, the date of Brown, Gilroy, and Kohen's comprehensive survey of this issue. I then summarize subsequent research in the United States and the available evidence from other countries. The latter is likely to be especially informative, since the uniformity of the policy across the U.S. labor market allows few opportunities for observing independent variation in its impact.

There are two major theoretical contributions to the analysis of the minimum wage. The first, Stigler (1946), treated the minimum wage as applying to the market for homogeneous labor that was coincident with an entire labor market. This by now textbook model demonstrated that the imposition of a minimum wage above the equilibrium wage reduces employment.

Perhaps prompted by the observation that higher wage minima did not seem to affect unemployment, Welch (1976) proposed a model in which the minimum wage applies to a covered sector, with an uncovered sector in which workers displaced by a higher minimum wage could find jobs. Figure 5.2 depicts the main points of this model. In the covered sector (C) a minimum wage is imposed, raising

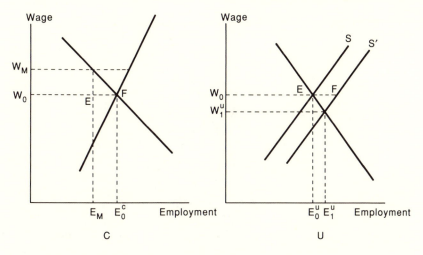

5.2 The Minimum Wage with Covered and Uncovered Employment

the wage from W_0 to W_M. Employment is reduced to E_M, with EF workers no longer employed (or not obtaining jobs) in the covered sector. These workers seek jobs in the uncovered sector (U), shifting the supply of labor rightward by an amount EF. This reduces the wage in the uncovered sector to W_1^u, but it increases employment there to E_1^u. The net impact is an economywide reduction in employment. Only if the elasticity of supply to the market is zero is there no net loss of employment. The decline is larger if the supply elasticity is greater, and it increases as the absolute value of the demand elasticity in the covered sector exceeds that in the uncovered sector.

Welch's model is a clever way of dealing with the apparent limitation of the impact of higher wage minima in the United States to employment only. It is appropriate for analyzing the policy where the uncovered sector provides a substantial outlet for workers who do not obtain jobs in the covered sector. That is a good description of developing countries, where minimum wages cover jobs in an urban industrialized sector but leave jobs in the large urban traditional sector uncovered. In the United States, though, it is difficult to believe that the small uncovered sector can provide an outlet for workers displaced by the minimum wage. In 1987 only 8.7 percent of private nonsupervisory workers were not covered by the minimum wage. Many of these were in high-wage jobs in which workers were unlikely to be affected by minimum wage laws in any case. In the United States Welch's model asks a very small sector to bear the en-

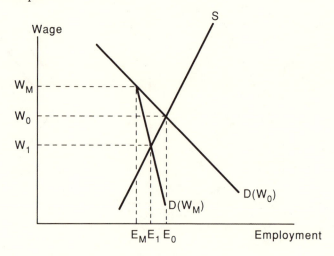

5.3 The Minimum Wage as a Tax Ceiling

tire burden of wage effects induced by raising minimum wages, a burden that is inconsistent with observed wage differentials.

An alternative approach recognizes that, in addition to covered and uncovered jobs, there exist jobs in the covered sector paying less than the minimum wage. Ashenfelter and Smith (1979) document this fact and attribute it in part to the low monetary penalties and imperfect enforcement of the U.S. minimum wage laws. The importance of maintaining a reputation as a "good employer" means that monetary penalties are not the only sanction for violating the law; but their evidence demonstrates that substantial violations do occur despite this additional indirect incentive.

An approach to modeling the minimum wage that recognizes the importance of noncompliance with the law can integrate its existence with reductions in employment in the absence of an uncovered sector. Assume labor is homogeneous, and consider the initial equilibrium in Figure 5.3 with a wage at W_0 and employment at E_0. Suppose a minimum wage of W_M is imposed on this market. This minimum is a tax ceiling, with the tax rate on employment paying less than the ceiling being an increasing function of the discrepancy between W_M and the wage rate paid. This assumption accords with the observation that, at least in the United States, attempts to ensure compliance with the minimum wage law are targeted disproportionately toward low-wage areas (Ashenfelter and Smith 1979). It means that the demand curve in Figure 5.3 shifts from $D(W_0)$ to $D(W_M)$. At wages farther below the minimum the demand curve is shifted farther to the left.

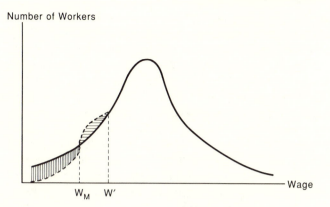

5.4 The Distribution of Wages Before and After a
Minimum Wage

With the leftward shift in the effective demand curve total employment drops to E_1. This consists of E_M workers at the minimum wage and $E_1 - E_M$ below the minimum. These subminimum wage workers are paid different wages, with some receiving rents and others earning W_1, just enough to induce them to remain in the labor force. In this model $E_0 - E_1$ workers leave the labor force.

The model could be revised to allow for queuing for jobs at the minimum wage, either by those earning less than W_M in jobs that are not in compliance or by those who drop out of the labor force. (Mincer 1976 develops a model with queuing.) The queuing, and the wait-unemployment that it produces, equilibrates the labor market by generating expected returns to seeking work in the covered sector equal to taking a job immediately in the uncovered sector. Adding this embellishment would add some flexibility to the model of Figure 5.3. It would not, though, alter the main point here, that one need not rely on an increasingly unimportant uncovered sector to explain the existence of secondary effects of minimum wages. Noncompliance by employers performs the same task. Also, the analysis suggests that the framework for studying a generalized P-specific policy can be readily adapted to discussing a minimum wage policy.

The assumption of homogeneous labor can be relaxed, and the effects of substitution to workers whose productivity is just above W_M can be analyzed.[13] The solid line in Figure 5.4 shows the number of workers at each wage rate before a minimum wage is imposed. This

[13] This discussion is based on Meyer and Wise (1983), except that unlike them I allow for the substitution of workers earning above W_M for those who previously earned less than the new minimum.

is not a density function of wages, since it shows numbers rather than percentages of workers at each wage. Let W_M be the minimum wage. Then the left tail of this histogram will thin out, especially as one moves farther to the left of W_M. At and just above W_M employment will increase, as employers increase their demand for workers who are close substitutes for others whose employment is no longer profitable (because of the implicit tax created by the minimum wage). As one moves farther above W_M this effect tapers off, for we assume that increasingly higher-skilled workers are decreasingly good p-substitutes for those earning below W_M. The minimum wage produces no impact on the employment of workers earning at least W'.

The imposition of the minimum wage creates a spike in the number of workers earning around W_M. Were we to graph the density of wages instead of this histogram, we would observe the same thing. Figure 5.4 also shows, though, that total employment decreases: The vertically shaded area exceeds the area shaded horizontally. This occurs because the average cost of labor has been increased, causing the usual substitution effects toward other inputs and, at least in the short run, a scale effect. The net result of imposing the minimum wage is a reduction of employment, especially of those whose previous wage was farthest below the minimum.

Before considering econometric evidence on the effect of minimum wage policies on employment, it is worth reviewing briefly the outlines of minimum wage policy in the United States. The minimum wage was created in 1938 by the Fair Labor Standards Act. Starting out at $0.25 per hour, it has been raised at discrete intervals, often with legislation specifying a series of increases over several years. Between legislated increases the minimum wage erodes relative to all other wages (moves to the left in terms of Figure 5.4). It eroded very far in the 1980s, since no increase became effective between January 1981 and April 1990. In the United States the federal minimum has covered an increasingly large fraction of employment. In most states, state minimum wage laws extended coverage still further. In some, especially during the late 1980s, state minimum wages were the effective wage floors for covered employees.

Many of the studies of the employment effects of minimum wages estimate some form of

$$\frac{E_i}{\bar{E}} = F(\frac{W_M}{\bar{W}}, t, U), \tag{5.18}$$

where E_i is employment of the ith group of workers, $\bar{E}$ is employment or population in some larger group, $\bar{W}$ is the wage in that group, t is a time trend, and U is some measure of cyclical activity. Since teenagers' wages are among the lowest of any demographic group, much of the interest in estimating equations like (5.18) for the United States and other countries has focused on them (has included them as group i).

Equation (5.18) is hardly a relative demand equation of the Type b discussed in Chapter 3: The minimum wage is not the price of all teenage labor. Rather, it is an ad hoc formulation whose virtue is that it controls for cyclical and secular changes in relative employment and attributes movements around them to changes in the effective minimum wage. It says nothing about the demand elasticity for workers in the ith group. More important, the estimates of the effect of the minimum wage on employment in group i vary depending on the density of wages in Figure 5.4. The elasticity of E_i with respect to the minimum wage is in no sense a parameter of any underlying production function. It will change even if there is no change in the structure of production.

Brown, Gilroy, and Kohen (1982) concluded that the bulk of estimates for the United States indicated that the elasticity of teenage employment with respect to the minimum wage during the postwar period through 1979 was between -0.1 and -0.3, with the smaller figure being more likely. The elasticities for other groups were less negative and perhaps zero. Indeed, there is some evidence from a system of demand equations (Hamermesh 1982) that a higher effective minimum wage increases the employment of adult workers. The firm conclusion from the literature was that the employment effects were limited to teenagers, but that for them those effects are clear-cut.

Very few studies of the employment effects of minimum wages in the United States have been conducted since the early 1980s. This relative paucity is probably due both to the tremendous outpouring of research on the subject in the few years before the Brown, Gilroy, and Kohen survey; to the lack of any new technique for evaluating the problem; and to the absence of any pressing concern of policy about this issue. Few new studies have been conducted along the lines of (5.18). As Table 5.3 shows, Solon (1985) produced the same sort of results as those summarized by Brown, Gilroy, and Kohen, demonstrating that paying more attention to econometric detail did not affect the size of the estimates. Alpert (1986) used the same technique to study employment in the restaurant industry during the 1960s and 1970s, when coverage of the minimum wage was extended to this industry. The similarity between his and Brown, Gilroy, and Kohen's estimates for the entire economy suggests that little is lost

TABLE 5.3
Studies of the Employment Effect of a Minimum Wage, United States, 1985–91, Other Economies, 1980–91

Study	Economy and Data		Elasticity with Respect to W_M
Solon (1985)	U.S. teens, 1954–79, attention to autocorrelation		$[-0.06, -0.11]$
Alpert (1986)	U.S. employment, restaurants 1966–78		$[-0.04, -0.10]$
Wellington (1991)	U.S., teens, 1954–86		$[-0.05, -0.09]$
Santiago (1989)	Puerto Rico, all workers, 1973–82		-0.12
Castillo-Freeman and	Puerto Rico, all workers, 1951–87;		-0.15
Freeman (1990)	industry panel, 1956–87		-0.59
Swidinsky (1980)	Canada, 1956–75.	Male teens:	-0.10
		Female teens:	-0.27
Schaafsma and Walsh	Canada, provinces, 1975–79.		
(1983)		Males, 15–19:	-0.17
		Males, 20–24:	-0.20
		Females, 15–19:	-0.28
		Females, 20–24:	-0.21
McKee and West (1984)	Canada, 1975–81, ratio of part-time to		
	full-time employment.[a]	Males:	-0.55
		Females:	-0.56
Bazen and Martin (1991)	France, 1963–86.	Youths:	$[-0.09, -0.23]$
		Adults:	$\cong 0$
Kaufman (1989)	U.K., misc. industries, selected years, 1963–79		$[-0.02, -0.14]$

[a] Averages of estimates for eight provinces.

by an inability to study the employment effects of the minimum wage using comparisons before and after its coverage is extended.

Wellington (1991) reestimated the basic version of (5.18) for the entire economy over an extended sample period that included much of the 1980s. Her results imply that the minimum wage elasticity of teenage employment is below that found by the bulk of studies summarized by Brown, Gilroy, and Kohen. The reason is clear: During the 1980s the effective minimum moved far into the left tail of the distribution in Figure 5.4, so that changes in it could not have had a very large effect on teenage employment.

That the minimum wage affects behavior in the labor market is also shown by Holzer, Katz, and Krueger (1991), who demonstrate that jobs paying around the minimum have greater numbers of applicants than other jobs. From this evidence they infer that the rents created by the imposition of the minimum wage are not fully dissipated. This is consistent with workers queuing for jobs paying artificially high wages. While this does not imply anything about employment effects, it does demonstrate the importance of considering where W_M falls in the distribution of wages, for the size of the queue for minimum wage jobs must depend on the thickness of the wage distribution near W_M. Card (1990b) finds no discernible employment effect of an increase in the state minimum wage in California in 1988. Finding absolutely no effect is surprising, though perhaps less so at a time when changing immigration laws affected the supply of low-wage labor; but we would expect any effect to be small in a high-wage state facing an increase in the minimum wage that occurs far into the left tail of the distribution of wages.

Two other studies have examined the employment effects of the U.S. minimum wage, but for Puerto Rico, where average wages are far below those on the mainland. The mainland minimum wage has covered Puerto Rico since the inception of the FLSA, but only in the 1970s were many exemptions to its application removed. During the 1970s the effective minimum wage in Puerto Rico rose rapidly, and the uncovered sector was not very large. The effective minimum rose well up into the distribution of wages of all workers, not only that of teenagers.

Santiago (1989) uses time-series methods that effectively hold constant for cyclical changes in employment demand to analyze the effects of a higher effective minimum on all employment, not just that of teenage workers.[14] As Table 5.3 shows, the impact of moving W_M to the right in the distribution of all wages was substantial. Because the minimum was so high relative even to adult wages, presumably the scale effects that were generated swamped any substitution effects toward high-wage adult workers and combined with the negative substitution effects on lower-wage workers. Castillo-Freeman and Freeman (1990) provide evidence for this using (5.18). The estimated employment elasticity for the entire Puerto Rican economy is −0.15. Much larger impacts of higher wage minima are produced if employment-demand equations are estimated over pooled cross-section time-series data. The estimates allow for both substitution and scale effects of higher minimum wages, and underscore how large

---

[14] His minimum-wage measure is a weighted average of the minimum relative to the average wage, with the fraction of covered workers used as weights. This "coverage-weighted effective minimum wage" has been used in most of the studies completed since 1970.

the employment effect can be when the minimum already cuts fairly far into the distribution of wages.

A major difficulty in evaluating the employment effects of the minimum wage in the United States is the relative lack of exogenous variation in the crucial variable, W_M. Since the statutory minimum is national in scope, and is altered only infrequently, most of the variation in $\dfrac{W_M}{\bar{W}}$ in (5.18) and modifications of it arises from variation in the possibly endogenous $\bar{W}$. We might thus learn more about the impact of minimum wages by studying economies where there is more independent variation in W_M.

Additional evidence on employment effects is provided by studies of Canada, where there are substantial interprovincial differences in the minimum, and where those provincial minima are effective. Swidinsky (1980) and Schaafsma and Walsh (1983) pool cross-section and time-series data to estimate the employment of teens and young adults as a function of the independent variables in (5.18). Their results for teenage employment are close to those for the United States. Since the economies have many similarities, and since the minimum wage in Canada lies roughly at the same point in the wage distribution as the U.S. minimum wage, this should not be surprising.

The effect of a higher minimum in the absence of a large uncovered sector is shown by McKee and West's (1984) study of part-time employment in Canada. They, too, take advantage of the substantial interprovincial variation in nominal minima to estimate an equation like (5.18), but based on the ratio of part- to full-time employment. There is evidence (e.g., Ehrenberg, Rosenberg, and Li 1988) that part-time workers' wages are on average below those of full-time workers. That fact and the nearly complete coverage of the law suggest that a higher minimum will shift employment away from part-time work, which is what McKee and West find.

There has been some study of the minimum wage in France (Bazen and Martin 1991). As in the United States, the French minimum is national in scope, so there is little independent variation in the effective minimum. Studying the minimum there does, though, expand slightly upon U.S. studies. Using a system of demand equations for adults and teenagers, and accounting for the effects of higher nominal minima on average wages, Bazen and Martin estimate roughly the same or a somewhat higher minimum-wage elasticity for youths as in American studies. They too find little or no effect of higher minima on adult employment. The larger estimates for youth may result from the authors' different, more soundly theoretically based methods. Because the effective minimum has generally been higher in France, though, they should arise even if the authors estimated (5.18).

The United Kingdom does not have statutory minimum wages. In several low-wage industries, though, industry wage councils set floors on wages that function like (imperfectly enforced) statutory minima. Kaufman (1989) examined their effect using estimates of η_{LL} and of the impact of the minima on average wages in the industry. The implied employment elasticities shown in Table 5.3 are in the same range as those for the United States and Canada.

The empirical studies of the minimum wage in the United States and elsewhere and the theory underlying its effects on the labor market make several points quite clear. Most important, raising the minimum wage has only a small negative effect on employment if the nominal minimum is far to the left in the wage distribution. Even though the demand elasticity for young workers may be high (see Chapter 3), the relatively low nominal minimum in the United States has meant that the effects on teenage employment have been small.[15] The results for Puerto Rico (and, to a lesser extent, for France) indicate that a substantial increase in the effective minimum generates major losses of employment. In sum, the minimum wage produces little loss of employment if it is kept low. The higher the effective minimum wage, the greater the impact of the policy.

B. Specific Employment Subsidies

Specific employment subsidies represent another example of a P-specific labor policy. They come in a huge variety of forms and serve many purposes. A synthesis of research in this area will be aided by defining terms that allow us to classify the various subsidy schemes. For analytical purposes a threefold typology is useful. First, are they *categorical*, applying to workers in some certain demographic category, or are they *noncategorical*, applying to all workers regardless of demographic group, as long as their earnings render them eligible for the subsidy? Next, are they *marginal*, paid only on employment in excess of some specific level, or are they *total*, paid on all employees in the firm (subject to the employee qualifying on the basis of membership in the subsidized category or on the basis of earnings)? Finally, is the subsidy on *employment*, applying during the worker's en-

---

[15] Of course, they are still detrimental from an efficiency viewpoint. Moreover, evidence on the location of minimum-wage jobs in the distribution of income suggests that the policy is not very helpful from an equity viewpoint (Browning and Johnson 1983).

tire tenure in the firm, or on *hiring*, applying only as a bounty when the worker joins the firm—or is it some combination of these two? These distinctions are applicable only to the panoply of specific employment subsidies; but without them, it is much harder to focus the discussion.

A huge literature analyzes the economics of these subsidies generally and offers specific evaluations in various countries. (See the studies in Haveman and Palmer 1982 for much of the analysis along these lines.) The examples of *P*-specific subsidies are too many and too diverse to allow for even a summary of their design and estimated impact. Instead, I deal with one specific conundrum. The evidence summarized in Chapter 3 provides the basis for an *ex ante* evaluation of the effects of such subsidies on employment. The effects implied by that approach are much larger than the evaluations of many of the subsidies suggest actually occurred. What is the source of this discrepancy, and what can be done to make *P*-specific policies generate the increased employment among specific groups that broad-based evidence on demand elasticities leads us to expect?

The United States has tried one noncategorical employment subsidy, the New Jobs Tax Credit (NJTC) of 1977. This subsidy, whose purpose was to stimulate employment after the 1973–75 recession, was in effect from mid-1977 through 1978. It provided a tax credit to the employer of 50 percent of the first $4,200 paid to a worker, as long as the firm's total wage bill rose by 2 percent over the previous year. It was thus a marginal subsidy that was noncategorical (but *P*-specific, in that it applied disproportionately to low-wage employment) and was a mixture of an employment and a hiring subsidy. The total amount a firm could claim as a tax credit was limited to $100,000 per year.

The evidence on the effect of the NJTC on employment growth is both positive and convincing. Perloff and Wachter's (1979) survey results show that those firms that responded that they were aware of the NJTC grew more rapidly than otherwise identical firms. Moreover, this was true especially among smaller firms (for whose growth rate the $100,000 limit was less likely to be binding). Bishop (1981) estimates Type b labor-demand equations to which a measure of employers' awareness of the NJTC was added, using long time series for retail, wholesale, and construction industries. He finds that the credit generated roughly 400,000 extra jobs, equivalent to an economywide increase in employment of 0.5 percent. This came at a cost to the U.S. Treasury of roughly $4.5 billion, resulting from firms claiming the credit on approximately 3.6 million hires (O'Neill 1982). The number of jobs created, and the total budgetary cost of creating them, are remarkably close to what would be predicted if one applied the "best guess" estimates of Chapter 3 to the particular incentives offered by the NJTC (cf. Hamermesh 1978).

Additional evidence on the efficacy of marginal, noncategorical employment subsidies is provided by the Canadian experience with its Employment Tax Credit Program between 1978 and 1981. This subsidy was structured like the NJTC in the United States, though it had an additional component that targeted high-unemployment regions. The program did not create as many jobs as its proponents hoped, but evaluations of its effects on employment show that it was as successful in terms of job creation and cost per job as the NJTC (Gera 1987).

The United States has instituted a variety of categorical P-specific subsidies. In the late 1960s the federal government offered to reimburse employers for the cost of hiring disadvantaged workers under the Job Opportunities in the Business Sector (JOBS) program. In 1971, the largest year of the program, only 93,000 placements were made under the contract part of JOBS. Beginning in 1971 a formal system of tax credits was instituted to encourage employers to employ welfare recipients under the Work Incentive Program (WIN). Employment tax credits were claimed on less than 10 percent of WIN participants who entered the labor market during the years 1973–75.

The Targeted Jobs Tax Credit (TJTC), in effect from 1978, offered employers tax credits on the first two years of employment of members of specific groups, including at various times ex-criminals, persons on general assistance, Vietnam veterans, and youths working under a cooperative education program. For the category "economically disadvantaged youth" one estimate is that less than 5 percent of workers in this group who were eligible and hired were employed under the program of tax credits. While the majority of firms in one survey knew of the TJTC, few had used it or planned to do so (O'Neill 1982). Even worse, an experiment that offered vouchers for tax credits to employers of targeted workers under restrictions similar to those of the TJTC found that otherwise identical but untargeted workers were *more likely* to become employed than were the workers on whom vouchers could be claimed (Burtless 1985).

Why is there such a discrepancy between the apparent inability of these categorical subsidies to create employment and the apparent success of the NJTC? Why did the TJTC, which applied to workers for whom Chapter 3 showed that the demand is relatively elastic, generate so little extra employment? One argument is that the burden of paperwork on employers caused them to shy away from applying for the credits. Indeed, under the JOBS program many employers voluntarily took on the targeted workers without even bothering to claim the subsidy. Yet if regulatory burden were the cause of the difficulty, employers would have been no more willing to claim the NJTC on their tax returns than they were to claim the WIN or TJTC. All three programs operated through claims on corporate and other income tax filings, and the reporting requirements on the categorical subsidies were not obviously more onerous than those under the noncategorical program. Something beyond "government red tape" caused the elasticity of employment demand with respect to this subsidy to be essentially zero.

The most probable cause of the failure of targeted employment subsidies in the United States is the stigma that targeting attaches to the worker whose employment the government seeks to advance. The fact of eligibility for the subsidy identifies the worker to potential employers as being of lower productivity than would be expected without the targeting. This is the only way to rationalize Burtless's findings with other experience with subsidies. It is also consistent with the observation that "the one nondemeaning targeting category . . . enrolled in a cooperative education course . . . had an 18-month take-up rate . . . considerably larger than that for the disadvantaged youth target group" (O'Neill 1982).

It is reasonable to ask why a few smart employers do not realize that whether or not the government targets a group has no effect on the workers' productivity, then hire the now-subsidized workers and increase their profits. Their success should induce their competitors to follow suit, leading to a new equilibrium with no observable effects of the stigma. This is similar to asking why some employers do not take advantage of the discriminatory tastes of other employers by hiring members of minority groups and eventually driving the discriminators out of the market. Here, too, the answer must be based on problems of information, in this case, that a worker's eligibility for a targeted credit provides information that his or her productivity is lower than that of an otherwise identical nontargeted worker (or that the targeting increases the employer's uncertainty about the worker's productivity).[16]

If one wishes to increase the demand for certain groups of low-wage workers, the experience with targeted subsidies suggests that explicitly targeting those workers is a poor way of doing so. While such targeting prevents spillovers to workers outside the favored groups, the stigma it imposes on those groups guarantees that their

---

[16] Aigner and Cain (1977) present the classic example of this informational problem in their study of labor-market discrimination.

employment opportunities will not be enhanced greatly. Instead, subsidies that are limited to earnings below some level, as was the NJTC, accomplish most of the purpose of targeted subsidies without stigmatizing the low-wage group. To minimize spillovers to less-favored groups, a subsidy might be based on both an earnings ceiling and a qualifying age. (For example, the P-specific policy might provide a tax credit of 50 percent up to the first $7,000 in wages on workers between the ages of eighteen and twenty-five.)[17] The crucial point is to avoid defining targeted categories in a way that reduces the subsidy's effectiveness by stigmatizing the worker.

C. Mandatory Benefits

The two previous examples were P-specific labor policies. Consider now a P-specific employment-hours policy, one that would change the relative prices of employment and hours for a particular group of workers. Few policies or proposals alter the relative price of employment and hours for just one group of workers. But most that change this relative price do so differentially across groups of workers, and in some cases the impacts are sharply different. In those cases it is sensible to consider issues of substitution of employment in one group for hours in other groups rather than the usual issues of labor-labor substitution that arise under P-specific labor policies.

Good examples of P-specific employment-hours policies are proposals to require employers to give part-time workers access to employer-provided benefits on the same basis as full-time workers. For example, bills have been repeatedly introduced in the U.S. Congress to require employers to offer any worker usually employed more than thirty hours per week the same health insurance provided to full-time workers, and to provide the same pension coverage to workers employed ten or more hours per week as is offered to employees working more hours.[18] Proposals have been made to require Canadian employers to prorate benefits for part-time workers (Reid and Swartz 1982). The European Community has urged member states to adopt the same access to employee benefits (and job security too) for part-time workers as they offer to full-time employees (Disney and Szyszczak 1984).

---

[17] The $7,000 figure is the Federal Unemployment Tax Act ceiling in 1991, the same mechanism that was used as the ceiling for payment of the credit under the NJTC.

[18] The proposed Part-time and Temporary Workers Protection Act, 101st Congress, H.R. 2563, provided for pension protection under ERISA, the basic U.S. legislation covering private pensions, and for the health insurance requirement under a new system of protection.

Insofar as the hourly labor costs of part-time workers differ from those of full-time workers, these proposals are P-specific labor policies and should be analyzed using the framework set out at the start of this section. Insofar, though, as the benefits proposed for mandated coverage among part-timers represent fixed costs to the employer, the proposals also amount to P-specific employment-hours policies. We have seen that part-time workers receive lower wage rates, and other evidence demonstrates that they are less likely to receive employer-paid medical benefits, sick leave, and life insurance.[19] Since employer-paid health coverage is a fixed cost, these proposals mandate policies that would increase the fixed costs of employing a group of low-wage workers. They would have less effect on the variable costs of employing part-time workers, and less or no effect on any of the costs of employing full-time workers.

As we saw in Chapter 3, beyond being fairly sure that businesses treat both employment and hours as p-substitutes for capital, we do not know very much about employment-hours substitution. We clearly know nothing about the substitution of hours of one group of workers for employment in another group. Thus we are unable to infer anything about the likely impact of such a policy on employers' relative demand for employment and hours of different types of workers. (We can, of course, analyze the impact on worker-hours of different groups of workers in the same way we discussed the minimum wage and employment subsidies.) Worse still, P-specific employment-hours policies must be analyzed in the same kind of labor-market equilibrium model used throughout this chapter. This means including an elasticity of labor supply to the market and a relative supply elasticity (as in the model earlier in this section). More important, it means recognizing the implicit contract that exists between many full-time workers and their employers but that is absent in part-time work, and understanding how the policy might affect outcomes by generating implicit contractual arrangements between employers and their part-time workers.

V. TYPE Q POLICIES

Let us turn now to Type Q policies, government efforts to affect labor-market outcomes by operating on the quantity side. These policies produce a change in long-run labor-market equilibria by shifting

[19] A survey of larger firms showed that the likelihood of coverage by benefits increases with the number of hours worked per week (U.S. Chamber of Commerce 1990). For example, 99 percent of firms paid medical benefits for full-time workers, but only 25 percent paid benefits for part-time workers. Comparable figures for retirement plans were 89 and 36 percent; for paid vacations they were 96 and 35 percent.

the total amount of labor supplied to the market; by increasing the supply of one type of labor, and thus changing relative supply; or by imposing restrictions on the number of workers of a particular type, or on the number of hours that can be worked.

The discussion in this section is less extensive than the analysis of Type P policies. That is because the greater thrust of labor-market policy has been of Type P, because much of the analysis of the two general types is similar, and because several of the major policies have been analyzed by others in great detail. It is worth noting, though, that just as in the case of those policies, one needs to keep in mind that the ultimate effects of Type Q policies must be analyzed at least within a labor-market equilibrium framework. Merely looking at the wages of some workers, or at all wages through labor demand alone, gives an incorrect evaluation of the policy (and, of course, of its effects on equilibrium employment as well). In this section I briefly review two Type Q policies to indicate the kind of analytical framework that should be applied. I then discuss at greater length a labor-market approach to analyzing another Q-specific labor policy—government-sponsored training programs.

A. Migration and Standard Hours

Immigration policy and the setting of standard hours can be viewed as Q-policies, for both operate directly on quantities to produce impacts on employment. Consider first the case of immigration. The relatively large net immigration means that U.S. policy toward migrants has functioned as a major Q-policy that has increased the supply of labor. It has also, though, varied over the past century in preferring different groups. This has in part determined the skill mix of new immigrants and has affected the nature of what has in fact been a Q-specific policy. (See Borjas 1990.) For example, the Immigration Reform Act of 1990 represented a shift in U.S. policy toward more skilled immigrants. It clearly has different effects on the labor market, and on various groups of native workers, than a policy that emphasizes admitting refugees or family members.

To evaluate the labor-market impact of immigration at any time, one thus needs to identify how the migration affects the relative supplies of labor by skill group. This is not an easy question to answer. It depends (Borjas 1987b) on both the level of earnings in the receiving and potential sending countries and on the distributions of earnings in both locations. The answer will vary over time and across countries; and the specific circumstances of time and place must be studied to evaluate the impact on the labor market.

Whatever the skill mix of immigrants, all the evidence summarized in Table 3.10 suggests that in the United States in the 1970s and 1980s their impact on the wages of native workers was small. Remember that this inference is based mostly on estimates of the extent of q-complementarity (that implicitly assumed no change in employment of native workers) between native and immigrant workers. To some extent, even the small wage changes of native workers will affect their labor supply, causing reductions if they are q-substitutes with immigrants, increases if they are q-complements. With the appropriate labor-market equilibrium framework the impacts on wages are even less than the evidence in Chapter 3 suggested. The changing employment levels of different groups of workers mitigates the effect of immigration on the price of skill.

In Table 3.11 I summarized the impact of policies on standard hours. When governments set these standards and require employers to pay overtime premia for additional hours, they are effectively imposing Type Q employment-hours policies. In the United States standard hours have been unchanged since 1938 (though attempts have been made during recessions to legislate permanent reductions), so the policy has not attracted much attention from American economists.[20] In other industrialized countries standard hours have been altered frequently.

Chapter 2 demonstrated that most of the interesting questions yield answers that are ambiguous theoretically and require solid empirical evidence. Chapter 3 showed that the only convincing evidence on the demand-side effects of policies that reduce standard hours is that they shorten the work week by roughly the same amount. Even if we had more evidence, we would not be able to provide an *ex ante* evaluation of policies on standard hours. Employment-hours policies in particular must be analyzed from the viewpoint of the worker's contract (explicit or implicit) with the employer. As we showed in Chapter 2, simply looking at the demand side is especially deficient here, though knowledge of demand parameters is crucial.

By raising workers' utility a reduction in standard hours will lower the equilibrium hourly wage. It raises the returns to working, so that employers need not pay so much per hour to induce workers to enter the labor market. Competition in the product market among employers with differing labor intensities of production will work in the same direction. The standard hourly wage rate may thus fall by nearly enough to offset the increased costs imposed by requiring premium pay earlier in the work week. The outcome depends on the

[20] For example, some proposals to raise the overtime pay premium to double-time have also included provisions to lower standard hours to thirty-five (e.g., H.R. 11,784, March 22, 1978, introduced by Representative Conyers of Michigan).

shapes and distributions of utility and profit functions. These effects on equilibrium wages will produce secondary effects on equilibrium employment and total hours. As with changes in the overtime premium, the contracting behavior of workers and employers will partly offset the effects on hours and employment that are predicted by a purely demand-side analysis.

B. Skills-training Programs

Skills training can be defined as the attempt to add human capital to workers. In the context of government policy it is part of a huge array of efforts, ranging from subsidized education to military service. For purposes of this chapter, though, I concentrate on the much smaller set of policies through which a government either subsidizes private training or institutes stand-alone programs whose exclusive function is providing training to (usually nonemployed) workers. A variety of such programs has existed both in the United States and elsewhere. (See, for example, Levitan and Mangum 1981, for a general history, and Levitan and Gallo 1988, for a specific discussion.) Many of the issues, even the economic ones, surrounding these programs are unrelated to labor demand and do not merit comment here.

One important part of the research on skills-training programs has been the increasingly subtle and complex efforts to analyze whether the labor-market experience of participants in these programs differs from otherwise identical individuals after the program has been completed. The success of the program is generally measured as

$$\Delta = [Y^T_{\text{Post}} - Y^T_{\text{Pre}}] - [Y^C_{\text{Post}} - Y^C_{\text{Pre}}],$$

where Y is some outcome of the program, perhaps a wage rate, employment experience, or earnings; T indicates trainee; and C denotes a "control." Attention has been devoted to the proper definition of the control group, including attempts to create a sound experimental design, of the appropriate outcomes to examine, and of the appropriate length of the period after the program has been completed.[21] Perhaps the best summary of this welter of empirical studies is that there is remarkably little consensus about the effects of such programs.

Researchers in this area have become increasingly sophisticated about the problems with these evaluations. They have not, however, varied the basic question being asked: What is the effect of the program on a particular outcome for the trainee compared to an otherwise identical nontrainee? This is not a question about the labor mar-

---

[21] Among the myriad studies, see Kiefer (1979), Ashenfelter and Card (1985), and Card and Sullivan (1988).

ket, about what happens to the earnings and employment of all workers, or even of other workers having the skills that the trainees had or acquired. Rather, it implicitly assumes that the program is successful if Δ is positive (abstracting from the program's cost). The program is judged beneficial on the basis of the outcomes experienced by the trainees.

Evaluation research has lost sight of the biases imparted by the problems of *labor-market displacement*, the impact of the training program on the wages and employment of other workers. We can view skills training as a Q-specific policy that attempts to convert unskilled to semiskilled or skilled workers and thus to shift the relative supply of labor. Like any Q-specific policy, it generates effects on the wages of all workers (or on their wages and employment if one or more wage rates are rigid). This means that Δ is a biased measure of the enhancement of the trainees' skill: Both Y^T_{Post} and Y^C_{Post} will be affected by the change in relative supply. Y^T_{Post} no longer measures the returns to the new skill absent the training program, and Y^C_{Post} no longer represents the baseline without the program. In the literature the assumption has always been made that this uncertainty principle is unimportant because the programs are small. This may perhaps be true, though even it is probably incorrect for the many programs that concentrate on a few narrowly defined skills within a small local labor market. Even if it is correct, so that the bias is unimportant, it does not obviate the problem of interpreting Δ. This measure merely shows the impact on the trainee and says nothing about the impact on the many other workers whose wages and/or probabilities of employment are changed by the program.

Assume that the program is not small relative to the labor market and the existing supply of workers with the skill, and also that the probability of employment within a skill group is unaffected by past status as a trainee.[22] Assume for simplicity that there are only two groups of workers, and that the training program attempts to shift trainees into the higher-skilled category. In this case the only outcome variable of interest is the wage rate. Then the program's initial effect on Δ will be to lower the wage rate of skilled workers and raise that of unskilled workers, assuming there is no wage rigidity. Thus $\Delta < \Delta^*$, where Δ^* is the true measure of the accretion of skills in the group of trainees. The bias is larger the larger is the program relative to the labor market; the smaller is the relative supply elasticity between the two groups of workers (θ in the model of Section IV); the less responsive workers are to changes in the relative returns to market work compared to leisure; and the larger is c_{us}, the partial elastic-

---

[22] Much of this discussion is due to Johnson (1980).

ity of complementarity between unskilled and skilled workers. Since supply elasticities to the market are probably quite small, and since the evidence suggests that unskilled and skilled workers are generally q-complements, this consideration implies that the bias in the estimate of Δ^* can be large.

If there is wage rigidity, it is probably downward in the wages of unskilled workers (perhaps due to minimum wage laws). In that case some unskilled workers will be unemployed. Offering skills training reduces the excess supply of unskilled workers and has no impact on their wage rate. The only bias in evaluating the program by estimating Δ based on wage rates is in the estimate of skilled workers' wages. The extent of the bias is determined by the same parameters as in the case of flexible wages.

Evaluating skills-training programs is a major industry, one to which the U.S. government has devoted hundreds of millions of dollars since the late 1950s. Yet the question most often asked by participants in that industry is the exceedingly narrow one of whether the trainees' labor-market experiences are improved by the program. Consideration even of this question in the context of models of labor demand demonstrates that unbiased estimates of the effects of the program cannot be obtained without examining its impact on the labor market. The more interesting question, whether the program raises welfare by improving outcomes for trainees without too great a loss for nontrainees, is not asked in the literature on evaluation. The concentration has instead been increasingly on technique, decreasingly on economic questions. Perhaps because of that we probably know less today about the impacts of and benefits from skills-training programs than we do about the other policies discussed in this chapter.

VI. Conclusions and New Directions

I have presented a way of organizing our thinking about a wide range of labor-market policies. Rather than viewing each particular policy as requiring an analysis de novo, I have outlined how current and *potential future policies* can be studied within one framework. These policies all involve intervention that is initially on the supply or demand side of the labor market, and that either changes the price or quantity of labor generally or of a particular class of workers. All can be fruitfully studied using a framework that involves the supply-demand analysis of a labor market containing several types of workers, or that involves the analysis of labor contracts. The particular policies I have analyzed are among the more important in the United States and other industrialized countries; but the discussion of them has been designed as much to demonstrate the method of analysis, and the importance of relying on more general knowledge to underlie policy evaluation, as it has been to present information.

The impact of existing policies can often be determined more appropriately using this kind of modeling based on knowledge of the underlying demand and supply parameters than through attempts to infer it directly. The direct approach necessarily restricts the researcher to asking an exceedingly narrow evaluation question, one that is only of interest if the sole concern is the welfare of the individuals who are directly affected by the particular program. The indirect approach forces the researcher to think about the labor-market impacts of the policy. To evaluate policy proposals this kind of *ex ante* evaluation is the only possible method.

Government agencies that fund evaluation studies want simple answers about specific policies and programs, and often want information about the effect of their programs on their clients, those workers who are directly affected. That does not mean, though, that policy evaluation needs to be narrowly focused on the standard control/ treatment methodology that seeks only to find the impact on those workers, and those specific outcomes, at which the policy is aimed. Instead, evaluation studies should abandon this often narrow focus that has in many cases demonstrably failed to provide answers even to narrow evaluation questions. It should focus instead on the economic analysis of the program's effects *both* on those workers and outcomes that the policy targets and on other workers and labor-market outcomes. Put more bluntly, useful program evaluation requires more of an economic focus, both in the questions asked and the methods used to answer them.

APPENDIX

The solutions for the variables in the model in Section IV are

$$lnL_2 = \frac{\sigma\epsilon}{\sigma+\epsilon[\sigma-1]}\left\{-ln\alpha - [1-\sigma]^{-1}ln\left([1-\alpha]Z^{\frac{\sigma+\theta-\sigma\theta-\sigma3}{[\sigma+\theta]\sigma}} + \alpha\right) + \frac{1+\epsilon}{\epsilon}ln\left(1 + Z^{\frac{\sigma[1-\sigma]}{\sigma+\theta}}\right)\right\} \quad (5.A.1)$$

and

$$lnw_2 = \epsilon^{-1}lnL_2 + \frac{1+\epsilon}{\epsilon}ln\left(1 + Z^{\frac{\sigma[1-\sigma]}{\sigma+\theta}}\right) - ln\left(1 + Z^{\frac{\sigma[2-\sigma]}{\sigma+\theta}}\right). \quad (5.A.2)$$

PART TWO

The Dynamic Demand for Labor

CHAPTER SIX

The Dynamic Theory of Labor Demand

I. Introduction—the Nature of Dynamics

All of the adjustments discussed in Chapters 2 through 5 take time. A rise in the price of energy does not immediately increase the demand for worker-hours. New profit opportunities do not cause an instantaneous jump in the birth rate of new firms, nor in the growth of new jobs; and it takes some time before an imposed increase in the minimum wage generates the full reduction in the employment of low-skilled workers. While Chapter 4 dealt with one sort of dynamics, the birth and death of firms, I discussed those as if they occurred instantaneously in response to shocks whose duration was ignored. True dynamic responses take time, because it pays employers to adjust slowly to whatever shocks have altered equilibrium factor demand. Indeed, for purposes of these three chapters I define the dynamics of labor demand as the process of moving toward new steady states—the time it takes and the paths traced out by the inputs.

Analyzing this process has practical importance in two major areas. The more heavily studied has been the path of changes in labor productivity over business cycles. It has long been suggested that labor productivity—output per worker-hour—declines in recessions and rises during expansions.[1] The modern explanation for this is *labor hoarding*, which can be defined as a less than proportionate decrease in worker-hours in response to a negative demand shock. In turn it has been rationalized as employers' optimal response to the presence of costs of adjusting labor demand (Oi 1962). To understand what causes productivity to vary cyclically it is thus important to understand how these costs might affect the paths of employment and hours, exactly what the costs might be, and how large they are. More basically, it is necessary to understand precisely what we mean by labor hoarding, in particular, what workers are doing during the time they are hoarded and presumably not producing at the customary rate.

The second area of more general interest concerns the effects of policies designed to enhance "job security"—policies aimed at reduc-

---

[1] This possibility and its incompatibility with the static theory in Chapter 2 was recognized by Dunlop (1938).

ing layoffs and fluctuations in employment. Since employers' responses to shocks to product demand, and output and input prices, are what generate job insecurity, and since the timing of these shocks is mediated by adjustment costs, any policy that seeks to mitigate their effects must operate by changing the costs of adjustment. To understand the economics of job-security policies one must understand how those costs affect dynamic labor demand and how the policies modify them.

In this and the next two chapters I discuss these issues. To start out we need to know the time paths of a typical profit-maximizing employer's responses to shocks to long-run factor demand. These responses will be affected by the structure of the costs of adjustment and by how employers forecast the path of shocks. Labor-demand dynamics may be affected by the costs of adjusting other inputs; and assuming that labor is heterogeneous requires examining how the costs of changing inputs of one type of labor affect the dynamics of demand for other workers. Distinguishing between employees and hours makes the discussion more realistic, because it generates predictions that allow inferences about the contribution of demand forces to the dynamics of unemployment. That distinction also leads naturally to the examination of the dynamics induced by long-term contractual arrangements, and to the study of how workers' effort on the job varies over time.

Chapters 7 and 8 examine the applied aspects of demand dynamics. In Chapter 7 I survey the very large literature, the long-run implications of much of which were presented in Chapter 3, that has estimated the speeds of adjustment of worker-hours, employment, and hours to demand shocks. Also of interest, and mostly ignored in Chapters 2 and 3, was the question of the degree of returns to labor, more particularly, whether shocks in demand eventually generate equiproportional changes in worker-hours. Answering these empirical questions is necessary in order to predict the extent of workers' insecurities in the face of labor-market fluctuations and how these differ among workers.

In Chapter 8 I use the synthesis of empirical work from Chapter 7 and the theoretical results from Chapter 6 to examine how various policies have affected changes in the demand for workers and hours. Of particular interest are policies that offer unemployment benefits or severance pay to employees who lose their jobs; requirements that employers notify workers of impending job loss; and, more generally, any policy that imposes *either* hiring or firing costs on employers.

II. The Costs of Adjusting Labor Demand—Characteristics and Direct Evidence

The typology presented in Figure 2.2 divided labor costs into fixed and variable costs. Within fixed costs the subcategory one-time costs represents the monetary loss to changing employment. One focus of the analysis in this chapter is on the crucial issue of how these costs vary with the size of the change. Are they completely lumpy, positive if a change occurs but invariant with the size of that change? Do they rise more or less proportionately as the change increases? Are they symmetric with respect to positive and negative changes?

Most of the costs discussed in Chapter 2 are explicit, the kind of cost that an accountant can measure and report on an income and expenditure statement. A large or even the major part of the costs of adjustment are implicit costs. For example, expansion of the work force may result in difficulties scheduling the flow of work across sites within an establishment, problems that in turn reduce average efficiency. Adding a few employees to a work crew may require senior workers to spend time training their new co-workers; hiring replacement workers for a work crew whose size is unaltered may have the same effect, and cutting employment may reduce the morale of the remaining employees and lower their efficiency. It is very difficult to measure the costs generated by any of these changes.

The main distinction in this chapter is between gross and net costs of adjustment. Some of the costs are occasioned by *gross changes in employment*—by adding new workers or by the departure of current employees. These costs may be important even if there is no change in the level of employment—no *net employment change*. For the same net change the costs will clearly be larger if more workers need to be hired to replace a larger flow of quits. Obversely, these net changes can produce costs independent of those produced by the new hires that make up the change. A good example is the cost of the disruption generated by the expansion of the total work force. This distinction is easy to identify, but very difficult to measure. It is important because the two types of adjustment cost affect employers' behavior differently, so that they cannot be modeled the same way.

The literature on dynamic factor demand has also distinguished between *internal* and *external* costs of adjustment (see Treadway 1971 for an example in the case of investment in physical capital). The internal costs of changing employment represent declines in output that are inherent in the production function. These are costs that would arise solely from the disruption to the accustomed flow of work among experienced employees. External costs are those generated by spending for such things as job advertisements, unemployment benefits, formal training—anything that increases costs but occurs off the shop floor.

There are no available data on the size of these dynamic costs, or on their breakdown into internal versus external or gross versus net costs. Indeed, few attempts have been made to measure them directly. What are available are a few surveys of broad groups of employers on some of the costs of hiring and firing, and several more careful attempts at inferring the accounting costs of turnover within particular firms. Taken together, they illustrate the difficulties of measuring these costs and their potential size.

To allow some comparability I report all the results in 1990 U.S. dollars. A survey of employers in the Rochester, New York, area in 1965–66 found an average hiring cost for all occupations of $910, but an average for professional and managerial workers of $4,660. A survey in Los Angeles in 1980 found hiring and training costs of $13,790 for salaried workers, and $5,110 for production workers. The same survey found separation costs to be much smaller, roughly $1,780 for salaried workers and $370 for production workers. In a nationwide survey of large employers in 1979 the cost of hiring a secretary was $680, but for a college graduate was $2,200. A similar survey in 1985 found the median cost of severance benefits among firms offering them to be $3,050 (though 18 percent of these very large companies offered no severance benefits). A broad survey of employers in twenty-eight cities in 1980 indicated that they spent 42.5 hours recruiting the typical new hire and training him or her during the first month on the job.[2]

Among the even fewer accounting estimates of the present value of the costs of turnover, those for a large pharmaceutical company placed the costs of training and what personnel specialists refer to as "career development" at between 1.5 and 2.5 times annual salary. A survey of automobile salespeople indicated these costs to be equal to annual salary (Cascio 1991, 19). A particularly careful attempt to measure the replacement costs of labor (of drivers in an Australian trucking firm) yielded costs of $7,000 per worker (Button 1990).

The diversity of the concepts behind these estimates makes their lack of agreement unsurprising. It is difficult to agree on what constitutes hiring costs, and how to measure those costs after a definition is settled upon. Most estimates ignore the cost of training new

[2] For Rochester, Myers (1969, Table 3-1); Los Angeles Merchants and Manufacturers Association, *Turnover and Absenteeism Manual*, Los Angeles, M & M Association, 1980; Bureau of National Affairs, *Personnel Policies Forum*, No. 126, July 1979, No. 143, December 1986, and Barron, Bishop, and Dunkelberg (1985).

workers. None attempts to account for the costs of disruption to the flow of output that can occur as adjustments are made. Despite this failure the measures demonstrate that the average cost of adjustment can be substantial; and their size justifies the amount of attention I devote to their effects. I follow the literature by representing adjustment costs very simply. Even the most complex representations in this chapter only account for the distinctions between gross and net costs, for how smooth costs are as a function of the size of the adjustment, and for possible asymmetries with respect to increases or decreases in the demand for labor. I do not analyze explicitly the other distinctions. But they are an important reminder that there are serious economic considerations behind the fairly technical discussion of dynamic factor demand.

III. Adjustment of the Demand for Homogeneous Labor—No Cooperating Factors

Assuming that labor is the only input into production is nonsensical. Similarly silly is the assumption that the employment-hours split can be ignored in analyzing adjustment. Both assumptions, though, permit the isolation of the role of adjustment costs and expectations in determining the path of labor demand. They allow us to see how different assumptions about the structure of adjustment costs and the nature of employers' expectations affect labor demand. That in turn provides the basis for empirical studies of dynamics and for the analysis of policies that affect the time path of the demand for labor. I therefore assume throughout this section that labor is the only input into production and that hours are fixed, and I equate worker-hours L with employment E for purposes of the analysis.

A. Net Costs of Adjustment under Static Expectations or Perfect Foresight

In order to focus attention more closely on the role of adjustment costs, I assume in this section that employment adjusts toward its static equilibrium value. I assume that employers project an equilibrium level of labor demand, L^*, from the current time through all future time. At each point in time the firm revises its forecast of L^* and assumes the new forecast is the new permanent value. Because this assumption is so unrealistic, though a good place to begin the analysis, I also discuss what the paths would look like under the alternative polar assumption that employers have perfect foresight about the entire future path of product and factor prices.

The most commonly—indeed, nearly universally—discussed example of factor-demand adjustment is that in which the costs are variable, with the average cost increasing in the size of the adjustment. The usual assumption is that adjustment costs are

$$C(\dot{L}) = a|\dot{L}| + b\dot{L}^2, \, a, \, b > 0, \tag{6.1}$$

and I have suppressed the t subscripts on the terms in $\dot{L}$, the change in L_t. Under this specific assumption the marginal adjustment cost of a small increase or decrease in labor demand is $a + 2b|\dot{L}|$. This means that it is very costly for the firm to move instantaneously between static equilibria, because compressing the change in employment into a very small period of time causes costs to rise with the square of the change. This particular structure of costs presumably rests on the notion that changing worker-hours more rapidly produces disproportionate increases in disruptions in output, and thus reduces labor productivity. The implicit assumption is that the costs of adjustment stem from the net change in employment.

Throughout this section I fix the product price and assume that all shocks are to wages. At any time $t = 0$ the employer seeks to maximize

$$\pi = \int_0^\infty \{F(L_t) - wL_t - C(\dot{L}_t)\}e^{-rt}dt, \tag{6.2}$$

where F is the production function (concentrated on the input of labor only), and I assume the employer discounts future profits at a constant rate r. The Euler equation describing the optimal path along (6.2) is[3]

$$2b\ddot{L}_t - 2br\dot{L}_t + F'(L_t) - w - ra = 0. \tag{6.3}$$

In the steady state the demand for labor is unchanging, so that $\dot{L} = \ddot{L} = 0$. Equilibrium labor demand is determined by

$$F'(L^*) = w + ra.$$

This is the standard result of equation (2.1): that the value of the marginal product of labor equals the cost of labor services. In this case, though, that cost includes both the wage and the amortized cost of increasing or reducing the work force by one worker.[4] L^* differs from

[3] This is a standard problem in the calculus of variations. Along the path that maximizes π the motion of L_t is obtained by solving the first-order condition

$$\frac{\partial \pi}{\partial L} - \frac{d}{dt}\left(\frac{\partial \pi}{\partial \dot{L}}\right) = 0$$

for L. The first term in this differentiation contributes $F'(L_t) - w$ to the left-hand side of (6.3); the second term contributes the rest of the expression. (Intriligator 1971, chap. 12, offers a good exposition of economic applications of the calculus of variations.)

[4] For expositional simplicity I have excluded voluntary turnover. If workers left the firm at a rate δ per period, the amortized cost of turnover would be $[r + \delta]a$. Anything

the static equilibrium demand only by the adjustment costs added to the static model of Chapter 2.

The more important issue for this chapter is how actual employment adjusts in response to shocks that alter L^*. Gould (1968) has shown that, assuming static expectations about wages and prices, the optimal path of employment is described by

$$\dot{L}_t = \gamma[L^* - L_t]. \tag{6.4}$$

Employment adjusts slowly toward what the firm views as equilibrium employment, L^*, with the size of the adjustment determined by γ and the extent of the disequilibrium. The rate γ at which employment adjusts toward L^* is an implicit function that decreases with the parameter b. Once the system has been shocked, employment is always changing: Equilibrium employment is reached only asymptotically.

Equation (6.4) can be linked to empirical work directly by writing it in discrete time and substituting the determinants of L^*:

$$\Delta L_t = \gamma'[G(X_t) - L_{t-1}], \tag{6.5}$$

where X_t is a vector of determinants of L^*, and $G(\cdot)$ is a function that relates L^* to X. The X vector should be composed of those variables that were included in the studies analyzed in Tables 3.1 through 3.5. If G is assumed to be linear, and all the determinants of the current target L^* are assumed to be current values of the X variables, equation (6.5) takes on the typical geometric distributed lag form of the empirical literature discussed in Chapter 7.

The time path of employment in a typical firm is shown in Figure 6.1. I assume that the *actual* static equilibria L^* are shown by the solid path in the figure. Then the profit-maximizing path of employment is shown by L^s, the dashed line in Figure 6.1. At each point the firm begins adjusting employment slowly toward the equilibrium that it sees at that instant. The important thing to observe is that the fluctuations in L^s are less sharp than those in L^*. The reason is that the existence of the quadratic adjustment costs slows the response to the shocks that alter L^*. That this is the optimizing response is intuitive. If the entire change in employment were made immediately, the marginal cost produced by adding (or dropping) the last employee would be huge, because of the quadratic term in (6.1). By smoothing adjustment over many time periods, the firm lowers the total cost of ad-

---

that shortens a worker's tenure, either in fact, such as an increase in δ, or from the employer's subjective view, as with an increase in the employer's rate of discount, raises employment costs. This standard model has its origins in Holt et al. (1960) and was formalized by Gould (1968) among others.

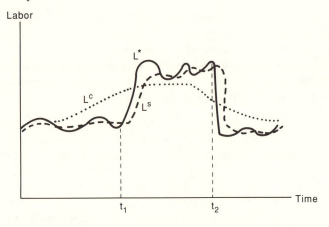

6.1 Demand Adjustment with Quadratic Variable Costs

justment by more than enough to offset the lost profits from failing to set $L_t = L^*$.

This model provides the standard explanation for procyclical labor productivity. Assume, as the evidence in Freeman (1977) suggests, that the biggest shocks to optimal employment come from shocks to product price (or, obversely, to product demand). The optimality of slow adjustment implies that observed labor demand will lag behind these shocks. To the extent that shocks to the demand for output underlie the changes, the ratio of output to employment will rise after positive shocks and fall after negative shocks due to the slowness with which employment is adjusted. This is precisely the cyclical pattern of productivity that we observe.

This explanation makes sense superficially. But how can productivity be changing if, as I assume, the capital stock is not varying, and if L measures worker-hours? The explanation makes little sense unless one assumes that the firm is operating inefficiently—it does not obtain all the output Y_t that its production function F would enable it to get out of its labor input L_t. Either it is off its production function and hoarding labor in varying amounts at all times, or it is hoarding labor as it adjusts to negative shocks and "sweating labor," deriving extra output from its work force, as it adjusts to positive shocks. As a theory of procyclical productivity change quadratic adjustment costs make sense only if one abandons the assumption of efficiency that underlies the static theory of production.

If the employer projects changing prices and wages, the explicit solution of (6.4) cannot generally be obtained. There is no single target toward which the firm is adjusting at each particular time. Consider, though, how replacing static expectations by perfect foresight alters the outcome. In Figure 6.1, for example, if the employer has perfect foresight about the entire path of L^*, the sharp increase in labor demand that occurred after t_1 must generate large adjustment costs. Higher profits could have been gained by adjusting employment to it before t_1 by moving along the path L^c, the dotted path in the figure. Similarly, if the employer were aware that the higher L^* between t_1 and t_2 is only temporary, the optimal demand for labor would not have risen so high as L^s. Again, knowledge of the future path of the determinants of L^* would enable the firm to avoid adjustment costs that reduce its profits.

Throughout the rest of this subsection I assume that employers' expectations are static. Nonetheless, for each example that I discuss one could present the same sort of graphical depiction of L^c as in Figure 6.1. In each case perfect foresight would lead to changes that enable the employer to avoid some of the costs of adjusting labor demand. Changes in employment would depend on future fluctuations in wages and prices, with the effect on current labor demand greater the nearer those fluctuations are. In these other models, as under quadratic costs, perfect foresight prevents one from deriving an equation or set of equations like (6.5).

Though the example of quadratic adjustment costs has been by far the most frequently used, it is not obvious that it characterizes the structure of production better than a variety of other assumptions that could be analyzed.[5] I consider just two, both based on the assumption that at least part of the costs of adjustment are independent of the size of the change in net employment. This implies that the firm incurs the same costs whenever it alters its labor demand. They could be independent, for example, if the remaining workers' productivity drops when they see any of their fellows laid off. An alternative is that there are substantial fixed costs of hiring—for example, the costs of maintaining a hiring office, advertising, filling out government forms—but that the marginal cost of attracting additional workers beyond the first is zero.

The cost of adjusting labor demand can be described as

$$C(\dot{L}) = \begin{bmatrix} k \text{ if } |\dot{L}| > 0 \\ 0 \text{ if } \dot{L} = 0 \end{bmatrix}, \tag{6.6}$$

[5] This case and that of combined fixed and variable costs is analyzed in Hamermesh (1992b). Davidson and Harris (1981) analyze (for the adjustment of investment) still other examples of adjustment costs. Rothschild (1971) discusses (again, for investment) the case of linear adjustment costs.

where k are the fixed costs of adjustment. These are incurred in each period that the firm changes its labor input. The employer again maximizes (6.2), except that $C(L)$ is now described by (6.6). Given the path of L^* (determined by the employer's static expectations about prices and wages), the firm either sets $\dot{L} = 0$ or sets $L_t = L^*$ (with the implied change in L_t). This assumption is analogous to that made in (S,s) models of inventories, where the cost of restocking is independent of the size of the order.[6] Under static expectations and this assumption about adjustment costs the firm's choice depends only on whether

$$k \gtreqless \frac{[F(L^*) - wL^*] - [F(L_t) - wL_t]}{r} . \tag{6.7}$$

If the costs of moving to the new static equilibrium level of employment are large relative to the lost profits from being out of equilibrium (if k exceeds the difference in the present value of the profit streams), the employer will not change labor demand. If the costs are small, or the lost profits from being out of equilibrium are large, the change will be made. The crucial difference between the results from assuming (6.6) and (6.1) is that now any change in employment, *if one is made*, will be a jump to the equilibrium level of labor demand. Since it incurs the fixed cost k in each period when employment is changing, the firm will complete any move to equilibrium in one period rather than spread the move over many periods.

Like quadratic variable adjustment costs, lumpy fixed adjustment costs imply that labor demand is slow to adjust to shocks to equilibrium employment. The optimal pattern of labor demand, though, is drastically different. Consider Figure 6.2, which shows the same path of equilibrium employment, L^*, as in Figure 6.1. With lumpy fixed costs the profit-maximizing employer only makes those changes in employment that are justified by large departures of L^* from current worker-hours. Small fluctuations in equilibrium employment leave actual labor demand unchanged, while large ones lead to jumps that equate L^s to L^*. At most times actual demand is not changing, but occasionally it changes sharply. This is exactly opposite the quadratic variable cost case, in which employment is always changing but those changes never remove the entire disequilibrium.

This example does not produce a simple explanation of procyclical labor productivity. It is not obvious that employment lags behind output when shocks occur, for if the shocks are sufficiently large

[6] The (S,s) model was developed in operations research and has been applied increasingly by economists studying inventories. Blinder (1981) presents a very clear exposition and application of the model.

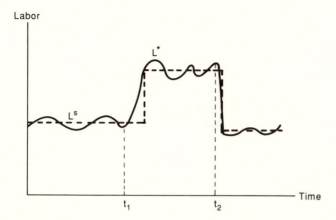

6.2 Demand Adjustment with Lumpy Fixed Costs under
Static Expectations

there is no lag. Even ignoring issues of aggregation (with which I
deal in Chapter 7), though, it is as satisfactory an explanation for productivity change as the standard approach. It too suffices only if one
appends a theory of variation in effort over the cycle.

As an additional example of how differences in the structure of
adjustment costs affect the path of labor demand, revise the assumption to allow both quadratic variable and lumpy fixed adjustment
costs:

$$C(\dot{L}) = a\left|\dot{L}\right| + b\dot{L}^2 + \begin{bmatrix} k \text{ if } |\dot{L}| > 0 \\ 0 \text{ if } \dot{L} = 0 \end{bmatrix}. \tag{6.8}$$

Under this assumption small shocks to L^* induce no change in employment demand, for the lost profits from being away from the
static profit-maximizing level of employment are less than the fixed
cost of changing labor demand. If the shocks are sufficiently large,
employment adjusts, but only slowly, because the costs are quadratic. That adjustment continues until employment gets close enough
to the static equilibrium level that the marginal cost of continuing the
adjustment (the per-period lumpy cost and the variable cost) exceeds
the increased profits that a further change would produce.

In Figure 6.3, with static expectations and the same path of equilibrium employment as in Figures 6.1 and 6.2, actual employment is still
unchanged in response to small fluctuations in L^*. Large gaps between L^* and L_t, though, are met by smooth changes in L_t rather than
the jumps in Figure 6.2. As with quadratic adjustment costs, changes

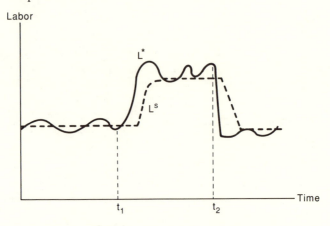

6.3 Demand Adjustment with Lumpy Fixed and
Quadratic Variable Costs under Static Expectations

in employment are continuous; but as with lumpy fixed costs, no changes occur when the disequilibrium is small.

Implicit in all three models is the assumption that net adjustment costs are symmetric with respect to increases or decreases in employment. There is no reason for this assumption to hold. If it does not, but firms still have static expectations, the conclusions in this subsection are only slightly modified. In each case two conditions describe changes in labor demand, one if current worker-hours are less than L^*, the other if they are greater.

B. Gross Costs of Adjustment under Perfect Foresight

The adjustment cost functions (6.1), (6.6), and (6.8) are all based on the costs of changing employment levels—on the net costs of adjusting employment. The paths they imply will track dynamic labor demand well only if there are no gross costs of employment adjustment. In this subsection I present an alternative polar case, in which only gross costs are present. Which polar case is closer to the truth is an empirical question, one which has not yet been addressed in the literature discussed in Chapter 7. Regardless of the general empirical importance of these two types of costs, the model examined here lends itself much more easily to examining asymmetries in adjustment costs. It is easy to see why hiring costs might differ from firing costs, but more difficult to argue that the costs of disruption are asymmetric. Also, the possibility of asymmetric gross adjustment costs provides a convenient basis for some of the analysis of policies in Chapter 8.

Let costs be symmetric linear functions of gross changes in employment:

$$C = [ah + af]L, \tag{6.9}$$

where $h \geq 0$ is the rate of hiring, $f \geq 0$ is the rate of firing, $a > 0$ is a parameter. The net change in employment is

$$\dot{L} \equiv [h - f - \delta]L,$$

where δ is the rate of voluntary quitting. Since the firm incurs costs if it hires or fires, and since simultaneously hiring and firing merely adds to costs without increasing output, it will never both hire and fire (under our assumption that workers are homogeneous).

If δ were zero—that is, if there were no voluntary mobility—the assumption in (6.9) would reduce to a simplified version of (6.1): symmetric linear costs of adjusting net employment. Equation (6.9) appears to be a slight modification of the simplest case of adjustment costs. Indeed, if we assume static expectations about L^*, so that the firm believes its target employment level is fixed forever, the problem reduces to maximizing (6.2) without the quadratic term in (6.1). In that case the optimal path of L_t in response to a shock coincides with L^*—there is no lag in the adjustment of labor demand. Assuming static expectations with linear gross adjustment costs is thus uninteresting. Maintaining the assumption of static expectations, but allowing the gross costs of adjustment to be quadratic, would lead to results just like those implied by the model consisting of (6.1) and (6.2).

Interesting results can be obtained using (6.9) if we make the polar assumption that firms have perfect foresight. This allows us to infer how changes in hiring (firing) costs affect the path of labor demand even at times when the firm is not hiring (firing). Unlike in the case of quadratic costs, only by assuming that adjustment costs are linear can we derive any explicit results under the assumption of perfect foresight. The two assumptions—linear gross adjustment costs and perfect foresight—jointly generate new insights into dynamic adjustment, though neither alone gives an explicit dynamic path that implies lagged adjustment.

Consider first what the solution looks like if $\delta = 0$.[7] At any time the firm is either hiring ($h > 0$), firing ($f > 0$), or holding employment constant. Consider the interval $[t_0, t_1]$ in which hiring occurs. The marginal hire must be justified by the marginal productivity condition

[7] The next set of results is a slight modification of Nickell (1986, sec. 3.3).

$$F'(L_t) = w_t + ra. \tag{6.10}$$

A worker will be hired only when the marginal product covers both the wage rate and the amortized cost of hiring.

Let the firm be firing workers on the interval $[t_2, t_3]$. Then the marginal fire must be justified by the marginal productivity condition

$$F'(L_t) = w_t - ra. \tag{6.11}$$

To justify firing a worker the marginal product must be so low that it cannot even cover the wage minus the amortized cost of firing (what would have to be paid to hire someone when labor demand rebounds). Notice that we have not determined the t_i; they result from firm's maximization of profits.

Equations (6.10) and (6.11) show that linear hiring and firing costs impose a wedge in the standard profit-maximizing marginal conditions. The wedge implies that in some cases when $F'(L_t) > w_t$ it does not pay the firm to hire more workers because the extra profits are insufficient to justify the hiring costs. Similarly, there are cases when $F'(L_t) < w_t$, but the gains from firing do not cover the firing costs.

This wedge defines the t_i and thus implicitly the period $[t_1, t_2]$ during which employment is held constant at some level $\bar{L}$. The marginal person hired at t_1 must justify his or her employment by generating a present value of profits just sufficient to offset the hiring costs:

$$\int_{t_1}^{\infty} \{F'(\bar{L}_t) - w_t\} e^{-r[t - t_1]} dt = a. \tag{6.12}$$

Similarly, at t_2 when the firm begins firing, separating the marginal person must be justified by a loss of profits sufficiently large to justify bearing the cost of firing:

$$\int_{t_2}^{\infty} \{F'(\bar{L}_t) - w_t\} e^{-r[t - t_2]} dt = -a. \tag{6.13}$$

Combining (6.12) and (6.13) and rearranging:

$$\int_{t_1}^{t_2} \{F'(\bar{L}_t) - w_t\} e^{-r[t - t_1]} dt = a[1 + e^{-r[t_2 - t_1]}]. \tag{6.14}$$

Moreover, since employment is constant at $\bar{L}$ over this interval:

$$F'(\bar{L}_t) = w_{t_1} + ra, \tag{6.10'}$$

and

$$F'(\bar{L}_t) = w_{t_2} - ra. \tag{6.11'}$$

The three equations (6.14), (6.10'), and (6.11') are defined over the three unknowns $\bar{L}$, t_1, and t_2. They determine the length of the interval when employment is held constant and its level during that interval. They show that an increase in hiring or firing costs, a, length-

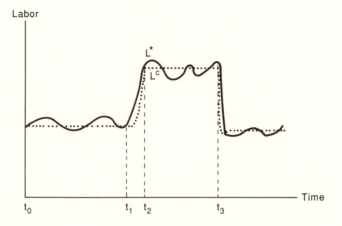

6.4 Demand Adjustment with Linear Costs and Perfect
Foresight

ens the interval. While I specified this for a period after hiring and
before firing (implicitly a business-cycle peak), I could have specified
equations mutatis mutandis that give the same results at a cyclical
trough. The main point is that employment is held constant at ex-
tremes of foreseen shocks to labor demand.

Because the costs of adjustment are linear, there is no reason to
smooth employment changes to reduce adjustment costs; and by
equating L_t to L^* if it pays to change employment, the firm maximizes
profits. Taken together, these considerations imply the adjustment
path shown in Figure 6.4. I assume that L^* is the same as in Figures
6.1 through 6.3. Labor demand follows the static-equilibrium path
when the latter is away from cyclical turning points (though the addition of the amortized training cost reduces actual labor demand
somewhat below what equilibrium demand would be without these
costs). Near troughs and peaks of L^* the demand for labor does not
change. These are the intervals $[t_0, t_1]$ and $[t_2, t_3]$ when the deviation
between the marginal revenue product and the wage lies within the
wedge created by firing and hiring costs.

Like the three models of net adjustment costs, symmetric linear
gross adjustment costs with perfect foresight generate slow adjustment of actual behind equilibrium labor demand. Like them this
model can be used to rationalize cyclical variations in productivity.
Unlike quadratic adjustment, though, but more like the models that
include fixed adjustment costs, the path of labor demand follows
fluctuations in L^* only when the latter is changing substantially and

away from peaks and troughs. Indeed, the path L^c in Figure 6.4 looks remarkably like L^s in Figure 6.3.

I have ignored the voluntary mobility that provided some of the motivation for the analysis. Adding turnover at a rate δ does not change the conclusions qualitatively. It merely shortens the time when the firm is firing workers (since the decline in labor demand can now be met partly by relying on voluntary quits). It lengthens the time when hiring occurs (since some hiring must continue near cyclical peaks to replace the quitters). The relationship between L^c and L^* in Figure 6.4 retains its general characteristics.

To see how asymmetric adjustment costs affect the results assume

$$C = [a_1h + a_2f]L, \tag{6.9'}$$

where the a_i are the adjustment costs per hire or fire. The analysis proceeds exactly as in the earlier case where $a_1 \equiv a_2$. a_1 is substituted for a in (6.10), (6.12), and (6.10'), and a_2 is substituted for a in (6.11), (6.13), and (6.11'). Equation (6.14) becomes

$$\int_{t_1}^{t_2} \{F'(\bar{L}_t) - w_t\}e^{-r[t-t_1]}dt = a_1 + a_2e^{-r[t_2-t_1]}. \tag{6.14'}$$

This modified system obviously yields the same sort of results as the simpler case and generates paths of actual employment demand like that shown in Figure 6.4. The novel and important implication comes from considering the effect of increased firing costs on the length of the interval $[t_1, t_2]$ and on the level of employment at that cyclical peak. With higher a_2 the interval $[t_1, t_2]$ lengthens; the profit-maximizing firm holds employment constant for a longer time *and at a lower level*. The obverse is true for employment near a cyclical trough. The crucial point is that, as long as employers' expectations are not completely static, changes in hiring or firing costs affect employment demand at all times, not only when the employer is hiring or firing.

C. Rational Expectations of the Determinants of Demand

The examples in this section have been based on the unrealistic assumptions that the employer's expectations about future wages and prices are static or are perfect. In reality the best employers can do is take account of the amount of labor (number of workers) currently employed and the likely future path of demand for labor. How they predict the future path of demand is not at issue here. I assume that at each point they take all the available information—the past history of wage, price, and other shocks—and form rational-expectations forecasts of their future values. Along with the inherited stock of labor, these forecasts determine the current-period demand for labor. During the next period (or the next instant if, as in the previous subsections, the problem is solved in continuous time) the forecasting and maximization are repeated.

Unless one assumes a quadratic production function and quadratic costs of adjustment, it is exceedingly difficult to derive an explicit solution for the demand for L_t.[8] But by making those very restrictive assumptions, we can obtain such a solution and explicitly link a realistic formulation of expectations to dynamic labor demand. To do so, assume that the employer wishes to maximize the expected value of the stream of future profits. The discrete-time analogue of (6.2) is

$$E_t \sum_{i=0}^{\infty} R^i \{ [\alpha_{0,t+i} + \bar{\alpha}_0] L_{t+i} - .5\alpha_1 L_{t+i}^2 - $$
$$w_{t+i} L_{t+i} - .5b[L_{t+i} - L_{t+i-1}]^2 \}, \quad (6.2')$$

where the α are parameters of the production function. The parameters $\alpha_{0,t+i}$ can be viewed as reflecting stochastic shocks to productivity and as having a mean of zero. Here and in Section VI only I use E_t to denote expectations at the time t, when the decision about current-period employment is being made. $R = [1 + r]^{-1}$, and the other parameters and notation are the same as before. In (6.2') adjustment costs are quadratic, just as in (6.1), but a $\equiv 0$ to make the derivation easier.

As in Subsection A, we can derive an Euler equation, now in discrete time, except that here there is one such equation for each period $t+i$:

$$RE_{t+i} L_{t+i+1} - [\alpha_1/b + 1 + R] L_{t+i} + L_{t+i-1} = $$
$$b^{-1}[w_{t+i} - \alpha_{0,t+i} - \bar{\alpha}_0], \quad i = 0 \ 1, 2, \ldots \quad (6.3')$$

The employer implicitly solves this equation for each period i based on the forecasts made at time t for all future values of w and α_0. Let

$$\kappa = [\alpha_1/b + 1 + R].$$

Then there exist parameters $0 < \lambda < 1$ and $\mu > 1 + r$ such that the coefficients of the second-order difference equation (6.3') can be factored as

$$1 - \kappa R^{-1} z + R^{-1} z^2 = [1 - \lambda z][1 - \mu z],$$

[8] A good exposition of some of these models (for the adjustment of investment) is Blanchard and Fischer (1989, sec. 6.3). A more complex exposition that is specific to employment adjustment and a particular set of aggregate data is Nickell (1984). The basic idea in the case of factor demand stems from Lucas (1976) and Sargent (1978). The exposition here is based on Sargent.

where z is an arbitrary variable in the factorization. This generates the nonexplosive solution

$$L_t = \lambda L_{t-1} - \lambda b^{-1} \sum_{j=0}^{\infty} \mu^{-j} E_t[w_{t+j} - \alpha_{0,t+j} - \bar{\alpha}_0]. \qquad (6.4')$$

This solution clarifies the link between the parameter λ that describes the length of the lag in a model with discrete time intervals and the degree of quadraticity of adjustment costs, b. Note that as $b \to 0$ (adjustment costs disappear), $\kappa \to \infty$. For the factorization to hold, μ must approach infinity; if it does, λ must approach zero. But if $b \to 0$, we are left with a solution to the Euler equation that has L_t depending only on w_t and $\bar{\alpha}_0 + \alpha_{0,t}$, the current realization of the shock to productivity. This is sensible, since the absence of adjustment costs should make labor demand in the current period independent of any past or future conditions. In that one special case how the firm forms expectations is irrelevant. Note too that this argument shows that the lag parameter is positively related to the curvature of the function relating the costs of adjustment to $L_t - L_{t-1}$.

The explicit solutions of the Euler equations (6.3') could have been offered in Subsection A had I made the same restrictive assumptions about production. What is novel is that they show explicitly how expectations enter into the firm's optimizing decision. If we were to assume static expectations, for example, the right-hand side of (6.4') would contain terms only in current w and α_0 no matter what the value of λ is. That would imply adjustment exactly as in (6.5). With the more general assumption that expectations of w_{t+j} and $\alpha_{0,t+j}$ are based on all information available to the employer through time t, estimating (6.4') requires specifying the process that generates these expectations. The major contribution of the literature on rational expectations in factor demand is to point out the need for basing such a specification on the stochastic processes that produce the shocks (in our formulation, to wages and productivity).

With great simplifying assumptions about these processes (6.4') can be converted into a form that is readily estimable and has very few data requirements. To see this, assume that the processes generating wage and productivity shocks are first-order autoregressions, with parameters ρ_w and ρ_α. Then the optimal forecasts of $\alpha_{0,t+j}$ and w_{t+j} are

$$E_t \alpha_{0,t+j} = \rho_\alpha^j \alpha_{0,t}$$

and

$$E_t w_{t+j} = \rho_w^j w_t ,$$

where for simplicity I now ignore the nonzero mean of the process generating the sequence of wages. Substituting in (6.4′) produces typical terms under the summation

$$\mu^{-j}[\rho_w^j w_t - \rho_\alpha^j \alpha_{0,t} - \bar{\alpha}_0].$$

The three infinite geometric series under the summation all converge (since each $\rho < 1$, and $\mu > 1$), so that (6.4′) can be rewritten as

$$L_t = \lambda L_{t-1} - \lambda b^{-1}\{w_t[1 - \rho_w/\mu]^{-1} - \alpha_{0,t}[1 - \rho_\alpha/\mu]^{-1} - \bar{\alpha}_0[1 - 1/\mu]^{-1}\}. \quad (6.4'')$$

This equation is completely observable. It solves the problem that the right-hand side of (6.4′) contains unobservable future values of the forcing variables. Note that (6.4″) uses no more data than an equation based on static expectations; but by specifying expectations explicitly, it provides a structural basis for estimating the optimizing dynamic path of labor demand that was missing from (6.5).

The processes generating w and α_0 will not usually be so simple. For example, if they were second-order autoregressions, (6.4″) would involve complex terms in w_t, w_{t-1}, and current and lagged productivity shocks. More generally, each will be based on a vector of current and past realizations of these variables and any others that provide information that is useful in predicting their paths. Assuming that expectations are formed as linear functions of the variables in this vector, we can write them as

$$E_t[w_{t+j} - \alpha_{0,t+j}] = \sum_{n=0}^{N} \psi_{nj} X_{t-n}, \quad (6.15)$$

where the ψ_{nj} are vectors of parameters, and N is the most distant past time period whose realizations of the exogenous variable(s) X add to the useful information available to the employer at time t. This means that we can write the empirical analogue to (6.5) as

$$L_t = \lambda L_{t-1} + \sum_{n=0}^{N} \psi_n X_{t-n}, \quad (6.16)$$

where ψ_n is a vector of parameters combining the sequences ψ_{nj}, $j = 1, 2, \ldots$ Equation (6.16) seems to yield no additional insights into the path of the demand for labor. That is not quite so. With sufficient manipulations and the assumption of linear forecasts it allows one to estimate a structural model of adjustment under rational expectations (and the simplifying assumptions about the structure of production and adjustment costs).

Consider what rational expectations imply about the firm's response to a shock (to wages, product price, or whatever), compared to the case when there can be no shocks because the entire future of

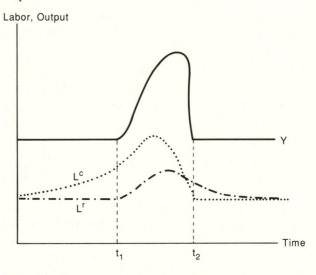

6.5 Demand Adjustment under Certainty or Rational
Expectations

these variables is certain. Complete knowledge of an impending
change in a forcing variable at some future time $t+j$ changes the entire previous path of L_t. The firm begins adjusting to the expected
future change long before it occurs. It can take advantage of its
knowledge of the change to increase the smoothing of its stock of
employment so as to increase profits. Once certainty is abandoned
this is not possible. The firm cannot preadjust to shocks (to unexpected changes in the forcing variables), so that the existence of adjustment costs leads it to forego some changes in labor demand that
would have raised its profits in response to the shock.

In Figure 6.5 I assume that the sole determinant of the long-run
demand for labor is some variable Y, perhaps exogenous product demand. The solid line shows the path of Y. With perfect certainty
about future Y the employer begins adjusting (along the dotted line)
to the shock to Y that occurs between t_1 and t_2 as soon as the firm
comes into existence. The adjustment is greater as t_1 nears, for discounting increases the effect of the blip in Y as $t \rightarrow t_1$. It is not immediate, though, because of the existence of quadratic adjustment
costs. Under the more realistic case of rational formation of expectations about Y, the blip is truly unexpected. The employer becomes
convinced only slowly after t_1 that the path of Y has changed. In this
case labor demand adjusts along the dotted-dashed line L^r. It only

begins to respond once the shock has occurred. The slow erosion of the employer's belief that the shock will recur leads to slower adjustment of employment after t_2 than in the certainty case.

Aside from replacing the unrealistic polar assumptions of the previous subsections by the realistic assumption of rational expectations, this approach provides a fundamental contribution by linking theory to empirical work. It yields an explicit solution for labor demand in which the equilibrium is determined within the model. No longer does the firm adjust toward a target L^*; instead, L^* is part of the firm's optimization. It also adds a new insight into understanding cyclical movements in employment demand by demonstrating that the firm reacts differently to unexpected than to expected changes in the underlying determinants of labor demand. This suggests that if we can distinguish between these kinds of changes we will predict the path of employment better. That will increase our understanding of how labor productivity varies over time and of the microeconomic determinants of fluctuations in aggregate employment. Introducing rational expectations does not, though, change the qualitative conclusions about sticky adjustment under quadratic costs. Adjustment is still smooth and slow.

The other examples of adjustment costs that I have analyzed under the assumption of static expectations can be modified in ways similar to the treatment of the quadratic case, though no explicit solutions are possible. The qualitative conclusions remain the same. The only difference is that, as with the quadratic case, distinguishing between expected and unexpected changes in the determinants of labor demand enhances the ability to predict variations in employment.

The models in this section clearly demonstrate the ways that employers' optimizing behavior can generate sticky employment. The diversity of the models allows for testing alternative structures that in turn might be used to analyze labor-market policies and perhaps even predict their impacts. Abandoning the assumption that employers have static expectations or complete certainty about all future developments allows one to distinguish stickiness of expectations from stickiness due to adjustment costs, and thus eventually to obtain better estimates of those costs.

IV. Adjusting the Demand for Employment and Hours

The discussion thus far has been technical, quite precise but very abstracted from the variety of possibilities available to the typical firm when its labor demand is shocked. In this section I allow homogeneous labor to have two dimensions, employment and hours, and I explore how this expands the firm's choices and generates a more flexible response to shocks. The chief issues are how and why the paths of employment and hours differ, and how these differences link back to explaining cyclical variations in labor productivity.

Consider again the typology of labor costs in Figure 2.2. A demand shock can be met by increasing employment or increasing hours of current employees. Whether a shock is temporary or permanent, the latter response generates costs per hour that at most equal the overtime wage rate (ignoring any effects on productivity, which I deal with below). Changing employment always generates adjustment costs, the fixed onetime costs in the figure. If the shock is permanent—if we are comparing long-run equilibria—changing employment will be the profit-maximizing response (following the assumption in Chapter 2 that the demand for hours is invariant to scale). But if the shock is temporary, those costs must be amortized very quickly, and changing hours will be a more attractive option. It is thus the permanence of the shock, as well as the relative costs of workers and hours and the breakdown into lumpy and divisible onetime fixed costs, that determines how employers respond.

A. Optimal Adjustment of Hours and Employment

The basis of the discussion in the previous section was the analytical solution (though under fairly restrictive conditions) of models of adjustment. In most of the literature on the dynamic demand for workers and hours such analysis is absent. Thus, the seminal studies of Oi (1962) and Rosen (1968) discuss informally, though highly insightfully, the choices facing a firm confronted by a temporary change in demand. Feldstein (1967) discusses at length the differences between workers and hours, but does not deal at all with issues of dynamics. Nadiri and Rosen (1973) recognize the interrelation between the lags in adjustment of employment and hours by specifying their paths as generalizations of the geometric adjustment derived for the case of quadratic costs and static expectations in (6.4). Hart (1987) repeats this formulation, as does the macroeconometric literature that has grown up since Nadiri and Rosen. Brechling (1975) formally models adjustment, but not in the context of the adjustment of employment and hours. Only Santamäki (1988) derives optimal paths of adjustment of employment and hours. The reason for this absence is clear: The models are extremely messy and yield no additional insight beyond what can be gathered from considering how rational actors respond to the existence of another margin in the models of Section III.

Following Chapter 2, assume that the employer takes all labor costs as given, and that a wage premium is required on hours worked beyond the standard workweek H_s. I assume throughout this section that there are no one-time costs of adjusting hours per worker. Consider how the firm responds to a temporary shock. If workers are employed H^* hours per week, $H^* < H_s$, the cost of an extra hour of work is wE^*, where E^* is the equilibrium employment before the shock. The additional employment needed to generate an equal increase in labor services is $\frac{E^*}{H^*}$.[9] Assuming there is no voluntary turnover, the total cost of these services is $E^*[w + \delta C\left(\frac{E^*}{H^*}\right)]$, where δ is

the rate at which the firm expects to amortize these fixed costs over the worker's tenure, and C are the costs of adjusting employment. This cost is clearly greater than the cost of adding an hour of work. If the firm need not pay an overtime premium, and if an additional hour worked by current employees is as productive as the average hour worked, no employer will respond to a shock by adding workers.[10] Adding hours is always preferred, and the problem is not very interesting.

The more interesting case arises if (homogeneous) workers already are employed at least H_s hours. For simplicity of exposition assume they work exactly H_s hours before the shock occurs, and assume too that the required overtime premium is 50 percent. Assuming again that there is no difference between the productivity of an additional hour and the productivity of the average hour worked by a new, fully trained worker, the relevant cost comparison is

$$1.5 \gtreqqless 1 + \frac{\delta}{w} C\left(\frac{E^*}{H^*}\right). \tag{6.17}$$

Whether the firm adjusts employment, hours, or both, and the path of that adjustment, depends on this comparison, in particular on the size of δ and C relative to the overtime premium. If the firm adjusts employment, the shape of C determines the path of adjustment (as it did in Section III). The path of adjustment of hours will in turn be affected by the rate at which employment is altered.

Consider the simplest case, in which the employer has perfect fore-

[9] This assumes that the production function for labor services is $L = EH$, which is clearly incorrect and inconsistent with the discussion in Chapter 2. It is a useful approximation, though. I return to the problem later in this section.

[10] For the United States there is some evidence (Hamermesh 1990b) that adding an extra hour of work to the schedule of the average worker does not reduce the worker's average productivity per hour.

sight about the entire path of product demand (and of prices and wages). In the case of quadratic costs of adjusting employment, it always pays the employer to *alter employment* as L^* changes, even if the shock is brief. $C'(\Delta E) \to 0$ as $\Delta E \to 0$, so that some change in employment will raise profits more than changing work schedules will. That $C'' > 0$ ensures that the adjustment of employment will be smooth and slow. The employer will always be changing employment, and may be changing employment and adding hours as well. Hours will adjust relatively more than employment the greater is C''—the greater the gain to spreading the adjustment of employment. The employer will rely more on changing hours the larger is δ—the shorter the duration of the shock, the higher the employer's rate of time preference and the shorter the worker's expected tenure in the firm.

In the case of lumpy adjustment costs k, the optimal response to a shock may be to do nothing if the shock is small and brief. The potential profits from responding to the shock may be less than δk, so that adding employees is an inferior strategy. Changing hours may also be inferior because the (premium) cost of an extra hour may exceed the gains in static profits that would be reaped. As in Section III, once the assumption of quadratic adjustment costs is abandoned, other structures of adjustment costs introduce a wedge between desired and equilibrium employment demand. The existence of a premium wage for overtime work introduces a wedge in the adjustment of hours if all employees must work the same hours per week. Three regimes, the probability of whose occurrence is linked to the size and permanence of the shock, are possible: (1) no changes in E or H; (2) H changes; and (3) E changes. Changes in E will be discrete and will not occur in every time period. The demand for hours may change each period, though, since there are no onetime costs of changing hours.

The employer's optimal response under lumpy fixed adjustment costs hints at the response when the costs of hiring and firing are linear (Santamäki 1988). As in the second subsection of Section III, firms are either holding employment constant (at the tops and bottoms of the cycle) or are varying employment (see Figure 6.4). The existence of another margin—hours—affords employers the opportunity to reap additional profits during booms and troughs by changing hours when it is not profitable to alter employment. The firm will either be: (1) holding employment constant and increasing H by demanding overtime hours; (2) varying employment but not using overtime hours; or (3) holding employment constant and cutting hours. The shorter the blips in L^*, the more the firm will rely on changing hours to meet the shocks, as implied by (6.17). Voluntary turnover and greater impatience by employers produce a similar reliance on variations in hours (and similar longer periods of unchanged employment).

None of these models differs qualitatively from those of Section III. They do point up, though, the importance of the term δ in (6.17). Its importance is made clearer when we abandon the assumptions of static expectations or perfect forecasting and assume, at the most, that employers have rational expectations about the path of demand. Deriving the rational-expectations equilibrium for a fully specified hours-employment model under the same restrictive assumptions as in Section III is fairly straightforward (and has been done by Sargent 1978 and many others).

The process of adjustment described above was made insightfully clear by Rosen (1968, 518):

> Suppose there is a permanent change in output that leads to a corresponding change in manhours employed in an occupation. Initially, most of the output change will be considered temporary and the firm will adjust to the situation by varying hours per man relatively more than employment. The cumulation of experience will lead the firm to view more and more of the change as permanent and hours will be readjusted toward their "normal" level and the level of employment will be changed.

To add just a bit to this description, consider the typical firm depicted in Figure 6.6. It has had no demand shocks for a very long time. It has therefore set employment at the profit-maximizing level for the expected output and factor prices, and has set hours at the long-run rate dictated by the relative prices of hours and workers and by their relative productivity. At t_1 a series of shocks to an underlying determinant of demand, Y, occurs. Initially the shocks are viewed as ephemeral, so that δ is perceived to be so high that adding more workers is not justified. Instead, the employer will increase the hours of existing employees. As the shocks persist, the perceived δ decreases, and the firm begins adjusting employment. (In Figure 6.6 I assume there are quadratic costs of adjustment.) When the blip in product demand begins to subside, employers still expect the shocks to continue, so they continue expanding employment. Soon, though, they begin to realize that the shocks are subsiding. Their initial response is to cut the demand for hours back toward normal hours, as that generates no costs of adjustment, but eventually they reduce employment too. In sum, absent any regulations that alter the incentives, the peak in hours precedes that in employment and represents a greater relative change.

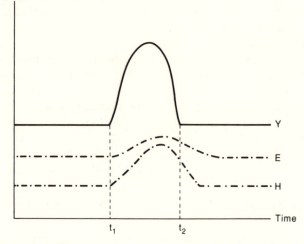

Employment, Hours, Output

6.6 Hours and Employment Adjustment under Rational Expectations

An important prediction of the theory of dynamic labor demand is implicit in this discussion: The demand for employment and hours will lag behind the shocks that determine their levels. The lag will be greater for employment than for hours and will be greater the larger are adjustment costs (the fixed one-time costs of employment), and the slower employers are to alter their expectations about product demand and input prices. The theory also implies that we will observe greater variations in hours than in employment, which is far from universally true. I deal with this apparent failure of the theory in Section VI.

B. Indivisibilities, Labor Hoarding, and Part-time Work

The entire discussion has assumed that hours and workers are infinitely divisible (or, what amounts to the same thing, that the typical firm is big enough that even small shocks can be profitably met by discrete changes in hours or employment). While the typical modern economy is so large that one need not be concerned about indivisibilities at the aggregate level, many firms are so small that these become important. One problem is easy to analyze. In a small firm experiencing a relatively small positive shock, hiring an extra employee may reduce profits, even ignoring the adjustment costs that are incurred. If workers are homogeneous and must work the same hours, an increase in hours may be inferior to doing nothing. If some worker(s) can be assigned overtime while others are not, or if all can work a small amount of overtime, this indivisibility can be overcome: A very small change in total hours can be made and profits can be increased. This type of indivisibility is yet another reason why shocks that are small, or are perceived as ephemeral, will lead to adjustments of hours rather than employment.

The need to use fixed capital at a given rate along with workers on shifts of fixed length can produce a different kind of short-run indivisibility. Assume that a plant that is running two eight-hour shifts per day experiences a positive shock. Unless the shock is sufficiently large, it is unprofitable to add another shift, so that hours cannot be adjusted. Adding employees may also not be profitable, for the capital might have to be used in fixed proportions with workers. This particular configuration of capital—the short-run fixity coupled with the fixed proportions—can mean that neither hours nor employment will respond to fairly large demand shocks. Only when the shock is sufficiently large will hours, or more likely employment, adjust. This will produce a path just like that in Figure 6.2. In this case, the lumpy adjustment stems from the nature of production technology.

Can such a firm circumvent this indivisibility to increase its profits? If the technology permits it, if the fixity involves worker-hours rather than intensity of work, the employer might induce workers to increase their effort. Even beyond the problems occasioned by indivisibilities, variations in effort must be a major cause of variations in output per worker-hour.[11]

Another way to deal with indivisibilities is to consider the notion of temporary part-time work—putting part or all of one's work force on a part-time schedule in response to a negative demand shock. In the United States the structure of the unemployment insurance system produces substantial incentives against doing this.[12] Nonetheless, employers do increase their use of part-time schedules during downturns. Consider the data in Table 6.1. In the recession years 1975 and 1982 more use was made of involuntary part-time work, and a larger fraction of part-timers were working part-time involuntarily, than in the subsequent peak years, 1979 and 1989. Still other

[11] The only alternative to this explanation derives from problems of measurement. Output per worker-hour is Y/EH; yet in the short run $Y = (K^*, L(E, H))$, where K^* is the fixed input of capital. The structure of the labor aggregator $L(E, H)$ may induce the firm to respond optimally to fluctuations in product demand by changing E and H in ways that depart from the values that maximize Y/EH.

[12] See, for example, Munts (1970).

TABLE 6.1
Cyclical Variations in Aspects of Part-time Work, United States, 1975–89

	Year			
	1975	1979	1982	1989
	Trough	Peak	Trough	Peak
Involuntary part-time employment (percent of all full-time workers)	5.6	4.4	8.1	5.3
Involuntary part-time employment (percent of all part-time employment)	24.9	19.1	32.0	23.7

Source: *Employment and Earnings*, January issues, 1976, 1980, 1983, and 1990.

possible responses to indivisibilities are subcontracting temporarily heavy workloads out and hiring temporary workers.

Since the employer must still bear the continuing fixed costs of employment, why not avoid them by laying off enough workers to keep the hours of the remaining workers at their usual rate? One answer ties into the discussion in the previous section: With uncertainty about the duration of the negative demand shock, the employer wishes to avoid the cost of firing experienced workers and then having to incur the cost of hiring new workers shortly thereafter. These one-time costs may outweigh the continuing fixed costs of employing part-time workers. A second answer is that it may be very costly in the short run to depart from using workers in fixed proportions with capital and from using the entire stock of plant and equipment.

V. Adjustment with Several Factors of Production

A. The General Model with Various Structures of Adjustment Costs and Expectations

The basic theory of adjustment with quadratic costs and static expectations that gave explicit paths of labor demand in Section III can be generalized to multiple factors, for example, labor and capital, or several types of labor (Lucas 1967). The multivariate analogue to (6.4) is

$$\dot{Z}_t = \Gamma[Z^* - Z_t], \qquad (6.18)$$

where Z is a vector of the N quasi-fixed inputs, Z^* is the vector of their targets, and Γ is an $N \times N$ matrix of adjustment parameters. The only novel result from making this generalization is that it becomes possible for disequilibria in the adjustment of the demand for one input to affect the path of adjustment of other inputs.

We can follow Nadiri and Rosen (1973) and write the general adjustment model (6.18) in discrete time as

$$Z_{it} = \lambda_{ii}Z_{it-1} + \sum_{k \neq i} \lambda_{ik}Z_{k,t-1} + \beta_i X_t, \, i = 1, \ldots, K, \qquad (6.19)$$

where the λ_{ik} are adjustment parameters, and each β_i is a vector of parameters linking variables in the vector X to the long-run equilibrium value of Z_i. The economic issue of interest here is the dynamic equivalent of the notion of p-substitution. In terms of the system of equations (6.19) the inputs i and k are *dynamic p-complements* if $\lambda_{ik} > 0$, and are *dynamic p-substitutes* if $\lambda_{ik} < 0$. If two inputs are dynamic p-complements, a greater disequilibrium in the demand for one factor slows adjustment of the demand for the other. If they are dynamic p-substitutes, when the demand for one input adjusts more slowly, the adjustment of demand for the other input is speeded up. There is no theoretical basis for expecting any particular sign of any of the λ_{ik} involving inputs of labor, though one would expect that $\lambda_{ik} = \lambda_{ki}$, that is, that input demands are dynamically symmetric.

This general model has been applied to the interrelated adjustment of various combinations of inputs. In each case the central items of interest should be the off-diagonal terms, the λ_{ik} in (6.19). If these are zero, an empirical researcher will learn just as much from equations like (6.5) separately for each variable (or jointly as part of a system of own-adjustment equations) as from this system.

If one abandons static expectations and specifies that the firm maximizes profits using rational expectations of future prices under quadratic adjustment costs and a quadratic production function, one can derive a multivariate analogue to equation (6.16) (see Meese 1980). As in Section III, rational expectations along with specific assumptions about the nature of the processes that generate the forcing variables allow estimation of a structural model. If one is unwilling to make these assumptions, one can derive an empirical version of (6.16), which looks just like (6.19) but for the addition of terms in the vectors of variables $X_{t-1}, X_{t-2} \ldots X_{t-N}$. As in Section III, all lagged values of the variables in the vector X that provide additional information about the processes generating the forcing variables belong in the equation.

Thus far in this section I have assumed that all factors are quasi-fixed. Assume for the moment that there are (quadratic) costs of adjusting the other factors Z_i, but that there are no costs of adjusting the demand for worker-hours. Then under static expectations about future prices and wages the firm's optimum paths for its inputs are described by the system of differential equations (6.18) for nonlabor inputs and

$$F'(L_t) = w. \tag{6.20}$$

Equation (6.20) looks like a standard static marginal productivity condition, and it is. It is not, though, the same static profit-maximizing condition as (2.5b), for the other factors of production, which are costly to vary, are not employed at their long-run profit-maximizing rates once a shock has occurred.

Consider the case with only capital and labor, with adjustment costs only on the former. Assume there is a one-time, permanent negative shock to product prices (decline in product demand). The employer will adjust the capital stock downward slowly by letting net investment be negative. Because of the stickiness in the adjustment of capital, the marginal revenue product of labor at the new price will be greater than it would be if capital were also a variable input. The demand for labor would not be cut instantly to the new, lower long-run profit-maximizing level, but would instead decrease over time as the input of capital is decreased.

This conclusion contains important implications for estimating equations like (6.5) or (6.19). Though the optimal path of labor demand in this case is not characterized by any costs of adjusting labor, the costs of adjusting capital will generate observations on the demand for labor that lag behind the values of X_t. Though the path of labor demand will not be (6.5), estimating such an equation will indicate that there are lags in adjusting labor demand. Estimates of a system like (6.19) will indicate that labor and capital are dynamic p-complements. These inferences have no basis in adjustment costs for labor; but the estimates will suggest that such costs exist. Moreover, the lags will be greater the larger are the costs of adjusting investment and the greater is the quadraticity of these costs. In short, we cannot infer from estimates of equations like (6.5), or from their rational-expectations counterparts (6.16), that there really are costs of adjusting labor demand, or what their sources are. Of course, the same argument applies in reverse to inferring the costs of adjusting the capital stock. Indeed, unless one specifies a model involving all inputs into production and allows for the possibility that each is quasi-fixed, one cannot determine the source of the apparent stickiness in the demand for any factors of production.

Abandoning the assumption of quadratic adjustment costs does not qualitatively change the conclusions of this section. Explicit solutions are very messy even with static expectations and are not available with rational expectations. With several quasi-fixed inputs characterized by lumpy adjustment costs, though, discrete adjustment of one input will affect the likelihood that another quasi-fixed input will jump to its new long-run equilibrium value. Similarly, lumpy adjustment costs will lead to discrete adjustment of a variable factor, as the marginal revenue product of the latter changes discretely when the input of the quasi-fixed factor is changed discretely. The results under lumpy one-time costs of adjustment match those under smooth one-time costs, except that they generate simultaneous discrete changes in the inputs instead of smooth changes.

B. Heterogeneous Labor

I have said nothing specific about the simultaneous adjustment of several types of labor—there has been no mention of a dynamic analogue to the substitution among types of heterogeneous workers discussed in Chapter 2. The reason is that there is little need for a specific discussion of this issue. Equations (6.18) and (6.19) apply equally well to the adjustment of, for example, skilled and unskilled workers as to capital and labor. Thus, the lag in adjusting a particular type of labor should be greater if its variable adjustment costs are more quadratic or if they are greater and employers are uncertain about the length of shocks. Similarly, the shock necessary to cause employers to change the input of one type of labor will be greater the greater are the lumpy one-time costs of adjusting the demand for that type of worker. Finally, as in the general case, stickiness in adjusting employment of one group will spill over into adjustment of the demand for other groups of workers, with the possibility that any pair of types of labor are dynamic p-substitutes or p-complements.

VI. IMPLICIT CONTRACTS, TEMPORARY LAYOFFS, AND OTHER MARGINS

Previous sections treated the dynamic demand for inputs as determined solely by technology, employers' expectations, and shocks to *exogenous* wages, prices, and output demand. This allowed a clear delineation of how different types of adjustment costs and different assumptions about expectations affect the path of employment demand. It also enabled me to focus on the dynamic interactions in the demand for several inputs. It is unlikely, though, that the path of wages is unaffected by these dynamics; and the feedback of wages to employment means that the former should be considered endogenous if we wish to explain factor-demand dynamics better. One of the two purposes of this section is to examine the implications for dynamic labor demand of treating wages as endogenous. As part of this I examine how the conclusions are modified by making alternative assumptions about the structure of adjustment costs.

Another difficulty is that the discussions of Sections III through V treated employment changes as resulting entirely from hires, quits, and fires. These last were implicitly viewed as permanent layoffs, workers separating from the firm with no chance of reemployment. Similarly, all hires were implicitly workers with no previous experience with the employer. Both implicit assumptions are incorrect: Establishment data for U.S. manufacturing in 1981 (the last year for which such data were collected) show that the rehire rate was 1.0 percent per month, while the rate of layoffs averaged 1.6 per month.[13] Household data for 1973–76 show that 41 percent of job leavers were on a layoff they believed to be temporary (Topel 1982). To understand the dynamics of labor demand, we need to account for the distinctions between permanent separations and temporary layoffs, and between new hires and recalls.

The costs of these different sources of separations and accessions differ, so that employers rely on one or the other depending on the nature of the underlying causes of the change in labor demand. Permanent layoffs generate higher costs, since severance pay beyond unemployment benefits may have to be offered, and any firm-specific human capital in whose investment the employer has shared is destroyed. These investments may also be lost should a temporary layoff find work elsewhere, and the temporary layoff also generates unemployment benefits. These differences in costs affect the path of employment and its apparent responsiveness to shocks to labor demand.

Assume hours per worker are fixed and output cannot be stored for future sale (there are no inventories of finished goods). The firm has a permanent work force L_t attached to it, though some workers may be on temporary layoff. Just as in Section III.B, $h_t L_t$ additional workers are added to the permanent work force at a onetime cost per new hire of a_1; $f_t L_t$ workers are fired from the work force at a cost per fire of a_2. Each period some fraction u_t, $0 \le u_t < 1$, of the permanent work force is on temporary layoff. The crucial assumption is that the firm incurs no one-time costs from altering the fraction u_t. This distinguishes temporary from permanent layoffs. While we saw that this is not entirely correct, it captures the direction of the difference between the two types of "involuntary" separations.

At each point a permanent employee can expect to receive a certain

---

[13] *Employment and Earnings*, March 1982, p. 109.

income of V per period in other firms. Ignoring workers' risk aversion, and setting the model in discrete time, this means that a worker with rational expectations expects an income Y_t such that

$$E_{t-1}(Y_t) \geq V/r, \tag{6.21}$$

or, more generally,

$$E_{t-1}\sum_{\tau=t}^{\infty} R^{\tau-t}\{[1 - u_\tau]w_\tau + u_\tau B\} \geq V/r, \tag{6.21'}$$

where B is the unemployment benefit per period (assumed costless to the employer), and I assume that the probability of being on temporary layoff, u_t, is the same for all workers. We can thus deal with a typical worker.

The employer wishes to maximize expected future profits:

$$E_{t-1}\sum_{\tau=t}^{\infty} R^{\tau-t}\{P_\tau F([1 - u_\tau]L_\tau) - w_\tau[1 - u_\tau]L_\tau - a_1 h_\tau L_\tau - a_2 f_\tau L_\tau\}. \tag{6.22}$$

In order to retain the permanent work force, though, (6.22) must be maximized subject to the weak inequality in (6.21'), lest the typical permanent employee quit the employer and take the certain income elsewhere. Assume for simplicity that (6.21') holds as an equality, which will be true under competition. In each period the employer must choose h_t and f_t, and thus its permanent work force L_t (since it "inherits" L_{t-1} workers from the previous period). It must also choose the fraction of the work force to have on temporary layoff, as well as the wage rate.[14] The only exogenous variables are B and V, though one should also view changes in P_t as exogenous shifts in product demand that are then processed through employers' expectations.

The constraint on employers' behavior means, for example, that any shock that causes the employer to raise u_t must for at least some $\tau \geq t$ increase the wages workers receive. The cost of a layoff is thus the higher wages needed to maintain the contract—to retain the firm's permanent work force. Workers remain with the firm, even though on temporary layoff for part of the time, because the alternative is less attractive. The employer gains by avoiding incurring the one-time costs of hiring and firing (of changing the permanent work force).

The firm's optimal plan under (6.21') and (6.22) cannot be characterized explicitly, though that can be done if the model is reduced to two periods. We can, though, characterize behavior generally in re-

---

[14] The model is a hybrid that stems from the early work of Feldstein (1976) and Baily (1977) (and the basic models of implicit contracts of Baily 1974 and Azariadis 1975). It is a simplified version of the model of Haltiwanger and Maccini (1990).

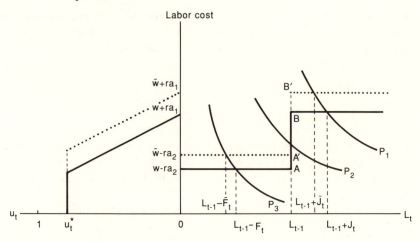

6.7 Temporary Layoffs, Hiring, and Firing

sponse to shocks of various sizes to P_t. Figure 6.7 illustrates the firm's responses to changes in P_t and V. In this graph J_t is the number of workers hired, and F_t is the number permanently laid off. The curves in the right quadrant are the equivalent of demand schedules. Consider first the cost structure that implies movements along the solid lines. In the left quadrant of the figure these illustrate the optimizing path of u_t as demand shocks occur. In the right quadrant they show the path of employment. I assume any induced changes in wages occur at $\tau > t$, so that I treat w as constant.

For high price levels, P_1, the firm expands employment by adding J_t workers to the permanent work force; their marginal revenue products exceed $w + ra_1$. As the demand shock becomes less positive—P_t shifts left from point B, for example to P_2—the firm begins laying off workers temporarily in an amount shown by u_t. It does not fire them, because their expected marginal revenue product exceeds $w - ra_2$. There is a large range of price shocks covering the vertical distance AB over which increasingly bad news—further decreases in P—just increases the fraction of the work force on temporary layoff. With low enough prices, say P_3, additional layoffs cease with a fraction u_t^* of the work force on layoff. The expected marginal revenue product is so low that it pays the firm to bear the cost of firing some of its permanent workers, decreasing its work force by F_t. If we were to draw the figure for period $t+1$, L_{t-1} would have shifted accordingly. With no change in the price shock between periods t and $t+1$, the firm would be setting $L_{t+1} = L_t$ and would set $u_{t+1} = u_t$.

What if something raises the right side of (6.21')? Assume for simplicity that this change is reflected initially entirely in the payment of a higher wage, say $\tilde{w}$. This generates an upward shift in the per-worker costs necessary to justify hiring or firing, so that the dotted lines in Figure 6.7 now form the basis for the firm's calculation. The same price shock now produces less hiring, a greater fraction of the work force on temporary layoff, or more firing.

In this model temporary layoffs are the source of endogeneity in wages. The model could be generalized to make the value of the contract also depend on the risk of permanent layoff. In a sense the model implicitly does that, for one of the costs of firing might be an increase in the compensating wage differential to workers who perceive that the probability of the contract being terminated rises with the rate of firing. Alternatively, the contract might depend explicitly on the risk of permanent layoff, with V viewed as the income stream offered on an alternative, riskless job. The solution to the model would be altered, with permanent layoffs being made later as P decreases, and with more reliance on temporary layoffs. With these respecifications, though, the same sequence of employer behavior, along with the endogeneity of wages, could be reproduced.

The firm will respond differently depending on its perceptions of the permanence of a price or cost shock. Take the extreme cases of a large negative price shock that employers and workers believe will last one period, and one that all expect to persist indefinitely. In the former case employers can raise u_t with at most a very small increase in wages for some $\tau \geq t$. This maintains the workers' implicit contract more profitably than firing people from the permanent work force. With a negative price shock that is perceived to be permanent the cost of relying entirely on temporary layoffs is raised by the large increase in wages necessary to prevent workers from leaving the firm's work force. Firing workers may be a more profitable option, since it allows the firm to maintain production without raising (current or future) wages, though the firm must bear the firing costs.

The model in (6.22) includes linear costs of hiring and firing. If instead there are lumpy one-time costs, the basic conclusions are not changed greatly. The main difference is that hiring to and firing from the permanent work force is done discretely. There will be longer sequences of temporary layoffs in response to the same set of shocks than under linear adjustment costs. At some sufficiently large (or more permanent) negative shock the firm will fire workers, but it will fire masses of workers at once (to minimize the burden of the lumpy costs). Obversely, it will recall temporary layoffs until u is zero, then forego some profits until it is fairly sure that hiring a large group of new permanent employees justifies bearing the one-time cost of hiring. The assumption of lumpy one-time costs in a world of implicit contracts leads to temporary layoffs proceeding continuously, while permanent layoffs, when they occur, are massive. Similarly, the firm only hires new workers in large groups.

The model of (6.21') and (6.22) can be expanded to allow for yet another margin of operation, hours worked. This reformulation, like that in Section IV, implicitly ignores costs of adjusting hours. With the worker's contract constraint specified solely in income terms, adding hours to the model adds little of interest. Like temporary layoffs, hours are just another margin that the employer can use in response to small and/or temporary negative demand shocks. Introducing hours in this way does not add to our understanding of employment dynamics.

Assume instead that the representative worker maximizes an expected utility function with the usual alternating-sign derivatives defined over income and leisure. Then the contract constraint becomes

$$E_{t-1}\sum_{\tau=t}^{\infty} R^{\tau-t}\{[1 - u_\tau]U(w_\tau H_\tau, T - H_\tau) +$$

$$u_\tau U(B,T)\} \geq U(V, T - \bar{H})/r, \quad (6.21'')$$

where T is the total available hours per time period and $\bar{H}$ are hours worked in the sector that provides the certain income. Equation (6.21'') is essentially a dynamic version of (2.59). Under this more realistic assumption a small decline in hours per worker produces a small reduction in expected utility for each worker. Assuming $U(w_t H_t, T - H_t) > U(B,T)$, a temporary layoff that reduces the wage bill by the same amount generates the risk (with probability u_t) that expected utility will fall by more. The employer can maintain the constraint and reap higher profits by reducing hours for all workers before temporarily laying off part of the work force. Temporary layoffs eventually become more profitable than continuing reductions in hours, as additional cuts in hours lower the utility of the typical member of the permanent work force by more than would a temporary layoff.

The exact point at which it pays the firm to switch to temporary layoffs will also depend on the structure of production. The extension in (6.21'') rationalizes reductions in hours as the first response to negative shocks, with temporary and then permanent layoffs responding more slowly. It thus provides an explanation that is consistent with profit and utility maximization for the ad hoc imposition of greater adjustment costs for employment changes than for changes in hours.

In this discussion I have assumed that all workers are identical, and that each faces the same probability of being placed on temporary layoff. This assumption produces the formulation of the problem as one of the employer maximizing profits subject to the constraint that the *representative worker's* income (utility in the formulation that includes hours and leisure) exceeds some level. In unionized plants layoffs are usually regulated by inverse seniority; and even in non-union plants inverse seniority may make the assumption of randomness that is implicit in (6.21″) irrelevant (Abraham and Medoff 1985). Assume that the tastes of the median worker determine employers' wage decisions, either because the median worker is the median voter in a unionized plant or because of some sort of solidarity among workers in a nonunion setting. Then constraint (6.21″) must be replaced by one based on the utility of that worker. If the employer reduces hours, the median worker is made worse off and requires a current or future wage increase to remain with the firm. If the negative demand shock is not too large, temporarily laying off junior workers generates the same reduction in worker-hours but has no effect on the utility of the median worker (Wright 1986). In that case temporary layoffs need not follow hours reductions.

The sequence of responses to demand shocks that was outlined above will be modified if temporary layoffs are nonrandom. Reductions in hours may not be made if the shock is small enough that there is no cost to the employer (in future wages) of using temporary layoffs of junior workers. This possibility may be what produces the failure to observe greater cyclical fluctuations in hours than in employment.

Yet another margin that can cushion the response to shocks to product demand is the inventory decisions of the firm. If output can be stored (at some cost), how employment responds to shocks depends on the costs of holding additional inventories compared to the costs of temporary or permanent layoffs. Modeling the firm's inventory decision makes the problem implied by (6.21′) and (6.22) still more complex and solvable only with still more simplifying assumptions. If, though, storage costs are relatively low, and the firm believes that the shocks are quite temporary, accumulating inventories may be its profit-maximizing response. It is sensible to treat the level of inventories of final goods as part of a dynamic system that also determines the demand for hours, employees, and capital goods, and to expect that employers will rely on layoffs more heavily in those industries where goods are not easily storable (Nadiri and Rosen 1973).

All of the models in this chapter develop the employer's side of decision-making in great detail. That is appropriate; our interest is, after all, in the demand for labor. Once one begins to include contracting, though, it becomes appropriate to develop the supply side and the workers' contracting constraint in more than the rudimentary way of (6.21) and its variants. A very simple extension postulates that workers have rational expectations about the future path of earnings. In that case the term V/r in (6.21') would be replaced by

$E_{t-1} \sum_{\tau=t}^{\infty} R^{\tau-t} V_\tau$. Then the information that enters into workers' and employers' forecasts of future values of V affects the outcome of the contracting problem under rational expectations (Card 1986). If, for example, a huge influx of skilled immigrants occurs at time $t-1$, skilled workers and their employers will expect future alternative wages to be on a lower path than they expected before $t-1$. The new information conditions expectations about the future path of V. The history of V is thus a determinant of the current contract values of wages, employment, hours, and the fraction of workers on temporary layoff.

A more complex extension would treat the demand and supply sides in a symmetric fashion by incorporating adjustment costs in labor supply that are analogous to adjustment costs in demand.[15] This essentially means generalizing the contract constraint (6.21') to include the worker's rational expectations about all future values. With the worker maximizing lifetime utility, employment and wage outcomes become functions of workers' tastes for leisure and income, both at a point in time and intertemporally, as well as of the technological parameters that determined the outcomes in the model of (6.21') and (6.22).

VII. Effort, Productivity, and Demand Shocks

A major reason for studying dynamic labor demand is to explain procyclical fluctuations in labor productivity. Yet none of the discussion thus far does so satisfactorily. Labor hoarding must reflect fluctuations in effort per worker-hour in the production of current output. Yet throughout the discussion all we have done is explain why there are lags in adjustment and how the adjustment depends on costs and expectations. No reason has been offered for the variation in effort over the cycle. Without that, we are left with the conundrum that the

---

[15] This merging of intertemporal choices on both sides of the market is in Kennan (1988). Including adjustment costs in labor supply makes the choice of the amount supplied a multiperiod problem. It is thus equivalent to including the intertemporal substitution in labor supply that underlies Lucas and Rapping's (1969) explanation of cyclical fluctuations in employment.

marginal productivity theory of demand implies *lower* productivity when employment rises (with a fixed stock of physical capital), though the facts show the opposite.

The notion of labor hoarding thus leads to the more basic question: Why does the employer tolerate inefficiency when product demand is low? A number of possibilities present themselves to explain this apparent departure from profit maximization: (1) Workers use their apparent leisure on the job to repair equipment, clean up the workplace, invest in their skills—in other words, to engage in activities that will raise output once product demand recovers. According to this view, productivity does not change cyclically; it is just not measured properly. (2) Perhaps more appealing, the workers enjoy their leisure, and it pays the employer to let them enjoy it because laying them off would lead to a greater reduction in profits. (3) Still more likely is this second explanation combined with an implicit contract that makes it optimal for the firm neither to lay off sufficient workers nor to reduce the hours of the remaining workers enough to hold output per worker-hour constant. Regardless of the cause, it is clear that labor hoarding cannot be explained by the slow adjustment of employment or hours alone. These are the result of some underlying behavior.

One way to rationalize labor hoarding is to let effort depend positively on the wage rate paid, and to assume that employers engage in monitoring to ensure that workers' efforts, which are costly to observe, do not fall below some acceptable minimum.[16] First assume that effort is either sufficient or not. In order to induce the worker to perform, the employer must pay a wage that makes performing more attractive than shirking. If the employer catches the worker goofing off, she fires him, and the worker must find a job elsewhere. When unemployment is high such jobs are difficult to find, and the expected duration of unemployment is longer. Thus, at high unemployment the wage needed to induce the worker to perform is relatively low, because the loss to the worker of getting caught shirking is substantial.

At lower unemployment employers must pay higher wages to induce workers to produce. Indeed, at very low unemployment the wage must approach infinity, as there is no cost to the worker of shirking. (If he is fired, he can find another, equally attractive job almost immediately.) The assumption that employers cannot police workers' efforts perfectly generates an upward-sloping relation, the

---

[16] The model is that of Shapiro and Stiglitz (1984). Attributing variations in effort to the effects of variations in wages along with shirking follows Akerlof and Yellen (1986b).

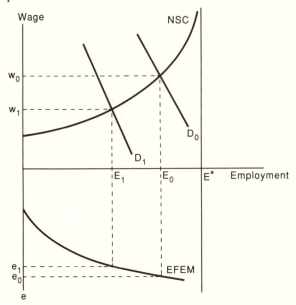

6.8 Cyclical Fluctuations in Effort under Efficiency
Wages and Shirking

no-shirking condition *NSC* in Figure 6.8, which relates the wage rate
and employment. Any wage on or above the *NSC* curve is sufficient
to elicit effort from the worker; and no profit-maximizing employer
will pay a wage above the curve. In Figure 6.8 E^* is full employment.
(The supply of labor to the market is assumed fixed.) In this model a
decline in aggregate demand, from D_0 to D_1, lowers the equilibrium
wage from w_0 to w_1: With the drop in demand the implicit contract
can be maintained at a lower wage rate.

Consider what happens if workers' efforts vary continuously with
wage rate. As before, employers will reduce wages as aggregate demand drops; but under this additional assumption the cut in wages
also reduces workers' efforts, which mitigates employers' incentives
for reducing wages. The relationship between the level of employment and effort is shown by the curve *EFEM* in Figure 6.8. With
lower employment (higher unemployment) the typical firm does not
need to pay so high a wage, and that lower wage reduces effort. The
size of the reduction in effort and wages depends on the interaction
between aggregate labor demand and the firm's choice of an optimal
wage-effort package.[17] In Figure 6.8, the negative demand shock re-

---

[17] In Figure 6.8 I ignore the fact that the shifts in the marginal product of labor that
underlie changes in the aggregate demand for labor depend on worker effort. As long

duces effort per worker from e_0 to e_1. The drop in effort is the worker's utility-maximizing response to the profit-maximizing, contract-maintaining behavior that leads employers to reduce wages when there are negative shocks to demand.

This model does not add to our understanding of the dynamics of factor demand; but it does solve the procyclical productivity conundrum that was one of the goals of analyzing dynamics. Procyclical variation in effort can result from the maximizing behavior of the typical worker and firm and from the technology that prevents employers from detecting shirking costlessly. While the reduction in worker-hours that occurs after a negative demand shock raises productivity per worker-hour *at a constant effort*, the shock reduces effort sufficiently to generate a net reduction in output per worker-hour.

Adding adjustment costs in labor demand to this model, and thus integrating the dynamics of factor demand into it, generates no major changes in the conclusions (Kimball 1989). It just produces lags in all the endogenous variables—wages, employment, and effort—with their relative sizes depending on the structure and size of adjustment costs, and the interactions of employment, wages, and effort in the firm's profit function. Similarly, adding in other margins, such as variations in hours, or the possibility that firms can accumulate inventories of final goods, does not alter the conclusion that effort will vary procyclically.

VIII. Conclusions, and Prospects for the Theory of Dynamic Labor Demand

This chapter illustrates the substantial progress that economists (few of them specialists in labor economics) have made in developing the dynamic theory of factor demand since 1960. The main advances have been in studying the implications of costs of adjustment, and different structures of those costs, for the observed paths of factor demand. A major success has been the integration of employers' expectations about the future paths of demand and cost shocks into models that include adjustment costs. These allow us to infer their separate effects on variations in labor demand. Also important has been the extension of the theory from one to several factors, in particular the analysis of interactions between the dynamic paths of several inputs. Despite these successes the theory cannot by itself achieve one of its goals, explaining cyclical variations in labor pro-

---

as the assumption about the effort-wage elasticity holds, shifts in D are in the direction shown in the figure.

ductivity. That requires appending a theory of procyclical variation in effort.

Nearly all of the theoretical developments have been based on the same set of highly restrictive assumptions about adjustment costs, namely that they are quadratic in the size of the per-period change in the amount of the input. This assumption was viewed as necessary to derive explicit solutions for the firm's decision rules. Imposing it, though, prevents one from thinking about the implications of alternative structures that may be just as satisfactory descriptions of the costs facing employers. That in turn prevents empirical research from investigating what the structure of adjustment costs looks like. Given the increased availability of techniques for obtaining solutions (albeit not analytical ones) to optimization problems under very complex sets of conditions, the assumption of smooth adjustment could be profitably abandoned. Doing so would enable researchers to study alternative implications of the interactions of adjustment costs and expectations, of the spillover effects of adjustment costs between multiple inputs, and of the interaction of these costs with variations in workers' effort.

As in the static theory of labor demand, there is a dearth of analysis that integrates the behavior of suppliers of labor into the dynamic theory of employment demand. Simply deriving paths of employment demand under the assumption that workers' utility must be maintained is only a first step in this integration. What is needed, and what the discussion in Section VII aims toward, is the inclusion of effort in the analysis of the effects of adjustment costs. How hard employees work may be modeled as a choice about labor supply, but it represents a choice about labor supply in the workplace rather than the usual margin between working and leaving the labor force. As such, it is as much an issue of demand, and it should be discussed along with the behavior resulting from costs of adjustment.

The entire discussion gets to a fundamental difficulty with the theoretical literature, a problem that is in sharp contrast to the static theory of factor demand. In the latter, as Chapter 2 made clear, the links between theory and empirical analysis are both explicit and close. In many cases fairly general estimating equations could be linked to the parameters underlying the structure of production. That is true here under rational or static expectations only if one makes very restrictive assumptions about the structure of both adjustment costs and production. Without them the link is fairly tenuous. Progress in narrowing the gulf between theoretical and empirical work would generate more rapid advances in our understanding of factor dynamics than any additional expansion of the theory *in vacuo*.

CHAPTER SEVEN

Estimates of the Dynamics of Employment and Hours

I. DYNAMIC ISSUES

The discussion in Chapter 6 raised questions that can only be resolved by examining empirical work on the dynamics of labor demand. As in Chapter 3, where I summarized the evidence on a variety of static issues, here too the evidence is mustered to infer a consensus about the sizes of the parameters of interest. As in that discussion, the purpose is aided by evaluating alternative approaches to generating parameter estimates, in particular, to issues of the appropriate kinds of data that should underlie the estimates.

One major issue in employment dynamics is the speed with which the demand for workers or worker-hours adjusts to price and quantity shocks. Every study of employment dynamics can be used to generate estimates of this, and thus allow us to infer the extent of changes in labor hoarding over the business cycle. Since the only way to evaluate the quality of the evidence on the issue is to compare studies, Section II tabulates the estimates using a typology similar to that used in Chapter 3. Examining differences in the speeds of adjustment of workers and hours also lends itself to consideration in this section.

We would like to know more than merely the speed of adjustment of the demand for homogeneous labor. For example, does the speed vary with the amount of skill embodied in workers? Are these and other differences reflected in international differences in adjustment paths? All of these questions deal with disaggregated demand dynamics and are considered in Section III.

In Section IV I examine the possibilities for linking estimated speeds of adjustment to the structure of the underlying adjustment costs to infer their sizes. More generally, I analyze the possibility of using evidence on employment dynamics to infer the structures themselves. As Chapter 6 showed, different hypotheses about these structures generate sharply differing adjustment paths; whether the available information suffices to discriminate among these hypotheses is central to discovering what the costs look like. Part of the discussion in Chapter 6 dealt with asymmetries in adjustment in response to positive and negative shocks. The evidence on these too is examined, with the goal of inferring its implications for the path of labor productivity over business cycles.

Chapter 3 did not discuss the effect of scale economies or diseconomies on labor demand, since this issue has been treated in empirical work partly as one of employment dynamics. In Section V I examine evidence on the elasticity of employment (or worker-hours) with respect to changes in product demand. Aside from its implications for changes in labor productivity, this evidence is central to evaluating the validity of the assumptions about functional form made in the estimates discussed here and in Chapter 3.

II. THE SPEED OF ADJUSTMENT OF DEMAND FOR WORKERS AND HOURS

This section focuses on the rate at which labor demand adjusts to shocks to product demand and factor prices. Like the estimates summarized and criticized in earlier chapters, those discussed here depend on the use of appropriate data and estimation methods. Those issues, though, are even more important in the study of employment dynamics for a variety of reasons.

A. Econometric and Measurement Considerations

A simple typical form of estimating equations that can measure the lag in the response of labor demand to exogenous variables is

$$L_t = \lambda L_{t-1} + \beta X_t + \epsilon_t, \tag{7.1}$$

where λ and β are parameters, X is a vector of variables that affect long-run equilibrium values of L, and ϵ is a disturbance term. This specification is the econometric analogue to (6.5). The median length of the lag (the time it takes the system to move halfway to the eventual equilibria in response to a shock) is obtained by solving for t^* in $\lambda^{t^*} = 0.5$.

A serious problem with applying (7.1) or extensions of it is that, even if the error terms ϵ are independently and identically distributed, aggregating the series L and X over longer time periods affects the estimate of t^* (measured in months or quarters) in fairly complex ways (Engle and Liu 1972). For one thing, it induces serial correlation in the errors where none previously existed. In the simplest case of exogenous regressors, Griliches's (1961) results, that positive serial correlation generates least-squares estimates $\hat{\lambda} > \lambda$, apply. Once this assumption is abandoned, the direction of the bias in $\hat{\lambda}$ is not generally clear. If, as is likely in most time-series estimation, there is positive serial correlation in the underlying ϵ that is not fully accounted for in the estimation, the situation is still more complex, and the biases in $\hat{\lambda}$ are still more difficult to determine. Taken along with the scant attention many studies pay to the serial structure of the disturbances, this possibility suggests that we take care in comparing estimates of employment dynamics based on data aggregated over different lengths of time.

A second potential difficulty arises from spatial aggregation. Chapter 3 showed that this could affect estimates of substitution parameters describing long-run labor demand, though empirically the problem did not seem very important. If equation (7.1) describes each subaggregate, estimating it over aggregates of L and X will give unbiased estimates of the parameters, in particular of the lag parameter λ, as long as the ϵ are identically distributed across units and any serial correlation is properly accounted for. One difficulty is that equations like (7.1) are typically estimated with L and X measured as logarithms of aggregates (linear sums). If the underlying relationship in microeconomic units is best described in terms of the logarithms of L and X, (7.1) cannot describe aggregate behavior, for the logarithm of a linear aggregate is not a linear aggregate of logarithms. Unless we believe underlying relationships are linear in the variables, which is inconsistent with most theories of production, the dynamic properties of estimates based on aggregates are not known.

The more serious problem generated by spatial aggregation is that it can obscure any nonlinearity or asymmetry in the underlying structure of adjustment costs. A nonlinear microeconomic relationship produced by adjustment costs cannot in general be recovered from aggregated data. As we saw in Chapter 6, quadratic symmetric adjustment costs are just one special case. Here and in Section III I deal only with studies that have made this special assumption and ignore the issue of the shape of the underlying adjustment costs. Section IV, though, discusses its robustness to spatial aggregation and summarizes empirical work that has relaxed or tested this assumption.

A third potential difficulty is with the time-series properties of the variables in (7.1). Most aggregate economic time series are nonstationary, which implies that estimating an autoregression in the levels of L_t makes no sense, as the process generating the sequence is explosive. In fact, we observe this difficulty in very few studies summarized in this section, in some cases because the L_t are first-differenced to make them stationary. In others the vector X includes a deterministic trend that makes deviations of L around that trend stationary.

Moving to other problems, an equation like (7.1) implies that the dynamics of the responses to shocks to each variable in the vector X are identical. The analysis in Chapter 6 shows that (7.1) can be derived by assuming that employers either have static expectations or that their expectations are rational based on processes that imply including only current values of the forcing variables in (7.1). Many studies have gone beyond this; but only a few of them have based the derivation in a theory of expectations, though they have allowed for more complex autoregressive processes in L_t and/or for moving-average processes in the X variables. Estimating equations are of the general form

$$L_t = \sum_{i=1}^{K} \lambda_i L_{t-i} + \sum_{m=1}^{M} \sum_{\tau=0}^{N_m} \mu_{m\tau} X_{m,t-\tau}. \tag{7.2}$$

The λ_i and $\mu_{m\tau}$ are parameters to be estimated, and I have explicitly written out the vector X to represent flexibility in the lag structure.

While (7.2) is less restrictive than (7.1), it lacks the basis in theory that would allow distinguishing the effects of expectations about the forcing variables from those of the costs of adjusting labor demand. Ideally one would be able to separate expectations formation from adjustment costs. Once expectations of the forcing variables are accounted for properly, any observed lags should reflect the cost of adjusting employment between its long-run equilibrium values and should be independent of the source of the shock. Ignoring issues of structure, this means that an equation that links the underlying adjustment costs to the estimated lagged parameters should be of the form

$$L_t = \lambda L_{t-1} + \sum_{m=1}^{M} \sum_{i=0}^{\infty} \beta_{im} E_t(X_{m,t+i}) + \epsilon_t, \tag{7.3}$$

where the operator $E_t(\ )$ denotes an expectation at time t.

Equation (7.3) shows that one must specify the formation of the agents' expectations extremely carefully to infer adjustment costs. Where this is done, optimal forecasting procedures generate the sequences $E_t(X_{t+i})$, and autoregressions of X or transfer functions generate forecasts for several values of i. Assuming these functions contain the appropriate information, this approach yields correct estimates of the lags generated by adjustment costs (ignoring other misspecifications).

The process of generating the sequences $E_t(X_{m,t+i})$ requires basing the forecasts only on past information on the variables in X. Ignoring any nonlinearities in the forecasting equations, the estimating form of (7.3) reduces to

$$L_t = \lambda L_{t-1} + \sum_{m=1}^{M} \sum_{\tau=0}^{N_m} \mu_{m\tau} X_{m,t-\tau}. \tag{7.3'}$$

This is the same equation as the generalized rational expectations form (6.16). It differs from the generalized ad hoc approach of equation (7.2) by its implicit assumption that one has specified the processes underlying the rational-expectations forecasts. This leads to the exclusion of any L_{t-2}, L_{t-3}, and so on, and to explicit restrictions on the μ_m, and allows the extent of adjustment costs to be inferred directly from the λ. The higher-order autoregression in (7.2) does, though, have the virtue of generating unconstrained estimates of the lag structure. Though it cannot produce structural estimates of adjustment cost parameters, it does allow one to infer the dynamics of lagged adjustment in a more general way than (7.3').

Equation (7.3) is itself useful. Suppose that one despairs of specifying the process by which employers form expectations about the forcing variables, but has extraneous estimates of forecasts of these shocks from surveys of employers' or consumers' expectations. Then (7.3) will generate estimates of the structural parameter λ that take advantage of this additional information.

In summarizing empirical studies of employment dynamics I rely on the same typology used in Chapter 3 (shown in Figure 3.1). In that system of classification the first level (I–III) shows the spatial disaggregation of the observations in the sample underlying the estimates (large sector, small industry, or micro data). The second level (A or B) denotes time-series or cross-section data, and the fifth (i or ii) shows whether the study is based on the United States or another country. I ignore the third level of the classification, which distinguished between establishment and household data, since all the studies are based on establishment data.

Since the focus is on dynamics rather than the structure of production, I abandon the distinction among studies using direct, labor-demand or system methods (Types a–c) in Chapter 3. Instead, this chapter distinguishes among different specifications of the lag structure. Type a denotes studies that use simple geometric lags of the labor input in ways similar to (7.1); Type b studies contain second- or higher-order lags in L, or include more than one lag in the X variables; and Type c studies pay explicit attention to distinguishing between the formation of expectations and adjustment costs (purport to be based on (7.3)).

While with this one exception the classification system is the same, the importance of various types of studies differs sharply. Since I concentrate on dynamics, the time/space dimension is necessarily restricted to time-series or pooled cross-section and time-series data. The availability of data underlying the estimates means that there are few studies based on micro units (Type III studies). Also, I include some studies that exclude factor prices from the vector X and were thus ignored in Chapter 3. Though they clearly lack a basis in the theory of production, they allow inferences about the speed of adjustment of worker-hours or employment, and perhaps labor demand, to shocks to product demand.

In summarizing the empirical research I focus on those issues that this discussion suggests are important: the degree of temporal aggregation, the amount of spatial aggregation, and the attention paid to extricating adjustment costs from lags in the formation of expectations. In the next subsection I present the median length of the lag of the measure of labor demand behind the forcing variable. Thereafter I present estimates of the λ_{ik} in (6.19) or of employment-wage or employment-output elasticities. Special attention is paid to whether the equation describes the adjustment of worker-hours ($L = EH$), employment (E), or hours (H). Unless otherwise noted, I summarize information from any study that applies the same model to several industries by taking a simple average of the underlying estimates. I present an abbreviated description in these tables of studies whose static properties were already discussed in Chapter 3.[1]

B. How Rapidly Does Labor Demand Adjust to Shocks?

In this subsection I summarize and examine a large number of studies that focus on the speed of adjustment of labor demand (or that allow its calculation) in models that ignore the dynamics of demand for other inputs. I leave to Subsection C research that treats labor as one of at least two factors whose adjustment is determined simultaneously as part of the firm's optimization process. I thus leave until then the question of whether interrelated factor-demand dynamics

---

[1] A few of these studies were not discussed in Chapter 3 even though they include factor prices among the forcing variables. The published versions of Sargent (1978) and Epstein and Yatchew (1985) did not allow calculating long-run wage elasticities. Brechling (1975) used a Cobb-Douglas specification, so that the long-run wage elasticities were constrained. Several of the studies of interrelated adjustment also did not provide sufficient information to allow those calculations.

are important in studying labor demand. Subsection D focuses on studies of the difference in the dynamics of demand for employment and hours.

Tables 7.1 through 7.3 present estimates of t^*, the half-life of the adjustment of labor demand. In these and subsequent tables I give a range of estimates for some studies that offer two or more sets of estimates that the authors prefer. All of the *calculations are in quarters*, to assure comparability across studies using annual, quarterly, and monthly data. Because of this need, I implicitly assume that adjustment is smooth within years in annual data.

Among those studies using Type b methods, and for some of the Type c studies that include higher-order lags in L, one cannot simply take an estimate of $\hat{\lambda}$ from (7.1) to calculate t^*, since no single lag parameter is estimated. For these studies I simulate the path of L_t in response to a permanent shock to an exogenous variable X_m that was assumed to occur at $t = 0$. For those studies that specified second- or higher-order lags in L, this means simulating the higher-order difference equation implicit in the lag structure. In such cases the estimates may imply that labor demand initially overshoots the eventual equilibrium, and/or that there are explosive cycles in the response.

Table 7.1 presents and summarizes the evidence on the median speed of adjustment from studies using annual data. Here and in Tables 7.2 and 7.3 the studies are grouped within each type of specification (a–c) according to the degree of spatial aggregation of the data, and in chronological order within those classifications. At the end of each table I summarize studies that exclude factor prices (that estimate employment-output relations).

The average of the estimates in Table 7.1 is 5.5 quarters, suggesting that lags of labor demand behind output and other shocks have a long half-life (relative to the length of the typical business cycle in industrialized economies). While a few of the Type c studies that used the KLEM data for U.S. manufacturing (see Chapter 3) generate rapid responses, most of these more careful studies produce long estimated lags. There is no obvious pattern of differences between the estimates of t^* among the three types of specifications.

Are these very long estimated lags believable? Using annual data in the specification (7.1), any $\hat{\lambda} > 0.0625$ will produce $\hat{t}^* > 4$ quarters. While I noted that the direction of the bias induced by aggregation in equations like (7.1)–(7.3) is unclear, there are good reasons to think that annual data are overaggregated temporally. The very long lags implied by these studies might suggest that the $\hat{\lambda}$ they generate imply adjustment speeds that are slower than those that would be pro-

TABLE 7.1
Estimates of the Speed of Adjustment of Labor Demand Using Annual Data

Study	Category	Description	Median Lag (quarters)
		Including Some Factor Prices	
Brown and de Cani (1963)	I.A.a.i	Private nonfarm worker-hours, 1933–58; K/L	10.2
David and van de Klundert (1965)	I.A.a.i	Private worker-hours, 1899–1960; K/L	8.5
Coen and Hickman (1970)	I.A.a.i	Private worker-hours, 1924–40, 1949–65; KL	1.8
Lucas and Rapping (1970)	I.A.a.i	Aggregate production-worker-hours, 1930–65; MP condition	5.1
Morrison and Berndt (1981)	I.A.a.i	Manufacturing, 1952–71; KLEM	1.9
Merrilees (1982)	I.A.a.ii	Aggregate, 1957–78; Canada; K, 4 labor types	4.6
Pencavel and Holmlund (1988)	I.A.a.ii	Blue-collar, manufacturing and mining, 1950–83; Sweden; KLEM	3.2
Boyer (1990)	I.A.a.ii	Aggregate, 1962–90; EC; E	4.2
McKinnon (1962)	II.A.a.i	2-digit SIC manufacturing, 1947–58; MP condition	1.7
Freeman (1975)	II.A.a.i	University faculty, 1920–70; MP condition	5.8
Stapleton (1989)	II.A.a.i	Ph.D. economists, 1960–85; MP condition	9.64
Brown and Ashenfelter (1986)	III.A–B.a.i	Typographers, estimated employment, 1948–65; MP condition	(2.5, 3.0)
Jones and Pliskin (1989)	III.A–B.a.ii	Firms in printing, footwear and clothing, employment, some beginning in 19th century; U.K.; MP condition	26.3
Schaafsma (1978)	I.A.b.ii	Manufacturing employment, 1949–72; Canada; K/L	12.5

Reference	Code	Description	Output	Wage
Layard and Nickell (1986)	I.A.b.ii	Aggregate, U.K.; 1954–83; K, import prices	3.2	
Andrews (1987)	I.A.b.ii	Aggregate, U.K.; 1950–79; supply-demand system, KLEM	1.75, cycles	
Pencavel (1989)	I.A.b.ii	Aggregate, 1953–79; U.K., KLM; supply-demand model	1.6	
Bean and Turnbull (1988)	III.A–B.b.ii	Coal mines, 1967–83; U.K.; MP condition, alternative wages	(10.1, 12.0)	
Card (1990c)	III.A–B.b.ii	Union contracts, employment, 1968–83; Canada; LM prices; attention to employment-contract-wage simultaneity; first differences	explosive	
Wadhwani and Wall (1990)	III.A–B.b.ii	Manufacturing firms' employment, 1974–82; U.K.; KLM	2.6	
			Output	*Wage*
			3.0	< 0
Epstein and Denny (1983)	I.A.c.i	Manufacturing, 1947–76; KLM	3.0	short
Pindyck and Rotemberg (1983)	I.A.c.i	Manufacturing, 1948–71; KLEM		overshooting,
Morrison (1986)	I.A.c.i	Manufacturing, 1949–80; KLEM; various specifications of expectations about quasi-fixed capital		or very short
de Regt (1988)	I.A.c.ii	Manufacturing employment, 1954–82; Netherlands	3.3	
Faini and Schiantarelli (1985a)	II.A–B.c.ii	5 2-digit industries, employment, 1970–79; southern Italy; KL	6.0	
		Factor Prices Excluded		
Smyth and Ireland (1967)	II.A.a.ii	2-digit industries, employment, 1945–63; Australia	2.0	

duced if observations on the data matched the timing of the decisions of the agents involved.

This consideration leads to the basic question: With no general prediction about the direction of aggregation biases, how can we tell *from the econometric estimates alone* what is the true lag describing the relation between labor demand and the forcing variables? Are estimates based on annual data the result of excessive temporal aggregation; or are those based on quarterly, or even monthly data, error-ridden because of excessive temporal disaggregation? Only by obtaining direct evidence on the timing of decisions about factor demand can this issue be resolved. There is no such evidence, so we must rely on intuition and anecdotes about (usually large) employers' responses to well-publicized shocks.

In some cases—for example, in the studies by Freeman (1975) and Stapleton (1989) of the demand for college faculty—the decision period may really be one year. A fair summary of most of the admittedly unsatisfactory evidence, though, is that in most industries the decisions are made over periods much shorter than a year. That suggests that estimates of the dynamics of factor demand based on annual data, though the direction of their bias is unclear, are inherently flawed because the intervals over which the data are collected do not match the timing of employers' decisions. To be fair, in many of the studies summarized in Table 7.1 the concentration was not on dynamics, but instead on generating estimates of long-run demand elasticities or testing theories of contracting. In some, though, the emphasis is on dynamics. For example, in Schaafsma (1978), Morrison and Berndt (1981), Epstein and Denny (1983), Pindyck and Rotemberg (1983), Morrison (1986), and de Regt (1988) that was the explicit purpose. The high degree of temporal aggregation renders the data used in these studies inappropriate for that purpose. The U.S. KLEM data used in four of these six studies, while readily available and helpful in examining factor substitution, are not much use in drawing inferences about the dynamics of labor demand.

The picture presented by studies using quarterly data, summarized in Table 7.2, is of more rapid adjustment than is implied by the studies based on annual data. The mean estimate in this table is that the median lag is 1.4 quarters. Here too, though, the range of estimates is quite wide. The early, mostly Type a studies, based on highly spatially aggregated data and including factor prices, imply more rapid adjustment of labor demand, with median lags on the order of one quarter.

The estimates generated by the Type a studies that are based on employment-output relationships and that used spatially aggregated

TABLE 7.2
Estimates of the Speed of Adjustment of Labor Demand Using Quarterly Data

Study	Category	Description	Median Lag (quarters)
		Including Some Factor Prices	
Dhrymes (1969)	I.A.a.i	Total private hours, 1948–60; MP condition	1.0
Chow and Moore (1972)	I.A.a.i	Private worker-hours, 1948–67; KL	1.3
Clark and Freeman (1980)	I.A.a.i	Manufacturing production workers, 1950–76; KL.	
		Employment:	1.1
		Worker-hours:	0.6
Kollreuter (1980)	I.A.a.ii	Manufacturing worker-hours, 1971–77; West Germany; KL	1.5
Rudebusch (1986)	I.A.a.i	Nonfarm business worker-hours, 1952–81; MP condition, disequilibrium supply-demand model	1.9
Faini and Schiantarelli (1985b)	I.A.a.ii	Aggregate, 1970–80; Italy.	
		Employment:	0.8
		Hours:	1.2
Nadiri (1968)	I.A.b.i	Manufacturing, 1947–64; K held constant.	
		Employment:	0.3
		Worker-hours:	0.3
Black and Kelejian (1970)	I.A.b.i	Private nonfarm worker-hours, 1948–65; MP condition, supply-demand system, employment slower than hours	< 1
Franz and König (1986)	I.A.b.ii	Manufacturing, 1964–83; West Germany; KLM prices	1.5

TABLE 7.2 (cont.)

Study	Category	Description	Median Lag (quarters)
Beach and Balfour (1983)	I.A.b.ii	Manufacturing operatives worker-hours, 1956–78; U.K.; MP condition, supply-demand systems	(1.1, 1.4)
Symons (1985)	I.A.b.ii	Manufacturing employment, 1961–76; U.K.; KL, import prices	2.4
Layard and Nickell (1986)	I.A.b.ii	Aggregate, 1957–83; U.K.; K, import prices	18
Wadhwani (1987)	I.A.b.ii	Manufacturing employment, 1962–81; U.K.; KLM prices; no Y or K	4.2
Nickell and Symons (1990)	I.A.b.i	Manufacturing employment, 1962–1984; attention to measuring wage deflators	> 3, damped cycles
Hall, Henry, and Pemberton (1990)	I.A.b.ii	Aggregate employment, 1966–88; U.K.; disequilibrium model	4.6
Card (1986)	III.A–B.b.i	7 airlines, maintenance-worker employment, 1969–76; MP condition, alternative wages	0.8
Sargent (1978)	I.A.c.i	Nonfarm employment, 1948–72	11.2
Kennan (1979)	I.A.c.i	Manufacturing, 1947–69.	
		Durables:	3.0
		Nondurables:	1.9
Nickell (1984)	I.A.c.ii	Manufacturing, 1958–74; U.K.; LEM prices	1.4, damped cycles
Kokkelenberg and Bischoff (1986)	I.A.c.i	Manufacturing production-worker hours, 1959–77; KLE prices	overshooting immediately

Study	Code	Description		Value
Kuh (1965)	I.A.a.i	Manufacturing employment, 1948–60		0.8
Soligo (1966)	I.A.a.i	Private employment, 1947–61		1.0
McCarthy (1972)	I.A.a.i	Manufacturing and mining, 1953–70.	E:	2.0
			L:	0.8
Taylor, Turnovsky, and Wilson (1972)	I.A.a.i	Manufacturing, 1949–69.		
		Straight-time hours:		0.9
		Production worker-hours:		0.6
Hazledine (1974)	I.A.a.ii	2-digit manufacturing industries, 1964–70; New Zealand		1.4
Ball and St. Cyr (1966)	II.A.a.ii	Industries, employment, 1955–64: U.K.		2.7
Hazledine (1978)	II.A.a.ii	2-digit manufacturing industries, 1964–73; U.K.	E:	2.2
			H:	2.5
Chang (1983)	II.A.a.i	Michigan automobile industry, 1962–79.	E:	7.1
			H:	0.9
Anderson (1992)	III.A–B.a.i	Retail firms' employment, 6 states, 1978–84		0.5
Fair (1985)	I.A.b.i	Manufacturing, 1952–82.	E:	4.6
			H:	2.1
Wren-Lewis (1986)	I.A.c.ii	Manufacturing employment, 1963–83; U.K.; extraneous expectations on output		4.0

data are also mostly quite short. Indeed, ignoring the issue of factor substitution (the central question in the analysis of labor demand in the long run) does not appear to affect the estimated speed of adjustment of labor demand given the use of a particular formulation of the lag structure. This should not be surprising: The variance in shocks to factor prices is far less than to output demand, so that most of the variance in labor demand will be generated by the latter.[2]

The inference is complicated by the results in the British Type b studies, by some of the Type c studies based on U.S. data, and by Chang's (1983) Type a study using data for one industry in one state. Except for Wren-Lewis (1986) and Hall, Henry, and Pemberton (1990), the British studies (Symons 1985; Layard and Nickell 1986; Wadhwani 1987) all exclude measures of product demand. As such, they are incapable of providing any implication about the response of labor demand to the main cyclical variable. Also, the lag must necessarily be long, for (like other Type b studies) it reflects the combined effects of the slow adjustment of expectations about changes in factor prices and the lags produced by the optimal smoothing of labor demand stemming from adjustment costs. These studies are unlikely to inform us about the speed of employment adjustment (and, of course, are inherently incapable of saying anything about cyclical variation in labor hoarding).

The Type c studies present a mixed picture of the speed of adjustment. The pioneering Type c study, Sargent (1978), estimates very slow employment adjustment; but the others suggest that adjustment (of both employment and worker-hours) to changed expectations about the forcing variables is mostly accomplished in one year. In particular, Nickell (1984), who carefully specified the formation of expectations about factor prices and output demand, finds lags on the same order as the other aggregate studies based on quarterly data. It is simply not clear why Sargent's work has such sharply differing implications from the others'.

The puzzle posed by the very slow adjustment of employment in Chang (1983), one of only three U.S. studies using quarterly data that are disaggregated spatially, is easily solved. The industry analyzed was automobile production, an activity in which union rules and/or the nature of production have ensured that it has been profitable for employers to respond to fluctuations in product demand, especially less severe ones, by altering hours rather than changing employment. Only when shocks are very large is employment adjusted. This nonlinear adjustment may be reflected in a high estimated λ when

---

[2] This is a cyclical version of the arguments and evidence in Freeman (1977).

an inappropriate equation like (7.1) is imposed. (See Section IV.C below.)

The anomalous results of the studies using quarterly data are, with the exception of Sargent (1978), readily explained. The overwhelming evidence of most of the studies suggests that the median lag in adjustment is on the order of one to two quarters. This conclusion is reasonable if we assume: (1) quarterly observations on the central variables—labor demand, output demand, and factor prices—correspond with the timing of employers' decisions, that is, quarterly data present the correct amount of temporal aggregation; and (2) the spatial aggregation in all the studies is justified by underlying microeconomic relationships that are linear (in logarithms). As noted earlier, econometric evidence and economic theory cannot shed any light on the first assumption. The second assumption is a major focus of Section IV.

As Table 7.3 shows, regrettably few studies use monthly data. This absence is especially disturbing in light of the near unanimity about the speed of adjustment of labor demand when such data are used. All but one of the studies implies that the majority of the adjustment is made within six months, and the mean of these median lags is 1.2 quarters. The problem is that one of the two studies that used Type c methods (Kennan 1988) is also the one that produced a much slower estimated speed of adjustment. Like the several British Type b studies using quarterly data, Kennan's work did not, though, allow for cyclical effects of output demand on labor demand. Thus, his estimates are plagued by the same difficulties that made the British studies less informative about dynamic labor demand.

The evidence based on monthly data strengthens the conclusion that the lags in labor demand are generally fairly short. The median lag behind expected changes in product demand is surely no more than two quarters and probably between one and two quarters. This conclusion is less secure than one would like because of the paucity of studies that consider problems of temporal aggregation carefully in the context of Type c methods. Just as important, none of these studies provides a link to adjustment costs; none examines whether the maintained assumption of symmetric quadratic adjustment costs is appropriate; and none considers whether the adjustment of labor demand is affected by disequilibria in the demand for capital goods, in other inputs, or in inventories.

Beyond the clear need to base one's inferences about the length of the lag in adjustment on high-frequency, at least quarterly, data, it is also worth considering whether using more elaborate specifications affects the estimated length of the lag of employment or worker-

TABLE 7.3
Estimates of the Speed of Adjustment of Labor Demand Using Monthly Data

Study	Category	Description	Median Lag (quarters)
		Including Some Factor Prices	
Liu and Hwa (1974)	I.A.a.i	Private worker-hours, 1961–71; MP condition, supply-demand system	0.4
Bernanke (1986)	II.A.a.i	Small manufacturing industries, production-worker employment, 1923–39; MP condition, supply-demand system[a]	0.5
Brunello (1989)	I.A.b.ii	Manufacturing, 1973–86; Japan.	
		E:	0.5
		L:	overshooting immediately
Kennan (1988)	I.A.c.i	Manufacturing production, worker-hours, 1948–71; MP condition, supply-demand system, no Y or K	3.4
		Factor Prices Excluded	
Miller (1971)	II.A.a.i	Production workers, small industries, 1947–66.	
		E:	0.4
		L:	0.4
Fair (1969)	II.A.b.i	3- and 4-digit manufacturing industries, production-worker employment, mainly 1947–65	2.1
Sims (1974)	I.A.b.i	Manufacturing, 1950–71.	
		E:	0.7
		L:	0.3
Topel (1982)	II.A.c.i	2-digit manufacturing industries, 1958–75; E, H, inventories simultaneous.	
		E:	1.4
		H:	0.4

[a] Weighted average using employment weights.

hours behind shocks. Examination of the results in Tables 7.1 through 7.3 suggests that this does not matter very much. Among those Type c studies that actually test the significance of forecasting errors on the forcing variables, though, the evidence is very strong that adding expectations to the specification improves the fits of the equations. Particularly clear on this point in these tables are Nickell (1984), Morrison (1986), and de Regt (1988). Several of the studies analyzed in Section C below suggest the same conclusion, and Wren-Lewis (1986) demonstrates the gains of using extraneous estimates of employers' expectations. This implies that the Type c approach, which formally accounts for the formation of expectations and provides at least some chance of distinguishing between them and costs of adjustment, is the preferred method for studying employment dynamics.

C. Are Interrelated Dynamics Important for Dynamic Labor Demand?

Whether the dynamics of employment demand are affected by employers' slow responses in adjusting the inputs of other factors of production depends on whether $\lambda_{ik} \neq 0$, $i \neq k$ in

$$Z_{it} = \sum_{k=1}^{K} \lambda_{ik} Z_{k,t-1} + \sum_{m=1}^{M} \sum_{\tau=0}^{N_m} \mu_{im\tau} X_{m,t-\tau}, \ i = 1, \ldots, K, \qquad (7.4)$$

where the Z_i denote the K inputs, one of which is employment or worker-hours. The system (7.4) is just (6.19) rewritten to make the variables in the vector X explicit. It can be viewed as a system in which each of the K decision variables responds to disequilibria in its own demand and those of all the other decision variables. System (7.4) can be expressed in terms of the disequilibria between the past period's values of the Z and the current period's equilibrium values, Z_t^*, as

$$Z_{it} - Z_{i,t-1} = [1 - \lambda_{ii}][Z_{it}^* - Z_{i,t-1}] -$$

$$\sum_{i \neq k} \lambda_{ik} [Z_{kt}^* - Z_{k,t-1}], \ i = 1, \ldots, K. \quad (7.4')$$

Without substantial restrictions the mappings from the Z^* in (7.4') to the combinations of the X_m in (7.4) cannot be identified. In any case, the studies that have used the interrelated dynamic approach have not been concerned with identifying these parameters and have instead concentrated on measuring the λ_{ik}.

Discovering whether there is dynamic p-substitution or dynamic p-complementarity is interesting in its own right, for it answers whether the dynamics of labor demand are affected by, for example, subsidies to investment or changes in the costs of holding inventories. The main interest, though, is that ignoring this possibility may bias estimates of the speed of adjustment of labor demand to a new equilibrium. Thus the focus in summarizing the empirical literature here is on the terms λ_{ik}, $i \neq k$, in the equations involving employment, worker-hours, or hours.

In Table 7.4 I present the matrices of the coefficients λ_{ik} characterizing the system (7.4). The literature in this area stems from the pioneering work of Nadiri and Rosen (1969, 1973). Unfortunately, the studies are more difficult to compare than those in Tables 7.1 through 7.3, for few of them specify interrelated adjustment among the same inputs. In a completely general system one would examine stocks and rates of utilization of relevant inputs, including labor and capital, along with buffers of inventories of finished and intermediate goods and materials. Decisions about the rates at which these are adjusted would be affected both by product prices and by the rate of incoming new orders. Such a complex system has not been estimated (though Rossana 1990 almost did this). Instead, each author implicitly assumes that the $\lambda_{ik} \equiv 0$ for the inputs k in this general system that are not included in the study.

The studies summarized in Table 7.4 are arranged in order of the size of the matrix $\|\lambda_{ik}\|$ of inputs, with those studies that include inventories listed at the end of the table. Examination of the terms $\hat{\lambda}_{iK}$ and $\hat{\lambda}_{Ki}$ for the various labor inputs i in the matrices in Table 7.4 shows these are small relative to the $\hat{\lambda}_{ii}$ and the $\hat{\lambda}_{KK}$. The only exception to this statement is Epstein and Yatchew (1985), which is based on the annual KLEM data that are not well suited to studying dynamics. Disequilibria in the *external* market for capital services do not appear to affect greatly the size of any disequilibrium in the labor market. This inference is supported by studies using both Type a and Type c methods, from both the United States and the United Kingdom, and using both monthly and quarterly data.

The same conclusion may not be correct for the firm's internal adjustments of its capital stock. In the equations describing capacity utilization in Harris (1985), Bergström and Panas (1990), Nadiri and Rosen (1969, or the 1973 study that includes both production- and nonproduction-worker employment), and Schott (1978), $\hat{\lambda}_{UE} < 0$. This suggests that the demand for workers is dynamically *p*-substitutable with the rate of utilization of capital, U, that is, that firms will adjust their use of equipment more rapidly when there is a larger disequilibrium in their input of workers. This conclusion is not very sure, as $\hat{\lambda}_{EU} > 0$ in two of the four studies, contrary to the notion of dynamic symmetry.[3] The appropriate inference is that these results are suggestive of what is an intuitively reasonable phenomenon, that they merit further examination, but that by themselves they are

---

[3] Schott (1978) arbitrarily restricts this and others of the λ_{ik} to be zero.

TABLE 7.4
Studies of Dynamic Complementarity and Substitution

Study	Category	Description and $\|\lambda_{ik}\|$
Brechling (1975)	I.A.a.i	Manufacturing production workers, quarterly, 1953–69; E, K simultaneous E 0.24 0.12 K 0.07 0.97
Meese (1980)	I.A.c.i	Manufacturing production-workers, quarterly, 1947–74; E, K simultaneous E 0.95 −0.04 K 0.11 0.95
Epstein and Yatchew (1985)	I.A.c.i	Manufacturing, annual, 1948–77; KLEM data L 0.63 −0.60 K 0.23 0.66
Hart and Kawasaki (1988)	I.A.c.ii	Manufacturing, annual, 1951–81; West Germany; attention to labor cost, E, H, K simultaneous E 0.93 0.66 −0.32 H −0.01 0.37 −0.13 K 0.14 −0.004 0.91
Harris (1985)	II.A.1–2.c.ii	Engineering worker-hours, quarterly, 1968–81; U.K.; L, K, U simultaneous, complex simultaneous lags L 0.68 −0.33 0.07 K −0.004 0.99 0.004 U −0.45 −0.42 0.67

λ_{ij} are sums of coefficients at various lag lengths

TABLE 7.4 (cont.)

Study	Category	Description and $\|\lambda_{ik}\|$

Bergström and Panas (1990) — I.A.a.ii

Mining and manufacturing worker-hours, quarterly, 1965–84; Sweden; L, K, U simultaneous

L	0.13	0.03	−0.07
K	0.19	0.77	−0.07
U	−0.08	0.03	0.74

Nadiri and Rosen (1969) — I.A.a.i

Manufacturing, quarterly, 1947–62; E, H, K, U simultaneous

E	0.65	0.78	−0.16	−0.28
H	−0.10	0.38	−0.19	−0.06
K	0.03	0	0.96[a]	−0.002
U	−0.07	0.37	−0.76	0.01

Schott (1978) — I.A.a.ii

All industry, annual, 1948–70; U.K.; E, H, K, U, stock of research (R) simultaneous

E	0.85	0		0.10	0.04
H	0	0.29	0.04	−0.11	0
K	0.07	−0.04	0.88	0	0.03
U	−0.21	0	0.29	0.35	−0.07
R	0.63	−0.74	−0.24	0	0.88

Nadiri and Rosen (1973) — I.A.a.i

Manufacturing employment, quarterly, 1948–65; E (production and nonproduction), H, K, U, inventories simultaneous

E_P	0.46	0.44	−0.06	0.18	−0.02	0.01
H_P	−0.10	0.85	0.05	−0.01	−0.08	−0.04
E_N	0.04	0.01	0.71	−0.01	0.04	0.02
K	0.04	0.02	0.08	0.91	−0.01	0.01
U	−0.23	−0.59	0.98	−0.28	0.20	−0.66
Inventories	0.31	0.56	0.34	−0.11	−0.09	0.62

Rossana (1985)   II.A.c.i   2-digit manufacturing industries, monthly, 1959–82; E, H simultaneous, with effects of inventories, orders

E	0.92	0.12
H	−0.02	0.69

Rossana (1990)   II.A.c.i   2-digit manufacturing industries, quarterly, 1958–85; E, H, equipment, plant simultaneous, with effects of 3 types of inventories, and new orders

	E_{-1}	H_{-1}	$Equipment_{-1}$	$Plant_{-1}$
E	0.60	−0.05	−0.35	0.33
H	−0.04	0.56	−0.05	0.04

[a] Sum of two lag coefficients.

hardly conclusive. Finally, though Crawford (1979) presents evidence (using data on employment flows) suggesting that workers are dynamic p-substitutes for inventories, the lack of symmetry of the $\hat{\lambda}_{ik}$ involving inventories and workers and hours in Nadiri and Rosen (1973) makes any conclusion about this effect very tenuous.

Other than the dynamic interactions between employment and hours, which I discuss in the next subsection, Table 7.4 provides only sparse evidence that the off-diagonal terms involving labor in the adjustment matrix are nonzero. Unfortunately, none of the studies formally tests the restriction that the λ_{ik}, $i \neq k$, are zero, so we cannot be sure whether they are small and variable, but statistically significant, or are truly zero. Given the paucity of comparable studies, more work in this area may be necessary. Based on existing research, though, the appropriate conclusion is that little additional is learned about the dynamics of labor demand by estimating it simultaneously with the dynamic demand for other inputs or with the dynamics of inventories.

D. The Dynamics of Employment and Hours

In Chapter 6 I presented several different models of the dynamics of demand for workers and hours that assumed that adjustment costs on hours are zero. Clearly this cannot be true; but is it even true that those costs are smaller than the costs of adjusting the demand for employment? While few studies explicitly measure these costs, a large number provide evidence on the relative speed with which employers adjust their demand for employees and for hours (the rate at which they utilize the stock of employees). Among the studies using quarterly data (Table 7.2), Nadiri (1968), Hazledine (1978) and Faini and Schiantarelli (1985b) fail to find that the demand for hours, or for worker-hours, adjusts more rapidly than the demand for employees. The other five studies that use quarterly data suggest this is the case. Though not quite comparable, Black and Kelejian's (1970) estimates indicate the same thing. Among the studies using monthly data that examined this, Sims's (1974) and Brunello's (1989) Type b studies also produce this result, as does Topel's (1982) Type c study (which included interrelated adjustment but did not report on the off-diagonal elements of the matrix of λ_{ik}). Miller's (1971) results suggest that the rates of adjustment are the same. With the exception of Nadiri and Rosen (1973), who examined the adjustment of production-worker hours along with their employment and that of nonproduction workers, the other five studies in Table 7.4 that considered interrelated dynamics demonstrated this same phenomenon.[4]

The overwhelming bulk of evidence and the unanimity of the Type c studies suggest strongly that employers adjust their demand for hours more rapidly than their demand for workers. As a description of observed behavior this finding is perfectly reasonable. We can be fairly sure that labor hoarding in response to negative shocks is the result of slower adjustment of employment than of hours. This conclusion is consistent with the theory of adjustment costs. It is reasonable to assume that the cost of hiring and training new workers increases more rapidly than that of increasing the hours of current employees. When demand drops, the fear of losing trained employees raises the costs of layoffs relative to those of cutting hours.

At a deeper level, though, the conclusion leaves a few nagging doubts. Does the result really reflect differences in adjustment costs, or does it instead stem from the failure to identify the impact of lower short-run elasticities of supply of new workers than of additional hours from current employees? None of the many studies considers both the demand for workers and hours and the supply of hours in a theoretically based econometric model. Such a model would be very difficult to estimate, and considering supply effects may well not alter the conclusion; but without such estimates, we cannot be certain that it does not stem from supply-side effects rather than from the nature of adjustment costs.

Consider finally whether there are any off-diagonal terms that describe the simultaneous adjustment of employment and hours. From the five studies in Table 7.4 that shed light on this by estimating λ_{EH} and λ_{HE} freely, there is some evidence that $\hat{\lambda}_{EH} > 0$, that is, that workers and hours are dynamic p-complements. The same studies that produce large estimates of this parameter, though, produce estimates of $\hat{\lambda}_{HE}$ that are small and insignificant. The result that larger disequilibria in the demand for employees generate larger disequilibria in the demand for hours (in the intensity with which employees are worked) is counterintuitive. This lack of symmetry between the estimates makes the evidence too sparse to allow even a shaky con-

[4] It is not possible to summarize Mundaca's (1989) evidence on interrelated adjustment based on Type c methods in Table 7.4; but she too finds more rapid adjustment of hours than employment in a model involving E, H, and K in Norway, but no evidence of any difference for the United States. Garber (1989) examined a cross section of small manufacturing industries during the 1974–75 recession (using data from the *Annual Survey of Manufactures*) and found no evidence that the establishments in these subaggregates adjusted employment more slowly than they adjusted hours.

clusion about whether E and H are dynamic p-complements or p-substitutes.

III. CORRELATES OF THE SPEED OF ADJUSTMENT OF LABOR DEMAND

This section examines evidence on the objective correlates of measured speeds of adjustment and their differences among countries and over time. Only a few of the studies make any attempt to measure the size of adjustment costs, and none examines their structure. Instead, most implicitly postulate that

$$\lambda_{ii} = \lambda_{ii}(Y), \tag{7.5}$$

where Y is a vector of variables that are hypothesized to affect the rate of dynamic adjustment because the researcher believes they affect adjustment costs. Some authors examine the effects of cross-section variation in the components of Y, others the effects of time-series variation. Only Burgess (1989) considers both types of effects on the speed of adjustment in the same model; but comparisons across studies enable us to examine the robustness of any conclusions. In making these comparisons, the diversity of the studies requires tabulating them slightly differently among the tables in this section.

The numerous studies of various economies that were summarized in Section II could be used to compare speeds of adjustment of employment, worker-hours, and hours across countries. In such a comparison it would, though, be difficult to disentangle the impact of differences in the specification of adjustment mechanisms and the extent of temporal and spatial aggregation from those that arise from true international differences. I thus restrict the comparisons to estimates generated using identical specifications.

The preponderance of American research on dynamic factor demand has meant that the main comparison must necessarily be between rates of adjustment in the United States and elsewhere. Consider the evidence from the eight studies summarized in Table 7.5. Where possible I present short- and long-run employment-output elasticities. In the other cases the specification either excluded output (Symons and Layard 1984), did not present the results involving output (Drazen, Hamermesh, and Obst 1984; Denny, Fuss, and Waverman 1981), or constrained the long-run response of output. Regrettably only Morrison (1988) used a Type c method, and her study is based on annual data. No study has used an appropriate temporal disaggregation along with some specification involving rational expectations on the forcing variables to make international comparisons of adjustment mechanisms.

TABLE 7.5
Comparisons of Short- and Long-run Employment Elasticities, U.S. and Other Economies

Study	Category	Description		
		Employment-output Elasticities		
			Immediate	*Long-run*
Brechling and O'Brien (1967)	I.A.a.i-ii	Manufacturing, quarterly, mostly 1952–64		
		Austria	0.10	0.81
		Belgium	0.17	0.89
		Canada	0.47	0.93
		France	0.07	0.31
		West Germany	0.16	0.98
		Ireland	0.21	0.68
		Italy	0.34	0.69
		Netherlands	0.15	0.55
		Norway	0.19	0.67
		Sweden	0.18	0.72
		United Kingdom	0.20	0.56
		United States	0.38	0.72
			Immediate	*Long-run*
Kaufman (1988)	I.A.b.i-ii	Aggregate economy, quarterly, 1979–85		
		Canada	0.30	0.57
		West Germany	0.04	0.16
		Japan	0.005	0.03
		Sweden	0.12	0.25
		United Kingdom	0.14	0.71
		United States	0.37	0.59
			Immediate	*Long-run*
Abraham and Houseman (1989)	I.A.b.i-ii	Manufacturing production workers, monthly 1970–85		
		United States	0.43	0.92
		Japan	0.03	0.28

TABLE 7.5 (cont.)

Study	Category	Description		
			Immediate	Long-run
		Employment-output Elasticities		
Mairesse and Dormont (1985)	III.A–B.b.i-ii	Manufacturing firms, annual, 1970–79		
		France	0.29	0.48
		West Germany	0.30	0.44
		United States	0.42	0.50
		Employment-wage Elasticities		
			Immediate	Long-run
Denny, Fuss, and Waverman (1981)	II.A.a.i-ii	2-digit manufacturing employment, annual		
		United States, 1948–71	−0.25	−0.56
		Canada, 1962–75	−0.15	−0.46
			Immediate	Long-run
Drazen, Hamermesh, and Obst (1984)	I.A.b.i-ii	Manufacturing production-worker employment, quarterly		
		United States, 1954–80	−0.21	−0.39
		United Kingdom, 1962–78	−0.06	−0.21
			Immediate	Long-run
Symons and Layard (1984)	I.A.b.i-ii	Manufacturing employment, quarterly, 1956–80		
		Canada	−0.50	−2.50
		France	0	−0.38
		West Germany	0.15	−0.46
		Japan	−0.09	−1.75
		United States	−0.07	−1.25
			Immediate	Long-run
Morrison (1988)	I.A.c.i-ii	Manufacturing employment, annual		
		United States, 1952–81	−0.35	−0.41
		Japan, 1955–81	−0.61	−0.66

Nearly of all the evidence shows that employment responds more rapidly to output or cost shocks in North America than elsewhere.[5] Some of the differences may be due to institutions or to differences in labor-market tightness that are discussed in Section IV and Chapter 8. Given these possible causes, though, the evidence of faster employment adjustment in the United States, especially Mairesse and Dormont (1985), one of the few studies of dynamics that use data on firms, is especially convincing. Only two pieces of evidence counter this conclusion. Morrison (1988) implies faster adjustment in Japan than in the United States, a result that may be due to the use of annual observations. Symons and Layard's (1984) evidence on employment-wage elasticities is from equations in which output shocks are not held constant, which, as already discussed, produces difficulties since these shocks are the major cause of employment dynamics. Beyond the distinction between adjustment in North America and elsewhere there is only one other apparent difference in the results. Employment adjustment in Japan is slower than in Western Europe in the two studies that examine both.

There are many easy explanations of why employment demand reacts more rapidly in North America than elsewhere. The lack of restrictive laws and penalties against rapid dismissals is a common explanation (and will be discussed at length in Chapter 8). Traditions, as embodied in various institutional arrangements, are also probably responsible. An additional explanation is that the North American economies are relatively sparsely unionized and that unions slow adjustment. The difficulty with this explanation is that there is good evidence for the United States that employers rely on layoffs in response to negative shocks to output. A careful Type A–B study (Medoff 1979) demonstrates that, given the size of output fluctuations, layoffs are more frequent in private-sector industries where the extent of unionization is greater. Corroboration of that conclusion is provided by Raisian (1979) using household data. Union decision making, which institutionalizes the preferences of the median worker (who is not likely to be laid off in response to most fluctuations), decreases the relative costs to employers of changing the employment of junior workers.

The five studies in Table 7.6 based their examination on employment-output relationships rather than on layoffs. The hypothesis has

---

[5] As is clear from the four studies that consider both the United States and Canada, it is difficult to distinguish the behavior of dynamic labor demand in the two economies. While there is substantial integration across the border, the differences in institutions—the extent of unionization, labor protection, and others—make this result somewhat surprising.

TABLE 7.6
Union-Nonunion Differences in the Speed of Adjustment

Study	Category	Description	
Greer and Rhoades (1977)	II.A–B.a.i	3-digit manufacturing industries, short-run employment-output elasticity, monthly, 1954–71	greater with unionization
del Boca (1990)	II.A–B.a.ii	22 manufacturing industries, employment, hours, quarterly, 1970–84; Italy	λ_{EE} ↑ with unionization; λ_{HH} ↓ with unionization
Burgess (1988)	I.A.b.ii	Manufacturing employment, quarterly, 1964–82; U.K.	λ_{EE} ↑ with unionization, ↓ over time
Hamermesh (1992a)	I.A–B.b.i	1-digit industries, employment, quarterly, 1973–88	λ_{EE} ↓ relatively in less unionized industries
Burgess (1989)	II.A–B.b.ii	4 manufacturing industries, employment, quarterly, 1964–82; U.K.	λ_{EE} greater with unionization, cross-section, but not over time

been tested using both cross-section and time-series estimates of the function λ_{ii} in (7.5). Burgess (1989) shows (though only for four manufacturing industries in the United Kingdom) that adjustment is slower where the fraction of workers unionized is greater, a result corroborated for one-digit industries in the United States by Hamermesh (1992a) and for two-digit industries in Italy by del Boca (1990). Examining time-series evidence on this, Burgess (1988) finds that the speed of adjustment in aggregate U.K. manufacturing slowed as the economy became more unionized. This result breaks down within the two-digit industries (Burgess 1989); and Greer and Rhoades's (1977) cross-section evidence shows that *more rapid* adjustment of employment to output shocks occurs in more heavily unionized (three-digit) industries. Clearly, the evidence on the issue is quite mixed. Sparse or ineffective unionism may well be the cause of rapid adjustment in North America; but the evidence, particularly that based on examining layoffs, hardly supports that conclusion.

Several studies have examined secular changes in λ_{EE}. The main motivation is to discover whether patterns in them are related to the timing of policies, such as the mandatory advance notice and severance pay that I discuss in Chapter 8, that might affect how rapidly employers alter their work forces in response to output and cost shocks. The results are quite mixed, and the studies examine different economies and industries, so they are not easily compared. Smyth and Karlson (1991) find a negative trend in λ_{EE} for U.S. automobile manufacturing using quarterly data on employment covering 1967–85. Burgess (1988) finds the same trend in U.K. manufacturing, once changes in the characteristics that might affect adjustment costs are accounted for. The finding is not corroborated within manufacturing industries (Burgess 1989); and Nickell (1979) for the United Kingdom and Hamermesh (1988b), both discussed in more detail in Chapter 8, show that λ_{EE} increased during the 1970s.[6] The effect of dynamic labor-market policy on these changes is discussed in Chapter 8. From the limited evidence, though, it is not clear that any generalized secular or structural change has occurred in the rate of adjustment of employment demand.

Table 7.7 tabulates studies that relate the speed of adjustment to the amount of human capital embodied in a group of workers. The first six studies distinguish between production workers (P) and nonproduction workers (N) (in manufacturing). Each finds that employ-

---

[6] Their findings are not necessarily inconsistent with Burgess's (1988) aggregate results. Unlike Burgess, they merely examine trends without controlling for measurable factors that might change the speed of adjustment.

TABLE 7.7
Differences in the Speed of Adjustment by Skill

Study	Category	Description	$\hat{\lambda}_{ii}$	Immediate	Long-run
Oi (1962)	I.A.a.i	Manufacturing, annual, 1920–39.			
		Production workers:	0.33		
		Nonproduction workers:	0.56		
Nadiri and Rosen (1973)	I.A.a.i	Manufacturing employment, quarterly, 1948–65.			
		Production workers:	0.46		
		Nonproduction workers:	0.71		
de Pelsmacker (1984)	III.A–B.a.ii	Five automobile manufacturing firms, annual, 1976–82; Belgium.			
		Production workers:	0.46		
		Nonproduction workers:	0.65		
Abraham and Houseman (1989)	I.A.b.i-ii	Employment-output elasticity			
		U.S.			
		Production workers:		0.43	0.92
		Nonproduction workers:		0.03	0.37
		Japan			
		Production workers:		0.02	0.03
		Nonproduction workers:		0.001	0.06

Shapiro (1986)	I.A.c.i	Manufacturing, quarterly, 1955–80; K, P, N, H	$\lambda_{NN} > \lambda_{PP}$
Palm and Pfann (1990)	I.A.c.ii	Manufacturing, quarterly, 1971–84; Netherlands; K, P, N	$\lambda_{NN} > \lambda_{PP}$
Rosen (1968)	II.A.b.i	Railroads, monthly, 1947–63; E/H, 7 occupations	λ_{ii} increases with skill
Nissim (1984)	II.A.b.ii	Mechanical engineering, annual, 1963–78; U.K.; K, 3 labor; wage elasticity	

	Immediate	*Long-run*
Skilled:	−0.39	−1.06
Semiskilled:	−0.81	−1.76
Unskilled:	−0.29	−2.31

ers adjust their demand for nonproduction workers more slowly. The six studies cover quite different time periods and several countries; and Shapiro (1986) and Palm and Pfann (1990) are based on Type c methods. If nonproduction workers are more skilled, we are justified in concluding that skill and adjustment speed are negatively correlated.

As noted in Chapter 3 (footnote 3), if we use earnings to measure skill, there is a substantial overlap in the skill distributions of production and nonproduction workers. The six studies suggest that employers view nonproduction workers as "overhead labor," workers who are not subject to the same immediate vagaries of product demand as other workers. Because of the difficulty in linking the blue-collar white-collar distinction to differences in skill, the studies are less easily interpretable as indicating that employers adjust their demand for human capital more slowly than for raw labor.

The best evidence on this issue is provided by Rosen (1968). Within three narrowly defined occupations, the demand for higher-skilled workers adjusts more slowly; and across these three occupations adjustment is slowest in the most skilled occupation. Nissim (1984) also demonstrates less rapid adjustment of demand for skilled than for semiskilled workers; but he finds that the employment of unskilled workers adjusts more slowly than that of semiskilled workers.

We can tentatively conclude that the demand for human capital responds less rapidly to product demand and input cost shocks than the demand for raw labor. It would be valuable, though, to have evidence based directly on the demand for skills rather than on differences among occupations (and still worse, between production and nonproduction workers). A dynamic version of Heckman and Sedlacek's (1985) method of aggregating skills (see Chapter 3) would be one useful way of approaching the issue.

IV. The Size and Structure of Adjustment Costs

Sections II and III concentrated on the speed of adjustment, with no attention at all to any direct link between the underlying adjustment costs and their supposed reflection in the parameters λ_{ik}. In this section I first consider studies that used methods like those discussed in Section II to infer the existence of asymmetric adjustment costs and possible cyclical variations in speeds of adjustment. I then examine what those studies, particularly the Type c research, say about the magnitude of the underlying adjustment costs under the assumption that those costs are quadratic. This issue is especially important in light of the very few direct measures even of hiring and separation costs (discussed in Chapter 6). The final subsection considers the validity of making inferences about structure from all of these studies and examines the implications of the few studies that test the assumption of quadratic costs of employment adjustment.

A. Asymmetry in Adjustment Costs

Examining asymmetries is of interest for several reasons. First, assuming that one can identify them as stemming from the structure of demand, their existence tells us something about the magnitude of costs, or the size of the parameter b, in an underlying function like (6.1). Second, if employment adjustment is asymmetric with respect to shocks to product demand, that informs us about the path of changes in labor productivity. Does procyclical labor productivity result more from labor hoarding when demand declines, or more from employers' reticence about hiring additional workers when product demand accelerates?

In discussing asymmetries, the difficulty of identifying variations in demand, and thus the nature of adjustment costs, separately from variations in supply becomes especially important. We may, for example, find that firms adjust employment more slowly in response to shocks to product demand when the short-run supply curve of labor is less elastic. Unless supply is specified very carefully, we would infer that adjustment costs are greater at such times (presumably times of low unemployment), even though the phenomenon has nothing to do with any underlying asymmetry in the costs of adjusting demand. This suggests care be taken in interpreting any alleged asymmetries: They may exist, but they need not stem from structural differences in the costs of adjustment.

Various methods have been used to test for asymmetries in employment adjustment. The simplest just modifies Type a or b studies by making λ a function of some variable(s) Y, as in (7.5). The most common choice is to let the speed of adjustment vary with the aggregate unemployment rate. Doing this, though, obviates any chance of identifying possible asymmetries as arising from adjustment costs, since the unemployment rate itself results from the dynamics of labor demand and supply. A better approach is to let Y represent measures of product demand covering aggregates of which a particular firm being studied is one small component. Still better is to specify the asymmetries explicitly by allowing changes in E and H to respond differently to changes in each of the forcing variables depending on whether those changes are positive or negative. A different method, which circumvents the problems with all of these, is to base the test on gross flows—hires and separations—and thus generate asymmetries without using (7.5).

Still another approach has been to separate the sample into periods when employment is increasing and those when it is decreasing, and then to estimate versions of (7.1) for the two subsamples. This approach has severe difficulties. Sample selection is based on the outcomes of the endogenous variable, so that realizations of the disturbance determine into which subsample a particular time period is classified. This is a well-known problem in cross-section econometrics, and it generates biased and inconsistent parameter estimates (Heckman 1979). Peculiar to time-series econometrics is the additional difficulty generated by the confusion in the serial structure of the disturbances when observations are truncated from one subsample and placed into the other. Because of these problems any estimates based on specifying λ as a function of ΔE or ΔL are highly suspect.

Consider first the five studies shown in Table 7.8 that specify λ as a function of the unemployment rate. Both over time (in three studies) and across countries (in the other two) we find that employment adjusts more slowly when labor markets are tight. Whether this reflects greater costs of hiring than of laying off or merely indicates the effects of relative shortages of workers is unclear from these five studies. None even attempts to identify whether these differences stem from supply effects instead of differences in adjustment costs. Such an attempt is made by Peel and Walker (1978), who use disequilibrium methods to classify observations into those generated when employment is demand or supply constrained. The results are consistent with those shown in the table. The difficulty is that, as with studies that separate the sample based on ΔE, realizations of the disturbances are used to construct the subsamples (though the errors here are in a complete structural model rather than just a demand equation). While an improvement over the studies that simply write λ(unemployment rate), this approach does not really identify lags that stem from the costs of adjusting labor demand.[7]

Now let us examine the research that uses other methods. Ambiguity about the existence of asymmetry is suggested by the two studies, Brechling (1965) and Bucher (1984), that separate subsamples based on realizations of ΔE. In these studies, though, we cannot tell if the conclusion stems from symmetric adjustment or from the econometric difficulties that the authors induced in testing for asymme-

[7] Another difficulty is that the classification of observations is treated as if it were deterministic rather than as in a probabilistic switching model.

TABLE 7.8
Asymmetry in Dynamic Employment Adjustment

Study	Category	Description	
		λ(*Unemployment rate*)	
Hughes (1971)	I.A.a.ii	Cross-section comparison based on Brechling and O'Brien (1967)	$\lambda' < 0$
Hazledine (1979)	I.A.a.ii	Manufacturing employment, quarterly, 1962–75; Canada	$\lambda' < 0$
Smyth (1984)	I.A.a.ii	Manufacturing employment, quarterly, 1960–81, 8 OECD countries	$\lambda' < 0$
Tinsley (1971)	I.A.b.i	Private nonfarm employment, quarterly, 1954–65;	$\lambda' < 0$
Fair (1969)	II.A.b.i	3- and 4-digit manufacturing industries, production-worker employment, mainly 1947–65	$\lambda' < 0$
		Other Methods	
		1. Aggregated Data	
Brechling (1965)	I.A.a.ii	Manufacturing employment, quarterly, 1950–62; U.K.; positive vs. negative ΔE	$\lambda^+ = \lambda^-$
Bucher (1984)	I.A.a.ii	Employment, quarterly, 1963–80; positive vs. negative ΔE.	
		France:	$\lambda^+ = \lambda^-$
		West Germany:	$\lambda^+ > \lambda^-$
Begg et al. (1989)	I.A.b.ii	Aggregate employment, annual; positive vs. negative expected ΔE.	
		United Kingdom, 1953–85:	$\lambda^+ > \lambda^-$
		Japan, 1953–86:	$\lambda^+ > \lambda^-$
		West Germany, 1953–86:	$\lambda^+ = \lambda^-$

TABLE 7.8 (cont.)

Study	Category	Description	
Burgess and Dolado (1989)	I.A.c.ii	Manufacturing employment, quarterly, 1965–82; U.K.	$\lambda^+ > \lambda^-$
Pfann (1989)	I.A.c.ii	Manufacturing, worker-hours, quarterly, 1971–84, Netherlands; annual, 1955–86, U.K.	
		Production workers:	$\lambda^+ > \lambda^-$
		Nonproduction workers:	$\lambda^+ < \lambda^-$
		2. Microeconomic Data	
Chang and Stefanou (1988)	III.A–B.a.i	Pennsylvania dairy farms, family workers, annual, 1982–84	$\lambda^+ > \lambda^-$
Pfann and Verspagen (1989)	III.A–B.a.ii	Manufacturing firms, employment, annual, 1978–86; Netherlands	$\lambda^+ > \lambda^-$
Rahiala and Teräsvirta (1990)	III.A.c.ii	Manufacturing firms' ΔE, quarterly, 1976–87; Finland; $\lambda(\Delta$ industry output)	mixed results on λ
Bresson, Kramarz, and Sevestre (1991)	III.A–B.c.ii	Manufacturing firms, employment, annual, 1975–83; France	$\lambda^+ > \lambda^-$ skilled, $\lambda^+ = \lambda^-$ unskilled,
Jaramillo, Schiantarelli, and Sembenelli (1991)	III.A–B.c.ii	52 large firms, employment, annual, 1963–87; Italy	$\lambda^+ < \lambda^-$
		Gross changes	
Hamermesh (1969)	II.A.a.i	3- and 4-digit manufacturing industries monthly, 1958–66, new hires and layoffs	$\lambda^{\text{hires}} > \lambda^{\text{layoffs}}$

try. Begg et al. (1989) separate their samples into times of increased and decreased labor demand, but the selection is based on deviations of predictions of labor demand from its value in the previous period. Ignoring difficulties induced by serial correlation in the presence of a lagged dependent variable, they may thus avoid the problem of sample selection. Their results provide some additional evidence that employment adjusts upward more slowly.

Two studies use standard Type c methods but specify nonlinear responses to expectations about the forcing variables. Pfann (1989) finds slower upward adjustment of the demand for production workers in both the Netherlands and the United Kingdom. The result is consistent with the same finding by Burgess and Dolado (1989) for all workers (since the overwhelming majority of workers in manufacturing are classified as production workers). These results thus accord with the evidence based on specifying λ as λ (unemployment rate). The interesting questions are: (1) Why, for both countries, do Pfann's estimates show slower downward than upward adjustment of the demand for nonproduction workers? (2) Why are hiring costs for them implicitly less than firing costs instead of the opposite, as is implicitly true for production workers? One way around this conundrum is to infer that net costs are generating the slow adjustment, that disruptions to production caused by having to train new production workers exceed those stemming from reducing their employment, but that the administrative necessities of handling those layoffs require that nonproduction-worker employment be maintained when product demand declines.

Far more interesting from a structural viewpoint are the results of the five studies in Table 7.8 that use microeconomic data. Chang and Stefanou (1988) decisively reject symmetry in adjustment parameters. Unfortunately the nature of their sample, and the inclusion of adjustment of only family labor, make the results difficult to compare to those in the other studies. Bresson, Kramarz, and Sevestre (1991) attempt to infer the magnitude of adjustment costs from the pattern of lagged responses, allowing for asymmetries. Within the assumptions about the underlying cost structure, hiring costs for skilled workers exceed firing costs for them, though no asymmetry is found for unskilled workers. Pfann and Verspagen (1989) alone try to measure adjustment costs (inferred from what are listed in firms' annual reports as "costs of reorganization") directly and relate them to net changes in employment. The results indicate that increases in employment lagged more behind employers' expectations about output changes than did decreases.

The other two studies use data on employment and product demand to examine asymmetries in adjustment as a function of output changes. The study of Italian companies used the firms' own output to measure shocks, while the Finnish study used industrywide output. The latter approach partly circumvents problems of identification, since the shocks that generate any asymmetric response are more likely to be exogenous than in the other studies. The results of the Finnish study, based on firms in just three industries, are mixed. The results for Italy are quite strong, but like the Dutch study and the example of dairy farms, they are clouded by the use of annual data.

An early effort (Hamermesh 1969) examined asymmetric adjustment by specifying estimating equations like (7.1) for new hires and layoffs of production workers in a number of three- and four-digit manufacturing industries. The implied speed of adjustment was significantly slower for new hires. While little effort was made in this Type a study to account for differences that might result from supply constraints, the results corroborate most of the other work discussed in this subsection.

Chapter 4 noted that the few studies that examined the issue report that gross increases in employment (due to births of new plants and expansion in existing plants) vary more over time than do gross decreases (due to deaths of plants and contraction in existing plants). Without a model that specifies the paths of the shocks that generate these changes, they provide no direct information about asymmetries in adjustment costs. If the sizes of shocks are the same, though, they suggest shorter lags in expanding employment than in cutting it, opposite the results discussed here.

There is fairly good evidence that employment demand adjusts more slowly in response to increases in product demand when unemployment is low. Whether this result stems from true differences in adjustment costs or merely from an inability to extricate those differences from the effects of supply constraints is not clear from the literature. Assume that it reflects the same slower adjustment of hires than of layoffs that was noted by Hamermesh (1969). If so, and if the results are not caused by identification problems, the inference that hiring costs exceed costs of separations corroborates the one survey presented in Chapter 6 that looked at this issue. Additional research should specify supply and demand dynamics jointly under asymmetric adjustment and examine the dynamics of hires and layoffs in a model that identifies demand responses. The only tentatively justifiable conclusion is that employers are slower to expand employment when unemployment is low than they are to reduce it when unemployment is high. Along with differences in the rate at which workers are required to exert effort, this asymmetry accounts for the rapid increases in productivity during cyclical recoveries.

B. The Magnitude of Adjustment Costs

Several studies have attempted to infer the size of the costs of adjusting labor demand or, equivalently, the amount that employers spend on hoarded labor. Consider first the two studies that have measured the stock of hoarded worker-hours. Rather than using any of the three general methods discussed in Section II, Fay and Medoff (1985) relied on a survey of manufacturing firms after the 1980–81 recession in the United States. Respondents were asked about declines in shipments, output, actual worker-hours used, and the potential cut in worker-hours if the firms' sole goal had been to produce current output most efficiently. The authors used the responses to calculate that 8 percent of worker-hours were hoarded at the trough of the recession, in the sense those hours were not directly used in production. Of the 8 percent, only half were used in activities (e.g., maintenance) that enhanced future productivity.

Fair (1985) provides a formal approach to measuring hoarded labor by assuming that the peak ratios of output to worker-hours are times of zero labor hoarding. The extent of labor hoarding is measured essentially as the excess of worker-hours paid for above the number required to maintain the trend in that ratio. Fair finds that the amount of hoarding ranged between 4.5 and 8.5 percent of worker-hours at postwar U.S. business-cycle troughs. He estimates hoarding was 4.5 percent during the 1980–81 recession, comparable to Fay and Medoff's (1985) estimate arrived at by an entirely different approach. A more complex version of Fair's approach was used by Aizcorbe (1992) to study automobile assembly plants. The results were strikingly similar, with hoarding accounting for between 4 and 9 percent of employment during declines in demand in the late 1970s and early 1980s.

Though none of these studies directly measures the costs of adjusting labor demand, their results can be used to infer limits on the magnitude of those costs. Presumably employers hoard labor because the cost of wages paid to hoarded labor is less than the cost of adjusting the work force completely. The Fay and Medoff, Fair, and Aizcorbe estimates thus suggest that the cost of adjusting worker-hours in response to shocks of the size that occurred during the 1980–81 recession was *at least* 4 to 5 percent of the wage bill.

Several Type c studies explicitly parameterize adjustment costs in rational-expectations models and allow us to infer their magnitude directly. To obtain the explicit decision rules that are required to derive these estimates, the specification must also make the highly questionable assumption that profit functions too are quadratic (see Chapter 6). Adjustment costs are specified as

$$C = 1 + c_E(\Delta E)^2, \tag{7.6}$$

and C is either included multiplicatively in the total cost function (Burgess and Dolado 1989) or is treated as a deduction from total output (Shapiro 1986; Mundaca 1989). Assuming that variations in supply constraints are properly accounted for, $\hat{c}_E$ can be used along with an estimate of the $(\Delta E)^2$ that occurs in a typical recession (or boom) to calculate the costs of adjusting labor demand.

Among the three studies that use this approach only Mundaca (1989) pays any attention to supply.[8] Perhaps that is the cause of what appear to be very low estimates of the cost of adjustment. Shapiro (1986) assumes that $\Delta E = 5$ percent and estimates that adjustment costs for nonproduction workers in U.S. manufacturing are 1.8 percent of output, while those for adjusting the employment and hours of production workers are zero. Burgess and Dolado (1989) estimate that adjustment costs on all manufacturing employment in the United Kingdom are 0.25 percent of the quarterly wage bill. Mundaca (1989) generates a very wide range of estimates of the cost of adjusting employment in several one-digit U.S. and two-digit Norwegian industries; but in most the cost is less than 2 percent of the quarterly cost of production.

These estimates are remarkably low, especially compared to the more straightforward estimates of Fair (1985); but are they low compared to the sparse evidence from the surveys discussed in Chapter 6? Take a high estimate from these Type c studies and assume that adjustment costs are 2 percent of the quarterly cost of labor (that is, are 0.5 percent of annual compensation). Assume further that in a typical business cycle employment varies by ±5 percent around its trend and that, as is implicit in all of these studies, adjustment costs are on net changes in employment. Then relative to the size of the average drop in employment during a recession, the costs of the reduction amount to 10 percent (0.5/5) of the annual compensation per worker. Given the level of compensation in the United States in 1990, this calculation implies that the cost of cutting employment by one worker was $3,100 (1990 dollars). This is within the range of estimates (of gross costs) presented in Section II of Chapter 6, though toward the lower end of that range. Clearly, the various sets of esti-

---

[8] Her approach is to specify an implicit contract that keeps the worker equally well off at all times. The dynamics of supply are ignored.

mates of costs are of different concepts. Nonetheless, the overlap suggests that it is reasonable to assume that the lags in employment behind cost and demand shocks that are implied by the Type c studies (as well as by the many other studies summarized in this chapter) are not completely inconsistent with the sparse direct evidence on the size of costs of adjusting employment.

Thus far the literature that attempts to measure adjustment costs has not added very much to the survey results on their magnitude. Grant the assumptions of quadratic variable and no fixed costs (and the other assumptions necessary to generate these estimates). Other problems, including the limitation of the studies to highly aggregated data and the virtual neglect of considerations of supply constraints, mean that we have made little progress thus far in actually measuring the magnitude of costs of adjusting labor demand.

C. Aggregation and Structure

These assumptions should not be granted. There is nothing inherently wrong with assuming quadratic adjustment costs, any more than with making linear approximations to general functions in the absence of better information. The problem is with making this assumption about costs at the micro level; using it as the basis for estimates covering the highly aggregated, often macroeconomic data employed in most of the studies discussed in this chapter; and then drawing inferences about underlying costs from those aggregate estimates.

To examine the problems of inferring the size of adjustment costs from macroeconometric estimates, consider a simple alternative structure. I assume that static-equilibrium employment is determined by the level of current output demand, denoted by Y_t in this section, and that expectations about shocks are static. The general point holds in a rational-expectations framework based on something more than first-order autoregressive processes, but the demonstrations are more complex. While the example is quite specific, any cost structure that is not *both* symmetric and quadratic, including the lumpy costs and linear hiring and firing costs in Chapter 6, gives the same result (Hamermesh 1992c). The results do not stem from heterogeneity in the firms' adjustment costs, but are produced solely by difficulties of aggregation.

The example implicitly underlies the aggregated studies discussed in Subsection A, namely that adjustment costs are quadratic but asymmetric. For expositional purposes assume that there are no costs of decreasing employment. With quadratic costs of increasing employment the ith firm's adjustment is described by

$$L_{it} = Y_{it}, \text{ if } y_{it} \le 0,$$
$$L_{it} = \lambda L_{it-1} + [1 - \lambda]Y_{it}, \text{ if } y_{it} > 0, \tag{7.7}$$

where y_{it} is a shock to the ith firm's labor demand at time t and Y is the sole determinant of the static equilibrium demand for worker-hours. Let the y_{it} be cross-sectionally and serially independently distributed as normal with mean $\bar{y}_t$ and variance $\sigma^2_{y_t}$.[9] The importance of the quadratic term in adjustment costs is reflected in λ. Aggregating (7.7) across all units i yields

$$L_t = g_t L_{t-1} + [1 - g_t]Y_t, \tag{7.8}$$

where

$$g_t = \lambda N\left(\frac{\bar{y}_t}{\sigma_{y_t}}\right),$$

and N is the unit normal distribution. Mutatis mutandis, equation (7.8) is the standard geometric lag structure that forms the sole basis for the Type a studies, and that is central to measuring adjustment in Type b and c studies.

Increases in the underlying adjustment costs raise λ, which in turn raises the observed lag parameter g_t:

$$\frac{\partial g_t}{\partial \lambda} = N\left(\frac{\bar{y}_t}{\sigma_{y_t}}\right) > 0.$$

Any differences in adjustment costs will be directly reflected in differences in the observed speed of adjustment in aggregated data.

It is incorrect to draw the obverse inference, that slower adjustment in aggregated data implies greater underlying costs. For example, a change in the variance of demand shocks will also change the observed g_t:

$$\frac{\partial g_t}{\partial \sigma_{y_t}} = -\frac{\lambda \bar{y}_t}{\sigma^2_{y_t}} n\left(\frac{\bar{y}_t}{\sigma_{y_t}}\right) \gtreqless 0 \text{ as } 0 \gtreqless \bar{y}_t,$$

where n is the unit normal density. The observer may attribute a change in the lag of adjustment of employment in the aggregate data to a change in adjustment costs, when in fact it arises from a change

[9] These assumptions of independence are essential to derive the simple results; but abandoning them does not vitiate the general result that one cannot infer either the structure or speed of microeconomic adjustment from aggregate data. Also, I assume that employment is deterministic, given the structure of the shocks. The addition of stochastic terms complicates the analysis without changing the qualitative conclusions.

in the variance of demand shocks. Even in this simple example, it is impossible to use changes or differences in the $\hat{\lambda}_{ii}$ to infer anything about the size of adjustment costs.

With this or any other asymmetric or nonquadratic structure we can learn nothing about the true structure of adjustment costs from spatially aggregated data. Equation (7.8) describes employment adjustment in the aggregate, yet the underlying mechanism stemmed from quadratic asymmetric adjustment costs. (As Chapter 6 showed, the standard case of quadratic symmetric costs yields this relationship even at the firm level.) Estimates from a model like (7.1) that is applied to aggregated data, or even the extended versions used in Type b and c studies, are consistent with a variety of sharply differing underlying cost structures.

While the results summarized in this chapter do indicate labor-marketwide average speeds of adjustment, the example illustrates the general impossibility of using aggregate dynamics to go beyond this to compare the structures or sizes of adjustment costs. Other models could be examined and would yield the same conclusion. Only if one makes the very restrictive assumption that adjustment costs are symmetric and quadratic are estimates of aggregate employment dynamics informative about the structure. Without this assumption *there is no representative firm* for purposes of studying the structure of dynamic factor demand, just as in Chapter 4 there was no representative firm for purposes of analyzing births and deaths of plants.

Studies using aggregate data are perfectly satisfactory for inferring aggregate (but nonstructural) relationships, such as patterns of changes in labor hoarding. The example suggests, though, that only by examining the dynamic adjustment of employment in individual firms or establishments will we be able to measure the size of adjustment costs or to infer their structure. Even though the readily available macro data have been a very tempting target for researchers studying dynamics, they should not be used if we are interested, as we should be, in the technological structure that underlies firms' behavior.

Heterogeneity of labor means that even establishment or firm-level data will mask any differences in employment dynamics between still finer disaggregations of workers, for example, by type of labor within the workplace. The problem here is analogous to one noted in Chapter 2, namely the desirability of identifying separate demand elasticities for every worker in the labor force. Further disaggregations below the level of the establishment are desirable; but the extent of disaggregation that is useful may not be very fine, as the studies in Chapter 3 of substitution among several types of workers showed.

While several of the studies presented above have been based on microeconomic data, only five studies have tried to examine what the structure of adjustment costs looks like using such data. All focus on changes in levels of employment, and thus, like the overwhelming majority of research summarized here, assume implicitly that those costs are net. Hamermesh (1989) ran a "horse race" between the conventional model (7.1) and a switching model specifying lumpy adjustment costs as in (6.6). Based on monthly data covering seven plants in a unionized durable-goods manufacturing firm, the estimates clearly demonstrated the superiority of the lumpy-cost model as a description of the adjustment of employment to shocks in output demand. Craig (1990) argued that the difficulties of specifying the processes that generate the shocks suggest the benefits of examining variations in L alone. His semiparametric tests of monthly data from 1968 to 1987 in four lumber mills reject smooth adjustment and imply that there are fixed costs of changing the level of employment.

Pfann and Verspagen (1989) suggest that the typical firm is best characterized as having both fixed and variable costs of adjusting employment (though the annual data make any conclusions highly tentative). Holtz-Eakin and Rosen (1991) specified a Type c model describing the demand for full- and part-time municipal employees over eight years. Their use of annual data also renders any conclusions about the structure of adjustment costs quite shaky. Nonetheless, a test for increasing marginal costs of adjustment could not reject the hypothesis that there are none, and thus that the costs are linear. In Hamermesh (1992b) a general model including both quadratic variable and lumpy fixed costs was estimated over the quarterly data on airline firms used by Card (1986). In this case neither quadratic costs alone nor lumpy costs describe the adjustment of labor demand. Rather, employment dynamics are consistent with a more complex structure like (6.8) that includes both types of costs.

These are the first studies to test the structure of adjustment costs, and thus to provide some empirical basis for choosing among the models developed in Chapter 6, Section III. Their admittedly tentative evidence suggests that the entire literature summarized in Tables 7.1 through 7.8 must be viewed as telling us little about the underlying structure of labor demand. The results in those tables are very useful as descriptions of aggregate employment dynamics, and thus as research into such issues as cyclical changes in the extent of hoarded labor in the aggregate. They are also good indications of differences in reduced-form lags in adjustment by skill level. Because the micro evidence suggests they are based on an assumption about technology that is at least not universal, they do not yield information about structural differences. This means that comparisons of speeds of adjustment over time or among economies are particularly suspect, since any differences could easily be caused by shifting distributions of demand shocks. Similarly, one cannot extricate these shifts from true asymmetries in underlying adjustment costs. In short, extreme care, even self-denial, is required in making any structural interpretations based on the vast literature that uses aggregated data.

These few studies are not sufficient to show the relative importance of various structures of adjustment costs. They also say nothing about the importance of the distinction made in Chapter 6 between gross and net costs of adjustment. They do suggest, though, that the assumption that the only adjustment costs are variable and quadratic in net changes in employment is demonstrably untenable. They cast severe doubt on any attempts to use estimates based on aggregated data to do more than infer average aggregate speeds of adjustment.

V. Returns to Labor and to Scale

Even if production functions are characterized by constant returns to scale, short-run increasing returns to labor are implicit in the lags of employment or worker-hours behind output. Indeed, these short-run increasing returns are what produces the observed procyclical labor productivity. As we have seen, they are very well documented. They imply that firms either disproportionately reduce their use of other inputs during contractions in demand or, more likely, that they reduce the efficiency with which inputs are combined during such times.

The maintained assumption in most of Chapter 2 was that production is characterized by constant returns to scale in the long run. Implicit in that assumption, if the production function is homothetic, is the long-run linear homogeneity of the demand for inputs, including labor. This assumption also underlies much of the empirical work summarized in Chapter 3. Some of that work, and most of the studies discussed in this chapter, allow examining whether expansions of output demand yield proportional *long-run* increases in labor demand once labor-saving technological change is properly accounted for. This is a very old issue in the study of production. I consider it here because much of the evidence comes from research on employment-output elasticities rather than labor-demand equations or systems of cost or production relationships. In discussing it I only add a compendium of the implications of the empirical literature discussed in this book and discuss some issues of measurement.

Whether returns to scale are constant is of course fundamental in production theory. It is also basic to the study of labor demand. Most important, if it is wrong, the structures used to generate much of the knowledge that was synthesized in Chapter 3 are incorrect, with errors whose directions are extremely difficult to gauge. Long-run nonconstant returns to scale would also imply that we could not so easily use the magnitude of permanent changes in output demand to predict changes in labor demand. This would cause problems for most theoretical models commonly used in macroeconomics. It would also mean that any attempt to simulate the effects on employment of policies that change factor prices or that stimulate the demand for final output cannot rely on the simplifying assumption of proportionality.

Returns to scale have in many cases been inferred from equations like (7.2) (or simpler versions such as (7.1)) as

$$
\hat{s} = \frac{\sum_{\tau=0}^{N_Y} \hat{\mu}_{Y_\tau}}{1 - \sum_{i=1}^{K} \hat{\lambda}_i} ,
$$

where the $\hat{\mu}_Y$ are estimates of the responses of current labor demand to various lags in output, Y. This measure is correct if: (1) factor prices are included in the vector X in (7.2), or are excluded because one correctly maintains the assumption that they are uncorrelated with output; (2) problems of measurement are avoided, particularly those of measuring the effective amount of labor adjusted for changes or differences in the skill of the work force; and (3) the labor-saving or using nature of technical change is properly accounted for, or is not considered, but its rate and direction are uncorrelated with changes in factor prices and output. Alternatively, returns to scale are inferred from extended versions of the translog tableau (2.26) that include a term in output (or if nonneutral technical change is also assumed, interactions of terms in output and a measure of technical change). Throughout I denote constant returns to scale by $\hat{s} = 1$, increasing (decreasing) returns by $\hat{s} < (>) 1$.

Consider the estimates of $\hat{s}$, compiled from all those studies summarized here and in Chapter 3 in which this parameter is not implicitly or explicitly constrained to equal one. Rather than classifying studies, to analyze this narrow, but very important question, I present in Table 7.9 statistics on the distribution of the 101 estimates of $\hat{s}$ from the studies that I have already tabulated. The sources are so

TABLE 7.9
Distribution of ŝ

	Total	Foreign	United States
Mean	.792	.767	.828
Standard deviation	.294	.318	.252
Median	.775	.761	.827
N =	101	59	42

diverse, in terms of method of estimation, type of specification, source of data, and underlying purpose of the model, that it is impossible to cross-classify them in a single typology that would usefully distinguish among the ŝ.

The summary in Table 7.9 makes it very clear that the literature suggests the presence of slight increasing returns to scale. The averages are below one, and the distributions around the means are not extremely dispersed. This is equally true among studies of the U.S. economy, or industries within that economy, as it is among those that examine other economies. This result does not stem from a few very low estimates of s: The median estimates differ little from the means.

Is the inference that the literature implies increasing returns to scale correct? Many of the studies included in the summary statistics simply calculate the employment-output elasticity, an incorrect measure of scale economies if variations in factor prices are correlated with variations in output and (as is surely the case) with changes in employment. Yet basing the calculations in the table only on those studies that account for wages, or wages and other factor prices, yields $\hat{s} = 0.83$. Failure to consider variations in factor prices has only a slight impact on estimates of the degree of returns to scale.

Another possibility is that most of the studies of employment-output relationships, marginal productivity conditions, and labor-demand equations (the Type a and b studies in Chapter 3) generate biased estimates of s because they do not specify a complete production or cost system. Yet among those studies that estimate an entire system of production relationships (the Type c studies in Chapter 3) and do not restrict the system to exhibit constant returns, $\hat{s} = 0.84$. The few estimates of this type differ only slightly from the other results. Even system estimation appears to imply increasing returns.

A third potential problem is excessive spatial aggregation, which we saw in the previous section can make any structural inferences in dynamic models difficult. Limiting the calculation to those few studies that use micro data yields $\hat{s} = 0.62$. If anything, spatial aggregation makes it less likely to reject the hypothesis of constant returns to scale. However, errors in measuring output at the plant level may impart a negative bias to estimates of s based on micro data.

A final possibility is that the research cannot distinguish between the effects of labor-saving technical change and increasing returns. This may be because it does not measure effective labor, adjusted for changes in the amount of human capital embodied in the work force. Several studies (most notably, Berndt and Khaled 1979, using aggregate annual data) do model nonneutral technical change. These too find increasing returns, though they do not try to account for changes in the stock of human capital. The paucity of research examining this issue and the lack of microeconomic studies of it leave it as a possible explanation of the generally increasing returns found in the bulk of the empirical literature.

We may conclude that there clearly are short-run increasing returns to labor. More important, the evidence suggests tentatively that there are also long-run increasing returns to scale, albeit not very large ones. If true at the micro level the finding is hard to rationalize in light of the failure in most industries for larger firms to become ever more dominant over long periods of time. If it is true only as a description of aggregates (but the literature suggests the result holds for micro data too), what aggregation mechanism generates increasing returns from underlying constant-returns functions? Even if correct only as a summary of economywide tendencies, the literature implies that one probably should not treat the scale effect on employment of a change in product demand as proportionate. Instead, one should assume in *both* the short and the long run that it is somewhat less than one-for-one.

VI. Conclusions and Difficulties

The literature on dynamic labor demand has not yielded as many or as certain conclusions as that on static labor demand. It has, however, demonstrated a number of results:

The speed of adjustment of employment or worker-hours in response to shocks is fairly rapid. Taking the approach of static expectations, most of the gap is made up within a year. Nearly half is covered within one quarter of a shock.

Employers are quicker to alter hours in response to shocks than they are to change levels of employment. Labor hoarding reflects "excess" work-

ers more than it does a smaller work force whose hours are spent at
reduced levels of effort.

There is little evidence that the rates at which employment and hours are
adjusted depend on the speeds of adjustment of other inputs. They
may, though, depend on each other.

Employment and hours in the United States adjust more rapidly to shocks
than is true in most other developed economies.

Adjustment of the employment of unskilled workers is faster than that of
skilled workers.

Employment responds less rapidly to shocks when unemployment is
lower.

Rapidly mounting evidence suggests that adjustment costs are not both
quadratic and symmetric.

Some problems with this literature can be highlighted by comparison to the empirical literature on long-run labor demand analyzed in
Chapter 3. There the estimates of the substitution and demand elasticities stem directly from underlying production functions. Here
there is little or no link between the parameter estimates and the underlying technological structure of the adjustment costs that are assumed to generate the lags. The only exceptions are the few cases
where authors (of Type c studies) have estimated a parameter like c
in (7.6) that reflects the size of quadratic costs. In those instances the
assumptions necessary to generate the estimates are remarkably restrictive. Substantial effort has been devoted to building complex
models based on microeconomic theory; but in their application to
data the link that would enable the researcher to estimate structural
parameters has been lost.

In the literature on multifactor production functions an increasingly complex array of assumptions about the structure of production
has been tested. In the literature on dynamic factor demand one assumption about technology, that the only adjustment costs are variable and quadratic, underlies nearly all research. The apparent problems with this assumption in every study that has tested it suggest
even more the breadth of the gulf between theory and empirical
work in this area. As important, little has been done to test whether
the dynamic costs are on net changes in employment, as in most of
the literature, or on gross changes.

Attempts to infer demand parameters in a model that properly
accounts for variations in supply are fairly uncommon in both literatures, but more effort has been made to examine the effect on
long-run parameters than on dynamic labor demand. Since long-run
supply curves to individual firms and industries are probably very

nearly horizontal, insufficient study of this issue probably does not greatly detract from our understanding of long-run parameters. Short-run supply curves are surely not horizontal. The failure to account for short-run supply dynamics in most studies means that the estimates of employment adjustment may not reflect behavior stemming from optimization in the face of adjustment costs that is unconstrained by limits on supply.

Related to this is the need to distinguish between slow adjustment to expected changes and employers' slow adjustment of their expectations. Only a few studies, though, model both demand and supply dynamics, and only one (Kennan 1988) specifies dynamic optimization on both sides of the labor market. Again, the empirical literature does well in informing us about the length of the (reduced-form) lag. It fails in indicating whether this lag is due to the adjustment costs that the authors adduce as its cause.

Even assuming that we can distinguish between the effects of lags in expectations and lags resulting from costs of adjustment, what are the costs that produce the lags? As Section V of Chapter 6 showed, a firm will lag the adjustment of an input for which there are no inherent costs of adjustment as long as such costs are associated with other inputs. The evidence in this chapter suggests that we do not go far wrong in inferring the length of the lag of employment or worker-hours behind shocks by treating it separately from the adjustment of other inputs. But that evidence tells us nothing about the source of the costs of adjusting the demand for labor. At this point we simply do not know what generates those costs, or even if there are any costs attached to adjusting labor other than those that stem from combining it with other factors whose adjustment is costly.

Spatial aggregation will confound any attempts to draw structural inferences from the estimates of the dynamics of factor demand and may even severely bias reduced-form estimates of lags. Biases to long-run elasticities seem less severe. Anomalously, much of the empirical literature summarized in Chapter 3 is based on microeconomic data, while such data underlie few of the studies discussed in this chapter. This imbalance stems partly from the existence of easily available sets of cross-section household data that are usable in estimating long-run parameters and the relative scarcity of comparably useful time-series data based on establishments. A few such sets of data are available, though; and, *horribile dictu*, even economists can collect their own data when the problem warrants. That we have not, and have instead concentrated on developing models that are increasingly ill suited to the data used to estimate them, suggests a misallocation of resources.

Another difficulty is the remarkably heavy use of quarterly and even annual data in this area of research. Unlike excessive spatial aggregation, which is partly excusable because of the difficulty of obtaining microeconomic time series, the existence of large numbers of monthly economic time series makes excessive temporal aggregation inexcusable. In the United States there are good monthly data on production-worker employment and industry output, the most important measure in the vector of forcing variables.[10] Monthly measures of earnings of production workers are also available by detailed industry. The focus on lower-frequency data is inexplicable given the ease of handling the larger sets of data that monthly observations represent. If we really believe that employers make decisions only once a year, this belief should be tested using higher-frequency data rather than imposed.

More research using high-frequency microeconomic data is essential if we are to achieve the same link of empirical work to theory as in the analysis of the demand for labor in the long run. With such data one can test alternative hypotheses about the structure of the technology of adjustment. That should be done properly, with a reasonable specification of the dynamics of labor supply facing the firm and with some generality in the structure of costs.

[10] The Federal Reserve Board Index of Industrial Production is a satisfactory measure for a number of small industries in which it is based on actual production rather than employment. Census reports on shipments and inventories allow construction of an alternative set of monthly measures of output.

CHAPTER EIGHT

Dynamic Demand Policies

I. Purposes and Typology

As in Part I, it makes sense to consider a variety of labor-market policies whose impacts can be analyzed using the theory and empirical work summarized earlier in this part. Most have not received the same detailed, theoretically based attention that has been given to the policies discussed in Chapter 5. Indeed, in some cases there has been no formal modeling and no even rudimentary testing. Partly this absence results from the lack of an obvious basis of many of the policies in labor demand and the apparent irrelevance of economic analysis for them. Partly, too, the novelty of some of the policies means that economists have yet to give them much substantive attention. Still more important, it stems from the complexity of the appropriate analysis.

This chapter provides some of the missing attention. As in Chapter 5, the goal is an analysis that accommodates the specific policies that are discussed, but that still outlines generally how alternative policies affect behavior. For several specific policies, including unemployment insurance and policies that affect employers' ability to fire at will, I examine their structure and present the same kind of evaluative survey of evidence on their impact that was included in Chapter 5. I deal with others, including several that would affect the dynamics of labor demand, in less detail, because no similar body of evidence exists.

To make these assessments I adopt a typology based on the kinds of adjustment costs discussed in Chapter 6. One of the distinctions made there was between external and internal costs of adjustment. The former reflect out-of-pocket costs of hiring and laying off workers, while the latter reflect disruptions to production when the level of employment is altered. Thus, the central distinction I make here is between policies that affect hiring/firing costs and those that reduce employers' ability to alter production relationships. This distinction is shown in the first line of the display in Figure 8.1.

Among external costs of adjustment the appropriate distinction is between those that accompany gross additions to the work force and those that accompany layoffs or firing. Policies affecting the former

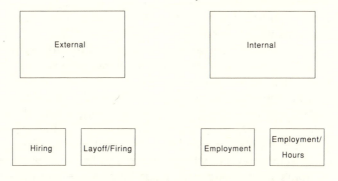

8.1 Schema for Classifying Dynamic Labor Demand Policies

include mandatory listing of job vacancies, the availability of registers of potential workers (in the United States, through the Employment Service), and to some extent the marginal employment subsidies that were discussed in detail in Chapter 5. Policies that raise the external costs of laying off workers include unemployment insurance benefits. Rather than repeating the several existing summaries of the effects of these benefits on unemployment, I restrict the discussion here to analyzing and summarizing the evidence on their effects on labor demand and employment.[1]

The best example of a policy that might alter the internal costs of adjustment is the erosion of the employment-at-will doctrine in the United States. This doctrine has implicitly been altered to limit employers' right to terminate workers without any quasi-judicial procedure and even without warning. Also included among such policies are requirements of advance notification of layoffs. The distinction between policies that affect external and internal costs becomes somewhat shakier when we analyze mandatory severance pay. While it could be viewed as generating external costs of reducing employment, it also is often a penalty for attempts to change technique. Accordingly, I analyze it too as affecting internal costs of adjusting employment. Internal costs are also altered by policies that change the relative prices of hours and workers. The long-run effects of mandatory wage premia for overtime work were discussed in Chapter 5; but such premia, and changes in the standard work week, also affect the dynamics of employment and hours in response to external

[1] Hamermesh (1977), Gustman (1982), and Cox and Oaxaca (1990) provide comprehensive surveys of the evidence on the effects of unemployment insurance benefits in the United States on workers' behavior.

shocks and deserve examination here. A similar analysis applies to any payroll tax with a ceiling.

In each case the link between the policy and the adjustment costs that cause it to affect dynamic labor demand underlies the discussion. A major purpose of this chapter is to demonstrate the importance of thinking about effects on the size and structure of adjustment costs of policies that are not obviously targeted on these costs. The discussion stresses dynamic effects and adjustment costs throughout; but the additional labor costs that most of these policies generate affect the level of labor demand and firms' choices of workers and hours in the long run. Their long-run impacts are understandable and predictable using the same analysis and evidence that was presented in Chapter 5.

Whether the imposition of any of these policies affects labor demand in the long run is the same problem as the static incidence of taxes/subsidies discussed in Chapter 5. If information about the policies is complete (presumably, if they have been in place for a long time), why does compensation fail to adjust fully to offset the effect of the policy? If it does, employment will be affected only in the short run, before expectations about changes in the policy have adjusted fully. If empirical research finds that employment is affected, it could merely be that the legislation has varied so much, or is so recent, that it is producing short-run effects on the labor market. Alternatively, even long-run effects can be produced if the structure of pay cannot adjust fully. I account for this difficulty by analyzing policies within labor-market equilibrium models.

II. Policies Affecting Hiring Costs

This section examines how policies affecting hiring costs change the path of employment. There has been little analytical research on the dynamics of these policies, so there are no evaluative results to be summarized. Indeed, little thought appears to have been given to their dynamic effects. That means that the purpose here is only to infer their potential economic effects, not to describe their magnitudes. The analysis can, though, be used mutatis mutandis to study the much more widespread job-security policies discussed in Section IV.

Since the goal of most dynamic labor-market policy is to increase employment or cushion layoffs, it is not surprising that there are few policies that directly aim at *increasing hiring costs*. Yet a few policies that are designed to stimulate employment effectively raise hiring costs. The mandatory listing of job vacancies with government employment agencies that exists in most Western European countries, and that has been proposed in the United States, falls under this rubric.[2] Other policies designed to stimulate employment of certain groups of workers also effectively increase the costs of hiring. Requirements that employers file affirmative-action plans, or that they advertise jobs in ways that are not narrowly profitable, increase the external cost of a positive gross change in employment.[3] So do limits on hiring, such as those imposed through collective bargaining in the German steel industry and elsewhere in the late 1970s (Gennard 1979).

More common are policies that reduce hiring costs to stimulate labor demand, either generally or for certain workers. Subsidized vocational programs with a component of firm-specific training reduce hiring costs. The marginal employment tax credits whose static effects were discussed at length in Chapter 5 also have dynamic effects like those of a subsidy to hiring costs. Particularly if the subsidy applies only to wages during an initial period of a worker's tenure in the firm, and if the typical worker's tenure is long, the subsidy is analytically equivalent to a reduction in hiring costs.[4]

The obvious way to analyze these subsidies/taxes on hiring costs is to consider how they affect adjustment costs. Consider the standard representation

$$C(\dot{L}) = a|\dot{L}| + b\dot{L}^2, \, a, b > 0, \tag{6.1}$$

repeated here for convenience. It is difficult to rationalize using this function to describe the effect of the subsidy/tax on adjustment costs. Even if employment is not being changed, the policy affects the firm that is replacing workers who quit. It applies to hires, not to the net changes in (6.1), and is on gross rather than net external adjustment costs. Ignoring this difficulty, it is also not clear how these policies would affect b, the convexity of adjustment costs. In order to use (6.1), one must argue that they raise costs disproportionately as the

[2] For example, see a proposal by the Lawyers' Committee for Civil Rights Under Law, *Falling Down on the Job: The United States Employment Service and the Disadvantaged* (Washington, D.C., Lawyers' Committee, 1971), that employers list all job vacancies with the federal Employment Service.

[3] The added costs may only be short-run, in that the policies overcome statistical or other information-based discrimination and eventually lead to higher profits and greater welfare economywide. All I am describing here is how the *individual* employer's hiring/employment behavior will react to these requirements.

[4] The Targeted Jobs Tax Credit in the United States can be viewed as a hiring subsidy. The analogy is muddied, though, by the likelihood that the low-skilled workers who are targeted have sufficiently high turnover rates that their wages are subsidized during most of their tenure. (For example, Mincer and Jovanovic 1981 show that half the workers with less than one year of job tenure are in different jobs two years later.)

Employment

8.2 Adjustment to a "Tax" on Hiring

amount of hiring increases. For the mandatory listing of vacancies, and the filing of affirmative-action plans, the opposite seems more likely; for marginal employment subsidies there is no obvious effect on b.

These policies can be represented either as changing k in the model of lumpy costs of adjustment in (6.6) or altering hiring costs, a_1 in (6.9'). Lumpy costs of changing employment capture the shape of the changed costs but still inappropriately base the analysis on net employment changes. The model of asymmetric costs of gross changes in employment characterizes these policies better. Either way, though, abandoning the standard model means that the empirical literature summarized in Chapter 7, based as it nearly entirely is on (6.1), is not much use in predicting the impact of these policies.

A. Increased Hiring Costs and Dynamic Labor Demand

With linear hiring and firing costs the path of employment is E^b in Figure 8.2. As the derivation of (6.14') showed, *both hiring and layoff costs* impose a wedge between a potential new hire's marginal product and wage rate. Consider a policy that increases the costs of hiring. (All the results work with opposite signs for an imposed decrease in hiring costs.) This increases the right side of (6.14'), enlarging the wedge between the excess of the worker's marginal revenue product over the wage rate by increasing the cost of making *any* change in employment. That a policy that effectively taxes hiring reduces it and thus leads to employment being held constant longer during an upturn in product demand is fairly obvious. The reduction in firing that it also produces can be understood by noting that any fired worker must eventually be replaced in a future boom. The rise in hiring costs raises the present value of the costs of a fire and thus reduces firing. The path of employment after the increase in hiring costs is E^a.

With this archetypal policy that raises hiring costs, employment fluctuates less than before the policy is imposed. Unless we observe employment over a sufficiently long period, its path may not reflect the theoretical results, for the timing of the (unexpected) policy may alter the conclusions. Further, the transition from the dynamic equilibrium before the policy is imposed to the new equilibrium may be long.

Assume initially that the typical firm stays in business after time t when hiring costs are increased. The seven possible outcomes differ by the time t at which policy is imposed relative to the state of product demand (and of the derived demand for labor). In terms of Figure 8.2 the specific cases are:

1. $t < t_1'$, $t_2' < t < t_3'$. Employment proceeds along the new steady-state path E^a from the time the policy is imposed. There is no immediate effect, but in the steady state employment fluctuations are reduced.

2. $t_1 < t < t_2$. Employment proceeds along the old path E^b until some time between t_2 and t_2', when firing begins. The policy has no immediate impact.

3. $t_3 < t < t_4$. As in Case 2, but with the reverse result that hiring begins between t_4 and t_4'. The policy has no immediate effect.

4. $t_1' < t < t_1$. Employers stop hiring. The immediate effect is a smaller expansion of employment.

5. $t_4 < t < t_4'$. Employers delay hiring. The observer sees a temporary reduction in hiring.

6. $t_2 < t < t_2'$. Employers delay firing workers who otherwise would have been let go. Eventually firing will put the firm on the new path E^a. The immediate result is less firing and more employment.

7. $t_3' < t < t_3$. Firing ceases because of the policy. Employment is held constant at a higher level than along E^b. The observer sees the policy as reducing firing and increasing employment.

These cases show that the policy may initially reduce hiring, reduce firing, or have no impact. The effect depends on the timing of the imposition of the policy relative to the future path of factor prices and product demand, and thus to the path of its steady-state labor demand. If the policy is fully expected sufficiently far ahead of its start, there will be no transition effect: The new dynamic equilibrium will have been approached closely by the time the policy takes effect (as in Figure 6.5).

This discussion ignores voluntary turnover. With increased hiring costs, greater voluntary quitting enhances the policy's impact, for the (taxed) rate of hiring for replacement alone is greater. On the other hand, the conclusions are weaker if wages are more flexible, for employers can absorb some of the output shocks by changing wages. Wages will rise during booms, inducing workers not to quit and reducing the loss of profits due to the increased cost of hiring replacements.

The example is based on firms in competitive product markets that face adjustment costs as in (6.9'). If firms are noncompetitive in product markets, the results are not changed substantively. The policy alters the amount of rents available for sharing, but there is no reason to presume that it changes the relative bargaining strengths of organized workers and the monopolistic employer.

This discussion may generate a sanguine view: *If the policy is an appropriately timed surprise*, it might achieve its other purposes without reducing employment. The difficulty is that this view is based on an infinitely lived firm. The policy also affects employment by altering rates of entry and exit of plants. The sparse evidence in Chapter 4 suggests that quasi elasticities of labor demand are not that different from standard labor-demand elasticities. Since the policy reduces profit opportunities, it will reduce the birth rate of new plants. Existing firms realize that they could not survive the losses they would bear if they stayed in business and had to incur the increased costs of hiring, so the death rate of existing firms rises. The view implied above is too optimistic even in the short run, for it ignores the dynamics of entry and exit.

In the new steady state the birth rate of firms will be lower. Prospective employers' reduced ability to use labor as efficiently during future business cycles as they envisioned before the policy was imposed reduces the number of firms that choose to enter the market. The hiring tax will reduce new firms' ability to generate additional competition in the product market. Plant closings are also reduced: By definition, deaths in the steady state must equal births, and the policy has reduced births.

Though fairly clear from the discussion here and a comparison to Chapter 5, it is worth considering the static effects of the policy on worker-hours and employment. The extra hiring costs must be amortized over the expected tenure of the worker. As the results in (6.10') and (6.11') imply, with the conventional shape of production functions the demand for worker-hours decreases. In Figure 8.2 the horizontally shaded area exceeds the vertically shaded area: Average inputs of worker-hours fall over the business cycle. The drop increases with the magnitudes of the tax on hiring and the long-run elasticity of labor demand. This conclusion is even stronger with respect to employment if we assume that firms are at least somewhat able to substitute hours for workers. The policy raises the cost of an additional worker relative to that of adding an hour to the work week. This induces the constrained profit-maximizing employer to maintain a smaller work force and vary its hours more over the cycle of product demand.

B. Increased Hiring Costs and Labor-Market Dynamics

The discussion thus far has dealt with a particular form of dynamic labor demand. As the discussion of the static impacts of payroll taxes in Chapter 5 showed, though, one must also account for the effect of the policies on supply. The issue there was how long-run supply behavior interacts with demand to generate simultaneous effects on wages and employment. Here the problem is how the policy can change the dynamics of labor supply and wages. If these are changed, one cannot infer the impact of the policy simply from the time path of labor demand.

I analyze this problem in a labor-marketwide context and impose the simplifying assumption that labor demand is characterized by quadratic adjustment costs that yield smooth adjustment of employment. The evidence in Chapter 7 suggests that this is not a good description of microeconomic behavior. Since the purpose is to demonstrate how employment and wages economywide (for the randomly selected firm) are affected by the interaction of dynamics of labor supply and demand, not to infer structure, it is probably satisfactory here. Without making the assumption the analysis is extremely complex. For labor demand rewrite (7.1) as

$$L_t^d - L_{t-1}^d = [1 - \lambda_1][L_{t-1}^{d*} - L_{t-1}^d]. \tag{8.1}$$

If t denotes years, the evidence in Chapter 7 is overwhelming that λ_1 is fairly small, that is, that labor demand adjusts rapidly to its long-run equilibrium. An increase in hiring costs effectively raises λ_1. The question is what this does to the dynamics of employment and wages.

I model aggregate labor supply analogously to (8.1) as

$$L_t^s - L_{t-1}^s = [1 - \lambda_2][L_{t-1}^{s*} - L_{t-1}^s], \tag{8.2}$$

where s denotes supply and λ_2 indicates the speed of adjustment of supply (with higher λ_2 implying slower adjustment). Presumably households adjust labor supply toward a target that is shocked by innovations in the processes generating market and reservation wages. The literature on the dynamics of labor supply is much more sparse than that on dynamic labor demand. One time-series study based on establishment data covering all of manufacturing (Freeman 1980) and two cross-section studies (Fleisher, Parsons, and Porter 1973; Kalachek, Raines, and Larson 1979) based on observations on individual workers suggest that λ_2 is large relative to λ_1. λ_2 may be such that the median lag of adjustment of labor supply in response to an exogenous shock is over two years.

To complete the generalized dynamic model of the labor market, specify the adjustment of wages as

$$w_t - w_{t-1} = \lambda_3[L_t^d - L_t^s], \tag{8.3}$$

a standard representation of Walrasian equilibration through changes in the price (of labor). What little evidence there is on the size of λ_3 suggests that the lag in (8.3) is also much longer than that in labor demand.[5] Also, note that anything that shocks (8.1) through (8.3) causes L^d to depart from L^s. That means that employment must differ from either L^d or L^s during the disequilibrium. The observed level of employment is

$$E = \min\{L^d, L^s\}. \tag{8.4}$$

Given the determinants of L^{d*} and L^{s*}, the system (8.1) through (8.4) can be used to examine how the time paths of employment and wages are affected by an identical shock before and after an increase in hiring costs raises λ_1. The evidence in Chapter 7 suggests that we can be fairly sure that half the adjustment of labor demand occurs in two quarters. Thus, a reasonable estimate is that $\lambda_1 = 0.25$ (0.5^2). Assume, as a conservative interpretation of the sparse evidence, that the median lag in labor supply is two years, and the median lag in the response of wage rates to excess labor demand is one year. With these assumptions, imposing an increase in hiring costs that is large enough to raise λ_1 to 0.5 (which increases the median lag in labor demand from six months to one year) has almost no impact on the time paths of employment or wages in response to either positive or negative shocks to long-run labor demand. Similarly, cutting hiring costs by enough to reduce the median lag in labor demand to just one quarter also works only small changes on the system's response to shocks.

The cause of what appear to be anomalous results is clear: The dynamics of the system are determined by the long lags in the adjust-

---

[5] Ashenfelter, Johnson, and Pencavel (1972) and Johnson (1977) provide evidence on this. Presumably the slow adjustment is due partly to rigidities induced by unions, partly to the effects of implicit contracts.

ment of labor supply and of wages in disequilibrium. This renders even important changes in hiring costs incapable of causing more than minor disturbances in the paths of aggregate employment and wages.

At this point it would be appropriate to summarize all the evidence that has been produced using models of hiring costs. There is no such evidence; the only guide is the prediction of the model that the policy will reduce fluctuations in employment. Requiring employers to list their vacancies with centralized employment registries, or insisting on certain forms of advertising, may achieve the goals of increased diversity of employment within the workplace and of more equal distribution of earnings by race or sex. They also generate the (at least short-run) economic cost of reduced flexibility of the labor market. (That result is consistent with Griffin's 1992 estimates of their impact on substitution possibilities in the long run.) More important than their dynamic effects are the reductions they induce in the long-run demand for worker-hours through the increase in labor costs.

III. Policies Affecting the Cost of Layoffs

In this section I discuss policies that affect the cost of layoffs but not internal adjustment costs. The archetypal policy is an unemployment benefit paid by the employer. One way of viewing such benefits is as affecting a_2 in the model of (6.9′). As such, they are no different from severance pay to workers who are permanently laid off. Unemployment benefits that are financed by taxes on employers not only raise the cost of separating workers from the firm, though. They also affect the cost of keeping attached workers idle, and as such must be viewed in the context of a model of implicit contracts and temporary layoffs (as in Figure 6.7). This section deals at length with such taxes on layoffs and the empirical evidence of their effects on employment fluctuations in the United States. The discussion of severance pay is in the next section.

To model the effect of unemployment insurance (hereafter UI) benefits and the taxes that finance them, I could use the complex contracting model of (6.21′) and (6.22) to distinguish between effects on permanent and temporary layoffs. To simplify matters, and to concentrate on the temporary layoffs that seem so important in the United States, I use a model that holds long-run employment fixed (a constant number of workers is attached to the firm).[6] The employer chooses both the wage and the fraction of workers on temporary lay-

[6] Topel (1982) presents Current Population Survey data for the mid-1970s showing that over one-third of all unemployed workers were on temporary layoff.

off. As in the contracting model of Chapter 6, these choices must maintain the worker's expected utility at the level available in a risk-free alternative employment.

The simplest way to model this is to assume that hours are fixed and the product price does not change, and to ignore the costs of capital.[7] The implied short-run approach seems sensible in a model of temporary layoffs. The employer's profits can be written as

$$\pi = P^*F([1-u]E^*) - w[1-u]E^* - euBE^*, \tag{8.5}$$

where P^* is the product price, B is the unemployment benefit per period, e is the fraction of UI benefits financed by charges on the employer, and E^* is the work force. u is the fraction of the firm's trained workers who are on temporary layoff (as in Section VI of Chapter 6). The firm chooses w and u to keep the typical worker's expected utility constant at

$$\bar{U} = [1-u]U(w,0) + uU(B,T), \tag{8.6}$$

where T is the leisure available to the laid-off worker. As in the United States after the early 1980s, and in most other countries, B is taxed at the same rate as wages, so that (8.6) reflects the utility from after-tax income.

The utility function generates indifference curves that are like $U(0)$ in Figure 8.3. That particular curve is based on the assumption that $B = 0$ and reflects combinations of w and u that suffice to keep workers' utility at $\bar{U}$. The firm's isoprofit curves π^* are negatively sloped and concave: With a higher wage the firm must lay off workers (raise u) to maintain profits. With the usual shape of production functions ($F'' < 0$), incremental reductions in employment (increases in u) cause increasing reductions in output, making constant profits consistent with ever-smaller rises in w.

Without UI benefits ($B = e = 0$) the behavior of the (constrained) employer leads to an equilibrium at point I in Figure 8.3, on the lowest isoprofit curve consistent with maintaining workers' utility at $\bar{U}$, labeled $\pi^*_{B=e=0}$. Consider what happens if UI benefits are paid ($B > 0$), but they are provided by government without being charged to the employer ($e = 0$). The same combination of wage rates and probabilities of working now yields a higher expected utility. The indifference curve that offers the same satisfaction as the risk-free alternative becomes $U(B)$. Even if U is homothetic, though, $U(B)$ is flatter in w—$[1-u]$ space than $U(0)$: A drop in 1-u generates some UI benefits,

---

[7] This presentation is a simplified version of Feldstein (1976) and Baily (1977) that allows the essence of those models to be shown in a simple graphical way. Extended discussions of this model are presented by Burdett and Hool (1983) and Burdett and Wright (1990).

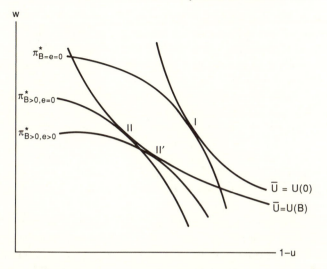

8.3 Equilibrium Wages and Temporary Layoffs with
Experience-Rated Unemployment Benefits

so the increase in the wage needed to maintain the typical worker's utility is less. This enables employers to operate on the more favorable isoprofit curve, $\pi^*_{B>0,e=0}$. The result is a new equilibrium at point II, with lower wages and a higher probability of layoff. UI benefits that are provided without charging the employer are a subsidy that gives an incentive to increase layoffs and/or reduce wages.

To circumvent this incentive for increased layoffs American systems of UI benefits *experience-rate* them by charging employers for some part of the benefits paid to their workers. In terms of (8.5) this means that they set $e > 0$. This does not directly alter the typical worker's utility, since e does not enter (8.6). It does, though, flatten the isoprofit curves in Figure 8.3: At a constant profit, any increase in u is now associated with additional (tax) costs, so that the wage increase that is consistent with constant profits must be smaller. The tilt in the map of isoprofit curves shifts the equilibrium along $\bar{U} = U(B)$ to point II′. Taxing employers to finance the benefits paid to their workers reduces layoffs. To the extent that the taxes reflect the benefits paid by the particular firm (are properly experience-rated), they will offset the subsidy to layoffs produced by the benefits.

In the broader contracting model of (6.21′) and (6.22), with margins of decision about hiring and firing, the same conclusions about wages and temporary layoffs still hold. Offering benefits without taxing the employer increases the size of the firm by increasing its hiring rate and enlarging its permanent work force. More generally, it enables those firms that experience greater fluctuations in product demand to use their unusually large rates of payout of UI benefits to expand relative to other firms. Requiring employers to pay taxes to finance these benefits reduces this subsidy to unstable firms.

If employers have a margin of choice between layoffs and reduced hours, the effects of these subsidies/taxes on layoffs become less clear. In the United States they are particularly muddied by the low tax base (see Chapter 5, footnote 17). Because the effects are on dynamic employment-hours substitution, I discuss them in Section V.

To understand the effects of taxes on layoffs it is first necessary to understand the institutions of the experience-rated UI tax system in the United States. To qualify for certain federal tax credits, all states have adopted systems of at least partial experience rating. Over half of all employees are in states where experience rating is based on the *reserve ratio*, the excess of the employer's prior taxes minus prior benefits relative to the company's taxable wages (Topel 1985). In reserve-ratio systems the typical tax structure can be described by Schedule A in Figure 8.4 (based on Brechling 1981). The tax rate cannot drop below a legislated minimum t_{min}, which is zero in some states, even if reserves rise above some maximum ratio, R^*. As the company's reserve-ratio drops, its tax rate rises in steps until it hits t_{max}, the highest tax rate on employers with positive reserves. In some states an extra tax on *negative-balance employers*—those whose reserve accounts are in deficit—makes the highest tax rate t_{neg}.

Schedule A in Figure 8.4 is not permanent. An employer's tax rate also depends on the experience of the entire state UI fund. If the state fund is low—it has been paying out more than it has recently taken in—a higher tax schedule is imposed statewide. There is some *least favorable* schedule, Schedule B in Figure 8.4, that relates a firm's tax rate to its reserve ratio when the state fund is weakest. Obversely, if the state fund has been bringing in more taxes than have been paid out in benefits, lower schedules are imposed. There is some *most favorable* Schedule C, which employers face if the state fund is very flush. Notice that t_{min}, t_{max}, and t_{neg} can differ along the various schedules (though few states have both different minimum and maximum tax rates on their most and least favorable schedules).

A company whose reserve ratio is above R^* when the state is on Schedule A cannot reduce its tax rate below t_{min}; and if the state were already on its most favorable schedule, the tax rate could never be reduced. Unless $t'_{min} = 0$, these limits mean that additional benefit payments will not raise the employer's tax bill; and lower benefit payments may not lower the tax bill. Additional benefits paid by an

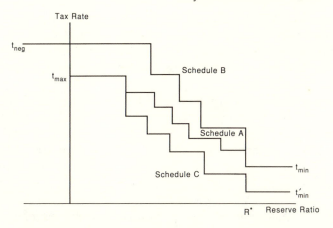

8.4 UI Tax Schedules, Tax Rates, and the Company's
Reserve Ratio

employer with a negative balance cannot raise the tax on a given schedule; and if the state is already on its least favorable schedule, those benefits cannot raise taxes in the future if the employer continues to pay very high UI benefits. Also, negative-balance employers do not accrue any interest charges; and positive-balance employers are not credited with interest. Other employers essentially provide interest-free loans out of their tax payments to finance benefits for employees of negative-balance firms.

This cross-subsidization exists within a state, and is applicable for limited times between states, because states that run deficits can borrow from the federal government. Since the early 1980s those loans accrue interest, and penalty tax rates have been assessed on employers in states that had borrowed. The average employer in a state is eventually charged for benefits paid in that state. Each state system is self-contained; but the charges are by no means directly on the firm where the layoffs occur.

State governments have made decisions that *noncharged benefits*— those paid to voluntary quitters and selected other categories of recipients—will not be financed by taxes on the employer from whose company the worker was separated. To some extent the heightened incentives to lay off workers are reduced by the existence of the multiple tax schedules depicted in Figure 8.4: Even though the benefits may not raise taxes this year, they may do so in future years as the state system shifts to a higher schedule (Wolcowitz 1984; Brown 1986). The limits on tax rates, the absence of interest credits to employers with positive balances and of interest charges on those with negative balances, and the noncharging of some benefits all imply that the UI tax is only *partly experience-rated*. The low limit on the tax base also makes experience rating imperfect. In terms of the model above, e is less than one.

Several studies support this conclusion. Substantial benefits are not charged or are charged to employers who already pay t_{neg}. Studies covering the 1970s (Wandner and Crosslin 1980; Hibbard 1980; Becker 1981) found that noncharged benefits amounted to roughly 15 percent of all payments, and that negative-balance employers account for around 20 percent of payments. Data for 1983 for twelve states show that benefits charged to positive-balance employers and to negative-balance employers up to their tax contributions equaled only 52 percent of all benefits (U.S. Department of Labor 1985). Finally, even ignoring noncharged benefits, data for nineteen states (Topel 1984, table 1) suggest that the cost to the typical employer of an extra dollar of UI benefits is only around eighty cents.

As with any economic policy, the actual size of e varies over time as laws, administrative rules, and economic behavior change. There is strong evidence, though, that e was between one-half and two-thirds during the 1960s and 1970s, but that it probably increased to between two-thirds and three-fourths in the late 1980s. This change was due to a widening of the range of tax rates in 1985 that more than sufficed to offset the decline in effective experience rating resulting from the decreasing fraction of total earnings that were taxable.[8]

This evidence on the actual degree of experience rating suggests that: (1) employers with substantial noncharged benefits, (2) negative-balance employers, (3) companies that are at t_{max}, and (4) firms whose reserve ratio exceeds R^* in states where $t_{min} > 0$ all increase layoffs above what they would be if experience rating were complete. The incentive is greater where the product-demand cycle is easily predicted, for employees are then more easily attracted to a company offering a slightly lower wage along with the chance to receive benefits while on layoff. This implies that seasonal and other temporary layoffs will be especially strongly affected by incomplete experience rating, as will permanent layoffs where business cycles are predictable. Other permanent layoffs, such as those stemming from in-

---

[8] This widening resulted from federal action that required states to raise t_{max} beginning in 1985 if they wished employers in the state to qualify for federal credits on the UI tax.

creased foreign competition and other demand shocks, are not likely to be affected so much.

Beginning in the late 1970s substantial research related partial experience-rating to employment fluctuations.[9] Table 8.1 summarizes the twelve studies of this effect, which have mainly attempted to discover the effects of the tax structure on the layoff rate or the rate of unemployment resulting from layoffs. They have tried to distinguish between effects on permanent and temporary layoffs, and to look for special impacts on seasonal variations in employment. Both efforts are based on the observation from the model in Figure 8.3 that the largest effects of partial experience rating should be on those flows into unemployment that are most expected and among those workers who are likely to retain an attachment to the employer who lays them off.

In some studies the impact of differences in the parameters of state UI tax systems, which are structured as nonlinear functions of firms' experience, is clouded by the use of industry-level data on turnover measures. In others the effects of the parameters of the tax systems on turnover are considered separately rather than through their impacts on e. Since it is differences in e that directly affect turnover, the best estimates of the impact of incomplete experience rating are in those studies that first construct measures of e and then relate these to disaggregated data on the turnover of individual workers or on the adjustment of employment in individual firms. All the studies advance our knowledge; but these considerations suggest that Saffer (1983) and especially Topel (1983, 1984, and 1985), Anderson (1992), and Card and Levine (1992) are the most reliable.

More research on the effect of these taxes on the rate of layoffs is clearly desirable. Especially useful would be a greater effort to link the policies to adjustment costs, since only Anderson (1992) does so explicitly. The evidence is sufficient at this point, though, to conclude that higher e, and thus higher taxes on layoffs, does reduce the layoff rate, the rate of layoff unemployment, and variability in employment. The major avenues through which changes in tax laws produce this impact are higher t_{neg} or t_{max}. The effect is mainly on temporary layoffs and seasonal unemployment; the evidence for effects on permanent layoffs is more mixed.

As Table 8.1 shows, the empirical research has demonstrated that a higher tax base relative to taxable wages also reduces layoffs and

[9] Only one empirical study (Warden 1967) was published before 1977. Though hardly at the same degree of sophistication as the studies published during the 1980s that linked data on workers to the characteristics and experience of the state UI tax systems, its conclusions are qualitatively similar to those in later work.

TABLE 8.1
Studies of Experience Rating and Layoff Unemployment

Study	Data	Results
Brechling (1981)	Reserve-ratio states, manufacturing industries, 1962–69	Higher t_{neg} sharply reduces layoff rate; smaller effect of lower t_{min}
Edebalk and Wadensjö (1986)	Sweden, 1954–69	Sharp decline in temporary layoffs after introduction of partial experience rating
Halpin (1979)	Three small manufacturing industries, 36 to 50 states, 1960–74	Less seasonal variability of employment where high tax base compared to wages; no consistent effects of other tax parameters
Halpin (1980)	41,000 individuals, 1976	Temporary layoffs less where: higher tax base compared to wages, higher t_{max}
Kaiser (1987)	Reserve-ratio states, manufacturing industries, 1964–69	Higher t_{neg} sharply reduces layoff rate. High tax base reduces layoff rate
Saffer (1982)	States, data on industries, 1967–75	Larger gap between t_{neg} (or t_{max}) and t_{min} reduces layoff rate
Saffer (1983)	15,000 individuals, 1975	Lesser chance of being on temporary or permanent layoff in states with larger gap between t_{neg} (or t_{max}) and t_{min}
Topel (1983)	8,000 individuals, 29 industries, 19 states, 1975	Lesser chance of temporary layoff, greater chance of returning to work with higher e. $e < 1$, not taxing benefits, produced 30% of temporary layoff unemployment
Topel (1984)	34,000 individuals, 29 industries, reserve- and benefit-ratio states, 1973–76	Lesser chance of being on temporary layoff in states and industries where e greater. Smaller effect on permanent layoff unemployment
Topel (1985)	76,000 men, reserve- and benefit-ratio states, 1975	Higher e lowers temporary layoffs more than permanent layoffs, quit unemployment. $e = 1$ reduces unemployment rate by 1.5 percentage points
Anderson (1992)	8,000 retail firms, 6 states, quarterly, 1978–84	Higher e increases employment level, decreases its seasonal variation
Card and Levine (1992)	180,000 individuals, 36 states, 1979–87; state employment by industry, 1978–87	Higher marginal e decreases temporary layoffs in recessions by 40%, decreases variability of employment

seasonal unemployment. For a particular set of tax rates, raising the tax base raises the tax liability of a negative-balance employer, or one at t_{max}, who lays off another worker. Raising the tax base is another way of increasing the extent of experience rating (Brechling 1977). Indeed, even though taxes in European UI systems are not experience-rated by law, European employers rely less on temporary layoffs to meet drops in product demand. One reason may be that, unlike in the United States, UI taxes in Europe are essentially a variable cost because the tax bases are very high relative to wages (Fitzroy and Hart 1985).

Topel (1990) brought together a variety of aspects of UI in an overall evaluation of the effect of incomplete experience rating in the United States. His calculations suggest that imposing complete experience rating would reduce unemployment by roughly 20 percent. It is hard to imagine that a program that taxes less than 1.5 percent of payroll can account for 1.5 percentage points of unemployment in the U.S. labor force. Put somewhat differently, with the relatively small fraction of the unemployed in the late 1980s who received UI benefits (Blank and Card 1991), it is difficult to believe that three-fourths of UI recipients would not have been unemployed if the program did not exist, or that it induces substantial unemployment among those who do not obtain benefits.

While we lack a good estimate of the net impact of imperfect experience rating, the research summarized in Table 8.1 makes it clear that greater experience rating reduces layoffs, and that the chief route for the reductions is through higher maximum tax rates, a higher tax base, and reduced noncharging of benefits. Imposing adjustment costs in the form of experience-rated UI taxes on employers partly offsets the incentives that the payment of UI benefits gives to firms and workers to increase layoffs.

IV. Policies Affecting Internal Adjustment Costs

A. General Considerations and Institutions

A wide variety of policies and institutions affect the internal costs of adjusting labor demand. Requirements that workers (or their representatives) receive advance notice of permanent layoffs imposes costs on the employer's efforts to reorganize production. Policies that restrict the use of temporary workers or that limit "contracting out" of production have qualitatively similar effects. So too do limitations on mandatory retirement. Trade unions, at least in the United States, engage in a variety of restrictive practices that can be construed as affecting dynamics. The diverse policies and their various impacts do not lend themselves easily to one particular line of analysis. Instead, in this section I consider them generally, provide specific discussions of the dynamic effects of trade union restrictions, and summarize the growing literature on the impact of changing job-security policies.

Policies affecting internal adjustent costs must affect $C(\Delta L)$ or $C(hL)$, the cost of hiring. In some cases the direct monetary costs are external, for example, penalties for separating workers. They indirectly generate internal costs, though, as the employers' responses to them change the nature of production—its rate and the profit-maximizing combinations of inputs that are generated by alternative sets of factor prices. In other cases the internal adjustment costs are generated directly, as restrictions are placed, rather than incentives merely given, on the rate and manner in which labor demand can be adjusted.

The model of (8.1) through (8.4) also applies to the discussion of internal adjustment costs. Higher costs of adjusting labor demand, either external or internal costs, slow the adjustment of employment only if they are sufficiently large that demand-side lags have important effects on the paths of employment and wages. As we saw in Section II, in general the lags in supply and wage adjustment are so much greater than those in demand that changes in the costs of adjusting labor demand have little effect on the path of employment. This means that the policies and institutions discussed here may not have obvious effects on the dynamics of employment *if we restrict attention only to existing firms.*

The more important effects of these policies may be on the birth and death rates of establishments. For continuing establishments that are not near the margin of closing, the analysis of Section II applies. Some labor costs that the employer had viewed as variable are converted into something more closely resembling fixed costs. As noted there, this partly insulates the work force from short-run fluctuations in demand; and the higher labor costs reduce the demand for worker-hours in the long run. An entrepreneur considering whether to open a business or continue as an employee elsewhere views all labor costs as variable. Imposing restrictions on the future ability to change the path of labor demand reduces the present value of the subjective potential stream of profits, thus reducing the rate of entry of new firms. Also, in the transition to the new long-run equilibrium with lower employment (dictated by the higher average costs of labor) the death rate of firms rises (temporarily) as businesses that were on the margin of profitability find that the increased costs make the expected profit stream negative.[10]

Another general consideration is the common limitation in many job-security laws on the size of the establishment to which the law applies or the size of the change in employment that is covered. A minimum firm size mainly produces static effects and alters entrepreneurs' choice of scale for new firms. A minimum on employment change alters the costs of adjustment and thus employment dynamics. Limiting the applicability of a job-security policy that regulates mass layoffs to layoffs of more than one hundred workers, for example, raises adjustment costs for $\Delta L \leq -100$, creating a discontinuity at that point.[11]

Depending on the size of the shock that generates pressure for layoffs and on the structure of adjustment costs before the policy is imposed, this discontinuity could smooth (and slow) adjustment by providing incentives to slow the rate of layoffs. By behaving this way employers can avoid incurring the discontinuous increase in costs. It is quite possible, though, that a firm would react by lumping all its layoffs together, since the policy creates what is essentially a fixed cost of changing employment (in amounts of at least one hundred workers). The actual impact is an empirical issue, but it is noteworthy that even the dynamic effects of such policies may be perverse.

The first example of imposed changes in internal adjustment costs is certain negotiated work practices in union contracts. Job security—the protection of current members' jobs and of employment opportunities for union labor generally—has been recognized as a major or even overarching goal of unions (Perlman 1928). A variety of union practices, including negotiated changes in work rules, limitations on contracting with outside suppliers, and restrictions on the utilization of labor that accompany process innovations, affect the demand for labor without directly affecting its price.[12] Some of these practices are static Q-policies that have no dynamic effects. Limits on external contracting are attempts to shift the derived demand for union labor by increasing the demand for goods and services produced by the union's members. Limits on the minimum number of workers in-

---

[10] This assumes that the firm does not incur internal adjustment costs if it declares bankruptcy. For single-establishment firms it is unclear how such costs could be imposed under existing laws. At least in the United States, the employer is not as yet obligated to bear them if the business closes permanently.

[11] This is exactly the limit contained in the U.S. plant-closing law, P.L. 100–379.

[12] Rees (1989) presents an overview of this issue, while Allen (1986) discusses in detail the imposition of union work rules in construction.

volved in a particular process are designed to tilt input ratios toward labor.[13]

Other practices, though, restrict the rate at which innovations can be introduced by limiting employers' ability to shed labor. Slichter, Healy, and Livernash (1960, 368) report on the Railway Clerks' efforts to ensure that labor-saving devices reduce employment only through natural attrition. Contracts in the automobile and longshoring industries have imposed similar requirements.[14] These practices require distinguishing between adjustments at the intensive margin within existing firms and adjustment in marketwide employment through the birth and death of firms and plants. For existing firms they impose an added cost to negative net changes in employment. As the theory in Chapter 6 predicts, and as the evidence in Chapter 7 implies, that should slow the rate of downward adjustment of employment by reducing the rate of layoffs. By adding to the costs of staying in business, though, the restrictions also increase the likelihood of plant closing in response to negative shocks to product demand or to other positive shocks to labor costs. As long as the employer is not liable if the plant is closed, and as long as the restrictions do not apply if it is sold, they imply a lumpy reduction in adjustment costs for a sufficiently large cut in employment (to zero workers). They thus increase the death rate of unionized firms and plants.

Within existing firms it is unclear whether the reduction in the rate of layoffs, and the greater employment of unionized workers that it generates, suffice to overcome the increased incentive to close plants and the concomitant (lumpy) decline in employment of union labor. There is little research on the effect of unions on the rate of permanent layoff (independent of differences in rates of unionization by industry). No studies of plant closings have addressed the specific effects of union restrictions. The theory suggests, though, that the policy does not obviously slow the rate of reduction of the demand for union labor. The rate of continuous reduction is slowed, but the rate of mass reductions through shutdowns is increased.

As noted earlier, imposing adjustment costs reduces the expected profit streams foreseen by prospective employers. That is equally

[13] Johnson (1990) discusses this sort of job-security provision in the context of a model of bargaining over wages and employment.

[14] For example, the 1987 contract between the United Auto Workers and the J. I. Case Company specified a Guaranteed Employment Level at each plant. Outsourcing, new technology, productivity improvements, and the like were not allowed to reduce employment, and even attrition could only reduce employment levels by one worker for each two workers who quit or retired (Bureau of National Affairs, *Collective Bargaining Negotiations and Contracts*, 60:315).

true for the adjustment costs represented by restrictions on the rate of layoffs that are negotiated by unions. As such, these union policies give prospective employers an incentive to avoid opening up unionized establishments. They shift the birth rate of plants toward the nonunion sector of an industry, generating a long-run equilibrium with a less heavily unionized industry.

B. Job-Security Policies

Included under this heading are a wide variety of legislation and legal decisions that affect the adjustment of labor demand. Consider first one specific policy, advance notice to workers of impending plant closings or mass layoffs, whose goal is to make it easier for workers to find new jobs. The only econometric evidence is on state-level policies (e.g., Folbre, Leighton, and Roderick 1984, for Maine). It and a rapidly growing literature on bargained or employer-granted notice suggests that the policy reduces the average duration of post-layoff unemployment (Addison and Portugal 1987; Ehrenberg and Jakubson 1988). Does this beneficial effect come at the cost of more rapid plant closings?

There is some evidence (Hamermesh 1987) that workers do not anticipate plant closings or seek wage adjustments to compensate for their impending losses. The legislation might change that, causing the demand for labor to drop and the layoff or plant closing to occur sooner. Since the constant-output elasticity of labor demand is negative (see Chapter 3), with sufficient notice some change in this direction will occur. In the United States, the Canadian provinces, and most European countries, though, the notice can hardly produce much effect. Three or even six months, the maximum reported (Ehrenberg and Jakubson 1988), are too short to allow wage effects to generate reduced demand, given the slow speed with which wages adjust to shocks. Ordinary movements up a labor-demand curve will not be important.

The demand for labor might drop if workers restrict output as morale falls. Similarly, workers with the best alternatives, presumably those less senior workers not earning the quasi rents that accompany long job tenure, may leave. The changes may accelerate the date of the layoff or plant closing. All we can be sure of is that, given the relatively short period of notice required, the acceleration cannot be too large. The demand-side costs of the policy thus do not appear to be important.

Severance pay to workers discharged because of insufficient product demand is mandated in many industrialized economies and in some developing economies too (see Chapter 10). In many the pay increases steadily with the worker's prior tenure with the company.[15] An equity argument for this link is that long-tenure workers have invested more in firm-specific human capital that is being wiped out by the permanent layoff. Given substantial evidence that the amount of such human capital peaks, or at least stops growing, after some years in a firm (Mincer and Jovanovic 1981; Topel 1991), this rationale cannot completely explain the pattern of severance pay; but for most dismissed workers it is a fairly good rationalization.

Yet another form of job-security arrangement is the penalty paid to the state by employers who violate laws governing individual or collective firings (see Gennard 1985). Even assuming that any penalties that generate government revenues are offset by reduced taxes, this type of restriction will alter patterns of layoffs and levels of employment. If penalties are paid, they do not necessarily accrue to workers, and thus will not be offset by changes in the structure of wages even in a frictionless labor market. Even if they are not paid, the threat they impose changes the path of labor demand and its long-run equilibrium level.

Mandatory severance pay is designed to increase incentives to maintain employment, or to compensate workers when those incentives are insufficient. In some cases governments recognize that a particular industry or region has suffered a permanent drop in demand or a permanent labor-saving change in technology and offer incentives to speed the internal adjustment toward a lower long-run level of employment.[16] These incentives are usually in the form of adjustment assistance to workers; but since they affect the wage at which workers are willing to supply their labor to new employers or to new geographic areas, they can be viewed as subsidies that encourage permanent layoffs. Their existence means that not all job-security policies need slow adjustment.

In most industrialized countries the panoply of job-security policy has been well developed since the early 1970s. In the United States, except for a history of aid for readjustment (subsidies to permanent layoffs) since the early 1960s, and the very weak advance notification law passed in 1988, there is no full-blown legislation mandating job

[15] Gennard (1985) presents a concise summary of issues involving severance pay and legislation in the OECD as of the mid-1980s. More recent information is provided by the sources in Lazear (1990).

[16] Houseman (1991) describes the reactions of the government of Luxembourg to long-term changes in its steel industry as fitting this model. The political mechanism that determines when policy will cease trying to prevent layoffs and begin encouraging adjustment is far beyond the scope of this book.

security. Instead, beginning in the mid-1970s, state courts and legislatures began limiting employment at will (EAW), nonunion employers' unlimited freedom to terminate employees.[17] The uncertainty surrounding the limitations on EAW makes it very unlikely, even assuming complete freedom to contract, that the labor market could have offset these changes. Thus, backed by government sanctions, these restrictions could alter the rate at which employers adjust labor demand. Moreover, since they impose added labor costs, or threaten to do so, they may reduce the long-run demand for labor.

In the rest of this section I summarize and discuss the evidence on the impact of this immense array of policies on the path and level of employment demand. The discussion of the effects on the demand for hours versus workers, or on the relative demand for part-time versus full-time employees, is left to Section V. Table 8.2 divides the econometric literature on job-security policies into two broad types. The first includes comparisons of employment dynamics before and after the time when job-security policies were believed to become effective. These pre-post comparisons do not use specific information about the importance of particular policies. Instead, they implicitly treat the policies as dichotomous, either fully effective or nonexistent. The second group of studies uses measures of the magnitude of the policy, for examples, the size of severance pay and the degree of the exception to employment at will, to examine their effect on employment dynamics or levels. With an otherwise equally careful research design this second approach is clearly preferable.

Most of the studies of both types that use macroeconomic data, or data from one large industry, find that the policies do slow employment adjustment. This inference is especially clear in the pre-post comparisons in Table 8.2 that are based on aggregated data; but it also is derivable from the explicit cross-section comparisons of employment variations in countries whose job-security policies differ (Bertola 1990; Bentolila and Bertola 1990). The conclusion almost disappears in Burgess (1989), based on time series covering two-digit manufacturing industries. It is not supported in the clever research design in Abraham and Houseman (1988), who showed little relative change in speeds of employment adjustment between Germany and the United States after the introduction of German job-security policies.

Among the pre-post comparisons using microeconomic data Ben-

[17] Krueger (1991a) presents a state-by-state chronology of changing exceptions to EAW and explains them as a response to the increased costs of lawsuits brought by dismissed workers. Dertouzos and Karoly (1990) offer a similar chronology and a discussion of changes in the case law.

TABLE 8.2
Studies of the Effects of Job-Security Policies

Study	Data	Results
	Pre-post Comparisons	
Nickell (1979)	Manufacturing employment and hours, quarterly, 1954–76; U.K.	Employment lag ↑, hours lag ↓
Abraham and Houseman (1988)	Manufacturing industries, employment and hours, annual, 1962–84; U.S. and West Germany	No ↑ in employment lag in Germany relative to U.S. after German JS
Hamermesh (1988b)	Employment and hours, annual, 1961–85; 12 OECD countries	Employment lag ↑, no change in hours lag
Fallon and Lucas (1991)	Manufacturing industries, employment, annual: India, 1959–82, Zimbabwe, 1960–85	No change in employment lag; ↓ in labor demand after JS
Houseman (1991)	Employment, steel plants, annual, 1974, 1977–82; 6 EC countries	Greater ↓ employment in U.K., with weaker JS, than in other EC countries; JS slows hiring
Bentolila and Saint-Paul (1992)	Employment, manufacturing firms, 1983–88; Spain	Employment lag ↓ after flexible contracts became more widespread
	Explicit Measures of Job Security: *1. Dynamic Adjustment Equations*	
Burgess (1988)	Manufacturing, employment, quarterly, 1964–82; U.K.	Employment lag ↑ with ↑ severance pay, ↑ penalty for unfair dismissal
Burgess (1989)	4 manufacturing industries, employment, quarterly, 1964–82; U.K.	In 1 industry ↑ severance pay and unfair dismissal penalty ↑ employment lag; no impact in other industries
Burgess and Dolado (1989)	Manufacturing employment, quarterly, 1965–82; U.K.	$C(L)$ ↑ when unfair dismissal penalty is ↑

TABLE 8.2 *(cont.)*

Study	Data	Results
	2. Other Methods	
Bentolila and Bertola (1990)	Simulation of linear C($\dot{L}$) model, 1960s–80s; France, West Germany, Italy, U.K.	↑ firing costs ↓ employment, but effects were small in 1970s
Bertola (1990)	Employment change, annual, 1962–86; 10 OECD countries	Greater variation in employment where job-security regulation less stringent
Dertouzos and Karoly (1990)	Employment, annual, 1980–86; states, large industries	Introducing greater exceptions to EAW ↓ employment by as much as 5%
Lazear (1990)	Employment, annual, 1956–84; 22 countries	Large negative effect of severance pay and advance notice on employment-population ratio

tolila's and Saint-Paul's (1992) study of Spanish manufacturing shows that labor demand fluctuated more in response to output shocks after flexible employment rules were adopted. Houseman's (1991) careful analysis of time series of employment in individual steel plants in Western Europe shows greater decreases in employment in the United Kingdom, where restrictions that provided job security in this industry were less stringent. Because the period covered by her analysis was quite short, this result could be showing that the policy slows the rate of (downward) employment adjustment. Even more interesting, she offers evidence that a more restrictive policy slowed hiring, as Section II suggested will happen.

The strongest possible conclusion is that there is only a weak indication that the policies have any effect on employment dynamics. This may be because they are imposed at times when, as Section II showed, the expected impacts will not be observed; it may be that their dynamic effects are too small to be observed; or perhaps the necessary degree of care in modeling and testing their effects has not yet been taken. With the limited empirical study that this diverse group of policies has attracted we should not in any case have expected a convincing answer on something as subtle as employment dynamics.

The conclusion about the effects of these cost-increasing policies on the level of employment is clearer, as it rests on the two most careful studies in the second part of Table 8.2, Lazear (1990) and Dertouzos and Karoly (1990). Bertola (1990) did not find any effect of job-security policies on employment levels; but he failed to model the policies as carefully as in the other two studies, and he used economywide aggregates.

Dertouzos and Karoly (1990) included variables indicating whether a state had allowed exceptions to EAW and the form of those changes. Their estimates show that employment was reduced more within particular industries in states that allowed stronger exceptions. By using data disaggregated below the national level, and by carefully tracing the timing of judicial changes in the EAW doctrine, they offer convincing evidence on the impact of restrictions on job security. Lazear (1990) used a similar research design on a panel of countries to show that greater required advance notice of job termination, and especially more generous severance pay, reduced employment. This careful research design provides some evidence that the policies' negative side effects on the level of employment may be at least as important as any protection they offer to workers.

Job-security policies are much more diverse than the unemployment insurance policies discussed in the previous section. Yet the amount of careful evaluation research on UI far exceeds that on job security. Unlike the best research summarized in Table 8.1, there are no studies of job security that contain the detailed microeconometric analysis and careful specification of the parameters describing the policies that are necessary to infer their effects. Also, no empirical research has separated the effects on employment levels that result from altered adjustment costs operating through conventional labor-demand elasticities from those that work through quasi elasticities of labor demand. Until additional research that deals with these problems is produced, advocates on both sides of the discussion about these policies have nearly but no longer completely free rein to espouse their positions.

V. Policies Affecting the Dynamics of Employment and Hours

Many policies are designed to increase the relative demand for employment when product demand drops. Included in this are the requirement for premium pay for overtime work and partial unemployment benefits or compensation for short-time work. They and the other policies discussed in this section may affect dynamics; they also affect the equilibrium combination of employment and hours, as we discussed in Chapter 5. Recognizing this fact, it is important to examine how they affect adjustment costs before concluding they have any effects on dynamics.

This consideration points up a conundrum common to many of the policies discussed here. They aim to spread work during recessions; yet if they are permanent, we know that they reduce the demand for worker-hours in the long run and lower real output, because they raise labor costs. They may even, as Chapter 5 showed, reduce the demand for workers in the long run. Is there any way to avoid the tradeoff between worsened average living standards and reduced fluctuations in employment that the cost structures of these policies imply? Can a policy be devised to spread employment without reducing worker-hours?

Before considering policies that aim explicitly at work sharing, I examine two types of public policy that can affect the dynamics of employers' choices between employment and hours. The first is a payroll tax with a ceiling on taxable earnings. The best example of this is the tax that finances unemployment benefits in United States, which limits the taxable amount to less than half the average worker's earnings. The low tax ceiling affects dynamics, particularly seasonal fluctuations in hours and employment. Take the example of a company in Pennsylvania in 1989, where the tax base was $8,000. Assume its workers earn $16,000 per annum working a forty-hour week, and the employer is already rated at the highest state tax rate of 9.2 percent. On July 1 the employer realizes that product demand is booming and decides to expand output by 25 percent. Many factors will affect the choice between hiring more workers and asking current employees to work overtime. An additional, potentially substantial one is that the employer must pay UI taxes of 9.2 percent of wages on each new worker, but incurs no immediate UI tax liability on overtime hours of current workers (because the $8,000 ceiling means the tax liability on them vanished on June 30 for the remainder of the calendar year). The limit on the tax base thus raises the cost of adjusting employment relative to that of adjusting hours.

Halpin's two studies (Table 8.1), the only evidence on the impact of a higher UI tax base, produce results counter to this analysis: Taxing a greater fraction of earnings reduces layoffs and seasonal fluctuations in employment (and increases fluctuations in hours). This does not mean the analysis is incorrect, only that it is incomplete. It ignores the fact that limits on UI tax rates can be overcome if the tax base is higher, so that, as we saw in Section III, a higher tax base implies greater experience rating of taxes and the reduction in layoffs attendant on it. Presumably if one could hold constant the marginal effect of a higher tax base on the extent of experience rating, its discouragement to seasonal fluctuations in hours would be observable.

In some countries job-security provisions do not apply to regular employees with less than a specified accumulated seniority. Other countries, in response to concerns about the effects of job-security policies on worker-hours and real output, passed legislation relaxing their provisions and allowing employers to hire "noncontract" workers not subject to the policies (Gennard 1985). Even before the legislation, though, a growing number of employers sought to use temporary and part-time workers to whom job-security policies did not apply and for whom other fixed costs of employment were lower.

Taken by themselves, job-security policies shift the adjustment of labor demand from employment to hours. They generate a shift in demand toward "irregular" workers and toward an increase in the long-run employment-hours ratio. More important for purposes of this section, they also reduce the costs of responding to demand shocks by adjusting employment (of temporary or part-time workers) instead of hours (of full-time, regular workers).[18] These policies create a two-tier labor market, one consisting of long-term covered workers with job security and little fluctuation in hours, the other consisting of irregular workers whose jobs provide a cushion to fluctuations in product demand. Mandating job security for the former group generates job insecurity for the latter group.

While some work has been done on the static effects of job-security policies on the relative demand for workers and hours, there has been little study of their effects on dynamic relative demand. Nickell (1979) found that λ_{HH} in the United Kingdom decreased along with the structural increase in λ_{EE}; but Hamermesh (1988b) did not find evidence for this among the same OECD countries in which λ_{EE} increased. Also, very little study has been made of the dynamics of the demand for irregular workers, whether voluntary part-time or temporary or noncontract workers, compared to regular employees. The only satisfactory econometric study is Abraham (1988), whose survey produced data on the characteristics of over three hundred companies and their use of irregular workers. In those firms where product demand was more seasonal and varied more from year to year the fraction of total employment accounted for by irregular workers was greater. Beyond this, we know very little about the dynamic impacts

---

[18] Their effect on hours and employment dynamics is analytically similar to that of the limit on the base of a payroll tax.

of policies, other than that reduced employment fluctuations must lead to greater fluctuations in hours.

The evidence and simulations in Chapter 5 on the effects of over-time penalties dealt with their long-run implications. No empirical work has explicitly examined how they affect the dynamics of employment and hours. Consider a firm's adjustment to a negative shock to the forcing variables. Assume the productivity of a particular hour of work time is the same whether it is labeled as a regular hour or as overtime. Overtime penalties do not alter adjustment costs. They just change the relative prices of employees and hours. As long as the employer had used some overtime hours, the penalty decreases the costs of cutting hours as compared to reducing employment, because they change (static) hours costs compared to (dynamic) costs of adjusting employment. The change in costs at this margin induces greater flexibility into the demand for hours. Of course, if the employer had not been using overtime before the shock occurred, the downward path of employment and hours would be unaffected by the overtime penalty.

The conclusion is weakened if the productivity of an hour of work is greater when it is part of overtime rather than standard hours.[19] The incentive to reduce overtime hours in response to negative demand shocks is reduced, because one is substituting less for more productive hours. (The opposite result holds if overtime hours are less productive than standard hours.)

The conclusion is strengthened if an *unexpected* increase in the overtime penalty is imposed after a negative shock. In that case employers face a rise in the relative static costs of hours compared to the costs of adjusting employment, so they have an incentive to rely on reduced hours. Governments cannot impose ever-higher penalty rates in successive recessions, both because those rates will reduce the long-run demand for worker-hours and because employers will come to expect their imposition and will at least partly offset their effects. There is some limited scope, though, for a decisive policy to surprise employers and increase the effectiveness of overtime penalties by inducing them to vary hours instead of employment.

The magnitude of the dynamic effects of the penalties is not known; but because they apply regardless of the state of labor demand, they are not just targeted to spreading work during cyclical declines. Rather than relying on overtime penalties or shorter stan-

[19] See Santamäki (1988). This might occur, for example, if workers' effort responds to the premium pay they receive for overtime work. This possibility relaxes the assumption made in the simulation in Chapter 5.

dard hours, some European countries have attempted to encourage work sharing in response to decreases in product demand by offering short-time compensation (STC) payments to workers for partial unemployment. France, for example, pays unemployment compensation equal to 50 percent of wages for reductions below standard hours to workers who are certified by their employers. A similar program had long existed in Germany and was greatly expanded in 1974 as part of broader job-security legislation.

The United States has no national system of STC. State UI systems do, though, alter the relative costs of adjusting workers and hours by affecting workers' willingness to accept cuts in hours or employment. Since the inception of the UI program most states have provided *partial UI benefits* to be paid when a worker is unemployed at least several days per week. These payments severely discourage workers and employers from using them (Munts 1970) by imposing nearly infinite marginal tax rates (in terms of reduced UI benefits) on additional earnings. By 1989 eleven states, compared to six in 1978, had made their partial benefits provisions more conducive to work sharing by specifying that benefits are reduced by only a fraction of each dollar of earnings. Except for Alaska and Montana, though, the states that structure partial benefits this way decrease them by at least sixty-six cents for each additional dollar earned.

Burdett and Wright (1989) show that in the United States and Canada (which has a similarly underdeveloped system of partial benefits) a much greater fraction of the variation in worker-hours is accounted for by variations in employment than in most European countries. This is consistent with the results in Table 7.5. It may stem from differences in the methods of financing UI benefits (see Section III), or it may be due to factors unrelated to labor-market policy; but it is also consistent with differences in incentives provided by benefits for partial unemployment.

Perhaps because of the growth of STC in Europe, in 1982 the United States encouraged experiments with it by authorizing federal assistance to states to set up STC programs. As of 1987 twelve states had implemented STC programs, though with sharply differing financial arrangements. In six states even companies whose UI tax rates are at t_{neg} in Figure 8.4 paid the costs of their employees' STC; in six others STC payments were treated the same as regular UI benefits that are charged to the employer (Johnson 1987) but often not effectively experience-rated.

Kerachsky et al. (1986) evaluated STC programs in Arizona, California, and Oregon by comparing employers that used STC to others. In all three total payments under STC were less than 1.5 percent of all UI benefits. Clearly, STC could not have had much impact even in the states that implemented it. Workers in companies that used STC had more total hours of compensated time (by STC and regular benefits together) than did employees in other, unfortunately not necessarily observationally identical, firms. The experience in these three states is probably unusually favorable compared to the other nine states, for in these three STC payments were more likely to be experience-rated than regular UI benefits. This implies that in other states, where STC payments are no better experience-rated than regular UI benefits, the program generated even larger increases in compensated hours.

These findings suggest that in the United States STC led to greater reliance on work sharing relative to layoffs; but it also produced a greater reduction in total worker-hours. Wider application of STC would probably reduce layoff unemployment and spread work. However, it would reduce total worker-hours in long-run equilibrium: Unless it is perfectly experience-rated, it raises the price of a worker-hour for the average employer. Current research does not provide enough evidence to infer the size of this effect.

The conundrum posed at the start of this section has a clear answer, the same one as in the similar general problem in macroeconomics (Lucas's 1976 critique). There is no way to circumvent permanently the tradeoff between increasing employers' reliance on varying hours to meet cyclical declines in product demand and reducing their long-run demand for worker-hours. Policy surprises, such as altering overtime penalties in recessions, break the tradeoff; but repeated surprises come to be expected, and employers adjust long-run demand accordingly. Moreover, the increased uncertainty that surprises engender will itself reduce employment (if we abandon the usual assumption of risk-neutral firms).

VI. Conclusions, and the Need for Serious Evaluation

The overarching and too often neglected conclusion about policies affecting dynamic labor demand is that they also affect long-run labor demand—they alter the average level of worker-hours. As Chapter 6 showed, changes in adjustment costs change both the rate of adjustment and the target toward which employers adjust. The specific policies discussed here must always be analyzed in terms of their dynamic and static impacts (which is why some aspects of the policies considered here were treated in Chapter 5). Any policy that increases adjustment costs, and thus that attempts to discourage employers from reducing employment, necessarily decreases the demand for worker-hours in the long run.

The second general theme is basically a response to the riposte by proponents of job security and other work-sharing policies that long-run effects are irrelevant if jobs can be protected in the short term. The empirical side of that riposte is that it is difficult to find evidence that the policies reduce employment (or the obverse, that relaxing the policies stimulates employment).[20] As the discussion in Section II showed, the timing of the imposition of a policy surprise that affects adjustment costs will determine its short-run impacts. It is perfectly possible to observe policies that have long-run negative impacts on employment but that do no immediate harm. Job-protection policies can provide "free lunches" in the short run to the extent that they are unexpected. This suggests that complete evaluations of policies under any of the rubrics discussed here require obtaining several years of data and experience.

Comparing the discussions here and in Chapter 5 reveals how much further advanced is the study of static labor-demand policies. There I used the general empirical results from Chapter 3 to evaluate policies on which no specific evaluations had been conducted. Indeed, general empirical analysis obviated the need for policy evaluation in many cases. The links between the empirical work discussed in Chapter 7 and the general types and specific examples of policies discussed here have been much more tenuous. This is partly because empirical research on dynamic labor demand has not been so closely based on the underlying theoretical parameters. Partly, too, it stems from a nearly universal failure to model the effects of dynamic labor-demand policies on adjustment costs, the theoretical construct through which we must view them as affecting the paths of employment and hours.

The greatest need in this area is for research that explicitly models policies as changing adjustment costs. With that modeling the more general theoretical and empirical literature becomes relevant for predicting the effects of proposed policies. With it, too, evaluation studies can have a common basis that allows comparisons among them. A wide range of research in this area is thus necessary and would provide the opportunity to study the dynamic effects of these policies properly for the first time. Given problems of timing and expectations, such studies cannot be based on limited pre-post evaluation research. Also, the discussions here and in Chapter 7 show that it is

---

[20] Buechtemann (1989) is a good example of this skeptical view of long-run effects.

impossible to use variations in highly aggregated data to infer the complex effects of these policies on the structure and size of adjustment costs. Both arguments suggest using longitudinal data that follow individuals and firms for at least several years before and after a change in policy.

PART THREE

Some Applications

CHAPTER NINE

Labor Demand and the Macroeconomy

I. Introduction

The previous seven chapters have demonstrated that economists have put empirical meat on the bones of the static and dynamic theories of labor demand that I have described. Part III uses that empirical knowledge and the theoretical approaches that were developed in Chapters 2 and 6 to examine a variety of related issues. Chapter 9 deals with the implications of the study of labor demand for macroeconomic outcomes, Chapter 10 with its implications for the analysis of labor markets in developing countries. Both chapters contain series of vignettes, each examining a particular issue within the general topic of the chapter in relation to labor demand. Each vignette is designed to explore that relationship and examine its implications, not to provide an exhaustive analysis. The purpose in both chapters is to consider whether the study of labor demand has anything useful to say about this variety of topics.

In many cases the empirical evidence discussed in previous chapters was inferred from highly aggregated data; but it was always designed to shed light on the underlying microeconomic parameters and was never linked to macroeconomic behavior. In this chapter I examine what the accumulated knowledge gleaned from these literatures implies about various aspects of macroeconomics. In some cases the knowledge is sufficiently secure that it can be used to concentrate the search for explanations of macroeconomic phenomena. For example, the overwhelming evidence on the relative long-run inelasticity of labor demand and the very rapid adjustment of actual to desired labor demand should constrain the types of explanations that describe economic fluctuations. Their implications for macroeconomic equilibrium are examined in Section II.

In other cases we have not inferred specific estimates of important structural parameters; but we have narrowed the range of debate over the signs of some, and we have drawn some more general inferences about the structure of labor demand. The second part of Section II examines the implications for macroeconomic adjustment of assuming that there are substantial fixed costs of changing labor demand. Similarly, the first part of Section III considers how differing demand elasticities and varying ease of skill substitution affect the inequality of wages.

Several important macro issues depend on labor demand and merit discussion here even though we have not provided specific evidence that can be linked to them. Instead, the theoretical discussion and a general consideration of the evidence are useful in understanding them. The second part of Section III therefore examines the effects of technical progress on labor demand and the supply of jobs, based in part on the theory in Chapter 2 and the theory and empirical evidence in Chapter 4. Section IV uses the material in Part I to infer the substantive content of the terms "job-creation policy" and policies to create "good jobs."

II. Labor Demand and Macroeconomic Equilibria

Explaining macroeconomic fluctuations was the core of debates between Keynes and the classical economists, and forms the basis of discussion between new classical and new Keynesian and, indeed, of all modern macroeconomics. What role can our enhanced understanding of labor demand play in describing fluctuations, or at least in informing the discussion among macroeconomists?

A. Is There an Aggregate Labor Demand Curve, and How Does It Help Explain Business Cycles?

The standard theory of the firm's static factor demand presented in Chapter 2 demonstrated the reasonableness of a *microeconomic* labor-demand relation, a negative relation between wages and worker-hours, other things being equal. Chapter 3 demonstrated its empirical validity on a huge variety of microeconomic, industry, and broad sectoral data. With this consistency of theory and empirical evidence, it would be as foolish to deny the existence of a microeconomic labor-demand relation as it would be to deny that the demand for any other particular service is negatively related to its price in the long run.

Does the existence of individual firms' labor demand mean that we can move to an aggregate labor-demand curve by summation? A simple answer is yes, based on the notion that "the measures obtained from aggregate series and those from individual panel data must be consistent. After all, the former are just the aggregates of the latter" (Prescott 1986). That simple view may suffice for some; but it is desirable at least to examine what kind of explanatory power one should want of an aggregate labor-demand curve.

Some of the central facts of aggregate labor markets over the business cycle are in doubt. Almost by definition *aggregate employment is procyclical*: In the United States from 1947 to 1982, for example, deviations of the logarithms of person-hours and real GNP from their trends were essentially coincident (Prescott 1986). The evidence on the cyclicality of real wages is much less clear. This issue was recognized early as being crucial to understanding the causes of business cycles; and empirical research followed shortly upon the publication of Keynes's *General Theory* (Dunlop 1938; Tarshis 1939).

A resurgence of research on this issue used microeconomic panel data on households to examine whether real wages vary cyclically. A major difficulty in evaluating this research is whether to concentrate on changes in the average wage of people working at each particular time; on the wage of the same group of people over the cycle; or still more narrowly, on the wages of those people working steadily and at the same job. If we wish to hold the mix of jobs and workers constant, the last should be our focus; but if we wish to include all cyclical variation in the labor market, we should look at the first. In fact, the degree of procyclicality of real wages appears to decrease as the underlying group studied is narrowed to exclude cyclical changes in the mix of jobs and workers (Bils 1985; Keane, Moffitt, and Runkle 1988). The best conclusion at this point is that *the aggregate real wage may be at most slightly procyclical*.

Instead of studying the cyclicality of employment and real wages separately, one might instead examine their unconditional temporal relationship. Using varieties of causality tests, Geary and Kennan (1982) find no relation between aggregate employment and real wages in twelve countries. The two series are independent, in the sense that variations in one are of no use in predicting variations in the other once the past history of the second series is accounted for.

Both univariate and bivariate examinations imply clearly that cyclical variation is not along an aggregate labor-demand curve. Indeed, if there is any correlation between aggregate employment and real wages, it may be positive. Does this mean that there is no aggregate labor-demand relation, or that it is not useful? One answer is to abandon the construct of an aggregate labor-demand curve entirely and to develop some other explanation for macro labor-market facts. The interpretations of McDonald and Solow's (1981) bargaining model, whose roots extend to Edgeworth's *Mathematical Psychics* (Creedy 1990), essentially do this. Consider Figure 9.1, which shows the convex indifference curves of a typical union that embodies its members' preferences, with $U_2 > U_1 > U_0$. It also shows the concave isoprofit curves of the typical firm, with $I_2 > I_1 > I_0$. The union and firm settle

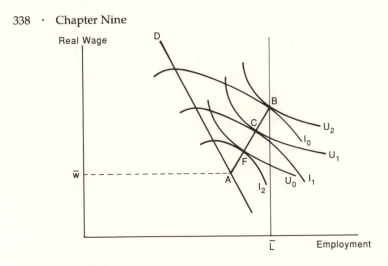

9.1 A Bargaining Approach to Aggregate Employment-
Real Wage Variation

on a wage-employment outcome along the line *AB*. Point *A* is given
by the wage $\bar{w}$ that union members might obtain at their next best
alternative employment. If one views the economy as consisting of
one large employer and one large union, it is the reservation wage of
labor-force participants. Point *B* is given by some maximum employment dictated by an eventually completely inelastic labor supply at
$\bar{L}$.

If cyclical shocks alter the relative bargaining power of the two parties, the economy moves along the line *AB*, for example, from *C* to *F*.
This movement does generate the possible procyclicality of both real
wages and employment. It implies that the typical worker is worse
off in a recession (when employment and wages decrease), which is
very likely. The difficulty is that the model is incomplete. In this standard form it also suggests that the firm is better off in a recession,
since it moves to a better (lower) isoprofit curve. This latter inference
is hard to credit and casts some doubt upon this model's ability to
explain aggregate phenomena without additional assumptions.[1]

The model does not explicitly contain a labor-demand relation, and
one is not necessary to obtain results from the model. Such a relation
is implicit, though, in that the peaks of the isoprofit curves trace out
the labor-demand curve *D*. While that curve is irrelevant for behavior

---

[1] Its ability to describe the behavior of individual unions and employers is another
issue, though one in which a firm-level labor-demand curve is assumed. That was the
main focus of the studies of union contracts whose estimates of labor-demand elasticities were presented in Table 3.5.

induced by cyclical changes in bargaining power, it is nonetheless there. Along with failures of exchange that probably accompany negative shocks, it might be useful in explaining northwest movements off the contract curve during recessions.

Does the failure to observe a negative correlation of aggregate employment and real wages over the business cycle deny the existence of an aggregate labor-demand curve? Obviously the answer is no, just as the failure to observe a negative simple correlation between the price and quantity of watermelons does not negate the existence of a conventional demand curve for watermelons. No aggregate relation of any sort exists; each is just a construct based on our theory and evidence on utility- or profit-maximizing microeconomic behavior. The existence of an aggregate labor-demand curve is not demonstrable or refutable; its existence at the firm level has been demonstrated. I believe, and the subsequent discussion suggests, that as with Voltaire's view of the deity, if aggregate labor demand did not exist we would have to invent it.

The most important inference from the empirical literature in Chapter 3 is the fairly low elasticity of demand for homogeneous labor, perhaps on the order of -0.30. The most important inference from the literature in Chapter 7 is that labor demand adjusts relatively rapidly in response to changing expectations about the structure of factor prices and about product demand. In the rest of this subsection I examine what the first major finding says about some simple textbook explanations of cyclical unemployment. I then consider how the observed rapid adjustment of labor demand affects those explanations.

Consider a simple "expectational" model of cyclical fluctuations in the labor market, shown in Figure 9.2. Assume the labor market is in equilibrium at a real wage of w_0 and employment, E_0. The rate of inflation has been constant at p_0 for a long time, so that expected inflation, p_0^*, equals p_0. Assume that some negative aggregate shock reduces the rate of inflation to p_1. The first crucial assumption in the model is that workers are slow to perceive this decline, so that their expectation of price inflation remains high, at $p_1^* > p_1$. The second assumption, which has led to extensive testing, is that labor supply falls in response to this shock because workers believe their real wages have fallen. Employers, whose perceptions of inflation are assumed to be correct, see the real wage as the true w_1, so that only labor supply shifts. This results in a rise in real wage rates and a fall in employment.[2]

---

[2] This is the model of Lucas and Rapping (1970). In its various forms and extensions it has become known as the expectational model, or the intertemporal substitution

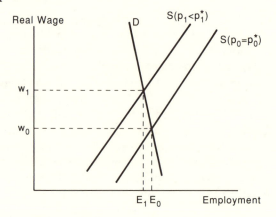

9.2 The Expectational Model with Inelastic
Labor Demand

I have drawn a fairly steep labor-demand curve in Figure 9.2 to
reflect the relative inelasticity demonstrated in Chapter 3.[3] Consider
what this implies. Assuming a parallel leftward shift in supply that
decreases employment by 1 percent, real wages must rise by 3.33
percent if the elasticity of labor demand is -0.30. This means that
our findings on this elasticity require that we should observe strongly
countercyclical real wages if the expectational hypothesis is to provide
a good explanation of cyclical fluctuations in employment.

Assume conservatively that employment declines by 3 percent
during the typical postwar U.S. recession. Then Figure 9.2 suggests
we should observe countercylical changes in real wages of over 10
percent around the trend. The micro evidence suggests in fact that
real wages are if anything slightly procyclical. There is no definition
of *the* average real wage that allows inferring the extent of variation
in real wages that is required to sustain the outcomes implied by applying $\eta_{LL} = -0.30$ to the expectational model in Figure 9.2.

Our inferences about the magnitude of the long-run elasticity of
labor demand lead to inferences about the nature of the labor-market

hypothesis. Whether labor supply fluctuates sufficiently over the cycle to generate the
observed variation in employment is a well-researched issue, and one on which the
evidence of a fairly low intertemporal substitution elasticity is quite overwhelming.
(See MaCurdy 1981; Altonji 1986; and Card 1990d for a summary.) I assume here that
such substitution is possible and see how it interacts with relatively inelastic labor
demand to generate wage and employment outcomes.

[3] The main point of this paragraph was made by Robert Solow (1980) in his presi-
dential address to the American Economic Association.

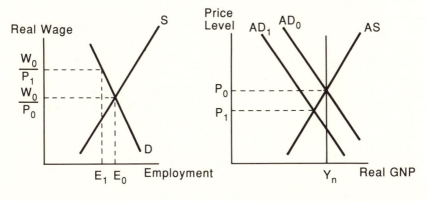

a. Labor market   b. Price and income determination

9.3 A General Model with a Negative Shock to Aggregate Demand

adjustment that is necessary to support macroeconomic models based on shocks to aggregate demand. Consider the textbook model in Figure 9.3 (from Parkin 1990). Figure 9.3b shows the short-run aggregate supply curve, AS, and the initial aggregate demand, AD_0. The economy is at long-run equilibrium real output Y_n, with a price level of P_0 and a money wage of W_0. In the labor market in Figure 9.3a this leads to employment of E_0. If there is an exogenous shock that drives aggregate demand to AD_1, the price level drops to P_1. If money wages are rigid downward, the real wage rises to $\dfrac{W_0}{P_1}$ and employment falls to E_1. Coupled with downward nominal wage rigidity, this aggregate demand story satisfactorily explains cyclical variations in employment.

The observation that labor demand is fairly inelastic also imposes another requirement on this simple story, namely that the nominal wage rigidity be associated with *strongly* countercyclical variations in real wages. As noted above, this is contrary to fact. Without a better theory of labor-market behavior, inelastic labor demand and the absence of countercyclical variation in real wages invalidate a simple demand-shock theory of cyclical fluctuations in aggregate employment and output.

The relative inelasticity of labor demand says nothing about the incarnation of the expectational models in the form of the "real business cycle" theories of Kydland and Prescott (1982) and their followers. These theories depend not on the slope of the labor-demand curve, but rather on its shifting cyclically due to shocks to technology. A major difficulty with this approach is that its proponents cannot identify these specific shocks, or even explain why shocks to technology are procyclical. It does not seem consistent with the evidence that the dynamic responses of labor demand in the United States during the 1930s Depression differed little from dynamics after the 1940s (Bernanke and Parkinson 1991). As Summers (1986) has noted, this difficulty and the very high degree of intertemporal substitution of leisure required by the theory make these conceptually neat models implausible.

These examples demonstrate that the secure knowledge that labor demand is fairly inelastic rules out some explanations of cyclical phenomena. It also suggests that some of the recent emphasis of new Keynesian economists on wage rigidity is likely to be useful (Gordon 1990). Though they have difficulties with some other macroeconomic facts, contracting models and efficiency-wage and insider-outsider theories provide rationales for the rigidity of real wages that circumvent the problems inelastic labor demand imposes. As such, they hold some promise of offering consistent explanations for labor-market fluctuations. These conclusions are underscored and strengthened by our distillation from the empirical literature on dynamic labor demand that adjustment is quite rapid. Labor demand is not sticky; it adjusts rapidly toward the level dictated by production technology and by expectations about product demand and product and factor prices. Whatever stickiness generates employment fluctuations presumably stems from some of the more subtle sorts of behavior in these other models.

B. Lumpy Adjustment Costs and Macroeconomic Equilibrium

In Chapter 7 I showed that there is growing evidence that the standard assumption that employers face increasing costs of adjusting employment may not be correct. Various kinds of nonconvex costs may characterize adjustment at the level of the firm, but discussions of macroeconomic equilibrium are based on the standard assumption. How must they be modified if we assume instead that the typical firm faces nonconvex costs, in particular, that it faces lumpy adjustment costs of the kind implied by (6.6)? Does changing this assumption alter any qualitative conclusions about how macroeconomic fluctuations proceed?

As a first step in examining whether lumpy adjustment costs are useful in explaining macroeconomic behavior, I ignore problems of aggregation. I thus examine its effects under the assumption that all firms are identical (or, if they are not, that they all experience shocks at the same time). More generally, we saw in Chapter 7 that aggregation can make employment fluctuations appear smooth and make it very difficult to infer nonconvex costs from aggregated data. Is there anything to be gained by assuming lumpy adjustment at the micro level in a world in which the aggregation of temporally separated shocks smoothes macroeconomic fluctuations?

A substantial literature in macroeconomics arose beginning in the mid-1980s in which the stickiness of macro quantities was generated by the costs of adjusting prices (e.g., Mankiw 1985). This menu-cost argument is based on the notion that price setters may maximize profits by holding prices constant after a negative macro shock to avoid incurring the costs of changing them. This leads to rigidities in both prices and quantities, as well as to a reduction in (static) economic welfare. In what follows I examine how stickiness—actually, lumpiness—in employment adjustment affects the path of output as well. Can this stickiness, which is documented at the micro level, generate fluctuations in output? Can it rationalize inventory cycles?

Throughout the analysis I assume that the only source of stickiness is the lumpy costs that characterize the adjustment of labor demand. The crucial assumption in the model is that real wages are constant. Presumably they are determined through bargaining in a unionized economy or through repeated adjustments of money wages to match price changes in nonunionized employment. These latter may be part of some implicit contract between the employer and the workers. Obviously this assumption is incorrect at the micro level. Yet as the evidence discussed in Subsection A suggested, real wages do not fluctuate very much over the cycle, so the assumption does not conflict sharply with reality.

Assume that a negative demand shock hits the product market and shifts the marginal revenue product curve leftward in the labor market in Figure 9.4 from MRP_0 to MRP_1^e. Employers expect that the product-market shock will result in lower prices, and their estimates of the value of what each employee produces drops. Initially the typical firm was employing L_0 workers at a real wage rate of w^*. It now sees the real wage as staying constant even while it expects the price of its own product to fall. By assumption, each employer views the shock as causing a decline in demand for labor; but institutional or other rigidities that appear to describe reality well, and whose genesis I am not trying to explain, keep real wages constant in response to this cyclical decline in product demand.[4]

[4] Holzer and Montgomery (1993) provide microeconomic evidence based on estab-

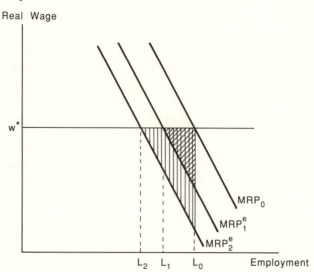

9.4 Employment Adjustment with Lumpy Adjustment
Costs

If there were no costs of adjusting labor demand, employment
would immediately drop to L_1. Even if such costs existed, but if they
were convex, employment would immediately begin adjusting to L_1.
If costs are lumpy, though, no change in employment might occur.
In particular, if the present value of the cross-hatched area in Figure
9.4 is less than the costs of changing employment, the profit-maximizing employer will keep employment constant at L_0. Employment
will be unchanged in the face of a decline in labor demand.

Consider now how the assumption of lumpy costs of adjusting employment, and the sticky short-run employment demand that it en-
genders, affect the product market. I assume that the employer is a
short-run price setter who sees the product-demand curve sloping
downward.[5] The firm depicted in Figure 9.5 had chosen to produce
at Q_0, *selling all its output* at a price P_0, following the textbook pricing
rule by producing where marginal revenue equals marginal cost. If it
can hold inventories (and they need enter the model only due to their
cyclical fluctuations), their level stays constant when demand is D_0.

The demand shock that caused the expected marginal revenue

---

lishment data that the correlation of changes in real wages with output changes is
positive only among firms whose output is increasing.

[5] Drazen (1980) surveys the literature on disequilibrium and short-run monopolistic
price setting by suppliers.

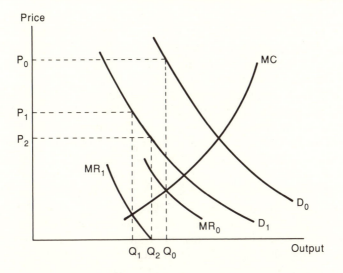

9.5 The Product Market with Lumpy Costs of Adjusting Employment

product curve to shift leftward also shifts the product-demand curve from D_0 to D_1 in Figure 9.5. If there were no costs of adjusting employment, the firm would follow the same pricing rule as before, setting output at Q_1 and price at P_1 (producing where marginal revenue equals marginal cost). No inventory buildup would occur. Because of the lumpy costs of adjusting employment, though, the amount of labor demanded remains at L_0. With this many workers employed, production is kept at Q_0, above the rate that would be optimal but for these adjustment costs. The extra static profits that would be generated by cutting output and price are insufficient to overcome the lumpy costs of adjusting employment.

With this rate of production the optimal pricing strategy is no longer the textbook one; the fixities in the labor market must be taken into account. With production at Q_0, the firm's goal should be to sell as much of the output as is consistent with minimizing its losses. This dictates a pricing strategy of revenue maximization. In terms of Figure 9.5 it means setting the price equal to P_2 and selling Q_2. Some amount of output, Q_0–Q_2, is accumulated as an addition to inventories of final goods, because cutting price sufficiently to sell this extra amount reduces total revenue.[6] We thus observe rigid employment

---

[6] There are obvious costs of storing the additional inventory. The model could be complicated by specifying them and showing that they must be weighed against the

and output in response to an initial negative shock to product demand; but inventories begin building up because of this rigidity.

This decline in prices increases agents' beliefs in the permanent nature of the negative shock. In the labor market this means that the expected marginal revenue product curve shifts further to the left, say to MRP_2^e. At this point the per-period loss in profit due to excess employment is the entire shaded area in Figure 9.4. Assume that the present value of this larger loss exceeds the (lumpy) cost of adjusting employment from L_0 to its new, lower profit-maximizing level. Then the firm will drop employment to L_2—a discrete decrease from the previous level, L_0.

In the product market this discrete move to a new static profit-maximizing position is reflected in a cut in output to Q_1. The product price is set equal to P_1, a price that *sells all output produced in the period*. Since employment is again variable, now that the decline in expected prices is sufficient to overcome the lumpy costs of adjustment, the firm maximizes profits in the static textbook manner. The cut in output halts the growth of inventories, and product prices rise, though not to their old level, P_0. It may seem strange that prices rise in response to the cut in employment, but this might be thought of as substituting cuts in list prices from P_0 to P_1 for discounting of the old list price, P_0, sufficient to generate the low price P_2.

Is there anything about this story that depends on the assumption of lumpy costs of adjusting employment? Had we assumed convex adjustment costs, the model would imply continuous movements from L_0 to L_2 in Figure 9.4, and from Q_0 to Q_1 and P_0 to P_1 in Figure 9.5. Cyclical inventory buildups would not have been generated endogenously in the model, but would instead have had to be imposed on the model as additional structure. Lumpy costs of adjusting employment generate inventories as a result of profit-maximizing behavior by the employer-producer. Since we know inventories of final goods are countercyclical, the model with lumpy costs and the discrete changes in employment that they imply is more powerful than one with convex costs and the implied continuous changes in employment.

The model developed in this subsection also implies that we will observe large, discrete changes in output and employment rather than continuous small changes. There is little doubt that this occurs at the micro level (see Chapters 4 and 7). At the macro level, though, the process seems much smoother, essentially a generalization of the

---

revenue losses that would occur if price were lowered below P_2. The qualitative conclusion, that some inventory may be accumulated, need not change.

result on aggregation in Chapter 7 to adjustment in the product market. In explaining the behavior of aggregate employment (and aggregate output too) the two models are observationally equivalent.

If we concentrate only on aggregate phenomena, Occam's razor implies continuing to use models with convex adjustment costs. There are two good counterarguments. First, it seems quite likely that models with convex costs, though analytically convenient, are incorrect at the micro level. It is not a matter of choosing a convenient model as opposed to a less convenient one that is no more clearly correct. Rather, the choice is between using a convenient model that the evidence shows to be fundamentally wrong, or one that is correct but less convenient. Second, based on this conclusion, the model that is correct at the microeconomic level is more likely to lead to new inferences about macroeconomic behavior.

This conclusion indicates where the study of macroeconomic employment dynamics should head. The crucial issue here is aggregation—how to move from the micro-level dynamics generated by nonconvex adjustment costs to aggregate employment and output dynamics. Once one admits the possibility that labor demand at the firm level adjusts discretely, one creates an opportunity to search for implications about aggregate dynamics that could not exist under the restrictive assumption of continuous adjustment by each firm. The nature of aggregation becomes important, and examining its effects can yield new theoretical results about aggregate dynamics and lead to the development of facts describing empirical regularities that would otherwise not have been noticed.

III. Labor Demand, Technical Change, and Wage Inequality

In this section I examine what the analysis of labor demand says about two issues that have long attracted public attention and on which economists have provided substantial comment and some attempt at measurement. The first is the effect of changes in technology on labor demand. The layman's response to technical change is to assume that it reduces the demand for labor; yet the simultaneous explosion in living standards and growth in the number of workers employed in the United States and other countries since the Industrial Revolution obviously demonstrates that response is incorrect. It is useful to inquire into and explain the integration between technical change at the firm level and the macroeconomic outcomes that we observe. The second issue is changing inequality in wages, particularly changes in wage differentials by skill level. It is interesting both because it is an important labor-market outcome and because it is a major determinant of changing inequality in the distribution of income. The second part of this section examines the short- and long-run aspects of this problem in the context of changes in earnings inequality in developed economies, especially the United States, since the 1960s.

A. Technical Change

Chapters 2 and 3 dealt with a world that was assumed to be technologically static. That assumption stemmed from the desire to focus on substitution relationships, for which the theory is developed in a static world. In this subsection I abandon this assumption and examine how technical change might affect the demand for homogeneous and then for heterogeneous labor. I present evidence on the directions of these effects, and consider how improvements at the micro level translate into changes in the demand for labor in the aggregate. The discussion of technical change and homogeneous labor produces conclusions that laypeople find surprising. The analysis of the effects on heterogeneous labor generates results that may be somewhat surprising to economists.

The discussion proceeds using the terminology of the theory of economic growth. Rewrite the two-factor production function (2.4) as

$$Y(t) = F(L^*(t),K(t)), \; F_{ii} < 0, \; F_{ij} > 0, \tag{9.1}$$

where $L^*(t)$ is "effective labor," and

$$L^*(t) = L(t) \cdot T(t), \tag{9.2}$$

that is, the actual number of workers times the level of *labor-augmenting* technology.[7] All technical change is assumed to be labor-augmenting. If society saves a constant fraction of its income, and savings are used to finance replacing depreciated capital and for net investment in new capital, the fundamental result of growth theory is that the economy can grow steadily, in the sense that output rises at a constant rate. That rate is faster the greater is $dlnT/dt$, the rate of augmentation of labor, and the greater is the natural growth of the labor force. The rate of growth of output does not depend on the saving rate.[8]

With this assumption about the nature of technical change, with the assumption that each factor receives its marginal product as its return, and under (static) constant returns to scale, the following out-

[7] Like most of the growth literature, and as in Sections II–V of Chapter 2, I ignore here the distinction between workers and hours.

[8] This and the next paragraph are based in part on the summary in Burmeister and Dobell (1970).

comes will be observed: (1) the capital-output ratio, K/Y, is constant over time; (2) the capital-labor ratio rises steadily at the rate of growth of $T(t)$; (3) the marginal product of capital is constant, as is the rate of return to capital; (4) the marginal product of labor rises at the rate of growth of $T(t)$, as does the wage rate; and (5) results (2)–(4) guarantee that the ratio of factor shares remains unchanged. These conclusions define *Harrod-neutral* technical change, which can result only if we can represent technology as purely labor-augmenting.

Surprisingly little effort has been devoted to examining explicitly whether or not technological change is Harrod-neutral. Indeed, it would be difficult to construct a test of what is necessarily a complex description of technology at the macro level. Rather, the general constancy over time of the capital-output ratio and of factor shares in industrialized economies makes the assumption of Harrod-neutrality a convenient description of technology. What has been examined in great detail is the role of technology, as represented always merely by a time trend, in labor-demand equations like (2.9a'), in systems of factor-demand equations, and in the generalized forms like the translog tableau in (2.26). Many of the Group I studies whose results on labor-demand and substitution elasticities are summarized in Tables 3.1 through 3.3 include this trend; and a smaller number of the Group II studies summarized in Table 3.4 do too.

The studies that involve factor-demand equations (Type b) uniformly find that, holding output and factor prices constant, the amount of labor demanded decreases over time. Unsurprisingly, the rate of decrease is roughly consistent with the rate of increase of labor productivity during the sample period (in accord with the observation that the biggest portion of most changes in employment demand results from changes in demand for final products). Some models involving system estimation (Type c) of homogeneous labor and several other factors allowed for the possibility that factor shares could change while factor prices remained constant. This kind of nonneutrality appears in the aggregate data on U.S. manufacturing, but has not received very much testing in Type c studies on data for other economies. It is not inconsistent with Harrod neutrality, since the result is inferred under the assumption of constant factor prices rather than the rising wage-rental ratio implicit in Harrod-neutral technical change.

All of these studies imply that technical improvements enable the firm to produce the same amount of output with fewer workers. What mechanism translates this reduction in firms' *constant-output* demand for labor into steady employment and rising output at the aggregate level? Technical change necessarily occurs at the micro

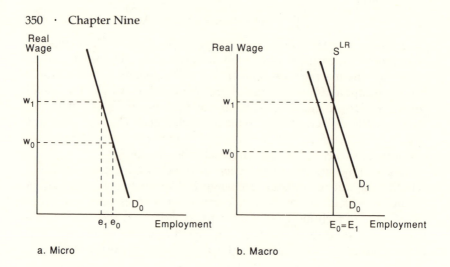

a. Micro   b. Macro

9.6 Micro-Macro Effects on Labor Demand of Labor-Augmenting Technical Change

level. In line with (9.1) it can be viewed as labor-augmenting, as raising the productivity of every employed worker. Since workers are assumed to be paid their marginal products, the real wage rises. This increase in real wages means national income will rise, as will aggregate demand. It is true that at a constant output the rise in the real wage, from w_0 to w_1 in Figure 9.6a, would lead to a reduction in employment from e_0 to e_1. At the macro level, though, output has not remained constant. Ignoring any long-run aggregate labor-supply elasticity, and ignoring population growth, the rise in aggregate product demand shifts the aggregate demand for labor from D_0 to D_1 in Figure 9.6b. As long as the long-run supply of labor to the market is fairly inelastic, as it appears to be, this is sufficient to generate a demand for E_0 workers at the new, higher wage w_1.

An interesting question is what is the locus of the growth in output that results from increased aggregate income? That is, does the expansion occur through rightward shifts in D in Figure 9.6a in existing firms; or does it occur through the replication of net new firms that are similar to existing firms, but whose demand for labor picks up the slack in employment? The studies summarized in Chapter 4 deal with the pattern of employment change over time in existing and new plants. To the extent that they examine changes in this pattern, though, they only consider its cyclical variation. The data used in those studies could easily be examined by industry to discern whether the sources of changes in employment—expansions, contractions, births, and deaths—differ among industries whose rate of technical progressivity differs. Better still, a detailed effort to identify the timing of important innovations and examine their effect on these patterns would go far toward answering this question.

How does technical change affect the demand for different types of workers? As Chapter 3 showed, economists have examined a large variety of interesting disaggregations of the work force. Rather than discuss one or several specific disaggregations, I simply assume that there are three inputs—physical capital, skilled workers, and un-skilled workers. (Alternatively, one might view this as a three-factor world with physical capital, raw labor, and raw labor augmented by embodied investments in skill.) Specify production technology analogously to (9.1) and (9.2) as

$$Y(t) = F(L_S^*(t), L_U^*(t), K(t)), \quad F_{ii} < 0, \tag{9.1'}$$

with

$$L_i^*(t) = L_i(t) \cdot T_i(t), \quad i = S, U, \tag{9.2'}$$

where S denotes skilled and U denotes unskilled labor. The T_i can be viewed as rates of augmentation of the two types of labor (of increase in the productivity of skill and raw labor).

Unless $T_S(t) \equiv T_U(t)$ and the L_i are separable from K, production in a world of balanced growth cannot be such as to allow the ratio of physical capital to each type of labor to grow at the same rate and the three factor shares to remain constant. The strongest conclusion of Chapter 3, Section IV, was that the L_i are not separable from K—that skill and physical capital are p-complements, or at least relatively p-complementary compared to unskilled labor and capital. Is that conclusion correct, or is it an artifact that results from ignoring differences in the rates of augmentation of skill and raw labor?

Many studies summarized in Tables 3.7 and 3.8 use cross-section data and are thus inherently incapable of shedding light on this issue. Many of the time-series studies summarized there do not allow for technical change. Indeed, only Bergström and Panas (1992) examine this issue (using a Type c, translog approach). They cannot reject the hypothesis that $T_S = T_U$, and they do suggest the standard result that skilled (salaried) workers are less easily substitutable for physical capital than are unskilled (wage-earning) workers.

Bartel and Lichtenberg (1987), and the studies discussed in Chapter 3 that relate to it, shed indirect light on this issue. All find that the productivity of skill (measured by education, on-the-job training or occupational category) is enhanced by more rapid technical progress. This might be interpreted as relatively greater augmentation of the productivity of skilled than of unskilled workers. Alternatively, one could interpret the result as a static reflection of capital deepening and the relative q-complementarity of capital with skilled workers.

The relative employment of skilled workers has increased over time in industrialized economies. It is convenient to interpret this change as the result of the capital deepening that has certainly occurred, coupled with capital-skill p-complementarity. The evidence is far too sparse, though, to infer whether this conventional interpretation is correct, or whether instead it is produced by technical change that augments different types of labor at different rates. Studies applying Type c methods to a variety of sets of aggregate time-series data that allow the disaggregation of labor by skill category and that test for possible nonneutrality of technical change across types of labor are needed. Also necessary, and probably eventually more useful, are studies that consider the effects of the introduction of specific new technologies on the paths of employment of different types of workers at the level of very small industries (essentially, careful *microeconomic* versions of Osterman 1986). Until such evidence is available, the conventional interpretation should stand; but it rests on remarkably little supporting evidence beyond the development of aggregate changes in the relative demand for skilled and unskilled labor, and in the capital-labor ratio, that could be explained instead by factor-augmentation rates that differ by skill.

B. Changing Wage Inequality

Through 1970 differentials between the pay of skilled and unskilled workers in the the United States declined, though not steadily. (I define skill in terms of occupation, white-collar versus blue-collar, or professional versus manual worker [Cullen 1956].) As I discuss at the end of this subsection, a massive amount of microeconomic evidence has demonstrated that wage differentials along various dimensions of skill rose in the United States between 1970 and 1990. There have been times in the history of Western economies when skill differentials increased, for example, in the early stages of the Industrial Revolution in Britain. There have been other times, such as most of the subsequent industrial history of Britain, and from the Civil War through the 1960s in the United States, when they decreased (Phelps Brown 1977). There is nothing unprecedented about reversals of secular trends in wage inequality. Indeed, the growing inequality from 1970 to 1985 just brought wage dispersion in the United States back to where it had been in 1940 (Goldin and Margo 1992).

A simple definition of wage inequality would compare wages across groups of workers defined by skill. Archetypically this would just be the ratio of the wages of skilled to those of unskilled workers, though more complex ways of combining two or more wage rates into a measure of inequality could be used. The difficulty with this approach, and a continuing point of confusion in the literature, is how to define skill, and thus how to decide on which wage differentials to focus. Do we mean educational attainment, something that is easily measured in today's household surveys for most developed countries? Do we mean the skill of a journeyman craft worker? Maintaining comparability of data over very long periods of time while focusing on wage differentials of current interest is difficult. Other than recognizing that the notion of skill is ill defined, and that this makes examining changes in the returns to skill quite problematical, I ignore the issue here. Instead, I assume we have an agreed-upon definition of skill and examine what might affect it in the intermediate and long run. I assume throughout that production takes place with two types of labor, skilled and unskilled, and with physical capital. The discussion thus parallels the taxonomy underlying much of the empirical literature presented in Tables 3.7 through 3.9.

Assume that the skill differential, $w^R = w^S/w^U$, has not changed for a long time. Assume there has been no change in capital-skill complementarity as technology has advanced; and the increase in the relative supply of skilled labor has progressed at the same rate as the growth in the relative demand for skill. Consider what might cause w^R to begin increasing. If there is an unexpected exogenous increase in the rate of capital deepening, the relative demand for skilled workers will increase (due to their complementarity with physical capital). This will increase w^R. The same result will occur if the relative quality of skilled workers increases.

These intermediate-run demand and supply effects are the only two general causes of changing wage inequality in a closed economy. In a highly skilled economy whose trade is opening up to a world economy with different endowments of skilled and unskilled workers the pressure of competition from trade in commodities that are unskilled-labor-intensive will raise w^R in the intermediate run. For example, increased foreign competition resulting from the lowering of tariffs in the 1960s and 1970s could have been one cause of the increases in w^R that occurred during the 1970s and 1980s in the United States.

Assume that a shock has increased the relative demand for skill from D_0 to D_1 in Figure 9.7. This raises the relative wage from w_*^R to w_1^R as the labor market moves along the short-run relative supply curve of skill, S^{SR}. This curve is presumably not vertical because some workers who possess the "skill" and are working at unskilled jobs because the relative wage w_*^R made skilled work unattractive can easily switch to skilled work when w^R increases. Over time, as new

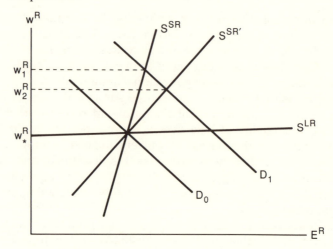

9.7 Short-run Wage effects of Skill-using Capital
Deepening

workers choose to invest in the now more attractive skilled occupation, the short-run supply curve becomes flatter; for example, it tilts
to $S^{SR'}$. Relative wage inequality will begin to drop back toward its
original level.

Can what we have learned about labor demand inform us about
the path of the skill differential in response to this shock? The evidence in Chapter 3 suggests that skilled and unskilled labor are fairly
easily substitutable. If that is true, the relative demand curves in Figure 9.7 will be fairly flat. As the short-run supply curve tilts forward
toward S^{LR}, the labor market will trace out equilibria along this flat
relative demand curve, D_1. (This assumes, as the discussion in Chapter 7 suggests is reasonable, that dynamic adjustments of demand are
more rapid than those of supply.) We will observe fairly substantial
increases in the number of skilled relative to unskilled jobs. At the
same time, it will appear that the rise in the skill differential to w_1^R is
being reversed only slowly. For example, it only falls to w_2^R by the
time the relative supply curve has tilted forward to the $S^{SR'}$ depicted
in Figure 9.7. The evidence on skill substitution and dynamic adjustment of labor demand suggests that relative demand shocks will generate an increase in the skill differential whose erosion appears slow
compared to the changes in skilled and unskilled employment.

Figure 9.7 suggests that in the long run w^R will return to w_*^R. This
will be true as long as there is no limiting factor on the supply of skill.
A physical characteristic such as raw strength may, though, limit

supply when skill is defined along a physical dimension. An intellectual factor—for example, the ability to handle mathematical concepts—may limit supply when skill is defined along that dimension. Independent of either of these limitations on endowments, workers' inherent tastes for undertaking the investments that generate an expansion of the skilled work force may differ. This heterogeneity may require employers to offer an increasing compensating wage differential in the long run in order to attract additional skilled workers.

These possibilities will generate an upward-sloping long-run relative supply curve in Figure 9.7. Its slope does not necessarily imply a long-run increase in the skill differential. Figure 9.7 is drawn for static supply and demand relations. Yet in reality, as the discussion that introduced it suggested, the relative demand is changing at varying rates. More important, we assumed that the nature of the technical changes that keep shifting the relative demand for skill is unchanging. In fact, these limitations are a necessary condition for long-run increases in the skill differential, but they are not sufficient.

Only if technical change is independent of w^R will relative demand shift outward over time, if not steadily, along an upward-sloping relative supply curve of skill. There is a long theoretical literature, which has not generated serious empirical work, on the role of induced innovation—technical change that is biased by relative factor prices (see Burmeister and Dobell 1970, 90–96, for a summary). If such arguments are valid for innovations that save labor, they should be equally valid for discussing the effect of fluctuations in the relative price of skill on the path of innovation.

Consider the labor market in the right panel of Figure 9.8. Skill-using technical change has shifted the relative demand for skill from D_0^* to D_1, raising the relative wage from w_0^R to w_1^R. In the absence of induced innovation that would be the end of the story. With induced innovation there is a frontier that links the technology that is adopted, as measured by σ_{su}, the partial elasticity of substitution between skilled and unskilled labor, with the skill differential. The rise in w^R alters the path of technical progress, inducing firms to choose techniques that use new capital that is less p-complementary with skill than before and in which skilled and unskilled workers are less easily substituted. That reverses the rightward movement of the relative demand for skilled labor and at least partially offsets the increase in wage inequality. Instead of shifting all the way to D_1, the relative demand for skill settles at D_2^*, a long-run equilibrium that is produced in part by the shift in the direction of technical change. The degree of substitution between the two types of labor settles at σ_{su}^2.

If the response of induced innovation is sufficient, any increase in

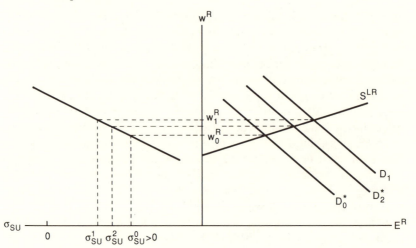

9.8 Induced Skill-saving Innovation and Wage Inequality in the Long Run

the relative demand for skill may produce no eventual impact on the skill differential, even if the long-run relative supply of skill is upward-sloping. If the path of technology is affected by relative factor prices, biased technical change may restore an initial skill differential and eliminate any trend toward increasing wage inequality. Obversely, induced innovation can work in the other direction to reduce declines in wage differentials associated with skills that were useful under an older technology. The main point is that there is no *necessary* long-run tendency for wage inequality to decrease or increase; and absent interference from policy, there may be natural economic forces that keep inequality within some range.

Whether we measure skill by education and experience (as in Katz and Revenga 1989 or Bound and Johnson 1992), or completely generally by examining the relative wages of individuals at different deciles of the wage distribution (Juhn, Murphy, and Pierce 1992), the extent of wage inequality in the United States increased from 1970 at least through the late 1980s. This increase was not just due to inter-industry shifts in employment; it occurred within narrowly defined industries as well. The consensus among these studies is that only a small part was due to changes in the importance of labor-market institutions, such as trade unions.

Aggregate data for Canada (Gunderson and Riddell 1991) suggest that the same general increase in wage inequality occurred there between 1967 and 1988. Such an increase most definitely is not observed in Japan (Katz and Revenga 1989); and the increase in inter-industry wage inequality in the United States did not occur in many Western European countries (Bell and Freeman 1991). This suggests that the causes of the reversal of the trend in wage inequality are specific to changes in the North American economy and to the institutions and policies, or lack thereof, that affect wage setting in North America. Slower growth in the relative supply of skill, unusually rapid skill-using technical change, and increased openness to foreign competition in unskilled-worker-intensive commodities have been identified by at least some of the research as causing these North American phenomena (particularly Bound and Johnson 1992; Juhn, Murphy, and Pierce 1992). What are unclear are their relative effects on the trend in wage inequality.

Just as the reversal of the trend in the United States suggests that industrial development need not continually narrow wage inequality, so too a comparison of the North American to the European and Japanese experiences indicates that a postindustrial economy need not generate increasing inequality. Instead, skill differentials, and wage inequality more generally, depend on workers' choices about supplying skill, and on employers' choices about technique and the relative demand for skill that those choices imply. Government policy designed to alter the results of these choices needs to be justified in light of possible mechanisms that can reverse intermediate-run trends and of the historical evidence that the trends do reverse themselves.

IV. Job Creation and Labor Demand

The term "job creation" seems to have no economic content and certainly is not obviously an issue in labor demand. Yet to government officials, and probably to the public generally, it subsumes the labor-demand questions of employment determination and adjustment that are the substance of this entire book. Is there any economic meaning to this term? Can job-creation policies alter unemployment rates beyond what can be accomplished by general macroeconomic stimuli to aggregate demand? If so, are they worth the effort?

Most of the policies discussed in the preceding chapters can be viewed mutatis mutandis as job-creation measures. The static policies analyzed in Chapter 5 are types of *indirect job creation*. For example, a special minimum wage increases demand for youths, thus creating jobs for them. Marginal or average employment subsidies are designed to increase the demand for workers generally, or for certain categories of workers, by altering the costs of employing them. The policies discussed in Chapter 8 are job-retention policies, the obverse of job-creation measures. Increasing the extent of experience rating in unemployment insurance, and raising the amount of payroll that is taxed to finance unemployment benefits, are *indirect job-retention* measures that help to reduce the magnitude of cyclical layoffs. Legislation requiring advance notice of plant closings and mass layoffs, or consultation before decisions are made to reduce employment, are *direct job-retention* policies that mandate the maintenance of employment (at least for some period of time).

Even though the policies discussed in Chapters 5 and 8 represent most of the instruments for job creation that are used in industrialized countries, most observers would not usually consider them in this light. Rather, most people would consider only *direct job creation*—the provision of jobs by some level of government in programs one of whose major purposes is providing employment; or they would include indirect measures other than wage subsidies, such as projects demonstrating new techniques, the creation of "incubators" for small businesses, and the dissemination of new technology.

Direct job-creation policies have run from the counterseasonal employment policies of the pharaohs (pyramid building) to countercyclical public-service employment programs in the United States and other industrialized countries in the 1970s and early 1980s. Substantial economic analysis of the micro- and macroeconomic impacts of these programs has been produced. To varying degrees such programs will always be a staple on the policy menu.

One issue was peculiar to programs in the United States beginning in the 1970s, because they consisted of federal grants to lower units of government: Did the "job-creation" programs even increase total government spending, since lower-level governments could engage in *fiscal substitution* of federal grants for taxes on their own citizens? From the viewpoint of the representative local taxpayer/consumer, a federal grant for any purpose constitutes unearned income that causes a reallocation of spending so that consumption of different goods and services increases only in proportion to their income elasticities of demand. Freedom to reallocate other spending and taxes would lead to only a tiny increase in total government spending through such grants. The literature on this issue is fairly clear that fiscal substitution was substantial, but because of federal restrictions on spending and lags in subgovernmental responses it was probably not complete (Wiseman 1976; Johnson and Tomola 1977).

The evidence makes it reasonable to assume that there was some scope for revenue-shared direct job creation to generate additional employment. The more important issue is whether even the direct provision of jobs by the national government can generate more employment, in the short or the long run, than a general policy of macroeconomic fiscal and monetary stimuli. Baily and Tobin (1978) compared the short-run effects of direct job creation (DJC) and general fiscal policy. Assume that there are two types of labor, skilled (S) and unskilled (U), and that the DJC program hires only U workers. It must compete with the private sector for such workers and can be viewed as shifting leftward the relative demand curve for skilled labor.

Under what conditions will the DJC program have more desirable macroeconomic consequences than a general policy that does not affect the relative demand for S and U? Consider first the short-run possibilities. If at the current level of aggregate demand the short-run Phillips curve for U workers is flatter than that for S workers, an increase in aggregate demand targeted at U workers will generate less wage inflation than a general fiscal stimulus. Whether this precondition holds is unclear, since the evidence on it is quite mixed. If it does, the DJC program can reduce unemployment and lower inflation. Changes in wages of S and U workers are obviously interdependent in the long run, but less so in the short run, as indicated by the difference between S^{SR} and S^{LR} in Figure 9.7. The slower the adjustment to the long-run relative supply curve, the greater the scope for a policy that tilts the relative demand for U to avoid additional wage and eventually price inflation.

An additional consideration for a successful DJC policy targeted at U workers is that the wage paid in the government jobs be low. The higher it is, the more likely such jobs are to attract currently employed U workers, so that the net effect of the additional spending will differ little from a general fiscal stimulus. The final consideration is that the policy will do better if the economy is further away from the long-run equilibrium rate of unemployment. With extra slack in labor markets, effects on wages and prices will be fewer; by directly increasing employment of U workers, the DJC will at least generate additional first-round effects beyond those produced by general spending measures.

While it seems possible that DJC policies can have beneficial short-run effects beyond those of standard fiscal stimuli, there is only very sparse evidence that they have.[9] Simply studying employment changes of type U workers cannot offer sufficient evidence, as it does

[9] There is remarkably little research on the labor-marketwide effects of these programs, as opposed to their impact on employment in the targeted groups. One effort (Skedinger 1990) does demonstrate that the dispersion of relative wages was narrowed in Sweden in the 1970s and 1980s by public spending on direct job creation.

not examine either employment of other workers or effects on prices. Examining total employment does not get at price effects. Only an evaluation within a complete short-run macroeconomic model would suffice; and given how tiny DJC programs in most countries are compared to total employment, such an econometric evaluation is unlikely to generate useful results. Reliance on the theoretical considerations discussed above is the best approach. It suggests there is some scope for a carefully targeted and, most important, short-term direct job-creation policy surprise.

Whether DJC can generate any long-run impact, presumably on the location of a vertical long-run Phillips curve, is a different question. Only if it can somehow shift aggregate long-run supply outward can this labor-demand policy succeed in the long run. The only argument for this possibility is based on hysteresis, that is, that a DJC program that is successful in the short run will enable new labor-market entrants to develop skills that are essential for eventual success in obtaining jobs, and that these skills must be developed early in a worker's labor-market experience.[10] There is no evidence in favor of this argument. To the extent that the jobs created are short-term and low-skilled, it seems very unlikely. Indeed, consideration of the microeconometric evidence on its obverse (Ellwood 1982) suggests it is incorrect. Any long-run effect of job-creation policy on the level of employment is at best a theoretical possibility for which there is no convincing evidence.

Other policies, in some cases initiated by subnational governments, are designed to generate long-run impacts on the labor market by improving the rate of dissemination of technology defined broadly. "Incubators" for new small businesses, usually in areas of advanced technology, effectively function to give the protected firms the time to grow to the point where they can take advantage of scale economies.[11] Programs to demonstrate and disseminate new production and managerial technology are similarly designed to shift labor demand rightward, especially for the high-skilled labor that is complementary with advanced technology.

Can these policies work, that is, might they do anything more *in the long run* than shift resources from the private to the public sector and create high-technology "sheltered workshops"? Consider a pro-

---

[10] Tobin (1972) was probably the first to raise the possibility that avoiding the sharpest cyclical declines might generate long-term benefits.

[11] General discussions of business incubators along with a series of case studies and surveys are presented by Smilor and Gill (1986) and Lyons (1991). A summary of European efforts to create jobs by stimulating entrepreneurship is provided by Schweke and Jones (1986).

gram that expands government in order to aid the private sector. The argument in favor of government employment for this purpose rests on the possible externalities that it might create. For example, private firms might innovate more rapidly with public demonstrations or dissemination of new technology. This is what publicly financed dissemination of agricultural technology appears to have accomplished (Griliches 1958). Whether the example of agricultural technology developed in the public sector is relevant is unclear; but it is conceivable that an "Industrial Extension Service" could produce a rightward shift in the demand for labor in the private sector. As this occurs there would be a temporary spurt in the growth of output and a once-and-for-all rightward shift in aggregate supply.

The opposite possibility is that public spending for these purposes removes resources from the private sector that would have been more productive in generating demand for workers complementary to the advanced technology. An alternative negative argument is that these subsidies insulate firms from competition and therefore reduce competition. Similarly, public efforts at disseminating technology may steer resources away from more efficient, but more diffuse and less visible, private efforts at acquiring new production and management methods. If these possibilities are correct, the net effect of these forms of "job creation" would be to reduce private-sector labor demand and reduce the total demand for labor. The long-run impact would be a less productive work force and a leftward movement in aggregate supply.

There is no evidence on the net effect on employment of programs of job development and information dissemination, much less on their long-run effects on the aggregate labor market. There is, though, no a priori argument that there are externalities or scale economies that might justify shifting resources from the private sector to subsidize protected jobs in markets that are not typically in the public sector or aided by public funds. The externality argument is plausible for public efforts to stimulate private-sector job creation through the dissemination of new technology; but here too there is no evidence outside agriculture of any net impact and none on the aggregate effects of such policies.

All jobs are not created equal; and throughout the modern history of government efforts have been made to create "good jobs." What is a good job? No doubt it is one with stable employment; where the working conditions are good (clean and not dangerous to health) and where there are good nonwage benefits. In developed labor markets all of these desiderata are observed where wages and salaries are high (Hamermesh and Rees 1993, chap. 13). We can therefore assume for argument that exhortations to create "good jobs" express a concern that these be high- or at least not low-paid jobs.

For a countercyclical program of direct job creation to generate "good jobs" it must target precisely those workers who are least likely to have difficulty finding work in a recession. Alternatively, it could offer high-wage jobs to unemployed low-skilled workers; but, as noted before, by attracting currently employed low-skilled workers this reduces the program's ability to cushion cyclical declines in aggregate labor demand. Worse still, a policy that seeks to create high-wage jobs will widen skill differentials in the short run, and perhaps to some extent in the long run as well. Generating "good jobs" as a matter of effective policy means targeting government aid to workers not among the least skilled.

In fact most government policy does directly create "good jobs," since on average government employees receive higher wages than the typical worker.[12] Whether this represents anything more than a shift of such workers from private to public employment is not clear; but the net impact of government on the relative demand for skill is unambiguous (and forms the focus of the analysis in Section III.B of Chapter 10). In addition, indirect effects on the demand for skill in the private sector, through subsidies to capital that is p-complementary with skill, or by the procurement of advanced-technology goods, may also shift the relative demand for skill to the right. It is likely that, at least in the United States, the government does create "good jobs."

V. Conclusions

This chapter demonstrates that thinking about labor demand and applying the estimates of important parameters describing it are useful in a variety of areas of macroeconomic theory and policy. Most important, it shows that the notion of a labor-demand relationship is a useful construct that can limit the discussions that should be acceptable as macroeconomic theory. Being able to describe the responses of a firm's labor demand to changes in wages, and knowing the speed of adjustment of its demand, inform us about the paths of labor-market aggregates and impose a burden on the descriptions that macro theory tries to provide. In other words, part of its usefulness is as a dose of reality to the more fanciful flights of macroeconomic theory.

---

[12] In 1989 in the United States the average wage/salary per full-time equivalent federal employee was $27,826; among state and local employees, $25,674; and among private-sector employees, $24,563.

Expectational models and, to lesser extent, real business cycle models too are examples where much of the outcome hinges on a parameter describing the labor market (the elasticity of intertemporal substitution of leisure). Most of the theory ignored what most labor economists knew is correct (the very low value of this elasticity) and what microeconomic evidence increasingly demonstrated. We know at least as much about the parameters describing labor demand, both the shape of labor-demand curves and the impact of shocks to them. That knowledge should limit the discussion of such topics as real business cycles and should be of increasing importance to the formalization of new Keynesian approaches to wage rigidity.

Several labor-market outcomes discussed here seem to be unrelated. Secular changes in earnings inequality have long attracted economists' attention; and more recently programs aimed at direct job creation have concerned both analysts of public policy and academic economists. Both discussions hinge upon issues in labor demand, particularly the shape of the relative demand for workers of different skills, and hence the degree of skill substitution. The theory and evidence on heterogeneous labor demand thus provide the basis for a unified analysis of these topics.

After a burst of interest in labor-market policy in the 1970s the attention of labor economists drifted away from these topics during the 1980s, at least in the United States. No doubt our interests depend partly on the vicissitudes of public clamor for these policies. This suggests that labor-market policy will someday attract more attention, and economists will again be attracted to studying it and providing guidance about the likely impacts and successes of various policies. The analysis in this chapter and the discussions in Chapters 5 and 8 provide a framework for studying future aggregate labor-market policies designed to change wages and employment.

CHAPTER TEN

Labor Demand and the Economics of Development

I. INTRODUCTION—IS THIS CHAPTER NECESSARY?

F. Scott Fitzgerald noted, "Let me tell you about the very rich. They are different from you and me."[1] To which Ernest Hemingway is said to have replied, "Yes, they have more money." Is the obverse of Hemingway's observation correct as applied to labor demand in developing countries? Is the only difference between previous descriptions in this volume and those characterizing labor demand in low-income countries the level of wages and the average amount of human capital embodied in the work force?

Economic theory should apply regardless of the location of the agents. That should be true for households and for the firms that are the central focus of this book. Similarly, the evidence summarized in Chapters 3, 4, and 7 included some econometric studies of developing economies. With those observations, why spend additional time on this issue?

There are two main reasons for devoting a separate chapter to issues in labor demand in developing countries. First, many policy issues in development, and the economic models that have been constructed to analyze them, depend on behavior in two or more related markets. A major determinant of equilibria and comparative statics in these models is the nature of labor demand. It is thus fruitful to see how what has been learned so far affects the inferences from the analysis. Second, the development literature has offered some useful conclusions based on models of production; but these models, and empirical research that stems from them, have paid relatively little attention to the heterogeneity of labor. A major focus of the discussions in this chapter is to discover how allowing for imperfect substitution among several types of labor modifies the conclusions of models describing labor-market problems in developing countries.

Perhaps the most striking feature of low-income developing coun-

---

[1] Fitzgerald, "The Rich Boy," in Malcolm Cowley, ed., *The Stories of F. Scott Fitzgerald* (New York: Scribner's, 1951).

TABLE 10.1
Percentage Rural Population, Developing and Developed Countries, 1965 and 1988

Country	1965	1988
	Low-income Developing Countries	
Bangladesh	94	87
India	81	73
Indonesia	84	73
Nigeria	83	66
Pakistan	76	69
	Middle-income Developing Countries	
Egypt	59	52
Malaysia	74	59
Mexico	45	29
Philipines	68	59
Thailand	87	79
Turkey	66	53
	Developed Countries	
Australia	17	14
Germany	21	14
Japan	33	23
Sweden	23	16
United Kingdom	13	8
United States	28	26

Source: World Bank, *World Development Report, 1990* (New York: Oxford University Press, 1990).

tries is the importance of agriculture and the rural economy more generally. Table 10.1 shows the percentage rural population in 1965 and 1988 in a variety of countries, ranging from low-income to highly developed. Beyond the steady decline between groups in the fraction of population that is rural, it is noteworthy that the population is mostly urban even in developed countries known for their primary exports, such as Australia.

Characteristic of the rural population in developing economies is the small landholder. Indeed, if we define firms as those units that employ workers (that demand labor), by far the largest number would be these small farms. They typically consist of the farm family occasionally supplemented by hired workers. Most of the labor is supplied by members of the (perhaps extended) family. This characteristic means that our treatment of labor demand as describing hiring the services of outsiders without a residual claim on the surplus is not necessarily applicable.

The closest analogy to the farmer-employer is the labor-managed firm discussed in Chapters 2 and 3. The issues are quite similar, though the literatures in the two areas have hardly overlapped. The most important theoretical and empirical question is how the agricultural household's consumption-leisure choices affect and are affected by its demand for inputs into production. Also of interest, and closely related, is the degree of substitution of hired labor for that supplied by household members, and of labor of one household member for that of another. In the standard discussion of labor demand the decision maker's own leisure choices are assumed away. In the small agricultural firm that assumption may be incorrect. I discuss these issues in Section II.

The other questions relate to the urban sector of a developing economy. As in developed countries, minimum wages, mandatory benefits, and severance pay raise labor costs and create a wedge between the covered and uncovered sectors. There is a quantitative difference, though, for the gap in labor costs and job protection between sectors is generally far wider in developing economies. Moreover, the high-wage, or at least high-skilled, sector in many developing countries is a large government sector. These institutional differences do not require changes in the basic theory of labor demand. With the link of these sectors to the farm sector, though, the analysis in Section III of their impacts must differ somewhat from that in developed economies.

Perhaps the most striking feature of urban labor markets in LDCs is the huge proportion of essentially unskilled industrial labor. This observation, and a simple two-factor model of production, lead to the prescription that appropriate technology must account for the differences between developed and developing economies and tilt toward relatively labor-intensive production in the LDCs. The implication is that capital is the scarce factor of production.

The development literature has paid substantial attention to whether technology adjusts to the differing factor (capital and labor) endowments in developing countries. Much less attention has been paid to the larger issue of what factors are truly scarce in a multifactor model that allows for worker heterogeneity. One observer of these labor markets noted, "The assumption of labor homogeneity also flies in the face of available evidence" (Kannappan 1983, 244). In Section IV I thus consider the nature of scarcity among productive inputs.

Tables 3.8 through 3.10 showed that labor economists in developed countries have begun the econometric examination of the effects of labor-market competition on wages of workers in different demographic and ethnic groups. In developing countries this line of research has barely begun; yet ethnic diversity in many of them is far greater than in developed economies. Section V proposes a number of potentially interesting topics in this and other areas of the demand for heterogeneous labor that should be examined using the techniques discussed in previous chapters.

II. Labor Demand in the Model of the Agricultural Household

This section examines the demand for labor by a farming household that uses a fairly labor-intensive technology involving little machinery and small landholdings. What distinguishes the model substantively, though, is the assumption that the farmer provides labor and entrepreneurial skill, and simultaneously chooses consumption. The main question of interest here is how this dual role affects the analysis of labor demand. I also examine the evidence on this issue and consider how the analysis of Chapters 2 and 3 applies to issues of agricultural development.

Consider a general model of the one-person consumer-entrepreneur-worker farm household.[2] The household maximizes a standard utility function defined over a staple that it produces, of which it consumes X_s, a purchased good X_m, and leisure:

$$U = U(X_s, X_m, T - L_h^o - L_h^f). \tag{10.1}$$

T is the total time endowment, L_h^o the time devoted to working off the farm, and L_h^f the time spent in farm work.

Temporarily assuming a one-person household enables me to ignore the household's allocation of consumption among its members and imperfect substitution among them in production. Especially considering that productive tasks and output may be divided by sex in ways that do not permit linear aggregation, these issues are clearly very important (e.g., Jones 1983). Subsuming them within the one-person household, though, enables me to clarify the exposition and concentrate on a different aspect of heterogeneity. Another issue, the potential endogeneity of fertility, which has received substantial at-

---

[2] The analysis of the most restricted case follows that of Singh, Squire, and Strauss (1986) in part. An alternative exposition of the basic model is Rosenzweig (1988). The discussion of specific cases here is new, though, as is the use of the particular expository devices.

tention in development economics, is outside the scope of this volume and will not be relaxed.

The household maximizes utility under the constraint

$$p_m X_m = p_s[Q - X_s] - w_r L_r + w_h L_h^o, \tag{10.2}$$

where the p_i are the goods prices, Q is the farmer's total production of the staple, the w are wage rates, and the subscript r refers to hired labor. Constraint (10.2) just states that the farmer can buy market goods using his net income from selling the surplus of the staple and his earnings from off-farm work, $w_h L_h^o$.

Rearranging (10.2), subtracting $w_h L_h^f$, and adding $w_h T$ on both sides,

$$p_m X_m + p_s X_s + w_h[T - L_h^f - L_h^o]$$
$$= p_s Q - w_r L_r - w_h L_h^f + w_h T. \tag{10.2'}$$

This is a full-income constraint, analogous to the constraint facing the consumer in Becker's (1965) model of household production. The left side is the value of all utility-increasing items, goods and leisure, that are "purchased"; the right side is the sum of the "profits" from production and the value of the farmer's endowment of time. Farm production is described by the general function

$$Q = Q(L_r, L_h^f, K), \tag{10.3}$$

where K denotes the composite of all the capital and land used.

In certain restrictive circumstances a very powerful result can be derived from this model. Assume $w_r = w_h$, hired and own labor cost the same, and hired and own labor are perfect substitutes in production, that is,

$$Q = Q(L, K), \tag{10.3'}$$

where $L = L_r + L_h$. The right side of (10.2') can then be rewritten as $p_s Q - wL + w_h T$. In maximizing utility with respect to the variables X_m, X_s, L_h^o, and L, the optimal L is independent of the other optimizing choices. The farmer's production decisions can be optimized independent of his consumption decisions, though the latter must be made in light of how X_s is produced. This *recursivity* or *separation* property allows us to treat the farmer just like an ordinary manager. That he also works on the farm and makes consumption-leisure choices is irrelevant for production.

Why this result occurs, and its effects on labor demand, can be seen in Figure 10.1. Let π be the farmer's profit function, which increases in K and decreases in w. X is a composite of X_s and X_m. The budget line with slope w_0 and intercept at $\pi(w_0, K)$ shows the choices available to him. The intercept functions exactly like unearned income in a model of labor supply. With this constraint the farmer uses L^* units of labor and supplies L_h^* of his own labor. Since $L_h^* > L^*$, the

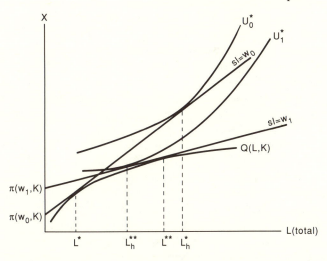

10.1 The Agricultural Household with Separation

farmer is willing to supply enough labor that he could fill the demand for labor on his farm and spend part of his time in off-farm work.

What happens if the wage decreases to w_1? The budget constraint rotates clockwise due to the greater profit from farm activity and the reduced marginal gain to extra hours of the farmer's own labor. Total hours of farm labor demanded rise to L^{**}; but total hours worked by the farmer fall to $L_h^{**} < L^{**}$. He can no longer fill his entire demand for farm labor by supplying it himself. Indeed, whether the farmer supplies any of his own time to farm work is irrelevant, since his full income is the same whether he works L^{**} hours off the farm and hires farm labor or works alongside his hired labor. The optimal L^{**} is reached as it would be in a standard firm. Under these assumptions a decrease in the wage rate has the same effect on employment as in the conventional model of Chapter 2, and that effect works solely through the parameters of the production function.[3]

Consider now whether the separation property stands up to various changes in the simplifying assumptions. First, assume that $w_r \neq w_h$. If $w_r < w_h$ and the supply of hired labor is unconstrained, the farmer's equilibrium is modified. It is no longer a matter of indif-

[3] The results on the farmer's labor supply are not standard (and not of particular interest in this book). The existence of profits from producing the staple generates an additional income effect opposite in sign from the usual effect of higher wage rates on labor supply. The elasticity of labor supply is thus more positive when the farmer's dual nature is accounted for (Rosenzweig 1980).

ference to him whether he uses his own or hired labor on the farm. It pays him to use only (cheaper) hired workers and devote all his work time to off-farm employment. The standard conclusions about the effects of a change in the wage rate w_r are unaffected.

It is more likely that $w_r > w_h$. First, in a multiperson household the average family laborer need not be the householder, and thus may not be as productive as a hired worker. Second, and probably more important, higher wages may be paid to hired workers to induce them to avoid shirking in an environment with costly monitoring. (See some of the studies in Binswanger and Rosenzweig 1984.) Monitoring costs probably apply in lesser degree to the labor of household members.

If $w_r > w_h$ the farmer's production choices are not independent of his consumption-leisure choices, even if L_h^f and L_r are perfect substitutes. The reason is that he will seek to use his own (cheaper) labor in producing the staple. His own wage w_h may, though, become so low that $L^{**} > L_h^{**}$, as in Figure 10.1. The decline in w_h reduces the utility-maximizing supply of his labor to where it falls short of the profit-maximizing input L^{**}. Further declines in w_h reduce L^{**} further (if leisure is a normal good), leading to a still larger demand for hired labor at the same w_r.

This second possibility, while implying a failure of the separation property, is hardly realistic. Why should hired and own labor be perfect substitutes in production yet receive different wages? A more interesting case that links the discussion to Part I of this book assumes the general model of (10.2') and (10.3). Assuming that hired and own labor must be used together has an intuitive appeal. It seems reasonable to argue that the hired farm laborer will be more productive, since his efforts are monitored more easily, when he is working along with the farmer. To the extent that the farmer's labor is supervisory, it will be q-complementary with that of the hired worker. The smaller is the supervisory component of his labor, and the greater the amount of labor supplied to agricultural production by other, nonsupervisory members of the household, the more likely that L_r and L_h are q-substitutes. That they are perfect q-substitutes, though, is difficult to believe.

These assumptions destroy the separation property. The reason is simple, and it is the same one that underlies its breakdown when L_r and L_h^f are perfect substitutes but $w_r > w_h$. With a reduction in w_h the optimal supply of L_h may decrease to the point where the equality $Q_1/Q_2 = w_r/w_h$ that is dictated by productive efficiency cannot be satisfied at the farmer's utility-maximizing point.[4] At that point his util-

[4] Similar arguments apply if the farmer's labor supply elasticity is negative.

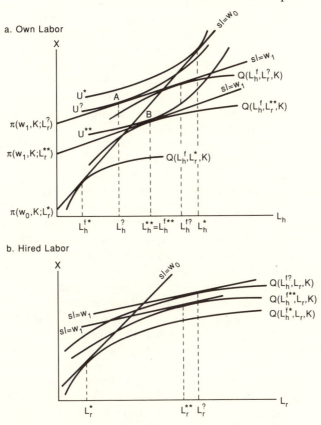

10.2 The Agricultural Household without Separation

ity is maximized at an L_h that affects his demand for the cooperating factor L_r.

This departure from recursivity can be seen with the aid of Figures 10.2a and 10.2b, drawn under the assumption that L_h and L_r are q-complements on the farm.[5] The wage rates w_h and w_r will probably differ, but ignoring that difference in the figures eases the demonstration. Figure 10.2b shows the farmer's demand for hired labor. At a high wage of w_0 he demands L_r^*, for he assumes that he will be using L_h^{f*} of his own labor on the farm. With a lower wage w_1 he would demand $L_{rr}^?$, since he notionally sets his own supply of labor to the farm at the higher $L_h^{f?}$. Not only is hired labor cheaper, so that the budget constraint is flatter; the notional increase in L_h^f raises the average productivity of L_r at each level of L_r used.

[5] If L_r and L_h^f are q-substitutes, the analysis will differ, but the conclusion of non-separability still holds.

The difficulty is that the notional amount, though it is dictated by the marginal productivity conditions for determining L_h^f, is predicated on using $L_r^?$ hired labor. But with the lower wage rate the notional amount of the farmer's own labor is more than the total amount he wishes to supply. At this low wage rate his desire for leisure constrains the amount of L_r he wishes to employ. He cannot optimize on the indifference curve $U^?$ in Figure 10.2a, because it is inconsistent with the constraint implied by choosing $L_r^?$.

The net result is that the profit- and utility-maximizing choices for the farmer dictate using L_r^{**} of hired labor and L_h^{f**} of his own labor in farm work. $L_h^{f**} = L_h^{**}$—he supplies no labor to off-farm employment. The farmer is forced to the lower indifference curve U^{**} in Figure 10.2a, supplying more labor at point B than at point A (because of the presumably negative income effect induced by the decline in profits from the notional $\pi(w_1, K; L_r^?)$ to $\pi(w_1, K; L_r^{**})$). His marginal product and that of hired farm workers vary together, and anything that constrains his own time affects his demand for hired labor.

The generalization from two types of labor, L_r and L_h, to $N-1$ types in an expanded version of (10.3) produces no qualitative changes in the conclusions. As long as a particular type of hired labor is not perfectly substitutable for his own labor, the farmer's utility function affects the mix of inputs chosen. An exogenous increase in the wage of such workers affects factor demand both through the parameters of the function Q and the farmer's utility-maximizing behavior. The direction of the effects depends on the q-substitutability or complementarity of his labor with that of the type of worker whose wage is changed.

A generalization to allow for a multiperson farm household is interesting if one abandons perfect substitution in production. In that case, even a simple multiperson household utility function requires that labor supply and the demand for farm labor be determined jointly. If the household's members are perfect substitutes in production and are perfectly substitutable for hired labor, though, the recursivity property holds. This is true regardless of the possibly complex nature of the family's utility function. While the household's choice of which of its members will work on or off the farm may be complex, the separation property that is guaranteed by perfect substitutability lets it treat the production side as parametric in its supply decisions.

These results underline the fact that the conventional theory of factor demand applies to the agricultural household's demand for labor as long as its members can be treated as identical in production and identical to (elastically supplied) hired farm labor. An important case in which the separation property breaks down even though workers are perfectly substitutable in production has productivity depending implicitly on consumption:

$$Q = Q(L_r + L_h^f(X_s), K), \quad \partial L_h^f / \partial X_s > 0. \tag{10.3''}$$

This is a basic version of an efficiency-wage model and was first discussed by Leibenstein (1957). Maximizing (10.1) when production is described by (10.3'') requires the joint solution of the production and consumption problems. Because the marginal product of labor depends on choices about how much to consume, the marginal productivity condition $p_s \partial Q / \partial L = w$ depends on X_s.

An increase in w when production is described by (10.3'') generates the usual negative substitution effect on the demand for the now more expensive labor. If the farmer's labor supply elasticity to on- and off-farm work exceeds -1, though, the higher wage rate also raises his earnings. This affects his consumption, probably raising X_s, which in turn raises his productivity and at least partly offsets the negative effect of the higher w on farm output, Q. Regardless of the direction of the effect, as long as labor supply is somewhat sensitive to changes in w, attempts to infer the effect of a wage change on farm employment must account for the farmer's consumption of X_s, because that affects his productivity.

Only two of the studies included in Chapter 3 shed direct light on the empirical validity of the separation property. Deolalikar and Vijverberg (1987) examined production in Indian and Malaysian agriculture based on heterogeneous (hired and own) labor. Their main result is that hired and own farm labor cannot be treated as perfect substitutes, which implies a failure of the separation property. Brown and Christensen's (1981) results for the United States suggest that the two types of labor are far from perfect substitutes.

Other empirical research on this issue has been indirect or has studied another problem that is related to the analysis of agricultural labor demand. Lopez (1986) estimated a joint system describing household consumption and farm production and found they are interdependent. The data, though, were aggregates of large areas containing many farms and, more important, covered Canada, hardly the developing country that the models seek to describe. Pitt and Rosenzweig (1986) found that profits of Indonesian farms are independent of whether the farmer was ill, suggesting that hired workers are easily substituted for farmers. Benjamin (1992) examined Javanese rice production. Though he did not specify a formal model of heterogeneous labor in production, his finding that the demographic mix of a farm's work force had no effect on η_{LL} suggests that the separation property is valid.

The other relevant strand of empirical research deals with the effect of higher consumption (actually, better nutrition) on agricultural productivity. The research provides an indirect test of the validity of (10.3″) and thus of the separation property. Strauss (1986) showed that higher wages among farmers in Sierra Leone enabled them to raise the nutritional content of their diets and improved agricultural productivity. Deolalikar (1988) estimated an agricultural production function (using a direct, Type a method) for Indian farms and showed that long-term nutrition, as measured by the weight-height ratio, augments raw labor.

These studies imply that $\partial L_h^f / \partial X_s > 0$, so that the separation property does not hold. Efficiency wages, if they operate at all in developed economies, function only through psychological mechanisms. It is reasonable to expect, though, that in lower-income developing economies they operate through actual improvements in workers' health and hence in their inherent physical productivity (Stiglitz 1987).

The admittedly sparse evidence does not generate much confidence in treating farmers' production decisions separately from their consumption-leisure choices. It is likely that the basic theory of labor demand must be modified to apply to agriculture in developing countries. In particular, the most basic parameter, η_{LL}, the constant-output elasticity of demand for (in this case) farm labor, may depend on the response of labor supply to wage changes as well as on technology.

Is this just a minor academic point, one that can easily be ignored at some small cost in realism but with little loss in the ability to analyze important issues of policy in developing countries? Compared even to the incomplete knowledge of substitution among heterogeneous workers in developed economies, we know very little about this sort of substitution in agriculture in developing economies; yet that knowledge is essential for evaluating policy.

Beginning in the 1980s a major emphasis of development policy was the growth of off-farm rural employment (see Chuta and Liedholm 1985). If these policies are successful, they increase the returns to off-farm work. As such, they will affect the income of rural households by altering the supply of farmers and hired labor to agriculture, while simultaneously affecting farmers' production decisions. Without knowing the extent of p-substitution between hired and own labor, and among family workers of different types, we cannot measure these effects. Absent this knowledge, it is possible to infer, though unlikely, that providing rural nonfarm employment might reduce landholders' incomes by raising the price of the hired labor whose nonfarm opportunities are increased. Alternatively, the income of hired labor might even be reduced, depending on its substitutability with farmers' own labor and the targeting of off-farm employment programs. The main point is that serious studies of substitution among heterogeneous groups of labor are required to evaluate the income and earnings effects of these policies.

If labor were homogeneous, it would be easy to gauge the impact of innovations in agricultural technology, such as the application of new fertilizers and the development of new strains of crops. Indeed, several of the studies summarized in Chapter 3 allow these inferences. Yet by assuming that all workers are identical they prevent us from inferring how innovations affect the distribution of earnings between the landed and landless rural population. Only studies of agricultural production that allow for heterogeneous labor working with other farm inputs can generate estimates that enable the researcher to infer the distribution of benefits from these innovations.

III. Market Interventions in the Modern Sector

Having considered how the theory might be modified to account for the peculiarities of agricultural production in developing countries, I spend the remaining sections of this chapter analyzing aspects of labor demand in the urban sector. This section concentrates on two aspects of the relationship among sectors and subsectors. The first subsection revises the analysis of minimum wages of Chapter 5 to consider the effects of the variety of mandated wage minima, benefits, and restrictions in developing countries. The second subsection analyzes the impact of the large, rapidly growing, education-intensive government subsector on employment, wages, and choice of technique in the private part of the modern sector.

A. Mandated Benefits and Minimum Wages

This subsection examines how wage/employment policy in modern industry can affect wages elsewhere in a developing economy. The links among sectors have been recognized in a number of computational general equilibrium models (see the review in Robinson 1989). The purpose here is to lay out these linkages and to show the importance of labor-demand parameters. The point is sufficiently general that it applies to the spillovers generated by restrictive policies in any sector, for example, in the rural sector too (Anderson 1990).

As Table 10.2 shows, nonwage labor costs are an important component of employee compensation in developing as well as devel-

TABLE 10.2
Nonwage Labor Costs as a Percent of Earnings, 1985

Less Developed Economies	
India	25
Kenya	13
Morocco	19
Pakistan	20
Peru	35
Developed Economies	
Canada	28
France	83
Germany	75
Sweden	67
United Kingdom	33
United States	37

Source: Mazumdar 1989, 55.

oped economies. While the (admittedly problematical) cross-country comparisons suggest that these costs are a smaller fraction of the total in developing countries, in many instances they are substantial and result from government mandates. Moreover, they surely exceed the importance that they had at the same stage of the development of today's developed economies. A similar difference between developing economies today and the now-developed economies during the early stages of their industrialization is today's widespread use of mandated minimum wages.

Assume that these minimum wages and mandated benefits are enforced, so they can produce some effect on employment and wages through their direct impact on labor costs.[6] Are these effects any different from what was discussed in Chapter 5? Is any additional analytical apparatus required? Assume that the developing economy consists of an urban modern sector, in which these minimum wages and mandated benefits raise labor costs; an urban traditional sector that contains self-employed workers not subject to these restrictions; and a rural sector as described in Section II.[7] In analyzing the restrictions' impact this trichotomy goes beyond the two-sector model of Chapter 5. It is necessitated by the importance of the agricultural sec-

---

[6] It is not clear that these laws are anywhere nearly fully enforced; but even their lax enforcement does induce substantial distortions into the labor market, especially for low-skilled industrial workers (Squire 1981, 125).

[7] This is the well-known breakdown analyzed by Harris and Todaro (1970) in the context of rural-urban migration.

tor, the links between the urban and rural sectors, and the behavior of urban workers.

Assume that only a fraction $1-u$ of the labor force located in the urban sector can be employed in the high-wage modern part of that sector at the mandated labor cost, $\bar{w}$.[8] Also, there is sufficient migration between the rural and urban sectors to keep expected earnings in the urban sector equal to the rural wage

$$w_r = uw_0 + [1-u]\bar{w}, \tag{10.4}$$

where w_0 are the returns to work in the urban traditional sector. To simplify the analysis I normalize on the number of people in the urban area by assuming that the urban sector is of size equal to 1.[9] Finally, I assume arbitrarily that the wage (returns to labor) of urban traditional workers, w_0, is the subsistence wage. The analysis could proceed equally well if w_r were fixed at an arbitrary level.

I analyze the imposition of a minimum wage/mandated benefit in the urban modern sector as equivalent to an increase in $\bar{w}$. The crucial point of this section is that this increase will affect rural wages, with the size of the impact depending on various characteristics of labor demand. Differentiating in (10.4), and remembering that a higher minimum wage will affect modern-sector employment, E_m, the effect on the rural wage is

$$\frac{\partial w_r}{\partial \bar{w}} = [\bar{w} - w_0] \frac{\partial E_m}{\partial \bar{w}} + [1-u] \tag{10.5}$$

Compare this to the effect of a higher minimum in the two-sector model of Chapter 5. In that model, as long as demand elasticities in the two sectors are the same and nonzero, a higher minimum wage unambiguously lowers wages in the uncovered sector if labor supply to the market is not infinitely elastic. In this three-sector model that is not necessarily so: A higher minimum wage, or the imposition of benefits that raise labor costs, may raise or lower the wage of rural labor. That wage is more like to decrease: (1) the more elastic is the demand for labor in the urban modern sector. This occurs because, as $\bar{w}$ is raised and workers in that sector are disemployed, the possibility of reverse migration (or reduced rural-urban migration) puts pressure on the rural wage. The rural wage is also more likely to de-

---

[8] Note that, unlike in Chapter 5, I assume here that the minimum wage is set sufficiently high that it is the sole price for covered workers. The notion of a distribution of wages whose lower tail is truncated by the minimum is less important in developing countries.

[9] This does not rule out migration. Indeed, it is migration that maintains the equilibrium condition (10.4). The assumption just allows me to abstract from changes in the sizes of the two sectors to concentrate on the impact on wage rates.

crease: (2) the greater is the gap between the minimum wage in the urban modern sector and the returns to work in the urban traditional sector. This works because, for a given drop in E_m, the loss in expected earnings in the urban sector is larger, thus putting more pressure on w_r through the equilibrium condition (10.4). Finally, the rural wage is more likely to decrease: (3) the smaller is the relative size of the modern sector. Implicitly, imposing higher wages or benefits on a smaller modern sector leaves fewer workers remaining to earn the new, higher wage rate within that sector.

This discussion demonstrates the importance of considering the economywide effects of minimum wages in developing countries. Imposing higher minimum wages on modern industry can generate secondary effects on wages in the traditional agricultural sector that accounts for such a large fraction of employment in developing countries. A major determinant of whether the rural wage rises or falls is the central parameter discussed in Part I, the demand elasticity for homogeneous labor. Especially if the demand for labor in modern industry is fairly elastic, the rural wage is more likely to drop.

If a minimum wage affects the well-being of rural hired labor, the discussion in Section II implies that it will also affect the well-being of farmers, whose output and leisure/consumption decisions partly depend on variations in the wage of hired labor. A useful and, given the growth of the urban sector and of labor-market regulation in developing countries, increasingly important line of theoretical and empirical research would link the behavior of the agricultural household to the policies imposed on modern industry. An important parameter in that research should be the elasticity of demand for industrial labor.

B. Government Employment and the Choice of Technology

In many developing countries public-sector employment has been expanding rapidly as a percentage of total employment. While the data presented in Table 10.3 are incomplete in terms of both the time periods and countries covered, they strongly suggest this conclusion. Whether or not the public sector pays higher wages for identical workers is not clear; but there is some evidence that its growth means that it has siphoned off from the private sector a disproportionate number of more educated workers.[10]

This unbalanced expansion in the relative demand for high-skilled

[10] For example, Stelcner, van der Gaag, and Vijverberg (1989) show that in Peru in the mid-1980s public employees had substantially greater educational attainment.

TABLE 10.3

Growth in Paid Employment, Public and Private Sectors, Developing Countries

| Country | Years | Annual Average Growth Rate | |
		Public	Private
Brazil	1973–83	1.4	0.0
Costa Rica	1973–83	7.6	2.8
Egypt	1966–76	2.5	−0.5
Ghana	1960–78	3.4	−5.9
India	1960–80	4.2	2.1
Kenya	1963–81	6.4	2.0
Panama	1963–82	7.5	1.8
Peru	1970–84	6.1	−0.6
Sri Lanka	1971–83	8.0	0.9
Tanzania	1962–76	6.1	−3.8
Thailand	1963–83	6.3	5.5
Trinidad	1970–84	4.7	1.2
Venezuela	1967–82	5.1	3.4
Zambia	1966–80	7.2	−6.2

Source: Mazumdar 1989, 94.

workers need not be restricted to public employment. In some developing countries and regions within them the growth of tourist and other enclave establishments has sharply increased the demand for indigenous skilled workers in managerial positions. (A good example is the Balinese tourist industry.) The main factor-demand-theoretic issue implied by this expansion, and by the much more important general expansion of the skill-intensive public sector, is how it affects growth and the path of development in the rest of the urban modern sector. Answering the larger question, about its further impact on the urban traditional and rural sectors, follows straightforwardly from the analysis of its effects on the urban modern sector.

Assume there are two parts of the urban modern sector, government (G) and private (P). In each there are three inputs: unskilled labor, L_U; skilled labor, L_S; and capital, K. The effect of an expansion of G depends partly on whether G is relatively unskilled- or skilled-labor intensive. Following the evidence, I assume that it is skilled-labor intensive. The impact on the private sector also depends on whether the supply of skilled workers expands to match the growth in demand for them generated by the expansion of the public sector. The supply of skill, mainly educated labor, depends on the government's allocating resources to the education sector. To the extent this

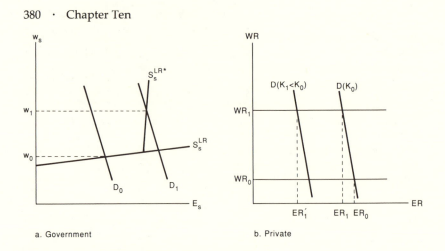

a. Government   b. Private

10.3 Expanding Public Employment and Choice of Technique

is done in conjunction with the growth of public employment, any effects on relative wages will be obviated.[11] I assume here, though, that either the expansion does not track the growth of public-sector demand for skilled labor one-for-one, or that it does so with a substantial lag. This means for our purposes that the supply of L_s to the government sector is insufficient to prevent the expansion of the demand for skill there from bidding up the wages of skilled workers.

We can analyze the effects of this expansion using Figure 10.3. In the government sector in Figure 10.3a the demand for skilled labor shifts from D_0 to D_1. Whether this occurs because the government pays premium wages, or because it sets employment targets that it fills no matter what, is unimportant. All that is necessary for the results is that a high-wage (or skill-intensive) sector expands relatively.

If the educational sector expands along with this shift, there may still be a small long-run effect on the wage rate of skilled workers, w_s, since there may be sector-specific capabilities that render the supply of skill to government less than infinitely elastic. I assumed, though, that educational facilities do not expand sufficiently to meet the shift to D_1, so that the effective supply of skill is S_s^{LR*}. This causes the skilled wage to rise to w_1.

I have drawn the labor market in the private sector in Figure 10.3b in terms of the relative wages and employment of skilled and unskilled workers. The relative supply curve is horizontal, or nearly so,

[11] A good early discussion of the need for appropriate planning of educational expenditures to meet the demand for skilled labor in developing countries is Tinbergen and Bos (1965).

over a broad range. (It may become very steep where the supply of skill is insufficient to meet the expansion of demand that occurred in G, but that section of the curve is not crucial for the basic point.) The relative demand for labor by skill level in the private sector is shown by D_0 at the initial capital stock, K_0. The growth of the public sector's demand for skill raises w_S. This causes the relative wage rate to increase from WR_0 to WR_1. Absent anything learned in previous chapters, we would infer that this would generate a reduction in the relative employment of skilled workers from ER_0 to ER_1.

We know more than that, though. Assuming, as the evidence strongly suggests, that capital and skill are p-complements, this increase reduces the amount of capital demanded to $K_1 < K_0$, and thus also shifts the relative demand for skill to $D(K_1 < K_0)$. Equilibrium relative employment in the private sector falls further, to ER'_1. Depending on the own- and cross-price elasticities, it is quite possible that most of the impact on relative employment comes from the indirect effect of a higher price of skill on the amount of capital installed rather than the direct effect through the substitution of unskilled for skilled labor with a fixed stock of capital.

The most important implication of this simple model is that the expansion of a skill-intensive government sector in developing countries, with no accompanying growth in the supply of skill, leads to a change in the choice of technology in the private sector. P-complementarity of capital and skill, coupled with the rise in the relative wage rate of skilled workers, leads private employers to choose less skill-intensive techniques, which are also less capital-intensive. Unless governments that expand their own employment make sure that they simultaneously invest sufficiently in developing a skilled labor force, their expansion alters the path of private economic development. It ensures that the private sector retains the low-skill-intensive production that economic planners may be seeking to change.

IV. Choice of Technology—Scarce Factors in Economic Development

An issue of continuing, though perhaps somewhat flagging interest in development economics is "choice of technique"—whether the technologies used in developing economies appropriately reflect existing factor prices. The fear is that, through planners' desires to emulate developed countries, or through miscalculations by investors, capital-labor ratios may be too high given the relatively low price of labor. There may, for example, be either explicit or implicit subsidies to the importation of relatively capital-intensive technologies (Krueger 1981).

Underlying this fear is a belief in the inability of decision makers to account properly for factor prices, and perhaps a belief that substitution away from technologies better suited for developed countries is impossible. Implicit too is the notion that the scarce factor in economic development is physical capital. This possibility motivated much of the empirical study of factor substitution in developing countries that is included in Chapter 3. It is noteworthy, though, that the conclusions about the constant-output demand elasticity for homogeneous labor reached there would not differ if they were based solely on estimates for developing countries. A welter of other, less direct evidence (summarized in Pack 1988) gives the same conclusion.

An especially convincing line of research has examined capital-labor ratios within international companies that operate in both developed and developing economies. The studies do not explicitly measure factor substitution (or do so only in the most rudimentary fashion); but their comparisons of these ratios for the same companies, across countries but within industries, are useful evidence on the issue. One of the best (Lipsey, Kravis, and Roldan 1982) examined U.S. and Swedish multinationals and found that they operated less capital-intensive technologies in developing economies. Whether the differences in input ratios fully reflect international differences in input prices and the possibilities for factor substitution is unclear, but at least some such substitution occurs.

This literature should at least partly reinforce our belief in the pervasiveness of economic behavior. It does that, yet it misses an interesting aspect of choice of technology in developing countries. Any visitor to urban areas of developing economies is struck by the modernity of much of the capital stock, particularly in larger industrial establishments and in offices, alongside the often antiquated (or even used imported) equipment. The simple theory of production with two factors, capital and homogeneous labor, would suggest that the abundance of labor should make the modern capital equipment highly productive. It does not. The same equipment does not function as well in developing countries as in developed economies.[12]

I believe the scarce factor in developing economies is skill, especially the skills necessary to organize production and deal with in-

---

[12] My favorite anecdote on this point stems from my experience teaching applied econometrics to young Indonesian university faculty. In the first class I distributed a diskette containing data files for use with a statistical package. One student promptly inserted the diskette into a personal computer, but stuck it not into a disk drive, but into the interstices between the drives! The machine had to be repaired.

dustrial technology, including modern capital equipment. This is, of course, the view implicit in T. W. Schultz's fundamental work on economic development (e.g., Schultz 1981). It is slightly different, though, in that I stress how production proceeds using three factors—physical capital, skilled labor, and unskilled labor—in order to use the evidence of p-complementarity between the first two of these.

This trichotomy subsumes the facts and concerns of the narrower two-factor literature on choice of technique, and it allows a broader understanding of the problems of industrial development. Other than anecdotes of visitors to developing economies, there is very little direct econometric evidence to support this view (note the relatively few studies of developing economies in Tables 3.7 through 3.9). There is, though, some striking evidence for small firms in Sierra Leone (Chuta and Liedholm 1985) of the importance of knowledge of even rudimentary management techniques in raising productivity.

The main point here is that industrial production in developing economies is efficient given the scarcity of skill. Clearly the importance of this approach differs across the incredibly diverse developing world. It is also not clear whether the problem is a scarcity of skill that is p-complementary in production with physical capital or of skill that organizes all inputs into production.[13] For simplicity, and to keep the analysis similar to the approaches of Chapters 2 and 3, I model the problem facing entrepreneurs and planners as one of choosing physical capital and unskilled labor with a constraint on the available input of skill.

Consider the behavior of the typical entrepreneur, shown in Figure 10.4. The available quantity of skilled labor is constrained to be L_S^0, so that the firm operates on the isoquant Q_0. Given the relative prices of the services of physical capital and unskilled labor, the firm chooses to produce at P_0, using L_U^0 unskilled workers. The total amount of labor employed is $L^0 = L_S^0 + L_U^0$. Labor productivity is Q_0/L^0. Assume that the supply of skill increases to L_S^1, because either private agents or government planners realized that skill is scarce and commands a high return. The isoquant shifts outward to $Q_1(L_S^1)$, which may be such, given the scarcity of skill, that $Q_1 >> Q_0$. At the new profit-maximizing point, P_1, there is a small decline in the demand for unskilled labor, no change in total labor input ($L^1 = L_S^1 + L_U^1 = L^0$), and an increase in the demand for physical capital.

With the appropriate numbers attached to the isoquants in $K-L_U$-

[13] The same implications could be derived using two factors, physical capital and unskilled labor, and allowing them to be augmented by the (quantity-constrained) input of skill.

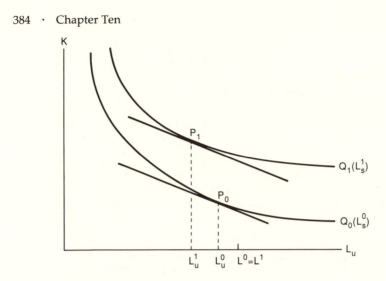

10.4 Capital-Unskilled Labor Substitution and Skill
Endowments

space, this figure implies a path of productivity change that is consistent with the path of economic development. With skilled labor scarce, total labor productivity is quite low, as is output per unit of capital. Relaxing the constraint on skilled labor raises output per worker substantially and can also raise output per unit of capital. These developments are generated by the p-complementarity of skill and capital that produces the particular heterotheticity of the isoquants shown in the figure.

What if a misguided planner, seeing the typical firm at P_0, decides an infusion of additional physical capital is required (or perhaps, that additional incentives should be provided for investment in physical capital)? Output will rise, but very slightly, because the limiting factor is L_S. (Indeed, in the case of perfect p-complementarity between L_S and K, this policy will generate no additional production.) Only by removing the limit on the supply of skill can large increases in production be realized.

The long-run implications of capital-skill p-complementarity can be analyzed most easily by making the extreme assumption of a fixed-coefficients technology for these two factors

$$Q(t) = F(\min\{a(t)K(t),b(t)L_S(t)\},c(t)L_u(t)),$$

where the a, b, and c are measures of factor augmentation, and $F(\cdot,\cdot)$ has the usual properties assumed in Chapter 2 for a two-factor production function. I assume that $a' = b' = 0$, but $c' > 0$, so that technical change is unskilled-labor-augmenting. Assume that population (the labor force) grows at a rate of n percent per year. Then the economy can grow along a nearly steady-state path, with

$$\dot{K} = \dot{L}_s = n + [1 - s(t)]c',$$

where $s(t)$ is the ratio $L_s/[L_U + L_s]$, and

$$\dot{L}_U = n - s(t)c'.$$

In this model $s(t) \to 1$ as $t \to \infty$, and the returns to skill and physical capital remain constant as their productivity remains constant. Output per unskilled worker rises steadily, as does the unskilled wage.

This very simple growth-theoretic approach obviously misses important issues in the development of the labor market. It does, though, demonstrate what one might expect of the growth of endowments and returns in a three-factor world. It stresses the dynamic importance of expanding the constraint imposed by the relative scarcity of skilled labor.

The notion of appropriate technology merits additional research. That study can benefit from greater recognition of the importance of capital-skill-labor substitution, not simply capital-labor substitution alone. That means that we will not learn much by examining capital-labor ratios or their response to differences in wages. Instead, useful work will examine how changes in the provision of skill alter choices of technique. It would study the transfer of technology from developed countries in specific industries, focusing on how the technology is adapted to international differences in endowments of skilled labor.

Capital-skill p-complementarity is an important issue in developing and planned economies that attempt to switch to more market-oriented approaches. Previously state-run (or heavily subsidized) enterprises appear to be given away at "fire-sale" prices, even though those prices reflect their market value *given their current stock of skilled and managerial capital*. That low market value, though, can be greatly increased with relatively small infusions of managerial skill, creating the opportunity for large profits. When barriers to the operation of markets are broken down, increases along the margin of skill as much as physical capital will lead to rapid increases in output and profits.

V. Other Applications of Labor Demand in Development

Our knowledge of labor demand can be used in studying other aspects of economic development. Here I do not propose to offer the same detail as in the previous sections. Instead, the discussion indicates how the analysis in Chapters 2 through 8 could be applied and how the findings of those chapters might condition consideration of the problems. Though in most cases I do not suggest applications to specific economies, knowledge of the idiosyncrasies of a particular labor market are essential to make these applications interesting. Just as essential, though, is the formalized structure of knowledge that has been developed in this volume.

A common thread in many developing economies, cobbled as they were out of locally homogeneous precolonial entities, is the fierce degree of ethnic rivalry and competition. One of the touchiest subjects in many such countries is the conflict over relative economic status and preferment for jobs. Looking only at Southeast Asia, resentment of the Chinese and Indian minorities by the Javanese and competition between ethnic Chinese and Malays in Malaysia are two among many possible examples. The actual effects of changes in the ethnic mix of developing economies on the wage and employment structure by ethnic status make an ideal application of the study of heterogeneous labor presented in Chapters 2 and 3. Studies of q-substitution among groups are necessary, yet apparently none has been conducted.

Substitution studies are admittedly broad-brush, in the sense that they implicitly assume that there is one national labor market in which several groups of workers compete, an obvious gross oversimplification of the facts, especially in developing countries. As such, they should be viewed as a potentially very useful way of evaluating the likely impact on wages and employment of alternative changes in the *relative* sizes of various ethnic populations. The producers and consumers of such research should also note that they focus solely on substitution effects and do not answer the potentially more important question of the likely scale effects of increases in the population of one or more groups of workers. That issue has also largely and regrettably been ignored in studies of developed economies summarized in Chapter 3. The low wages in developing economies make taking them into account there even more important.

There is an immense literature consisting of studies of the rates of return to different types of schooling and training in developing countries (e.g., Psacharopoulos and Woodhall 1985). This literature has been extended to examine the effects of changes in the distribution of education on income inequality, both economywide and among regions (Knight and Sabot 1990; Almeida dos Reis and Paes de Barros 1991). These studies are helpful and important, especially as short-term guides to educational investment. In the longer run they are less useful, since they do not pay sufficient attention to the macroeconomic effects of changes in the distribution of education on the returns. In estimating the rate of return to education most researchers implicitly take the relationship between wages and schooling as fixed.

Differences in wages among workers at various education and skill levels are not permanent, as the discussion in Section III of Chapter 9 made abundantly clear. Indeed, the main message there and in the first part of this volume is that they will change in predictable ways if the distribution of workers arrayed, for example, by education changes. To infer the long-run effect of additional resources that a developing economy invests in schooling, one must know not only the static wage-schooling relationship, but also the effects on that relationship of changing the relative supplies of skill (education).

Assuming nothing else changes, the negative effect of relative increases in the supply of education on the returns to education biases cross-section estimates of the rate of return upward. The degree of optimism implicit in rate-of-return studies should be investigated in specific economies by analyzing factor-price elasticities and the extent of q-substitution among workers with different educational attainments. While there is some recognition of this in related empirical work on cohort effects on the returns to education in developing labor markets (e.g., Behrman and Birdsall 1988), there has been little study of substitution parameters among heterogeneous labor in those markets. The importance of accounting correctly for the dynamic effects of investment in education is heightened by their potential effects through their impact on the rate of technical progress (e.g., Romer 1990).

The fundamental demographic phenomenon in developing countries is the so-called transition, the initial sharp drop in mortality rates, especially infant and child mortality, and the subsequent slower decline in fertility. Together they imply a temporary bulge in the age structure of the population (and hence the labor force), as the decline in child mortality reduces the population's average age. The labor-market impact of the transition is qualitatively the same as, though probably quantitatively more important than, the effect of cycles in fertility in developed economies discussed in some of the substitution studies summarized in Chapter 3.

The research question is how the demographic transition affects the structure of wages by age in different economies. Perhaps more important, as the transition proceeds and the new steady-state population with low mortality and fertility is approached, what is the time path of the structure of wages by age? The answer will differ among economies, depending on the nature of production (and no doubt, too, on cultural differences); but isolating the impact of demographic change on wages in countries that have experienced the transition should be a useful guide to predicting labor-market developments in economies in the middle of the transition. This requires obtaining actual or artificial cohort data that are uncommon in developing countries but are available for this purpose in a few of them.

Many models of international trade by developing countries have examined the effects of changing tariff policy on employment and wages (for example, Edwards and Edwards 1993, which cites much of the extensive literature). Nearly all have several sectors (usually tradeable and nontradeable goods) with capital and homogeneous labor as inputs into different production functions. Very few allow for any kind of heterogeneity in the work force (Findlay and Kierzkowski 1983 is among the few), and none takes into account substitution among workers or explores how sectoral differences in the elasticity of demand for homogeneous labor might affect the conclusions.

Interesting additional paths for research in this area arise from the discussions in the previous chapters. For example, we know that the demand elasticity for labor decreases with skill level. Implicit in the designation of sectors in these trade/development models are notions of real-world industries. Tradeables usually are assumed to include manufacturing, while nontradeables include construction, with other industries classified in varying ways. Knowledge of differences in η_{LL} across sectors should condition the conclusions about the impact on wages of relaxing tariffs on goods competing with the tradeables sector.

Another approach is to assume that production requires physical capital, skilled and unskilled labor. Different assumptions about the relative skill-intensities of the tradeable and nontradeable sectors generate different conclusions about the effect of reducing trade barriers, and these theoretical possibilities have been extensively worked out. The evidence that physical and human capital are relatively p-complementary is so strong that it should narrow the range of predictions in these models about the effect of a change in trade policy.

Even more than developed countries, nearly all developing economies are pervaded by low-interest loans, preferment on taxes for businesses that locate in certain areas, wage subsidies, and other gimmicks designed to stimulate growth in particular industries and regions. Some of these subsidies involve encouraging growth in existing plants and businesses, while others aim at the entry of new businesses and the construction of new plants.

Chapter 4 showed that over one-third of net employment growth stems from births and deaths of plants rather than from expansions and contractions of employment in existing establishments. To what extent should subsidies designed to create jobs be targeted to new versus existing business, or new instead of existing plants? The evidence from studies such as those summarized in Chapter 4 does not permit strong conclusions about the relative sizes of the quasi labor-demand elasticities η^o_{LL} and η^c_{LL} compared to the usual η_{LL}. As more evidence becomes available, though, development planners seeking to maximize employment creation should be able to economize by taking advantage of any differences between the wage elasticities of labor demand through these two routes. Subsidies should be offered on that margin along which the responsiveness of employment is the greatest.

Employment dynamics and, more generally, the demand for labor over business cycles are not major issues in the study of development. Yet some of the policies discussed in Section III, and others that impose restrictions on gross changes in employment in developing economies, add substantially to the cost of labor. Knowing the size of these cost increases would enable planners to gauge how much employment they are trading off, or what effect on wages elsewhere they are producing, to protect existing employees. That knowledge can only be gained by modeling the policies as changing adjustment costs and inferring the size of those changes from employment dynamics. At least as much as in developed economies, studies that enable us to infer the magnitude of adjustment costs are essential for understanding the impact of policies that, directly or indirectly, alter the employer's costs of adjusting the work force.

VI. CONCLUSIONS

The general theme of this chapter is that consideration of multifactor production functions, with imperfect substitution among groups of workers, is essential to analyzing a wide range of issues in economic development. This sounds trivial and unimportant; it is not. For example, I showed that the central result in the analysis of the peasant household, the separation of production choices from decisions about leisure/consumption, breaks down in the realistic case when hired and own labor are imperfect substitutes and where household members' labor is not perfectly substitutable.

I also showed that recognizing the heterogeneity of labor in production allows one to demonstrate the effects on the rural sector of policies that impose restrictions on the urban modern sector. Related to this is an awareness that the rapid growth of an education-intensive government sector affects the path of development of private industry and can confound attempts to generate private employment. Finally, the main concern in the study of "appropriate technology" for developing economies ought not be the choice of a capital/labor ratio. Rather, it should be the choice of the appropriate mix of capital, labor, *and skill*, focusing on the development of the skill necessary to increase the productivity of both capital and labor.

As in the analysis of labor markets generally, the most profound analytical focus has been on labor supply. There has been substantial integration of the theoretical and empirical apparatus of labor supply into the study of economic development. Much less work has been done on low-income countries using the lines of research discussed in Chapters 2 through 8. Given the importance of insufficient employment opportunities, low wages, and the development of skills, this emphasis seems unbalanced. Without much more study of these issues in the context of specific countries, little progress can be made on them. The discussion in the preceding sections should, though, illustrate the richness of the implications of the literature on labor demand for such study.

CHAPTER ELEVEN

Conclusions, Data Requirements, and New Directions

THE PURPOSE OF THIS VOLUME has been to assess the broad outlines of one major part of the subfield of labor economics, the demand for labor. Included in this assessment have been the theory of labor demand, evidence on the major parameters implicit in the theory, and the nature of and evidence on a wide variety of policies whose basis or effects are on the demand side of the labor market. In addition to to summarizing what we know, I have tried throughout to demonstrate various applications and to indicate what is not known but merits further investigation. In this Chapter I synthesize these findings and implications, offer suggestions for improving the data to overcome the severe limitations on research that are created by existing data on establishments, and present several broader directions for research on labor demand.

I. WHAT HAS BEEN ACCOMPLISHED?

The first major task was to lay out the static theory of the demand for labor. The novelty here, as opposed to what appears in textbooks in microeconomics, is the emphasis on the degree of substitution among *several* factors of production and on the rates at which inputs are utilized. The first emphasis arises from the intellectual and policy interest in disaggregating labor into various groups. The second is important because the intensity with which labor works is subject to variations that affect its productivity.

The second standard aspect of economic theory is the dynamic demand for productive inputs, including labor. Most of the concern in the general literature on this topic stems from interest in the path of investment demand; but the analysis applies as well to labor generally and to specific disaggregations of the work force. Crucial to this analysis, probably much more so than to the analogous exposition for investment demand, is a concentration on the structure and sources of the underlying adjustment costs that generate dynamic responses to output and cost shocks. As in any dynamic problem, the agents' expectations—in this case, those of employers—also had to be considered.

The least familiar part of the theoretical analysis dealt with the long-run manifestations of changes in labor demand through firms' entry to and exit from the labor (and inferentially the product) market. The issue here is the nonmarginal impact on product demand of changes in factor prices. Rather than the infinitely lived firm that underlies the standard static and dynamic analysis of factor demand, this analysis required constructing theories that can explain entry and exit. Particularly important for purposes of this volume, it was necessary to explain how these vary with changes in the exogenous determinants of the path of labor demand, especially changes in factor prices.

By far the greatest number of empirical studies have been produced on the static demand for labor. Nearly two hundred studies have been summarized here; and I do not pretend to have discovered every work that might be pigeonholed in one of the tables presented in Chapter 3. On some things so much work has been done, and the issues are sufficiently narrowly defined, that we can be fairly certain about the conclusions. Chief among these is the nature of the demand for homogeneous labor. Consideration of the many studies of this issue and of those that incidentally produce estimates of this parameter suggests reasonably securely that the long-run constant-output own-price elasticity of demand for *homogeneous* labor is between -0.15 and -0.75, with -0.30 being a good single estimate. Given the size of labor's share of total costs, this implies that a reasonable estimate of the elasticity of substitution between capital and homogeneous labor is one. A Cobb-Douglas function is a good approximation to the structure of two-factor production.

This does not mean that the immense theoretical-empirical literature expanding upon the Cobb-Douglas representation has been fruitless. If nothing else, it was necessary in order to test propositions about the ease of capital-labor substitution. Also, the development of more flexible representations of substitution among several inputs opened the way for insightful study of how demand for different types of workers differs and how employers substitute among workers.

The tremendous variety of possible disaggregations of labor makes it difficult to draw very secure conclusions about demand for or substitution among particular groups of workers without much more empirical study. The broad similarities among many of the results, though, allow some reasonably certain inferences. Chief among these is the apparent decline in the long-run own-wage demand elasticity for labor as the amount of skill embodied in a group of workers increases. This is inherent in employers' responses to long-run changes in relative factor prices. It must thus stem from current technological relationships among workers of different skill and between groups of workers and services from the stock of capital.

The other result that pervades the literature on the demand for heterogeneous labor is the apparent relative p-complementarity between skilled labor and physical capital, as compared to p-substitution between capital and unskilled labor. This conclusion means that we know something about how changes in the cost of capital affect the relative demand for different types of labor, and about how changes in the wage rates of different groups of workers affect the demand for investment.

There is also a weaker but still indicative set of results that suggests that the degree of q-complementarity or substitutability between most groups of labor is fairly low. Apparently, the nature of production is such that major shifts can occur in the supply of one type of labor with only fairly small effects on the wages of other types of workers.

The sparse research on the demand for hours and workers in the long run suggests that they are not easily substituted. Implicitly this reinforces the evidence that the demand side of the labor market does not figure importantly in explaining long-run variations in the average number of hours worked by participants in the labor force.

A large array of estimates describing the dynamic behavior of employment demand has been produced. Regrettably, though, the link between them and the underlying theory is much looser than in studies of the long-run demand for labor. We can be quite sure that labor demand adjusts fairly rapidly to changes in employers' expectations about product demand and factor prices, more rapidly than investment demand does.

A large array of evidence indicates that employers adjust hours more rapidly in response to shocks than they adjust employment. One might envision employers as responding to a shock first by altering the intensity with which they use worker-hours, then by changing hours, and finally by choosing a different-sized work force. The evidence also shows that employers are slower to change the employment of more-skilled workers (consistent with the notion of quasi fixed labor).

Despite these facts about the outcomes of adjustment, we know little about the structures that underlie them. In particular, there is very little econometric evidence on the magnitude of the costs that generate the lags. There has been a bit more analysis relating these costs to the time paths of adjustment that we observe, including evidence that the standard assumption of convex adjustment costs (and the implied smooth adjustment) is incorrect; but we lack the same detailed knowledge about these costs as we have of static cost functions.

The empirical study of labor demand through the entry and exit of firms and plants really began only in the late 1970s. The only fairly solidly established fact is that perhaps one-third of changes in employment within an industry arise out of the births and deaths of plants rather than from expansions or contractions in continuously operating plants. We do not know much about how the mix of sources of employment changes is affected by variations in factor prices or product demand. We thus have few estimates of what I have called *quasi elasticities of labor demand* that reflect the impact of changes in factor prices on employment changes resulting from the birth or death of firms and establishments. Research on this nonstandard topic is far behind that based on the standard theory, despite its apparent importance.

In examining how the theory and evidence relate to policy, I have consistently tried to go from particular policies to the archetypes they represent. That approach is essential if the framework and evidence are to have any more than the most ephemeral value. In the case of policies relating to the long-run demand for labor, the general approach used the synthesis of the empirical evidence on substitution parameters to infer the employment and wage effects of such existing specific policies as minimum wages, payroll taxes and subsidies, and limits on immigration. Using the same evidence, though, the approach can easily be applied by other researchers to different current policies and, perhaps more important, can be applied to generate *ex ante* analyses of alternative policy proposals. Because the evidence on many of the general issues of substitution is fairly secure and is linked directly to theoretical constructs, its application to evaluating policies rests on secure grounds.

The evaluation of policies that affect the dynamics of employment and hours suffers from the previously noted difficulty that the basic empirical work is only weakly linked to the underlying theory. This means that it is much more difficult to take the general evidence and apply it to an arbitrarily chosen policy proposal. The discussion instead involved analyzing specific policies and could only offer partial guidance to the evaluation of archetypal policies. In the example of financing unemployment benefits, the empirical literature sufficed to provide a useful evaluation. For other policies, such as requiring advanced notification of layoffs, instituting penalties on employers who separate workers, or seeking to alter employers' willingness to use layoffs instead of hours reductions, the literature is too diffuse and too loosely linked to the necessary basic theory to allow many useful conclusions. The only general conclusion is that, though these policies may smooth fluctuations in employment, they also reduce average inputs of worker-hours because they raise labor costs.

The last broad theme of the book has been the demonstration that the knowledge developed here has implications outside the subdiscipline of labor economics. Labor demand underlies a broad range of issues in macroeconomics, including the central question of employment determination. While the leap from substitution parameters describing the individual plant to aggregate employment is a difficult one, knowledge of those parameters does somewhat delimit the set of reasonable theories of macroeconomic adjustment. For example, along with information on the cyclicality of real wages, knowing that the own-price elasticity of labor demand is nonzero, but not very large, casts doubt on some of the more extreme supply-based theories of adjustment. The development of aggregate skill differentials in wages is of major interest to anyone concerned about income inequality. Knowing the possibilities for substitution among workers of different skills helps explain the paths of these differentials. Finally, the solid theoretical-empirical basis for labor demand allows putting the very loose notion of "job-creation" policy into proper perspective. We can then discover if the phrase has any useful meaning that goes beyond the framework for studying static and dynamic policies that is developed in Chapters 5 and 8.

The demand for labor figures importantly in the study of developing economies. Knowledge of the extent of substitution among workers makes it difficult to accept the dichotomy between the agricultural household's role as producer and consumer and suggests the need for greater generalization in the study of rural labor markets. The size of the elasticity of demand for homogeneous labor (based in part on the fairly large number of estimates of this parameter for developing countries) should affect evaluations of the impact of regulations on wages in urban industry and on the wages and well-being of both landless agricultural workers and landowners. Knowing that capital and skill are relative p-complements should affect the analysis of the impact of governments' demand for educated workers on private industry in many developing countries. It also increases our understanding of the long and extensive debate over problems of "appropriate technology" in developing economies by expanding beyond the narrow focus on substitution between capital and homogeneous labor.

II. The Need for Improved Data

Next to the cry "More research is needed," the subcry "More data are needed" is most often heard at academic conferences and seen in scholarly journals. Though nearly always valid, it is especially correct in the study of labor demand. In discussing many of the suggestions for research in this volume, I have indicated cursorily where more data are required. It is worth bringing these indications together and considering them more carefully in terms of the appropriateness of the data used. Much of this review is based on difficulties with American data; but since American research forms nearly a majority of that summarized in Chapters 3 and 7, this approach is useful.

Those chapters demonstrated the magnitude of the empirical literature on substitution among groups of workers, between employment and hours, and on the dynamics of employment and hours. Very little of it is based on microeconomic, establishment data, as a perusal of Tables 3.7 through 3.11 and 7.1 through 7.8 shows. Much is based on highly aggregated establishment data; a large part of the remainder uses household, often Census, data.

The commonly used establishment KLEM data suffer from problems of representativeness, since they cover only manufacturing. Their high degree of temporal aggregation is not a severe problem for measuring long-run labor-demand elasticities, but it generates problems in inferring the length of lags and makes it impossible to infer the structure of adjustment costs. The aggregation of all workers into at most two groups limits the applicability of these data to questions of substitution.

The excessive spatial aggregation of most of the commonly used establishment data also poses problems. The underlying static and dynamic theories yield relationships that can involve nonlinear transformations of the data. There is no reason to assume that aggregating relationships that are based on individual establishments will produce the same results as estimates based on aggregated data.

The problems with the household data are even more severe. The main difficulty is their general inappropriateness for estimating demand relationships due to their potentially severe unrepresentativeness. Essentially each worker in the household survey represents the establishment that employs him or her. Many plants have none, while others have several representatives in the survey. There is no reason to expect biases due to this unusual sampling procedure, but it is hardly designed to minimize sampling error in data used to describe the behavior of plants. Many of the studies also are based on data that are aggregated spatially (often to the level of metropolitan areas), which causes problems due to any nonlinearity of the relationships.

The study of the dynamics of employment change through the births and deaths of establishments and firms that was discussed in Chapter 4 has proceeded using laboriously constructed sets of longitudinal data in a number of economies. As noted there, the high degree of temporal aggregation generates both negative and positive biases in the estimated fraction of net employment change that is accounted for by births and deaths of plants. Also, many of the sets of data underlying the empirical work summarized in Chapter 4 are restricted to manufacturing, making the studies increasingly unrepresentative of developed economies.

Still more important, in most of the data the amount of temporal aggregation prevents one from inferring anything about the short-run causes of employment change. Even with higher-frequency data, the absence of good, or in most cases even any data on output and labor costs makes structural inferences impossible. None of the available sets of data provides any information on disaggregations of workers by demographic group (and most do not even distinguish between production and nonproduction workers). Any attempt to generalize studies of substitution in continuing plants to establishment dynamics is obviated.

At least as important as these problems with specific data sets is the lack of a generally available useful set of data for analyzing labor demand. This has no doubt inhibited advances in areas that would be explored were better data available. As noted in Chapter 1, exactly the opposite has occurred in the analysis of labor supply, which was rejuvenated by the development of large longitudinal household surveys. A major purpose of any new set of data for studying labor demand should be to stimulate new theoretical and policy inquiry, as well as to answer existing questions.

In the United States we do have the Longitudinal Research Database (LRD), an annual establishment-based file constructed from the same sources that generate the published data in the *Annual Survey of Manufactures*. Though this set of data does overcome problems of spatial aggregation, annual observations are too infrequent to capture many of the dynamic phenomena of interest. Also, the restriction to manufacturing means the data are seriously unrepresentative. Worse still, they are not generally available to researchers outside of government, and they offer essentially no disaggregation of the work force and no detail on the costs of labor.

In other English-speaking countries establishment-based data sets do exist and are generally available to researchers. Great Britain has the Workplace Industrial Relations Survey (WIRS), which contains most of the variables one might wish for studying labor demand. Only three waves of interviews had been produced as of 1991, so that the WIRS is not an ongoing longitudinal data base like the major household surveys. It cannot generate satisfactory inferences about establishment dynamics (births/deaths) or about the dynamics of demand in continuing establishments. The Australian WIRS, though it provides most of the desired data series at the plant level, offers only one cross section of information.

In non-English-speaking countries, perhaps the closest approximation to the ideal set of data is the Danish Integrated Database for Labor Market Research (IDA), though several other European countries have begun constructing similar sets of data. It provides annual data beginning in 1980 on all establishments in the country and offers detailed demographic information on each establishment's work force, flows of labor, and labor costs. Its only drawbacks are the absence of data on production or sales and its restriction to annual observations. While it comes closest, even the IDA is not an entirely satisfactory vehicle for the specific research ideas I have suggested. It could lead to entirely new types of study of labor demand, but those are more likely to be stimulated by data sources that remove more of the problems that arise in existing data.

The ideal set of data for studying labor demand is longitudinal, available at regular short intervals, and based on random samples of establishments. It should have information on all the forcing variables that determine long-run factor demand, including detailed information on types of labor costs. Employment and hours (worked as well as paid for) by type of worker should be available, as should information on flows of workers into and out of establishments. Some information on other inputs into production is also necessary.

Specifically, what is needed is a quarterly or, even better, a monthly longitudinal survey of an appropriately stratified sample of establishments that is representative of all private nonfarm business. This survey should be establishment-based, should replace defunct establishments with appropriate substitutes, and should be benchmarked at regular intervals to available censuses (in the United States, to the Censuses of Business, Manufactures, Mining, and the like). Given the required frequency of observations, only a small sample is feasible, but with careful sampling it can be reasonably representative.

The survey should contain data on total employment and on employment disaggregated into several meaningful skill and demographic categories, including at least sex, race, broad occupation, and age intervals. The number of workers hired each period in each group is also needed, as are hours worked per week. Payroll costs and the costs of other benefits are necessary for each type of worker, as is information on the cost of the establishment's personnel operation.

Information on output measured in physical units is desirable, but failing that, series on revenue along with good industry identifiers may suffice to allow the use of appropriate deflators.[1] To infer the rate of production, the value of finished-goods inventories is also necessary. Information on the replacement value of the establishment's plant and equipment is also desirable, but in its absence a series on investment in the establishment is a partial substitute.

This part of the proposed data collection effort is mostly an extension and rationalization of what already exists in the United States. The survey expands the monthly BLS-790 or the OSHA sampling frame, requires mandatory reporting, and makes the data set available in an appropriately constructed longitudinal format. Nonwage labor costs are already collected through the mechanisms that produce the Employment Cost Index. It should be possible to use the procedures that generate the inputs into the Index to construct the proposed longitudinal file. The only new information is that on output and sales, and on the disaggregations by type of worker. At least for manufacturing establishments, all but the work force disaggregations are already collected on an annual basis.

Studies of particular urban labor markets were conducted beginning in the 1940s and continuing to Rees and Shultz (1970). These involved micro data on *both* firms and households. Such data provide the best possible way to describe the inherently market phenomena that the authors were trying to examine and that still interest us today. A revival of the kinds of data collection that underlay the labor-market studies would yield very high returns.[2]

With this purpose in mind, samples of workers from the plants in the longitudinal establishment file should also be followed during their tenure in the establishment (though only at annual intervals), with replacements substituted for them as they separate from their employer. Information on their detailed demographic characteristics,

---

[1] Even detailed industry identifiers may not account for intraindustry heterogeneity in the mix of products, so that the appropriate deflator may be very difficult to obtain (Berndt, Griliches, and Rosett 1990).

[2] There were a few efforts at obtaining matched cross-section data on employers and their workers in the 1980s. One was tied to the Panel Study of Income Dynamics (Duncan and Hill 1985). The other assembled data for workplaces in six British cities (Elliot and Sandy 1991).

including the characteristics of other members of their households, should be obtained. Their self-reported hours, both with the employer and on other jobs, and their earnings and those of any other household members, are also desirable.

This proposed exercise in data collection is a fairly tall order. It is no taller, though, than the proliferation in developed economies of longitudinal data sets based solely on household data. As such, it provides a counterweight to the concentration on information on labor supply that has led to the imbalance in our knowledge of the two sides of labor markets, and to our inability to analyze those two sides jointly. If it is too costly, or too difficult conceptually (which I do not believe is so), the collection of only the longitudinal establishment data would be a major step in enabling us to acquire knowledge about employers' behavior.

The major longitudinal sets of household data in the United States (National Longitudinal Surveys, Panel Study of Income Dynamics, and others) and elsewhere are usually available to researchers with few or no restrictions. If the same progress is to be made in the study of labor demand, similarly few restrictions must be imposed on the data whose collection I propose or on any similar set of data. With sufficient care the data can be sanitized for public use to prevent disclosures that might cause companies competitive harm. With the comprehensive set of information proposed here, there is less need for identifiers that allow researchers to link the data to other information. The privacy arguments that have necessitated remarkably convoluted research gymnastics become an excuse for inaction when the data are sufficiently comprehensive.[3]

III. Where Should the Study of Labor Demand Go?

Throughout the volume I have indicated important specific studies that would extend research on labor demand. Though these merit investigation, and in many cases are quite basic, each is confined to the topic of a particular chapter. There are a few broader research topics that cut across several of the major issues in labor demand and that also merit attention in future studies. Much of that research will be conditioned by the availability of data, as past study has been. The data outlined in Section II could provide just such a useful basis for research. Some interesting questions cannot be dealt with using

[3] For example, users of the Longitudinal Research Database were required to become sworn employees of the U.S. government and conduct their research at the Bureau of the Census. Early users had the hard disk drives of the personal computers on which they worked destroyed when they left their project!

those data alone, though, and I turn to these in this concluding section.

The data collection proposed in Section II does not allow for the detailed investigation of labor costs—attaching numbers to the typology in Figure 2.2—that is necessary to measure the cost of labor to employers properly. A serious accounting is necessary, in part to provide a background and basis for collecting more generally usable data on labor costs. Also, this accounting is important in measuring the impact of most of the policies I have discussed. Since both static and dynamic demand policies function through altering labor costs, better knowledge of the magnitude of those costs is essential for understanding and predicting their effects.

Concerns about aggregation pervaded the discussion of both static and dynamic labor demand. This appeared, for example, in worries about inferring substitution parameters from nonlinear microeconomic relations estimated over aggregated (linearly summed) data, and about the problems of inferring the structure of adjustment costs. Still more important, it underlay the move from the maximizing models that generate the firm's demand for labor to the analogue of labor demand in macro models. These problems all require serious research, not merely the usual perfunctory nod by economists to the aggregation problem as we derive our theories and blithely estimate our models. Without more work on aggregation, the basis for many of the inferences that we seek to draw about labor demand is disturbingly weak.

In Chapter 2 I discussed whether wages or employment should be considered exogenous in the discussion of substitution. A similar issue underlies employment dynamics in Chapter 6, to the extent that supply constraints interact with adjustment costs to affect the path of employment. In Chapter 8 I discussed a similar problem in the context of the dynamic incidence of tax/subsidy policies. All of these topics show the need for empirical work that accounts for the interaction of labor demand with labor supply. This is, of course, a common problem in empirical economics generally.

A far-reaching area of research recognizes the need for economists to "get our hands dirty" by observing what actually occurs in the workplace, essentially renewing the path-breaking work of Holt et al. (1960). While available data and, to a greater extent, the data proposed in Section II show us the outcomes of decisions about labor demand, they cannot enable us to infer what generates those decisions. We cannot infer how workers use their time on the job, how they are supervised or what leads employers to conclude that a vacancy exists. These issues are important both for obtaining better estimates of the relationships dealt with in this volume and for inferring how behavior in the workplace generates aggregate labor-market outcomes and macroeconomic adjustment. This is not the kind of study we usually undertake. Without it, though, we cannot really understand the structure that produces the outcomes that interest us.

It is easy to conclude, despite all the evidence to the contrary in this volume, that theoretical, econometric, and data difficulties mean that we really know nothing about labor demand. Nihilism is a standard technique of academic game playing. It is never attractive; and to varying degrees it is incorrect in the study of labor demand. Nonetheless, by building ever more complex theoretical and econometric models that we estimate using inappropriate data, by our unwillingness to study labor demand at the level of the decision maker, and by failing to consider just what it is that we are trying to learn, we invite nihilism by other academics and neglect by policy makers and the public. Taken as a whole, the existing body of research in labor demand deserves neither response. The new directions and approaches that I have outlined here and throughout the volume should make nihilism and neglect even less appropriate. They will strengthen further the intellectual basis of the study of labor demand and will make research in this area even more useful in constructing labor-market policy.

References

Abraham, Katharine. 1988. "Flexible Staffing Arrangements and Employers' Short-term Adjustment Strategies." In Robert Hart, *Employment, Unemployment and Labor Utilization*. Boston: Unwin Hyman.

Abraham, Katharine, and Susan Houseman. 1988. "Employment and Hours Adjustment: A U.S./German Comparison." Unpublished paper, University of Maryland.

———. 1989. "Job Security and Work Force Adjustment: How Different Are U.S. and Japanese Practices?" *Journal of the Japanese and International Economies*, 3:500–21.

Abraham, Katharine, and James Medoff. 1985. "Length of Service and Layoffs in Union and Nonunion Work Groups." *Industrial and Labor Relations Review*, 38:87–97.

Addison, John, and Pedro Portugal. 1987. "The Effect of Advance Notification of Plant Closings on Unemployment." *Industrial and Labor Relations Review*, 41:3–16.

Aigner, Dennis, and Glen Cain. 1977. "Statistical Theories of Discrimination in Labor Markets." *Industrial and Labor Relations Review*, 30:175–87.

Aizcorbe, Ana. 1992. "Procyclical Labor Productivity, Increasing Returns to Labor, and Labor Hoarding in U.S. Auto Assembly Plant Employment." *Economic Journal*, 102:860–73.

Akerlof, George, and Janet Yellen, eds. 1986a. *Efficiency Wage Models of the Labor Market*. Cambridge, England: Cambridge University Press.

———. 1986b. "Introduction." In Akerlof and Yellin, eds., *Efficiency Wage Models of the Labor Market*. Cambridge, England: Cambridge University Press.

Allen, R.G.D. 1938. *Mathematical Analysis for Economists*. London: Macmillan.

Allen, Steven. 1986. "Union Work Rules and Efficiency in the Building Trades." *Journal of Labor Economics*, 4:212–42.

———. 1991. "Technology and the Wage Structure." Unpublished paper, North Carolina State University.

Almeida dos Reis, Jose, and Ricardo Paes de Barros. 1991. "Wage Inequality and the Distribution of Education." *Journal of Development Economics*, 36:117–43.

Alpert, William. 1986. *The Minimum Wage in the Restaurant Industry*. New York: Praeger Press.

Altonji, Joseph. 1986. "Intertemporal Substitution in Labor Supply." *Journal of Political Economy*, 94:S176–215.

Altonji, Joseph, and David Card. 1991. "The Effects of Immigration on the Labor Market Outcomes of Less-skilled Natives." In John Abowd and

Richard Freeman, eds., *Immigration, Trade, and the Labor Market*. Chicago: University of Chicago Press.

Anderson, Joseph. 1977. "Labor Force Age Structure Changes and Relative Wages." Unpublished paper, Harvard University.

Anderson, Julie. 1990. "Legislation, Development and Legislating Development in Brazilian Rural Labor Markets." Unpublished paper, Stanford University.

Anderson, Patricia. 1992. "Linear Adjustment Costs and Seasonal Labor Demand: Unemployment Insurance Experience Rating in Retail Trade." Princeton University, Industrial Relations Section, Working Paper No. 293.

Anderson, Richard. 1981. "On the Specification of Conditional Factor Demand Functions in Recent Studies of U.S. Manufacturing." In Ernst Berndt and Barry Field, eds., *Modeling and Measuring Natural Resource Substitution*. Cambridge: MIT Press.

Ando, Albert, Franco Modigliani, and Robert Rasche. 1972. "Equations and Definitions of Variables for the FRB-MIT-Penn Econometric Model, 1969." In Bert Hickman, ed., *Econometric Models of Cyclical Behavior*. New York: Columbia University Press.

Andrews, Martyn. 1987. "The Aggregate Labour Market: An Empirical Investigation into Market-Clearing for the UK." *Economic Journal*, 97:157–77.

Armington, Catherine, and Marjorie Odle. 1982. "Small Business—How Many Jobs?" *Brookings Review*, 1:14–17.

Arrow, Kenneth, Hollis Chenery, Bagicha Minhas, and Robert Solow. 1961. "Capital-Labor Substitution and Economic Efficiency." *Review of Economics and Statistics*, 43:225–50.

Ashenfelter, Orley, and David Card. 1985. "Using the Longitudinal Structure of Earnings to Estimate the Effect of Training Programs." *Review of Economics and Statistics*, 67:648–60.

Ashenfelter, Orley, and Ronald Ehrenberg. 1975. "The Demand for Labor in the Public Sector." In Daniel Hamermesh, ed., *Labor in the Public and Nonprofit Sectors*. Princeton: Princeton University Press.

Ashenfelter, Orley, and Richard Layard, eds. 1986. *Handbook of Labor Economics*. Amsterdam: North-Holland Press.

Ashenfelter, Orley, and Robert Smith. 1979. "Compliance with the Minimum Law." *Journal of Political Economy*, 87:333–50.

Ashenfelter, Orley, George Johnson, and John Pencavel. 1972. "Trade Unions and the Rate of Change of Money Wages in United States Manufacturing Industry." *Review of Economic Studies*, 34:27–54.

Atkinson, Scott, and Robert Halvorsen. 1984. "Parametric Efficiency Tests, Economies of Scale, and Input Demand in U.S. Electric Power Generation." *International Economic Review*, 25:647–62.

Azariadis, Costas. 1975. "Implicit Contracts and Underemployment Equilibria." *Journal of Political Economy*, 83:1183–202.

Baily, Martin N. 1974. "Wages and Employment under Uncertain Demand." *Review of Economic Studies*, 41:37–50.

————. 1977. "On the Theory of Layoffs and Unemployment." *Econometrica*, 45:1043–64.

Baily, Martin N., and James Tobin. 1978. "Inflation-Unemployment Consequences of Job Creation Policies." In John Palmer, ed., *Creating Jobs: Public Employment Programs and Wage Subsidies*. Washington, D.C.: Brookings Institution.

Baldwin, John, and Paul Gorecki. 1988. "Job Turnover in Canada's Manufacturing Sector." In Baldwin and Gorecki, eds., *Structural Change and Adjustment: Perspectives on Job Change and Worker Turnover*. Ottawa: Economic Council of Canada.

Ball, R. J., and E.B.A. St. Cyr. 1966. "Short-term Employment Functions in British Manufacturing Industry." *Review of Economic Studies*, 33:179–208.

Baltagi, Badi, and James Griffin. 1988. "A General Index of Technical Change." *Journal of Political Economy*, 96:20–41.

Barron, John, John Bishop, and William Dunkelberg. 1985. "Employer Search: The Interviewing and Hiring of New Employees." *Review of Economics and Statistics*, 67:43–52.

Bartel, Ann, and Frank Lichtenberg. 1987. "The Comparative Advantage of Educated Workers in Implementing New Technology." *Review of Economics and Statistics*, 69:1–11.

————. 1991. "Technical Change, Learning and Wages." *Economics of Innovation and New Technology*, 1:215–31.

Bartik, Timothy. 1985. "Business Location Decisions in the United States: Estimates of the Effects of Unionization, Taxes and Other Characteristics of States." *Journal of Business and Economic Statistics*, 3:14–22.

Bazen, Stephen, and John Martin. 1991. "The Impact of the Minimum Wage on Earnings and Employment in France." *OECD Economic Studies*, 199–221.

Beach, Charles, and Frederick Balfour. 1983. "Estimated Payroll Tax Incidence and Aggregate Demand for Labour in the United Kingdom," *Economica*, 50:35–48.

Bean, Charles, and P. J. Turnbull. 1988. "Employment in the British Coal Industry: A Test of the Labour Demand Model." *Economic Journal*, 98:1092–104.

Bean, Frank, B. Lindsay Lowell, and Lowell Taylor. 1988. "Undocumented Mexican Immigrants and the Earnings of Other Workers in the United States." *Demography*, 25:35–52.

Becker, Gary. 1965. "A Theory of the Allocation of Time." *Economic Journal*, 75:492–517.

Becker, Joseph M. 1981. *Unemployment Insurance Financing*. Washington, D.C.: American Enterprise Institute.

Begg, David, Assar Lindbeck, Chris Martin, and Dennis Snower. 1989. "Symmetric and Asymmetric Persistence of Labor Market Shocks." *Journal of the Japanese and International Economies*, 3:554–77.

Behrman, Jere, and Nancy Birdsall. 1988. "The Reward for Good Timing: Cohort Effects and Earnings Functions for Brazilian Males." *Review of Economics and Statistics*, 70:129–35.

Bell. Linda, and Richard Freeman. 1991. "The Causes of Rising Interindustry Wage Dispersion in the United States." *Industrial and Labor Relations Review*, 44:275–87.

Benjamin, Dwayne. 1992. "Household Composition, Labor Demand and Labor Markets: Testing for Separation in Agricultural Household Models." *Econometrica*, 60:287–322.

Bentolila, Samuel, and Gilles Saint-Paul. 1992. "The Macroeconomic Impact of Flexible Labor Contracts, with an Application to Spain." *European Economic Review*, 36:1013–47.

Bentolila, Samuel, and Giuseppe Bertola. 1990. "Firing Costs and Labor Demand: How Bad Is Eurosclerosis?" *Review of Economic Studies*, 57:381–402.

Berger, Mark. 1983. "Changes in Labor Force Composition and Male Earnings: A Production Approach." *Journal of Human Resources*, 18:177–96.

———. 1984. "Increases in Energy Prices, Costs of Production, and Plant Size." *Journal of Economics and Business*, 36:345–57.

———. 1985. "The Effect of Cohort Size on Earnings Growth: A Reexamination of the Evidence." *Journal of Political Economy*, 93:561–73.

Berger, Mark, and John Garen. 1990. "Heterogeneous Producers in an Extractive Industry." *Resources and Energy*, 12:295–310.

Bergström, Villy, and Epaminondas Panas. 1990. "Does Inflation Hurt Productivity Growth: An Estimation of Interrelated Factor Demand Functions." Stockholm, Trade Union Institute for Economic Research, Working Paper No. 74.

———. 1992. "How Robust Is the Capital-Skill Complementarity Hypothesis?" *Review of Economics and Statistics*, 74: in press.

Bernanke, Ben. 1986. "Employment, Hours and Earnings in the Depression." *American Economic Review*, 76:82–109.

Bernanke, Ben, and Martin Parkinson. 1991. "Procyclical Labor Productivity and Competing Theories of the Business Cycle: Some Evidence from Interwar U.S. Manufacturing Industries." *Journal of Political Economy*, 99:439–59.

Berndt, Ernst. 1976. "Reconciling Alternative Estimates of the Elasticity of Substitution." *Review of Economics and Statistics*, 58:59–68.

———. 1981. "Modelling the Simultaneous Demand for Factors of Production," in Zmira Hornstein et al., eds., *The Economics of the Labor Market*. London: Her Majesty's Stationery Office.

Berndt, Ernst, and Laurits Christensen. 1974. "Testing for the Existence of an Aggregate Index of Labor Inputs." *American Economic Review*, 64:391–404.

Berndt, Ernst, Zvi Griliches, and Joshua Rosett. 1990. "On the Accuracy of Producer Indexes for Pharmaceutical Preparations: An Audit Based on Detailed Firm-Specific Data." National Bureau of Economic Research, Working Paper No. 3490.

Berndt, Ernst, and Mohammed Khaled. 1979. "Parametric Productivity Measurement and Choice Among Flexible Functional Forms." *Journal of Political Economy*, 87:1220–45.

Berndt, Ernst, and Catherine White. 1978. "Income Redistribution and Employment Effects of Rising Energy Prices." Unpublished paper, University of British Columbia.

Berndt, Ernst, and David Wood. 1975. "Technology, Prices, and the Derived Demand for Energy." *Review of Economics and Statistics*, 57:259–68.

———. 1979. "Engineering and Econometric Interpretations of Energy-Capital Complementarity." *American Economic Review*, 69:342–54.

Bertola, Giuseppe. 1990. "Job Security, Employment and Wages." *European Economic Review*, 34:851–86.

Bils, Mark. 1985. "Real Wages over the Business Cycle: Evidence from Panel Data." *Journal of Political Economy*, 93:666–89.

Binswanger, Hans, and Mark Rosenzweig, eds. 1984. *Contractual Arrangements, Employment, and Wages in Rural Labor Markets in Asia*. New Haven: Yale University Press.

Birch, David. 1981. "Who Creates Jobs?" *Public Interest*, 65:3–14.

Bishop, John. 1981. "Employment in Construction and Distribution Industries: The Impact of the New Jobs Tax Credit." In Sherwin Rosen, ed., *Studies in Labor Markets*. Chicago: University of Chicago Press.

Black, Stanley, and Harry Kelejian. 1970. "A Macro Model of the U.S. Labor Market." *Econometrica*, 38:712–41.

Blackorby, Charles, and Robert Russell. 1989. "Will the Real Elasticity of Substitution Please Stand Up?" *American Economic Review*, 79:882–88.

Blanchard, Olivier, and Stanley Fischer. 1989. *Lectures on Macroeconomics*. Cambridge: MIT Press.

Blanchflower, David, Neil Milward, and Andrew Oswald. 1991. "Unionism and Employment Behaviour." *Economic Journal*, 101:815–34.

Blank, Rebecca. 1988. "Simultaneously Modeling the Supply of Weeks and Hours of Work among Female Household Heads." *Journal of Labor Economics*, 6:177–204.

Blank, Rebecca, and David Card. 1991. "Recent Trends in Insured and Uninsured Employment: Is There an Explanation?" *Quarterly Journal of Economics*, 106:1157–90.

Blinder, Alan. 1981. "Retail Inventory Behavior and Business Fluctuations." *Brookings Papers on Economic Activity*, 443–505.

del Boca, Daniela. 1990. *Relazioni Industriali e Mercato del Lavoro*. Rome: Nuova Italia Scientifica.

Borjas, George. 1983. "The Substitutability of Black, Hispanic and White Labor." *Economic Inquiry*, 21:93–106.

———. 1986a. "The Demographic Determinants of the Demand for Black Labor." In Richard Freeman and Harry Holzer, eds., *The Black Youth Employment Crisis*. Chicago: University of Chicago Press.

———. 1986b. "The Sensitivity of Labor Demand Functions to Choice of Dependent Variable." *Review of Economics and Statistics*, 68:58–66.

———. 1987a. "Immigrants, Minorities, and Labor Market Competition." *Industrial and Labor Relations Review*, 40:382–92.

Borjas, George. 1987b. "Self-selection and the Earnings of Immigrants." *American Economic Review*, 77:531–54.

———. 1990. *Friends or Strangers: The Impact of Immigrants on the U.S. Economy*. New York: Basic Books.

Bound, John, and George Johnson. 1992. "Changes in the Structure of Wages during the 1980's: An Evaluation of Alternative Explanations." *American Economic Review*, 82:371–92.

Bowles, Samuel. 1970. "Aggregation of Labor Inputs in the Economics of Growth and Planning: Experiments with a Two-Level CES Function." *Journal of Political Economy*, 78:68–81.

Boyer, Robert. 1990. "The Impact of the Single Market on Labour and Employment." *Labour and Society*, 15:109–42.

Brechling, Frank. 1965. "The Relationship between Output and Employment in British Manufacturing Industries." *Review of Economic Studies*, 32:187–216.

———. 1975. *Investment and Employment Decisions*. Manchester: Manchester University Press.

———. 1977. "The Incentive Effects of the U.S. Unemployment Insurance Tax." *Research in Labor Economics*, 1:41–102.

———. 1981. "Layoffs and Unemployment Insurance." In Sherwin Rosen, ed., *Studies in Labor Markets*. Chicago: University of Chicago Press.

Brechling, Frank, and Peter O'Brien. 1967. "Short-run Employment Functions in Manufacturing Industries: An International Comparison." *Review of Economics and Statistics*, 49:277–87.

Bresson, Georges, Francis Kramarz, and Patrick Sevestre. 1991. "Labor Demand for Heterogeneous Workers with Nonlinear Asymmetric Adjustment Costs." Unpublished paper, Université Paris XII.

———. 1992. "Heterogeneous Labor and the Dynamics of Aggregate Labor Demand: Some Estimations Using Panel Data." *Empirical Economics*, 17:153–67.

Brittain, John. 1972. *The Payroll Tax for Social Security*. Washington, D.C.: Brookings Institution.

Brown, Charles, Curtis Gilroy, and Andrew Kohen. 1982. "The Effect of the Minimum Wage on Employment and Unemployment." *Journal of Economic Literature*, 20:487–528.

Brown, Eleanor. 1986. "Unemployment Insurance Taxes and Cyclical Layoff Incentives." *Journal of Labor Economics*, 4:50–65.

Brown, James, and Orley Ashenfelter. 1986. "Testing the Efficiency of Employment Contracts." *Journal of Political Economy*, 94:S40–87.

Brown, Murray, and John de Cani. 1963. "A Measure of Technological Employment." *Review of Economics and Statistics*, 45:386–94.

Brown, Randall, and Laurits Christensen. 1981. "Estimating Elasticities of Substitution in a Model of Partial Static Equilibrium: An Application to U.S. Agriculture, 1947–74." In Ernst Berndt and Barry Field, eds., *Modeling and Measuring Natural Resource Substitution*. Cambridge: MIT Press.

Browning, Edgar, and William Johnson. 1983. "The Distributional and Efficiency Effects of Increasing the Minimum Wage." *American Economic Review*, 73:204–11.

Brunello, Giorgio. 1989. "The Employment Effects of Shorter Working Hours: An Application to Japanese Data." *Economica*, 56:473–86.

Bruno, Michael, and Jeffrey Sachs. 1982. "Input Price Shocks and the Slowdown in Economic Growth: The Case of UK Manufacturing." *Review of Economic Studies*, 49:679–706.

Bucher, A. 1984. "Marché du Travail et Stabilité des Fonctions d'Emploi: Le Cas de la France et de la R.F.A." In Daniel Vitry and Bernadette Marechal, eds., *Emploi-Chomage: Modelisation et Analyses Quantitatives*. Dijon: Librairie de l'Université.

Buechtemann, Christoph. 1989. "More Jobs through Less Employment Protection? Evidence for West Germany." *Labour*, 3:23–56.

Burdett, Kenneth, and Bryce Hool. 1983. "Layoffs, Wages and Unemployment Insurance." *Journal of Public Economics*, 21:325–57.

Burdett, Kenneth, and Randall Wright. 1989. "Unemployment Insurance and Short-time Compensation: The Effects on Layoffs, Hours per Worker, and Wages." *Journal of Political Economy*, 97:1479–96.

———. 1990. "Optimal Firm Size, Taxes and Unemployment." *Journal of Public Economics*, 39:275–88.

Burgess, Simon. 1988. "Employment Adjustment in UK Manufacturing." *Economic Journal*, 98:81–103.

———. 1989. "Employment and Turnover in UK Manufacturing Industries, 1963–82." *Oxford Bulletin of Economics and Statistics*, 51:163–92.

Burgess, Simon, and Juan Dolado. 1989. "Intertemporal Rules with Variable Speed of Adjustment: An Application to UK Manufacturing Employment." *Economic Journal*, 99:347–65.

Burmeister, Edwin, and A. Rodney Dobell. 1970. *Mathematical Theories of Economic Growth*. London: Macmillan.

Burtless, Gary. 1985. "Are Targeted Wage Subsidies Harmful? Evidence from a Wage Voucher Experiment." *Industrial and Labor Relations Review*, 39:105–14.

Button, Peter. 1990. "The Cost of Labour Turnover: An Accounting Perspective." *Labour Economics and Productivity*, 2:146–60.

Cain, Glen, and Harold Watts, eds. 1973. *Income Maintenance and Labor Supply*. Chicago: Markham.

Card, David. 1986. "Efficient Contracts with Costly Adjustment." *American Economic Review*, 76:1045–71.

———. 1990a. "The Impact of the Mariel Boatlift on the Miami Labor Market." *Industrial and Labor Relations Review*, 43:245–57.

———. 1990b. "Minimum Wages and the Teenage Labor Market: A Case Study of California, 1987–89." *Industrial Relations Research Association, Proceedings*, 234–42.

———. 1990c. "Unexpected Inflation, Real Wages and Employment Determination in Union Contracts." *American Economic Review*, 80:669–88.

Card, David. 1990d. "Intertemporal Labor Supply: An Assessment." Princeton University, Industrial Relations Section, Working Paper No. 269.

Card, David, and Phillip Levine. 1992. "Unemployment Insurance Taxes and the Cyclical Properties of Employment and Unemployment." National Bureau of Economic Research, Working Paper No. 4030.

Card, David, and Daniel Sullivan. 1988. "Measuring the Effect of Subsidized Training Programs on Movements in and out of Employment." *Econometrica*, 56:497–530.

Carlton, Dennis. 1979. "Why New Firms Locate Where They Do: An Econometric Model." In William Wheaton, ed., *Interregional Movements and Regional Growth*. Washington, D.C.: Urban Institute.

———. 1983. "The Location and Employment Choices of New Firms: An Econometric Model with Discrete and Continuous Endogenous Variables." *Review of Economics and Statistics*, 65:440–49.

Carlton, Dennis, and Jeffrey Perloff. 1990. *Modern Industrial Organization*. Glenview, Ill.: Scott, Foresman.

Carruth, A. A., and Andrew Oswald. 1985. "Miners' Wages in Post-War Britain: An Application of a Model of Trade Union Behaviour." *Economic Journal*, 95:1003–20.

Cascio, Wayne. 1991. *Costing Human Resources: The Financial Impact of Behavior in Organizations*. Boston: PWS-Kent.

Castillo-Freeman, Alida, and Richard Freeman. 1990. "Minimum Wages in Puerto Rico: Textbook Case of a Wage Floor?" *Industrial Relations Research Association, Proceedings*, 243–53.

Cerasani, Giulio. 1990. "Labour On-Costs—Who Bears the Burden?" *Labour Economics and Productivity*, 2:27–45.

Chang, Ching-chen, and Spiro Stefanou. 1988. "Specification and Estimation of Asymmetric Adjustment Rates for Quasi-Fixed Factors of Production." *Journal of Economic Dynamics and Control*, 12:145–51.

Chang, Julius. 1983. "An Econometric Model of the Short-run Demand for Workers and Hours in the U.S. Auto Industry." *Journal of Econometrics*, 22:301–16.

Chapman, Bruce, and Hong Tan. 1992. "An Analysis of Youth Training in Australia, 1985–88: Technological Change and Wages." In Robert Gregory and Tom Karmel, eds., *The Australian Longitudinal Survey: Social and Economic Policy Research*. Canberra: Australian National University, Centre for Economic Policy Research.

Chetty, V. K., and James Heckman. 1986. "A Dynamic Model of Aggregate Output Supply, Factor Demand and Entry and Exit for a Competitive Industry with Heterogeneous Plants." *Journal of Econometrics*, 33:237–62.

Chiswick, Carmel U. 1979. "The Growth of Professional Occupations in U.S. Manufacturing, 1900–73." *Research in Human Capital and Development*, 1:191–217.

Chow, Gregory, and Geoffrey Moore. 1972. "An Econometric Model of Business Cycles." In Bert Hickman, ed., *Econometric Models of Cyclical Behavior*. Vol. 2. New York: National Bureau of Economic Research.

Christensen, Laurits, Dale Jorgenson, and Lawrence Lau. 1973. "Transcendental Logarithmic Production Frontiers." *Review of Economics and Statistics*, 55:28–45.

Christofides, Louis, and Andrew Oswald. 1991. "Efficient and Inefficient Employment Outcomes: A Study Based on Canadian Contract Data." *Research in Labor Economics*, 12:173–90.

Chung, Jae Wan. 1987. "On the Estimation of Factor Substitution in the Translog Model." *Review of Economics and Statistics*, 69:409–17.

Chuta, Enyinna, and Carl Liedholm. 1985. *Employment and Growth in Small-scale Industry*. New York: St. Martin's Press.

Clark, Kim, and Richard Freeman. 1977. "Time-Series Models of the Elasticity of Demand for Labor in Manufacturing." Unpublished paper, Harvard University.

———. 1980. "How Elastic Is the Demand for Labor?" *Review of Economics and Statistics*, 62:509–20.

Cobb, Charles, and Paul Douglas. 1928. "A Theory of Production." *American Economic Association, Papers and Proceedings*, 18:139–65.

Coen, Robert, and Bert Hickman. 1970. "Constrained Joint Estimation of Factor Demand and Production Functions." *Review of Economics and Statistics*, 52:287–300.

Cogan, John. 1980. "Labor Supply with Costs of Labor Market Entry." In James Smith, ed., *Female Labor Supply*. Princeton: Princeton University Press.

Considine, Timothy, and Timothy Mount. 1984. "The Use of Linear Logit Models for Dynamic Input Demand Systems." *Review of Economics and Statistics*, 66:434–43.

Contini, Bruno, and Riccardo Revelli. 1987. "The Process of Job Creation and Job Destruction in the Italian Economy." *Labour*, 1:121–44.

Costrell, Robert, Gerald Duguay, and George Treyz. 1986. "Labour Substitution and Complementarity among Age-Sex Groups." *Applied Economics*, 18:777–91.

Cox, James, and Ronald Oaxaca. 1990. "Unemployment Insurance and Job Search." *Research in Labor Economics*, 11:223–40.

Craig, Ben. 1990. "A Semi-parametric Test of Fixed Costs of Employment Adjustment." Unpublished paper, Indiana University.

Crawford, Robert. 1979. "Expectations and Labor Market Adjustments." *Journal of Econometrics*, 11:207–32.

Creedy, John. 1990. "Marshall and Edgeworth." *Scottish Journal of Political Economy*, 37:18–39.

Cullen, Donald. 1956. "The Interindustry Wage Structure, 1899–1950." *American Economic Review*, 46:353–69.

Currie, Janet. 1991. "Employment Determination in a Unionized Public-Sector Labor Market." *Journal of Labor Economics*, 9:45–66.

Daughety, Andrew, and Forrest Nelson. 1988. "An Econometric Analysis of Changes in the Cost and Production Structure of the Trucking Industry, 1953–1982." *Review of Economics and Statistics*, 70:67–75.

David, Paul, and T. van de Klundert. 1965. "Biased Efficiency Growth and Capital-Labor Substitution in the United States, 1899–1960." *American Economic Review*, 55:357–94.

Davidson, Russell, and Richard Harris. 1981. "Non-Convexities in Continuous-Time Investment Theory." *Review of Economic Studies*, 48:235–53.

Davis, Steve. 1990. "Size Distribution Statistics from County Business Patterns Data." Unpublished paper, University of Chicago.

Davis, Steve, and John Haltiwanger. 1989. "Gross Job Creation, Gross Job Destruction and Employment Reallocation." Unpublished paper, Hoover Institution.

Dennis, Enid, and V. Kerry Smith. 1978. "A Neoclassical Analysis of the Demand for Real Cash Balances by Firms." *Journal of Political Economy*, 86:793–814.

Denny, Michael, and Melvyn Fuss. 1977. "The Use of Approximation Analysis to Test for Separability and the Existence of Consistent Aggregates." *American Economic Review*, 67:404–18.

Denny, Michael, Melvyn Fuss, and Leonard Waverman. 1981. "Substitution Possibilities for Energy: Evidence from U.S. and Canadian Manufacturing Industries." In Ernst Berndt and Barry Field, eds., *Modeling and Measuring Natural Resource Substitution*. Cambridge: MIT Press.

Dennis, Michael, Melvyn Fuss, C. Everson, and Leonard Waverman. 1981. "Estimating the Effects of Diffusion of Technological Innovations in Telecommunications: The Production Structure of Bell Canada." *Canadian Journal of Economics*, 14:24–43.

Deolalikar, Anil. 1988. "Nutrition and Labor Productivity in Agriculture: Estimates for Rural South India." *Review of Economics and Statistics*, 70:406–13.

Deolalikar, Anil, and Wim Vijverberg. 1987. "A Test of Heterogeneity of Family and Hired Labour in Asian Agriculture." *Oxford Bulletin of Economics and Statistics*, 49:291–305.

Dertouzos, James, and Lynn Karoly. 1990. "Labor Market Responses to Employer Liability." Unpublished paper, RAND Corporation.

Dertouzos, James, and John Pencavel. 1981. "Wage and Employment Determination under Trade Unionism: The International Typographers Union." *Journal of Political Economy*, 89:1162–81.

Devine, Theresa, and Nicholas Kiefer. 1991. *Empirical Labor Economics: The Search Approach*. New York: Oxford University Press.

Dhrymes, Phoebus. 1969. "A Model of Short-run Labor Adjustment." In James Duesenberry et al., eds., *The Brookings Model: Some Further Results*. Chicago: Rand McNally.

Diewert, W. Erwin. 1971. "An Application of the Shephard Duality Theorem: A Generalized Leontief Production Function." *Journal of Political Economy*, 79:481–507.

Diewert, W. Erwin and Terence Wales. 1987. "Flexible Functional Forms and Global Curvature Conditions." *Econometrica*, 55:43–68.

Disney, R., and E. M. Szyszczak. 1984. "Protective Legislation and Part-time Employment in Britain." *British Journal of Industrial Relations*, 22:78–100.

Dixit, Avinash. 1976. *Optimization in Economic Theory*. Oxford, England: Oxford University Press.

Dougherty, C.R.S. 1972. "Estimates of Labor Aggregation Functions." *Journal of Political Economy*, 80:1101–19.

Douglas, Paul. 1976. "The Cobb-Douglas Production Function Once Again: Its History, Testing, and Some Empirical Values." *Journal of Political Economy*, 84:903–16.

Drazen, Allan. 1980. "Recent Developments in Macroeconomic Disequilibrium Theory." *Econometrica*, 48:283–306.

Drazen, Allan, Daniel Hamermesh, and Norman Obst. 1984. "The Variable Employment Elasticity Hypothesis: Theory and Evidence." *Research in Labor Economics*, 6:286–309.

Due, John. 1961. "Studies of State-Local Tax Influences on Location of Industry." *National Tax Journal*, 14:163–73.

Duncan, Greg, and Daniel Hill. 1985. "An Investigation of the Extent and Consequences of Measurement Error in Labor-Economic Survey Data." *Journal of Labor Economics*, 3:508–32.

Dunlop, John. 1938. "The Movement of Real and Money Wage Rates." *Economic Journal*, 48:413–34.

Dunne, Timothy, and Mark Roberts. 1989. "Wages and the Risk of Plant Closing." Unpublished paper, Pennsylvania State University.

Dunne, Timothy, Mark Roberts, and Larry Samuelson. 1989. "Plant Turnover and Gross Employment Flows in the U.S. Manufacturing Sector." *Journal of Labor Economics*, 7:48–71.

Dye, Richard. 1985. "Payroll Tax Effects on Wage Growth." *Eastern Economic Journal*, 11:89–100.

Edebalk, Per Gunnar, and Eskil Wadensjö. 1986. "Temporary Layoff Compensation and Unemployment: The Case of Sweden." Unpublished paper, University of Stockholm, Swedish Institute for Social Research.

Edwards, Sebastian, and Alejandra Cox Edwards. 1993. "Labor Market Distortions and Structural Adjustments in Developing Countries." In Dipak Mazumdar, ed. *Labor Markets in an Era of Adjustment*. Washington, D.C.: World Bank, in press.

Ehrenberg, Ronald. 1971a. *Fringe Benefits and Overtime Behavior*. Lexington, Mass.: D. C. Heath.

———. 1971b. "The Impact of the Overtime Premium on Employment and Hours in U.S. Industry." *Economic Inquiry*, 9:199–207.

Ehrenberg, Ronald, and George Jakubson. 1988. *Advance Notice Provisions in Plant Closing Legislation*. Kalamazoo, Mich.: W. E. Upjohn Institute.

Ehrenberg, Ronald, and Paul Schumann. 1982. *Longer Hours or More Jobs?* Ithaca: Cornell University Press.

Ehrenberg, Ronald, Pamela Rosenberg, and Jeanne Li. 1988. "Part-time Employment in the United States." In Robert Hart, ed., *Employment, Unemployment and Labor Utilization*. Boston: Unwin Hyman.

Elliott, Robert, and Robert Sandy. 1991. "Adam Smith May Have Been Right After All: Another Look at Compensating Differentials." Unpublished paper, University of Aberdeen.

Ellwood, David. 1982. "Teenage Unemployment: Permanent Scars or Temporary Blemishes." In Richard Freeman and David Wise, eds., *The Youth Labor Market Problem: Its Nature, Causes and Consequences*. Chicago: University of Chicago Press.

Engle, Robert, and T. C. Liu. 1972. "Effects of Aggregation over Time on Dynamic Characteristics of an Econometric Model." In Bert Hickman, ed., *Econometric Models of Cyclical Behavior*. Vol. 2. New York: National Bureau of Economic Research.

Epstein, Larry, and Michael Denny. 1983. "The Multivariate Flexible Accelerator Model: Its Empirical Restrictions and an Application to U.S. Manufacturing." *Econometrica*, 51:647–73.

Epstein, Larry, and Adonis Yatchew. 1985. "The Empirical Determination of Technology and Expectations." *Journal of Econometrics*, 27:235–58.

Evans, David, and Boyan Jovanovic. 1989. "An Estimated Model of Entrepreneurial Choice under Liquidity Constraints." *Journal of Political Economy*, 97:808–27.

Evenson, Robert, and Hans Binswanger. 1984. "Estimating Labor Demand Functions for Indian Agriculture." In Hans Binswanger and Mark Rosenzweig, eds., *Contractual Arrangements, Employment, and Wages in Rural Labor Markets in Asia*. New Haven: Yale University Press.

Faini, Riccardo, and Fabio Schiantarelli. 1985a. "Oligopolistic Models of Investment and Employment Decisions in a Regional Context." *European Economic Review*, 27:221–42.

———. 1985b. "A Unified Frame for Firms' Decisions: Theoretical Analysis and Empirical Application to Italy, 1970–1980." In Daniel Weiserbs, ed., *International Studies in Economics and Econometrics*. Amsterdam: Martinus Nijhoff.

Fair, Ray. 1969. *The Short-run Demand for Workers and Hours*. Amsterdam: North-Holland Press.

———. 1985. "Excess Labor and the Business Cycle." *American Economic Review*, 75:239–45.

Fallon, Peter, and Richard Layard. 1975. "Capital-Skill Complementarity, Income Distribution, and Output Accounting." *Journal of Political Economy*, 83:279–302.

Fallon, Peter, and Robert E. B. Lucas. 1991. "The Impact of Job Security Regulations in India and Zimbabwe." *World Bank Economic Review*, 5:395–414.

Fay, Jon, and James Medoff. 1985. "Labor and Output over the Business Cycle." *American Economic Review*, 75:638–55.

Feldstein, Martin. 1967. "Specification of the Labour Input in the Aggregate Production Function." *Review of Economic Studies*, 34:375–86.

———. 1972. "The Incidence of the Payroll Tax: Comment." *American Economic Review*, 62:735–38.

―――. 1976. "Temporary Layoffs in the Theory of Unemployment." *Journal of Political Economy*, 84:937–58.

Ferguson, Brian. 1986. "Labour Force Substitution and the Effects of an Ageing Population." *Applied Economics*, 18:901–13.

Ferguson, Charles. 1969. *The Neoclassical Theory of Production and Distribution.* Cambridge, England: Cambridge University Press.

Field, Barry, and Charles Grebenstein. 1980. "Capital-Energy Substitution in U.S. Manufacturing." *Review of Economics and Statistics*, 62:207–12.

Field, Elizabeth. 1988. "Free and Slave Labor in the Antebellum South: Perfect Substitutes or Different Inputs?" *Review of Economics and Statistics*, 70:654–59.

Findlay, Ronald, and Henryk Kierzkowski. 1983. "International Trade and Human Capital: A Simple General Equilibrium Model." *Journal of Political Economy*, 91:957–78.

Fitzroy, Felix, and Robert Hart. 1985. "Hours, Layoffs and Unemployment Insurance Funding: Theory and Practice in an International Perspective." *Economic Journal*, 95:700–713.

Flaig, Gebhard, and Viktor Steiner. 1989. "Stability and Dynamic Properties of Labour Demand in West-German Manufacturing." *Oxford Bulletin of Economics and Statistics*, 51:395–412.

Fleisher, Belton, Donald Parsons, and Robert Porter. 1973. "Asset Adjustments and the Labor Supply of Older Workers." In Glen Cain and Harold Watts, eds., *Income Maintenance and Labor Supply.* Chicago: Markham.

Folbre, Nancy, Julia Leighton, and Melissa Roderick. 1984. "Plant Closings and Their Regulation in Maine, 1971–1982." *Industrial and Labor Relations Review*, 37:185–96.

Fortin, Pierre. 1979. "L'Effet du Salaire Minimum sur les Prix L'Emploi et la Repartition des Revenus: Le Cas du Quebec." *Relations Industrielles*, 34:660–72.

Franz, Wolfgang, and Heinz König. 1986. "The Nature and Causes of Unemployment in the Federal Republic of Germany since the 1970s: An Empirical Investigation." *Economica*, 53:S219–44.

Freeman, Richard. 1975. "Demand for Labor in a Nonprofit Market: University Faculty." In Daniel Hamermesh, ed., *Labor in the Public and Nonprofit Sectors.* Princeton: Princeton University Press.

―――. 1977. "Manpower Requirements and Substitution Analysis of Labor Skills: A Synthesis." *Research in Labor Economics*, 1:151–83.

―――. 1979. "The Effect of Demographic Factors on Age-Earnings Profiles." *Journal of Human Resources*, 14:289–318.

―――. 1980. "Employment and Wage Adjustment Models in U.S. Manufacturing, 1950–1976." *Economic Forum*, 11:1–27.

Freeman, Richard, and James Medoff. 1982. "Substitution between Production Labor and Other Inputs in Unionized and Nonunionized Manufacturing." *Review of Economics and Statistics*, 64:220–33.

Fullerton, Donald, and Yolanda Henderson. 1985. "Long-run Effects of the

Accelerated Cost Recovery System." *Review of Economics and Statistics*, 67:363–72.

Fuss, Melvyn. 1977. "The Demand for Energy in Canadian Manufacturing." *Journal of Econometrics*, 5:89–116.

Fuss, Melvyn, and Daniel McFadden. 1978. *Production Economics: A Dual Approach to Theory and Applications*. Amsterdam: North-Holland Press.

Garber, Steven. 1989. "The Reserve-Labor Hypothesis, Short-run Pricing Theories and the Employment-Output Relationship." *Journal of Econometrics*, 42:219–45.

Garofalo, Gaspar, and Devinder Malhotra. 1984. "Input Substitution in the Manufacturing Sector during the 1970s: A Regional Analysis." *Journal of Regional Science*, 24:51–63.

Geary, Patrick, and John Kennan. 1982. "The Employment–Real Wage Relationship: An International Study." *Journal of Political Economy*, 90:854–71.

Gennard, John. 1979. *Job Security and Industrial Relations*. Paris: OECD.

———. 1985. "Job Security: Redundancy Arrangements and Practices in Selected OECD Countries." Unpublished paper, OECD, Social Affairs, Manpower and Education Directorate.

Gera, Surendra. 1987. "An Evaluation of the Canadian Employment Tax Credit Program." *Canadian Public Policy*, 13:196–207.

Gerhart, Paul. 1987. *Saving Plants and Jobs*. Kalamazoo, Mich.: W. E. Upjohn Institute.

Gerlach, Knut, and Joachim Wagner. 1993. "Gross and Net Employment Flows in Manufacturing Industries." *Zeitschrift für Wirtschafts-und Sozialwissenschaften*, in press.

Goldin, Claudia, and Robert Margo. 1992. "The Great Compression: The Wage Structure in the United States at Mid-Century." *Quarterly Journal of Economics*, 107:1–34.

Gordon, Robert. 1972. "Wage-Price Controls and the Shifting Phillips Curve." *Brookings Papers on Economic Activity*, 385–421.

———. 1990. "What Is New-Keynesian Economics?" *Journal of Economic Literature*, 28:1115–71.

Gould, John. 1968. "Adjustment Costs in the Theory of Investment of the Firm." *Review of Economic Studies*, 35:47–55.

Grant, James. 1979. *Labor Substitution in U.S. Manufacturing*. Unpublished Ph.D. dissertation, Michigan State University.

Grant, James, and Daniel Hamermesh. 1981. "Labor Market Competition Among Youths, White Women and Others." *Review of Economics and Statistics*, 63:354–60.

Greer, Douglas, and Stephen Rhoades. 1977. "A Test of the Reserve Labour Hypothesis." *Economic Journal*, 87:290–99.

Griffin, James, and Paul Gregory. 1976. "An Intercountry Translog Model of Energy Substitution Responses." *American Economic Review*, 66:845–57.

Griffin, Peter. 1992. "The Impact of Affirmative Action on Labor Demand: A Test of Some Implications of the Le Chatelier Principle." *Review of Economics and Statistics*, 74:251–60.

Griliches, Zvi. 1958. "Research Costs and Social Returns: Hybrid Corn and Related Innovations." *Journal of Political Economy*, 66:419–31.

———. 1961. "A Note on Serial Correlation Bias in Estimates of Distributed Lags." *Econometrica*, 29:65–73.

———. 1969. "Capital-Skill Complementarity." *Review of Economics and Statistics*, 51:465–68.

Grossman, Jean Baldwin. 1982. "The Substitutability of Natives and Immigrants in Production." *Review of Economics and Statistics*, 64:596–603.

Gunderson, Morley, and W. Craig Riddell. 1991. "The Economics of Women's Wages in Canada." *International Review of Comparative Public Policy*, 3:149–74.

Gustman, Alan. 1982. "Analyzing the Relation of Unemployment Insurance to Unemployment." *Research in Labor Economics*, 5:69–114.

Gyapong, Anthony, and Kwabena Gyimah-Brempong. 1988. "Factor Substitution, Price Elasticity of Factor Demand and Returns to Scale in Police Production: Evidence from Michigan." *Southern Economic Journal*, 54:863–78.

Hall, S. G., S.G.B. Henry, and M. Pemberton. 1990. "Testing a Discrete Switching Disequilibrium Model of the U.K. Labour Market." Bank of England Discussion Paper No. 28.

Halpin, Terrence. 1979. "The Effect of Unemployment Insurance on Seasonal Fluctuations in Employment." *Industrial and Labor Relations Review*, 32:352–62.

———. 1980. "Employment Stabilization." In National Commission on Unemployment Compensation, *Unemployment Compensation: Studies and Research*. Vol. 2. Washington, D.C.: NCUC.

Haltiwanger, John, and Louis Maccini. 1990. "The Dynamic Interaction of Inventories, Temporary and Permanent Layoffs." Unpublished paper, Johns Hopkins University.

Halvorsen, Robert, and Tim Smith. 1986. "Substitution Possibilities for Unpriced Natural Resources: Restricted Cost Functions for the Canadian Metal Mining Industry," *Review of Economics and Statistics*, 68:398–405.

Hamermesh, Daniel. 1969. "A Disaggregative Econometric Model of Gross Changes in Employment." *Yale Economic Essays*, 9:107–45.

———. 1976. "Econometric Studies of Labor Demand and Their Application to Policy Analysis." *Journal of Human Resources*, 11:507–25.

———. 1977. *Jobless Pay and the Economy*. Baltimore: Johns Hopkins University Press.

———. 1978. "Subsidies for Jobs in the Private Sector." In John Palmer, ed., *Creating Jobs: Public Employment Programs and Wage Subsidies*. Washington, D.C.: Brookings Institution.

———. 1979a. "New Estimates of the Incidence of the Payroll Tax." *Southern Economic Journal*, 45:1208–19.

———. 1979b. "Econometric Studies of Labor-Labor Substitution and Their Implications for Policy." *Journal of Human Resources*, 14:518–42.

Hamermesh, Daniel. 1980. "Factor Market Dynamics and the Incidence of Taxes and Subsidies." *Quarterly Journal of Economics*, 95:751–64.

———. 1982. "Minimum Wages and the Demand for Labor." *Economic Inquiry*, 20:365–79.

———. 1983. "New Measures of Labor Cost: Implications for Demand Elasticities and Nominal Wage Growth." In Jack Triplett, ed., *The Measurement of Labor Cost*. Chicago: University of Chicago Press.

———. 1986. "The Demand for Labor in the Long Run." In Orley Ashenfelter and Richard Layard, eds., *Handbook of Labor Economics*. Amsterdam: North-Holland Press.

———. 1987. "The Costs of Worker Displacement." *Quarterly Journal of Economics*, 102:51–75.

———. 1988a. "Plant Closings and the Value of the Firm." *Review of Economics and Statistics*, 70:580–86.

———. 1988b. "Labor Demand and Job Security Policies." In Robert Hart, ed., *Employment, Unemployment and Labor Utilization*. Boston: Unwin Hyman.

———. 1989. "Labor Demand and the Structure of Adjustment Costs." *American Economic Review*, 79:674–89.

———. 1990a. "Aggregate Employment Dynamics and Lumpy Adjustment Costs." *Carnegie-Rochester Conference Series on Public Policy*, 33:93–130.

———. 1990b. "Shirking or Productive Schmoozing: Wages and the Allocation of Time at Work." *Industrial and Labor Relations Review*, 43:121S–33S.

———. 1990c. "Unemployment Insurance Financing, Short-time Compensation, and Labor Demand." *Research in Labor Economics*, 11:241–69.

———. 1990d. "Data Difficulties in Labor Economics." In Ernst Berndt and Jack Triplett, eds., *Fifty Years of Economic Measurement*. Chicago: University of Chicago Press.

———. 1992a. "Employment Protection: Theoretical Implications and Some U.S. Evidence." In Christoph Buechtemann, ed., *Employment Security and Labor Markets*. Ithaca: Cornell University Press.

———. 1992b. "A General Model of Dynamic Labor Demand." *Review of Economics and Statistics*, 74: in press.

———. 1992c. "Spatial and Temporal Aggregation in the Dynamics of Labor Demand." In Jan van Ours, Gerard Pfann, and Geert Ridder, eds., *Labor Demand and Equilibrium Wage Formation*. Amsterdam: North-Holland Press.

Hamermesh, Daniel, and Robert Goldfarb. 1970. "Manpower Programs in a Local Labor Market." *American Economic Review*, 60:706–9.

Hamermesh, Daniel, and Albert Rees. 1993. *The Economics of Work and Pay*. New York: HarperCollins.

Hanoch, Giora. 1971. "CRESH Production Functions." *Econometrica*, 39:695–712.

Harcourt, Geoffrey. 1972. *Some Cambridge Controversies in the Theory of Capital*. Cambridge, England: Cambridge University Press.

Harper, Carolyn, and Barry Field. 1983. "Energy Substitution in U.S. Manufacturing: A Regional Approach." *Southern Economic Journal*, 50:385–95.

Harper, Michael, and William Gullickson. 1989. "Cost Function Models and Accounting for Growth in U.S. Manufacturing, 1949–86." Unpublished paper, Bureau of Labor Statistics.

Harris, John, and Michael Todaro. 1970. "Migration, Unemployment and Development: A Two Sector Analysis." *American Economic Review*, 60:126–42.

Harris, Richard I. D. 1985. "Interrelated Demand for Factors of Production in the U.K. Engineering Industry, 1968–81," *Economic Journal*, 95:1049–68.

———. 1990. "Employment Functions for New Zealand: An Example of the Cointegration Approach." Unpublished paper, University of Waikato.

Hart, Robert. 1984. *The Economics of Non-Wage Labour Costs*. London: George Allen and Unwin.

———. 1987. *Working Time and Employment*. Boston: Allen and Unwin.

Hart, Robert, and Seiichi Kawasaki. 1988. "Payroll Taxes and Factor Demand." *Research in Labor Economics*, 9:257–85.

Hart, Robert, and Peter McGregor. 1988. "The Returns to Labour Services in West German Manufacturing Industry." *European Economic Review*, 32:947–63.

Hart, Robert, and T. Sharot. 1978. "The Short-run Demand for Workers and Hours: A Recursive Model." *Review of Economic Studies*, 45:299–309.

Hart, Robert, and Nicholas Wilson. 1988. "The Demand for Workers and Hours: Micro Evidence from the UK Metal Working Industry." In Robert Hart, ed., *Employment, Unemployment and Labor Utilization*. Boston: Unwin Hyman.

Hause, John, and Gunnar Du Rietz. 1984. "Entry, Industry Growth and the Microdynamics of Industry Supply." *Journal of Political Economy*, 92:733–57.

Haveman, Robert, and John Palmer. 1982. *Jobs for Disadvantaged Workers*. Washington, D.C.: Brookings Institution.

Hazledine, Tim. 1974. "Employment and Output Functions for New Zealand Manufacturing Industries." *Journal of Industrial Economics*, 22:161–98.

———. 1978. "New Specifications for Employment and Hours Functions." *Economica*, 45:179–93.

———. 1979. "Constraints Limiting the Demand for Labour in Canadian Manufacturing Industries." *Australian Economic Papers*, 18:181–91.

Heckman, James. 1979. "Sample Selection Bias as a Specification Error." *Econometrica*, 47:153–61.

Heckman, James, and Guilherme Sedlacek. 1985. "Heterogeneity, Aggregation, and Market Wage Functions: An Empirical Model of Self-selection in the Labor Market." *Journal of Political Economy*, 93:1077–125.

Hibbard, Russell. 1980. "Solvency Measures and Experience Rating." In National Commission on Unemployment Compensation, *Unemployment Compensation: Studies and Research*. Vol. 2. Washington, D.C.: NCUC.

Hicks, John. 1932. *The Theory of Wages*. New York: Macmillan.

Holmlund, Bertil. 1983. "Payroll Taxes and Wage Inflation: The Swedish Experience." *Scandinavian Journal of Economics*, 85:1–16.

Holt, Charles, Franco Modigliani, John Muth, and Herbert Simon. 1960.

Planning Production, Inventories and Work Force. Englewood Cliffs, N.J.: Prentice-Hall.

Holtz-Eakin, Douglas, and Harvey Rosen. 1991. "Municipal Labor Demand in the Presence of Uncertainty: An Econometric Approach." *Journal of Labor Economics*, 9:276–93.

Holzer, Harry, and Edward Montgomery. 1993. "Asymmetries and Rigidities in Wage Adjustments by Firms." *Review of Economics and Statistics*, 75: in press.

Holzer, Harry, Lawrence Katz, and Alan Krueger. 1991. "Job Queues and Wages: New Evidence on the Minimum Wage and Inter-Industry Wage Structure." *Quarterly Journal of Economics*, 106:739–68.

Houseman, Susan. 1991. *Industrial Restructuring with Job Security: The Case of European Steel*. Cambridge: Harvard University Press.

Howland, Marie. 1988. *Plant Closings and Worker Displacement: The Regional Issues*. Kalamazoo, Mich.: W. E. Upjohn Institute.

Hsing, Yu. 1989. "Testing for the Flexible Employment Elasticity Hypothesis: Application of an Expanded Box-Cox Model to U.S. Manufacturing." *Quarterly Review of Economics and Business*, 29:96–107.

Hughes, Barry. 1971. "Supply Constraints and Short-term Employment Functions: A Comment." *Review of Economics and Statistics*, 53:393–97.

Hunt, Jennifer. 1992. "The Impact of the 1962 Repatriates from Algeria on the French Labor Market." *Industrial and Labor Relations Review*, 45:556–72.

Intriligator, Michael. 1971. *Mathematical Optimization and Economic Theory*. Englewood Cliffs, N.J.: Prentice-Hall.

Jacobson, Louis. 1988. *Structural Change in the Pennsylvania Economy*. Unpublished manuscript, W. E. Upjohn Institute, Kalamazoo, Mich.

Jaramillo, Fidel, Fabio Schiantarelli, and Alessandro Sembenelli. 1991. "Are Adjustment Costs for Labor Asymmetric? An Econometric Test on Panel Data for Italy." Unpublished paper, Boston University, Department of Economics.

Jensen, Gail, and Michael Morrisey. 1986. "The Role of Physicians in Hospital Production." *Review of Economics and Statistics*, 68:432–42.

Johnson, Esther. 1987. "Short-time Compensation: A Handbook of Source Material." U.S. Department of Labor, Employment and Training Administration, Unemployment Insurance Service Occasional Paper 87–2.

Johnson, George. 1970. "The Demand for Labor by Educational Category." *Southern Economic Journal*, 37:190–204.

———. 1976. "Evaluating the Macroeconomic Effects of Public Employment Programs." In Orley Ashenfelter and James Blum, eds., *Evaluating the Labor-Market Effects of Social Programs*. Princeton: Princeton University, Industrial Relations Section.

———. 1977. "The Determination of Wages in the Union and Non-Union Sectors." *British Journal of Industrial Relations*, 15:211–25.

———. 1980. "The Theory of Labor Market Intervention." *Economica*, 47:309–29.

———. 1990. "Work Rules, Featherbedding, and Pareto-Optimal Union Management Bargaining." *Journal of Labor Economics*, 8:S237–59.

Johnson, George, and Arthur Blakemore. 1979. "The Potential Impact of Employment Policy on the Unemployment Rate Consistent with Non-Accelerating Inflation." *American Economic Association, Papers and Proceedings*, 69:119–23.

Johnson, George, and James Tomola. 1977. "The Fiscal Substitution Effect of Alternative Approaches to Public Service Employment Policy." *Journal of Human Resources*, 12:3–26.

Jones, Christine. 1983. "The Mobilization of Women's Labor for Cash Crop Production: A Game Theoretic Approach." *American Journal of Agricultural Economics*, 65:1049–54.

Jones, Derek, and Jeffrey Pliskin. 1989. "British Evidence on the Employment Effects of Profit-Sharing." *Industrial Relations*, 28:276–98.

Jovanovic, Boyan. 1982. "Selection and the Evolution of Industry." *Econometrica*, 50:649–70.

Juhn, Chinhui, Kevin M. Murphy, and Brooks Pierce. 1992. "Wage Inequality and the Rise in Returns to Skill." *Journal of Political Economy*, 100:in press.

Kaiser, Carl. 1987. "Layoffs, Average Hours, and Unemployment Insurance in US Manufacturing Industries." *Quarterly Review of Economics and Business*, 27:80–99.

Kalachek, Edward, Fredric Raines, and Donald Larson. 1979. "The Determination of Labor Supply: A Dynamic Model." *Industrial and Labor Relations Review*, 32:367–77.

Kannappan, Subbiah. 1983. *Employment Problems and the Urban Labor Market in Developing Nations*. Ann Arbor: University of Michigan, Graduate School of Business Administration.

Karlson, Stephen. 1986. "Multiple-Output Production and Pricing in Electric Utilities." *Southern Economic Journal*, 53:73–86.

Katz, Lawrence, and Ana Revenga. 1989. "Changes in the Structure of Wages: The United States vs. Japan." *Journal of the Japanese and International Economies*, 3:522–53.

Kaufman, Roger. 1988. "An International Comparison of Okun's Laws." *Journal of Comparative Economics*, 12:182–203.

———. 1989. "The Effects of Statutory Minimum Rates of Pay on Employment in Great Britain." *Economic Journal*, 99:1040–53.

Keane, Michael, Robert Moffitt, and David Runkle. 1988. "Real Wages over the Business Cycle: Estimating the Impact of Heterogeneity with Micro Data." *Journal of Political Economy*, 96:1232–66.

Kennan, John. 1979. "The Estimation of Partial Adjustment Models with Rational Expectations." *Econometrica*, 47:1433–41.

———. 1988. "An Econometric Analysis of Fluctuations in Aggregate Labor Supply and Demand." *Econometrica*, 56:317–34.

Kerachsky, Stuart, Walter Nicholson, Edward Cavin, and Alan Hershey. 1986. "An Evaluation of Short-time Compensation Programs." U.S. Department of Labor, Employment and Training Administration, Unemployment Insurance Service Occasional Paper 86–4.

Kesselman, Jonathan, Sam Williamson, and Ernst Berndt. 1977. "Tax Credits for Employment Rather Than Investment." *American Economic Review*, 67:339–49.

Kiefer, Nicholas. 1979. "The Economic Benefits from Four Government Training Programs." *Research in Labor Economics*, 2:159–86.

Killingsworth, Mark. 1983. *Labor Supply*. Cambridge, England: Cambridge University Press.

Kim, H. Youn. 1988. "Analyzing the Indirect Production Function for U.S. Manufacturing." *Southern Economic Journal*, 55:494–504.

Kimball, Miles. 1989. "Labor Market Dynamics When Unemployment Is a Worker Discipline Device." National Bureau of Economic Research, Working Paper No. 2967.

King, William. 1980. *A Multiple Output Translog Cost-Function Estimation of Academic Labor Services*. Unpublished Ph.D. dissertation, Michigan State University.

Klein, Lawrence. 1974. *A Textbook of Econometrics*. Englewood Cliffs, N.J.: Prentice-Hall.

Klotz, Benjamin, Rey Madoo, and Reed Hanson. 1980. "A Study of High and Low Labor Productivity Establishments in U.S. Manufacturing." In John Kendrick and Beatrice Vaccara, eds., *New Developments in Productivity Measurement and Analysis*. Chicago: University of Chicago Press.

Knight, John, and Richard Sabot. 1990. *Education, Productivity and Inequality*. New York: Oxford University Press.

Kokkelenberg, Edward, and Charles Bischoff. 1986. "Expectations and Factor Demand." *Review of Economics and Statistics*, 68:423–31.

Kokkelenberg, Edward, and Jeong Poy Choi. 1986. "Factor Demands, Adjustment Costs and Regulation." *Applied Economics*, 18:631–43.

Kokkelenberg, Edward and Sang Nguyen. 1989. "Modelling Technical Progress and Total Factor Productivity: A Plant Level Example." *Journal of Productivity Analysis*, 1:21–42.

Kollreuter, Christoph. 1980. "Recent and Prospective Trends of the Demand for Labour in the Federal Republic of Germany." In Edmond Malinvaud and Jean-Paul Fitoussi, eds., *Unemployment in Western Countries*. New York: St. Martin's Press.

König, Heinz, and Winfried Pohlmeier. 1988. "Employment, Labor Utilization and Procyclical Labor Productivity." *Kyklos*, 41:551–72.

———. 1989. "Worksharing and Factor Prices: A Comparison of Three Flexible Functional Forms for Nonlinear Cost Schemes." *Journal of Institutional and Theoretical Economics*, 145:343–57.

Kotlikoff, Laurence, and Lawrence Summers. 1987. "Tax Incidence." In Alan Auerbach and Martin Feldstein, eds., *Handbook of Public Economics*. Amsterdam: North-Holland Press.

Krueger, Alan. 1991a. "The Evolution of Unjust-Dismissal Legislation in the United States." *Industrial and Labor Relations Review*, 44:644–60.

————. 1991b. "How Computers Have Changed the Wage Structure: Evidence from Microdata, 1984–89." Princeton University Industrial Relations Section, Working Paper No. 291.

Krueger, Anne. 1981. "The Framework of the Country Studies." In Anne Krueger, Hal Lary, Terry Monson, and Narongchai Akrasanee, eds., *Trade and Employment in Developing Countries*. Vol. 1. Chicago: University of Chicago Press.

Kuh, Edwin. 1959. "The Validity of Cross-sectionally Estimated Behavior Equations in Time-Series Applications." *Econometrica*, 27:197–214.

————. 1965. "Income Distribution and Employment over the Business Cycle," in James Duesenberry, Gary Fromm, Lawrence Klein and Edwin Kuh, eds., *The Brookings Quarterly Econometric Model of the United States*. Chicago: Rand McNally.

Kuhn, Peter. 1988. "A Nonuniform Pricing Model of Union Wages and Employment." *Journal of Political Economy*, 96:473–508.

Kydland, Finn, and Edward Prescott. 1982. "Time to Build and Aggregate Fluctuations." *Econometrica*, 50:50–70.

LaLonde, Robert, and Robert Topel. 1991. "Labor Market Adjustments to Increased Immigration." In John Abowd and Richard Freeman, eds., *Immigration, Trade, and the Labor Market*. Chicago: University of Chicago Press.

Laudadio, L., and M. Percy. 1973. "Some Evidence on the Impact of Non-Wage Labour Cost on Overtime Work and Environment." *Relations Industrielles*, 28:397–403.

Layard, Richard. 1982. "Youth Unemployment in Britain and the United States Compared." In Richard Freeman and David Wise, eds., *The Youth Labor Market Problem: Its Nature, Causes and Consequences*. Chicago: University of Chicago Press.

Layard, Richard, and Stephen Nickell. 1986. "Unemployment in Britain." *Economica*, 53:S121–69.

Lazear, Edward. 1990. "Job Security Provisions and Employment." *Quarterly Journal of Economics*, 105:699–726.

Leibenstein, Harvey. 1957. "The Theory of Underemployment in Backward Economies." *Journal of Political Economy*, 65:91–103.

Leonard, Jonathan. 1987. "In the Wrong Place at the Wrong Time: The Extent of Frictional and Structural Unemployment." In Kevin Lang and Jonathan Leonard, eds., *Unemployment and the Structure of Labor Markets*. New York: Basil Blackwell.

Leonard, Jonathan, and Marc van Audenrode. 1991. "Corporatism Run Amok: Job Stability and Industrial Policy in Belgium and the United States." Unpublished paper, University of California at Berkeley.

Leslie, Derek, and John Wise. 1980. "The Productivity of Hours in U.K. Manufacturing and Production Industries." *Economic Journal*, 90:74–84.

Lester, Richard. 1948. *Company Wage Policies*. Princeton: Princeton University, Industrial Relations Section.

Leuthold, Jane. 1975. "The Incidence of the Payroll Tax in the United States." *Public Finance Quarterly*, 3:3–13.

Levitan, Sar, and Frank Gallo. 1988. *A Second Chance: Training for Jobs*. Kalamazoo, Mich.: W. E. Upjohn Institute.

Levitan, Sar, and Garth Mangum. 1981. *Human Resources and Labor Markets*. New York: Harper and Row.

Lewis, H. Gregg. 1986. *Union Relative Wage Effects: A Survey*. Chicago: University of Chicago Press.

Lewis, Philip E. T. 1985. "Substitution between Young and Adult Workers in Australia." *Australian Economic Papers*, 24:115–26.

———. 1987. "Short-run Substitution in the Sheep and Beef Industries." *Australian Journal of Agricultural Economics*, 31:266–71.

Lewis, Philip E. T., and Michael Kirby. 1988. "A New Approach to Modelling the Effects of Incomes Policies." *Economics Letters*, 28:81–5.

Lilien, David, and Robert Hall. 1986. "Cyclical Fluctuations in the Labor Market." In Orley Ashenfelter and Richard Layard, eds., *Handbook of Labor Economics*. Amsterdam: North-Holland Press.

Lipsey, Robert, Irving Kravis, and Romualdo Roldan. 1982. "Do Multinational Firms Adapt Factor Proportions to Relative Factor Prices?" In Anne Krueger, ed., *Trade and Employment in Developing Countries*. Vol. 2. Chicago: University of Chicago Press.

Liu, T. C., and E. C. Hwa. 1974. "A Monthly Econometric Model of the U.S. Economy." *International Economic Review*, 15:328–65.

Lopez, Ramon. 1986. "Structural Models of the Farm Household That Allow for Interdependent Utility and Profit-Maximization Decisions." In Inderjit Singh, Lyn Squire, and John Strauss, eds., *Agricultural Household Models: Extensions, Applications and Policy*. Baltimore: Johns Hopkins University Press.

Lovell, C.A. Knox. 1973. "CES and VES Production Functions in a Cross-Section Context." *Journal of Political Economy*, 81:705–20.

Lucas, Robert E. 1967. "Optimal Investment Policy and the Flexible Accelerator." *International Economic Review*, 8:78–85.

———. 1976. "Econometric Policy Evaluation: A Critique." In Karl Brunner and Allan Meltzer, *The Phillips Curve and Labor Markets*. Amsterdam: North-Holland Press.

Lucas, Robert E., and Leonard Rapping. 1969. "Real Wages, Employment and Inflation." *Journal of Political Economy*, 77:721–54.

———. 1970. "Real Wages, Employment and Inflation." In Edmund Phelps, ed., *Microeconomic Foundations of Employment and Inflation Theory*. New York: Norton.

Lyons, Thomas. 1991. *Birthing Economic Development: How Effective Are Michigan's Business Incubators?* Athens, Ohio: National Business Incubation Association.

McCarthy, Michael. 1972. *The Wharton Quarterly Econometric Model Mark III*. Philadelphia: Wharton School.

McDonald, Ian, and Robert Solow. 1981. "Wage Bargaining and Employment." *American Economic Review*, 71:896–908.

MacDonald, James. 1986. "Entry and Exit on the Competitive Fringe." *Southern Economic Journal*, 52:640–52.

McElroy, Marjorie. 1987. "Additive General Error Models for Production, Cost, and Derived Demand or Share Systems." *Journal of Political Economy*, 95:737–57.

McKee, Michael, and Edwin West. 1984. "Minimum Wage Effects on Part-time Employment." *Economic Inquiry*, 22:421–28.

McKinnon, Ronald. 1962. "Wages, Capital Costs and Employment in Manufacturing." *Econometrica*, 30:501–21.

McMullen, B. Starr, and Linda Stanley. 1988. "The Impact of Deregulation on the Production Structure of the Motor Carrier Industry." *Economic Inquiry*, 26:299–316.

McQuaid, Ronald. 1986. "Production Functions and the Disaggregation of Labor Inputs in Manufacturing Plants." *Journal of Regional Science*, 26:595–603.

MaCurdy, Thomas. 1981. "An Empirical Model of Labor Supply in a Life-Cycle Setting." *Journal of Political Economy*, 89:1059–85.

MaCurdy, Thomas, and John Pencavel. 1986. "Testing between Competing Models of Wage and Employment Determination in Unionized Markets." *Journal of Political Economy*, 94:S3–S39.

Magnus, Jan. 1979. "Substitution between Energy and Non-Energy Inputs in the Netherlands, 1950–1976." *International Economic Review*, 20:465–84.

Mairesse, Jacques, and Brigitte Dormont. 1985. "Labor and Investment Demand at the Firm Level: A Comparison of French, German and U.S. Manufacturing, 1970–79." *European Economic Review*, 28:201–31.

Maki, Dennis, and Lindsay Meredith. 1987. "A Note on Unionization and the Elasticity of Substitution." *Canadian Journal of Economics*, 20:792–801.

Mankiw, N. Gregory. 1985. "Small Menu Costs and Large Business Cycles: A Macroeconomic Model of Monopoly." *Quarterly Journal of Economics*, 100:529–38.

Marshall, Alfred. 1920. *Principles of Economics*. 8th ed. New York: Macmillan.

Martinello, Felice. 1989. "Wage and Employment Determination in a Unionized Industry: The IWA and the British Columbia Wood Products Industry." *Journal of Labor Economics*, 7:303–30.

Mazumdar, Dipak. 1989. "Microeconomic Issues of Labor Markets in Developing Countries." World Bank, EDI Seminar Paper No. 40.

Meade, James. 1972. "The Theory of Labour-managed Firms and of Profit-Sharing." *Economic Journal*, 82:402–28.

Medoff, James. 1979. "Layoffs and Alternatives under Trade Unions in U.S. Manufacturing." *American Economic Review*, 69:380–95.

Meese, Richard. 1980. "Dynamic Factor Demand Schedules for Labor and Capital under Rational Expectations." *Journal of Econometrics*, 14:141–58.

Merrilees, William. 1982. "Labor Market Segmentation in Canada: An Econometric Approach." *Canadian Journal of Economics*, 15:458–73.

Meyer, Robert, and David Wise. 1983. "The Effects of the Minimum Wage on the Employment and Earnings of Youth." *Journal of Labor Economics*, 1:66–100.

Michl, Thomas. 1987. "Is There Evidence for a Marginalist Demand for Labour?" *Cambridge Journal of Economics*, 11:361–73.

Miller, Roger. 1971. "The Reserve Labor Hypothesis: Some Tests of Its Implications." *Economic Journal*, 81:17–35.

Mincer, Jacob. 1976. "Unemployment Effects of Minimum Wages." *Journal of Political Economy*, 84:S87–104.

Mincer, Jacob, and Boyan Jovanovic. 1981. "Labor Mobility and Wages." In Sherwin Rosen, ed., *Studies in Labor Markets*. Chicago: University of Chicago Press.

Montgomery, Mark. 1988. "On the Determinants of Employer Demand for Part-time Workers." *Review of Economics and Statistics*, 70:112–17.

Morrison, Catherine. 1986. "Structural Models of Dynamic Factor Demands with Nonstatic Expectations: An Empirical Assessment of Alternative Expectations Specifications." *International Economic Review*, 27:365–86.

———. 1988. "Quasi-fixed Inputs in U.S. and Japanese Manufacturing: A Generalized Leontief Restricted Cost Approach." *Review of Economics and Statistics* 70:275–87.

Morrison, Catherine, and Ernst Berndt. 1981. "Short-run Labor Productivity in a Dynamic Model." *Journal of Econometrics*, 16:339–65.

Mosak, Jacob. 1938. "Interrelations of Production, Price and Derived Demand." *Journal of Political Economy*, 46:761–87.

Mundaca, Gabriela. 1989. "Nonlinear Rational Expectations Model of Demand for Inputs for the U.S. and Norwegian Economies." Unpublished paper, University of Oslo.

Munts, Raymond. 1970. "Partial Benefit Schedules in Unemployment Insurance: Their Effect on Work Incentive." *Journal of Human Resources*, 5:160–76.

Myers, John. 1969. *Job Vacancies in the Firm and the Labor Market*. New York: National Industrial Conference Board.

Nadiri, M. I. 1968. "The Effect of Relative Prices and Capacity on the Demand for Labor in the U.S. Manufacturing Sector." *Review of Economic Studies*, 35:273–88.

Nadiri, M.I., and Sherwin Rosen. 1969. "Interrelated Factor Demand Functions." *American Economic Review*, 59:457–71.

———. 1973. *A Disequilibrium Model of Production*. New York: National Bureau of Economic Research.

Nakamura, Shinichiro. 1990. "A Nonhomothetic Generalized Leontief Cost Function Based on Pooled Data." *Review of Economics and Statistics*, 72:649–56.

Nelson, Randy. 1984. "Regulation, Capital Vintage, and Technical Change in the Electric Utility Industry." *Review of Economics and Statistics*, 66:59–69.

Nelson, Randy, and Mark Wohar. 1983. "Regulation, Scale Economies, and Productivity in Steam-Electric Generation." *International Economic Review*, 24:57–79.

Neubig, Thomas. 1981. "The Social Security Payroll Tax Effect on Wage Growth." *Proceedings of the National Tax Association*, 196–201.

Newman, Robert, and Dennis Sullivan. 1988. "Econometric Analysis of Business Tax Impacts on Industrial Location: What Do We Know, and How Do We Know It?" *Journal of Urban Economics*, 23:215–34.

Nickell, Stephen. 1979. "Unemployment and the Structure of Labor Costs." *Carnegie-Rochester Conference Series on Public Policy*, 11:187–222.

———. 1984. "An Investigation of the Determinants of Manufacturing Employment in the United Kingdom." *Review of Economic Studies*, 51:529–57.

———. 1986. "Dynamic Models of Labour Demand." In Orley Ashenfelter and Richard Layard, eds., *Handbook of Labour Economics*. Amsterdam: North-Holland Press.

Nickell, Stephen, and Jim Symons. 1990. "The Real Wage-Employment Relationship in the United States." *Journal of Labor Economics*, 8:1–15.

Nissim, Joseph. 1984. "The Price Responsiveness of the Demand for Labour by Skill: British Mechanical Engineering, 1963–78," *Economic Journal*, 94:812–25.

Norsworthy, J. Randall, and Michael Harper. 1981. "Dynamic Models of Energy Substitution in U.S. Manufacturing." In Ernst Berndt and Barry Field, eds., *Modeling and Measuring Natural Resource Substitution*. Cambridge: MIT Press.

Nussbaum, Joyce, and Donald Wise. 1977. "The Employment Impact of the Overtime Provisions of the FLSA." Final Report, U.S. Department of Labor.

Oakland, William. 1978. "Local Taxes and Intraurban Industrial Location: A Survey." In George Break, ed., *Metropolitan Financing and Growth Management Policies*. Madison: University of Wisconsin Press.

Oi, Walter. 1962. "Labor as a Quasi-Fixed Factor of Production." *Journal of Political Economy*, 70:538–55.

Okunade, Albert. 1991. "Translog Cost Estimates of Labor-Labor Substitution in U.S. Hospital Pharmacies." *Journal of Research in Pharmaceutical Economics*, 3:91–113.

O'Neill, Dave. 1982. "Employment Tax Credit Programs: The Effects of Socioeconomic Targeting Provisions." *Journal of Human Resources*, 17:449–59.

Organization for Economic Cooperation and Development. 1983. *Lay-offs and Short-time Working in Selected OECD Countries*. Paris: OECD.

———. 1987. *Employment Outlook, 1987*. Paris: OECD.

———. 1990. *Employment Outlook, 1990*. Paris: OECD.

Osterman, Paul. 1986. "The Impact of Computers on the Employment of Clerks and Managers." *Industrial and Labor Relations Review*, 39:175–86.

Oswald, Andrew. 1985. "The Economic Theory of Trade Unions: An Introductory Survey." *Scandinavian Journal of Economics*, 87:160–93.

Owen, John. 1979. *Working Hours*. Lexington, Mass.: D. C. Heath.

Pack, Howard. 1988. "Industrialization and Trade." In Hollis Chenery and T. N. Srinivasan, eds., *Handbook of Development Economics*. Vol. 1. Amsterdam: North-Holland Press.

Paldam, Martin. 1979. "Towards the Wage-Earner State: A Comparative Study of Wage Shares, 1948–75." *International Journal of Social Economics*, 6:45–62.

Palm, Franz, and Gerard Pfann. 1990. "Interrelated Demand Rational Expectations Models for Two Types of Labour." *Oxford Bulletin of Economics and Statistics*, 52:45–68.

Papke, Leslie. 1991. "Interstate Business Tax Differentials and New Firm Location: Evidence from Panel Data." *Journal of Public Economics*, 45:47–68.

Parkin, Michael. 1990. *Macroeconomics*. Reading, Mass.: Addison-Wesley.

Peel, D. A., and Ian Walker. 1978. "Short-run Employment Functions, Excess Supply and the Speed of Adjustment: A Note." *Economica*, 45:195–202.

de Pelsmacker, Pierre. 1984. "Long-run and Short-run Demand for Factors of Production in the Belgian Car Industry." In Daniel Vitry and Bernadette Marechal, eds., *Emploi-Chomage: Modelisation et Analyses Quantitatives*. Dijon: Librairie de l'Université.

Pencavel, John. 1972. "Wages, Specific Training, and Labor Turnover in U.S. Manufacturing Industries." *International Economic Review*, 13:53–64.

———. 1989. "Employment, Wages, and Unionism in a Model of the Aggregate Labor Market in Britain." National Bureau of Economic Research, Working Paper No. 3030.

Pencavel, John, and Bertil Holmlund. 1988. "The Determination of Wages, Employment and Work Hours in an Economy with Centralised Wage-Setting: Sweden 1950–83." *Economic Journal*, 98:1105–26.

Perlman, Selig. 1928. *A Theory of the Labor Movement*. New York: Macmillan.

Perloff, Jeffrey, and Michael Wachter. 1979. "The New Jobs Tax Credit: An Evaluation of the 1977–78 Wage Subsidy Program." *American Economic Association, Papers and Proceedings*, 69:173–79.

Pfann, Gerard. 1989. *Stochastic Adjustment Models of Labour Demand*. Maastricht, The Netherlands: Rijksuniversiteit Limburg.

Pfann, Gerard, and Bart Verspagen. 1989. "The Structure of Adjustment Costs for Labour in the Dutch Manufacturing Sector." *Economics Letters*, 29:365–71.

Phelps Brown, Henry. 1977. *The Inequality of Pay*. Berkeley: University of California Press.

Pindyck, Robert. 1979. "Interfuel Substitution and the Industrial Demand for Energy: An International Comparison." *Review of Economics and Statistics*, 61:169–79.

Pindyck, Robert, and Julio Rotemberg. 1983. "Dynamic Factor Demands and the Effects of Energy Price Shocks." *American Economic Review*, 73:1066–79.

Pitt, Mark, and Mark Rosenzweig. 1986. "Agricultural Prices, Food Consumption, and the Health and Productivity of Indonesian Farmers." In Inderjit Singh, Lyn Squire, and John Strauss, eds., *Agricultural Household Models: Extensions, Applications and Policy*. Baltimore: Johns Hopkins University Press.

Pollak, Robert, Robin Sickles, and Terence Wales. 1984. "The CES-Translog:

Specification and Estimation of a New Cost Function." *Review of Economics and Statistics*, 66:602–7.

Prescott, Edward. 1986. "Theory Ahead of Business Cycle Measurement." *Federal Reserve Bank of Minneapolis Quarterly Review*, Fall:9–22.

Psacharopoulos, George, and Maureen Woodhall. 1985. *Education for Development*. New York: Oxford University Press.

Quandt, Richard, and Harvey Rosen. 1988. *The Conflict between Equilibrium and Disequilibrium Theories: The Case of the U.S. Labor Market*. Kalamazoo, Mich.: W. E. Upjohn Institute.

———. 1989. "Endogenous Output in an Aggregate Model of the Labor Market." *Review of Economics and Statistics*, 71:394–400.

Rahiala, Markku, and Timo Teräsvirta. 1990. "Labour Hoarding in Finnish Manufacturing Industries." Unpublished paper, Research Institute of the Finnish Economy.

Raisian, John. 1979. "Cyclic Patterns in Weeks and Wages." *Economic Inquiry*, 17:475–95.

Reder, Melvin. 1975. "The Theory of Employment and Wages in the Public Sector." In Daniel Hamermesh, ed., *Labor in the Public and Nonprofit Sectors*. Princeton: Princeton University Press.

Rees, Albert. 1989. *The Economics of Trade Unions*. Chicago: University of Chicago Press.

Rees, Albert, and George Shultz. 1970. *Workers and Wages in an Urban Labor Market*. Chicago: University of Chicago Press.

de Regt, Erik. 1988. "Labor Demand and Standard Working Time in Dutch Manufacturing, 1954–1982." In Robert Hart, ed., *Employment, Unemployment and Labor Utilization*. Boston: Unwin Hyman.

Reid, Frank, and Gerald Swartz. 1982. *Prorating Fringe Benefits for Part-time Employees in Canada*. Toronto: University of Toronto, Industrial Relations Centre.

Rice, Patricia. 1986. "Juvenile Unemployment, Relative Wages and Social Security in Great Britain." *Economic Journal*, 96:352–74.

Rich, Daniel. 1990. "On the Elasticity of Labor Demand." *Quarterly Review of Economics and Business*, 30:31–41.

Rivera-Batiz, Francisco, and Selig Sechzer. 1988. "Substitution and Complementarity between Immigrant and Native Labor in the United States." Unpublished paper, Rutgers University.

Roberts, Mark, and Emmanuel Skoufias. 1991. "Plant Characteristics and the Demand for Skilled and Unskilled Labor in the Colombian Manufacturing Sector." Unpublished paper, Pennsylvania State University.

Robinson, Sherman. 1989. "Multisectoral Models." In Hollis Chenery and T. N. Srinivasan, eds., *Handbook of Development Economics*. Vol. 2. Amsterdam: North-Holland Press.

Romer, Paul. 1990. "Endogenous Technological Change." *Journal of Political Economy*, 98:S71–102.

Rosen, Sherwin. 1968. "Short-Run Employment Variation on Class-I Railroads in the U.S., 1947–63." *Econometrica*, 36:511–29.

Rosen, Sherwin. 1974. "Hedonic Prices and Implicit Markets." *Journal of Political Economy*, 82:34–55.

———. 1978. "The Supply of Work Schedules and Employment." In National Commission for Employment Policy, *Work Time and Employment*, Special Report No. 28. Washington, D.C.: NCEP.

———. 1983. "A Note on Aggregation of Skills and Labor Quality." *Journal of Human Resources*, 18:425–31.

Rosenzweig, Mark. 1980. "Neoclassical Theory and the Optimizing Peasant: An Econometric Analysis of Market Family Labor Supply in a Developing Economy." *Quarterly Journal of Economics*, 94:31–56.

———. 1988. "Labor Markets in Low-income Countries." In Hollis Chenery and T. N. Srinivasan, eds., *Handbook of Development Economics*. Vol. 1. Amsterdam: North-Holland Press.

Rossana, Robert. 1983. "Some Empirical Estimates of the Demand for Hours in U.S. Manufacturing Industries." *Review of Economics and Statistics*, 65:560–69.

———. 1985. "Buffer Stocks and Labor Demand: Further Evidence." *Review of Economics and Statistics*, 67:16–26.

———. 1990. "Interrelated Demands for Buffer Stocks and Productive Inputs: Estimation for Two-digit Manufacturing Industries." *Review of Economics and Statistics*, 72:19–29.

Rothschild, Michael. 1971. "On the Cost of Adjustment." *Quarterly Journal of Economics*, 85:605–22.

Rowter, Kahlil. 1990. "Gross Employment Change in Indonesian Medium and Large Manufacturing Firms, 1975–84." Unpublished paper, Michigan State University.

Rudebusch, Glenn. 1986. "Testing for Labor Market Equilibrium with an Exact Excess Demand Disequilibrium Model." *Review of Economics and Statistics*, 68:468–76.

Saffer, Henry. 1982. "Layoffs and Unemployment Insurance." *Journal of Public Economics*, 19:121–29.

———. 1983. "The Effects of Unemployment Insurance on Temporary and Permanent Layoffs." *Review of Economics and Statistics*, 65:647–52.

Santamäki, Tuire. 1988. "Implications of the Non-Homogeneity of Standard and Overtime Hours on the Structure and Cyclical Adjustment of Labor Input." in Robert Hart, ed., *Employment, Unemployment and Labor Utilization*. Boston: Unwin Hyman.

Santiago, Carlos. 1989. "The Dynamics of Minimum Wage Policy in Economic Development: A Multiple Time-Series Approach." *Economic Development and Cultural Change*, 38:1–30.

Santoso, Bagus. 1988. *Permintaan Masukan Dalam Produksi Padi Pada Padi Sawah di Indonesia, 1976–1985* (The Demand for Productive Inputs in Rice Paddies in Indonesia, 1976–1985). Unpublished dissertation, Gadjah Mada University, Indonesia.

Sargent, Thomas. 1978. "Estimation of Dynamic Labor Demand Schedules under Rational Expectations." *Journal of Political Economy*, 86:1009–44.

Sato, K. 1967. "A Two-level Constant-Elasticity-of-Substitution Production Function." *Review of Economic Studies*, 34:201–18.

Sato, Ryuzo. 1975. *Production Functions and Aggregation*. Amsterdam: North-Holland Press.

———. 1977. "Homothetic and Nonhomothetic CES Production Functions." *American Economic Review*, 67:559–69.

Sato, Ryuzo, and Tetsunori Koizumi. 1973. "On the Elasticities of Substitution and Complementarity." *Oxford Economic Papers*, 25:44–56.

Schaafsma, Joseph. 1978. "On Estimating the Time Structure of Capital-Labor Substitution in the Manufacturing Sector: A Model Applied to 1949–72 Canadian Data." *Southern Economic Journal*, 44:740–51.

Schaafsma, Joseph, and William Walsh. 1983. "Employment and Labour Supply Effects of the Minimum Wage: Some Pooled Time-Series Estimates from Canadian Provincial Data." *Canadian Journal of Economics*, 16:86–97.

Schmenner, Roger. 1982. *Making Business Location Decisions*. Englewood Cliffs, N.J.: Prentice-Hall.

Schott, Kerry. 1978. "The Relation between Industrial Research and Development and Factor Demands." *Economic Journal*, 88:85–106.

Schultz, T. W. 1981. *Investing in People*. Berkeley: University of California Press.

Schweke, William, and David Jones. 1986. "European Job Creation in the Wake of Plant Closing and Layoffs." *Monthly Labor Review*, 109:18–22.

Segerson, Kathleen, and Timothy Mount. 1985. "A Non-Homothetic Two-stage Decision Model Using AIDS." *Review of Economics and Statistics*, 67:630–39.

Shapiro, Carl, and Joseph Stiglitz. 1984. "Equilibrium Unemployment as a Worker Discipline Device." *American Economic Review*, 74:433–44.

Shapiro, Matthew. 1986. "The Dynamic Demand for Capital and Labor." *Quarterly Journal of Economics*, 101:513–42.

Sims, Christopher. 1974. "Output and Labor Input in Manufacturing." *Brookings Papers on Economic Activity*, 695–728.

Singh, Inderjit, Lyn Squire, and John Strauss. 1986. *Agricultural Household Models: Extensions, Applications and Policy*. Baltimore: Johns Hopkins University Press.

Skedinger, Per. 1990. "Real Wages, Unemployment, and Labor Market Programs: A Disaggregative Analysis." Stockholm, Trade Union Institute for Economic Research, Working Paper No. 83.

Slichter, Sumner, James Healy, and E. Robert Livernash. 1960. *The Impact of Collective Bargaining on Management*. Washington, D.C.: Brookings Institution.

Smilor, Raymond, and Michael Gill. 1986. *The New Business Incubator*. Lexington, Mass.: Lexington Books.

Smyth, David. 1984. "Short-run Employment Functions When the Speed of Adjustment Depends on the Unemployment Rate." *Review of Economics and Statistics*, 66:138–42.

Smyth, David, and N. J. Ireland. 1967. "Short-term Employment Functions in Australian Manufacturing." *Review of Economics and Statistics*, 49:537–44.

Smyth, David, and Stephen Karlson. 1991. "The Effect of Fringe Benefits on Employment Fluctuations in U.S. Automobile Manufacturing." *Review of Economics and Statistics*, 73:40–49.

Soligo, Ronald. 1966. "The Short-run Relationship between Employment and Output." *Yale Economic Essays*, 6:161–215.

Solon, Gary. 1985. "The Minimum Wage and Teenage Employment: A Reanalysis with Attention to Serial Correlation and Seasonality." *Journal of Human Resources*, 20:292–97.

Solow, Robert. 1980. "On Theories of Unemployment." *American Economic Review*, 70:1–11.

Sosin, Kim, and Loretta Fairchild. 1984. "Nonhomotheticity and Technological Bias in Production." *Review of Economics and Statistics*, 66:44–50.

Squire, Lyn. 1981. *Employment Policy in Developing Countries: A Survey of Issues and Evidence*. New York: Oxford University Press.

Stafford, Frank. 1980. "Firm Size, Workplace Public Goods, and Worker Welfare." In John Siegfried, ed., *The Economics of Firm Size, Market Structure and Social Performance*. Washington, D.C.: Federal Trade Commission.

———. 1986. "Forestalling the Demise of Empirical Economics: The Role of Microdata in Labor Economics Research." In Orley Ashenfelter and Richard Layard, eds., *Handbook of Labor Economics*. Amsterdam: North-Holland Press.

Stapleton, David. 1989. "Cohort Size and the Academic Labor Market." *Journal of Human Resources*, 24:221–52.

Stapleton, David, and Douglas Young. 1984. "The Effects of Demographic Change on the Distribution of Wages, 1967–1990." *Journal of Human Resources*, 19:175–201.

Stelcner, Morton, Jacques van der Gaag, and Wim Vijverberg. 1989. "A Switching Regression Model of Public-Private Sector Wage Differentials in Peru, 1985–86." *Journal of Human Resources*, 24:545–59.

Stigler, George. 1946. "The Economics of Minimum Wage Legislation," *American Economic Review*, 36:358–65.

———. 1987. *The Theory of Price*. New York: Macmillan.

Stiglitz, Joseph. 1987. "The Causes and Consequences of the Dependence of Quality on Price." *Journal of Economic Literature*, 25:1–48.

Strauss, John. 1986. "Does Better Nutrition Raise Farm Productivity?" *Journal of Political Economy*, 94:297–320.

Summers, Lawrence. 1986. "Some Skeptical Observations on Real Business Cycle Theory." *Federal Reserve Bank of Minneapolis Quarterly Review*, Fall:23–27.

Swidinsky, Robert. 1980. "Minimum Wages and Teenage Unemployment." *Canadian Journal of Economics*, 13:158–71.

Symons, Jim. 1985. "Relative Prices and the Demand for Labour in British Manufacturing." *Economica*, 52:37–49.

Symons, Jim, and Richard Layard. 1984. "Neoclassical Demand for Labour Functions for Six Major Economies." *Economic Journal*, 94:788–99.

Tarhouni, Ali. 1983. *A Production Approach to Regional Economic Integration*. Unpublished Ph.D. dissertation, Michigan State University.

Tarshis, Lorie. 1939. "Changes in Real and Money Wages." *Economic Journal*, 49:150–54.

Taylor, Lester, Stephen Turnovsky, and T. Wilson. 1972. *The Inflationary Process*. Toronto: Institute for Quantitative Analysis.

Theil, Henri. 1954. *Linear Aggregation of Econometric Relations*. Amsterdam: North-Holland Press.

Thornton, Robert. 1979. "The Elasticity of Demand for Public School Teachers." *Industrial Relations*, 18:86–91.

Tinbergen, Jan, and H. C. Bos. 1965. *Econometric Models of Education*. Paris: OECD.

Tinsley, Peter. 1971. "A Variable Adjustment Model of Labor Demand." *International Economic Review*, 12:482–510.

Tobin, James. 1972. "Inflation and Unemployment." *American Economic Review*, 62:1–18.

Topel, Robert. 1982. "Inventories, Layoffs and the Short-run Demand for Labor." *American Economic Review*, 72:769–87.

———. 1983. "On Layoffs and Unemployment Insurance." *American Economic Review*, 73:541–59.

———. 1984. "Experience Rating of Unemployment Insurance and the Incidence of Unemployment." *Journal of Law and Economics*, 27:61–90.

———. 1985. "Unemployment and Unemployment Insurance." *Research in Labor Economics*, 7:91–136.

———. 1990. "Financing Unemployment Insurance: History, Incentives and Reform." In W. Lee Hansen and James Byers, eds., *Unemployment Insurance: The Second Half Century*. Madison: University of Wisconsin Press.

———. 1991. "Specific Capital, Mobility and Wages: Wages Rise with Job Seniority." *Journal of Political Economy*, 99:145–76.

Treadway, Arthur. 1971. "The Rational Multivariate Flexible Accelerator." *Econometrica*, 39:845–55.

Trejo, Stephen. 1991. "Compensating Differentials and Overtime Pay Regulation." *American Economic Review*, 81:719–40.

Turnovsky, Michelle, and William Donnelly. 1984. "Energy Substitution, Separability and Technical Progress in the Australian Iron and Steel Industry." *Journal of Economics and Business*, 2:54–63.

U.S. Chamber of Commerce. 1990. *Employee Benefits, 1989*. Washington, D.C.: Chamber of Commerce.

U.S. Department of Labor, Office of the Inspector General. 1985. "Financing the Unemployment Insurance Program Has Shifted from a System Based on Individual Employer's Responsibility Towards a Socialized System." Audit Report No. 03-3-203-03-315.

Uzawa, Hirofumi. 1962. "Production Functions with Constant Elasticities of Substitution." *Review of Economic Studies*, 29:291–99.

Vanek, Jaroslav. 1970. *The General Theory of Labor-managed Market Economies.* Ithaca: Cornell University Press.

Varian, Hal. 1984. *Microeconomic Analysis.* New York: Norton.

Vroman, Wayne. 1974a. "Employer Payroll Tax Incidence: Empirical Tests with Cross-Country Data." *Finances Publiques,* 29:184–200.

———. 1974b. "Employer Payroll Taxes and Money Wage Behaviour." *Applied Economics,* 6:189–204.

Wadhwani, Sushil. 1987. "The Effects of Inflation and Real Wages on Employment." *Economica,* 54:21–40.

Wadhwani, Sushil, and Martin Wall. 1990. "The Effects of Profit-sharing on Employment, Wages, Stock Returns and Productivity: Evidence from UK Micro-Data." *Economic Journal,* 100:1–17.

Wandner, Stephen, and Robert Crosslin. 1980. "Measuring Experience Rating." In National Commission on Unemployment Compensation, *Unemployment Compensation: Studies and Research.* Vol. 2. Washington, D.C.: NCUC.

Warden, Charles. 1967. "Unemployment Compensation: The Massachusetts Experience." In Otto Eckstein, ed., *Studies in the Economics of Income Maintenance.* Washington, D.C.: Brookings Institution.

Waud, Roger. 1968. "Man-Hour Behavior in U.S. Manufacturing: A Neoclassical Interpretation." *Journal of Political Economy,* 76:407–27.

Wedervang, Fröystein. 1965. *Development of a Population of Industrial Firms: The Structure of Manufacturing Industries in Norway, 1930–1948.* Oslo: Universitetsforlaget.

Weiss, Randall. 1977. "Elasticities of Substitution among Capital and Occupations in U.S. Manufacturing." *Journal of the American Statistical Association,* 72:764–71.

Weitenberg, Johannes. 1969. "The Incidence of Social Security Taxes." *Finances Publiques,* 24:193–208.

Welch, Finis. 1969. "Linear Synthesis of Skill Distribution." *Journal of Human Resources,* 4:311–27.

———. 1970. "Education in Production." *Journal of Political Economy,* 78:764–71.

———. 1976. "Minimum Wage Legislation in the United States." In Orley Ashenfelter and James Blum, eds., *Evaluating the Labor-Market Effects Social Programs.* Princeton: Princeton University, Industrial Relations Section.

———. 1979. "Effects of Cohort Size on Earnings: The Baby Boom Babies' Financial Bust," *Journal of Political Economy,* 87:S65–98.

Welch, Finis, and James Cunningham. 1978. "Effects of Minimum Wages on the Level and Age Composition of Youth Employment." *Review of Economics and Statistics,* 60:140–45.

Wellington, Alison. 1991. "Effects of the Minimum Wage on the Employment Status of Youths: An Update." *Journal of Human Resources,* 26:27–46.

Wiseman, Michael. 1976. "Public Employment as Fiscal Policy." *Brookings Papers on Economic Activity,* 67–104.

Wolcowitz, Jeffrey. 1984. "Dynamic Effects of the Unemployment Insurance Tax on Temporary Layoffs." *Journal of Public Economics*, 25:35–51.

Woodbury, Stephen. 1978. "Is the Elasticity of Demand for Labor Subject to Cyclical Fluctuation?" Unpublished paper, University of Wisconsin.

Wren-Lewis, Simon. 1986. "An Econometric Model of U.K. Manufacturing Employment Using Survey Data on Expected Output." *Journal of Applied Econometrics*, 1:297–316.

Wright, Randall. 1986. "The Redistributive Roles of Unemployment Insurance and the Dynamics of Voting." *Journal of Public Economics*, 31:377–99.

Wylie, Peter. 1990. "Scale-biased Technological Development in Canada's Industrialization, 1900–1929." *Review of Economics and Statistics*, 72:219–27.

Index